Exploratory Musicism
Ideas for Spontaneous Composition

By Karlton Hester

University of California, Santa Cruz

cognella™
San Diego, CA

Bassim Hamadeh, Publisher
Christopher Foster, Vice President
Michael Simpson, Vice President of Acquisitions
Jessica Knott, Managing Editor
Stephen Milano, Creative Director
Kevin Fahey, Cognella Marketing Program Manager
Melissa Accornero, Acquisitions Editor

First published in the United States of America in 2012 by University Readers, Inc.

15 14 13 12 11   1 2 3 4 5

Printed in the United States of America

ISBN:978-1-60927-132-9

www.cognella.com 800.200.3908

Contents

Chapter 9

Chapter 10

Appendix

Preface

M usic, an art form whose medium is sound organized in time, uses sonic vibrations to communicate ideas that reflect the universe around and within us. We sometimes use symbols to signify certain aspects of the musical process, but music is an expressive and dynamic symbolic language that transcends any form of visual representation. This is especially true when it comes to the creation of spontaneous composition.

People often try to reduce music to theories that govern its functions. Western Music theory is a field of study that deals with how music works through an examination of the language and notation of music. Although every musician needs to know the basics of music theory to have command over music production, many masters of music learn its modes of communication without note reading, or through dissecting intervals, scales, and chords the way we do in the West. Most musicians are concerned with composing interesting melodies using different pitches, assorted durations, and mixtures of harmonic progression organized linearly in time (rhythm). As composers worldwide learn to construct logical harmonic framework and to bind melody and harmony together meaningfully, some have the luxury of time to review their decisions (premeditated composers) while others have to make the same range of decisions primarily in real time (spontaneous composers). In both cases, however, the listener is looking for the same outcome: beautiful and logical musical construction.

One thing that binds musicians together, especially those who feel that there is a field of consciousness that connects with the universe at large, is a view that musical inspiration resides in a universal spirit or consciousness. Some consider divine inspiration to be a central source of musical creativity. Other composers conclude that the source of inspiration comes from within yourself and attempt to inspire others to discover ways to get that source to arise from within them. In any case, all agree that inspiration can come from many sources, both musical and extra-musical. The purpose of this book is to share some of the ideas and concepts that have inspired and shaped my approach to music and art. Although they may appear somewhat disparate at first glance, I trust that the connection between various subjects will become increasingly more apparent as you apply them to your own creative process.

Karlton E. Hester

Chapter One
Introduction: Creative Process

"All a musician can do is to get closer to the sources of nature, and so feel that he is in communion with the natural laws."

—John Coltrane

Ideas for Spontaneous Composition

We cannot isolate a particular musical secret, chemical formula, philosophical postulate, or theoretical genetic code that defines music definitively, thus anything that we say about music composition is largely speculative, hypothetical, and subjective. Music is not a phenomenon to simply quantify or define, but is a human endeavor that exists for all to appreciate, understand, and enjoy. Despite its ambiguity, music performance definitely has an *actual* effect during its process of transmission and reception. Like many aspects of actuality, especially the intangibles, that which is *real* often defies the capacity of words to contain them. Thus music's power and efficacy seems to reside far beyond the capacity of language.

It seems that music's abstract character demands that it be examined from an abstract conceptual perspective. Regardless of how dogmatically or unswervingly insistent we become about the superior, classic, universal, or serious nature of any musical approach, we cannot prove empirically that one brand of music is qualified to be elevated above another. In a continual search for inspiration and ideas for composition, many musicians worldwide observe and study nature. The intended goal is to promote creativity through relating things in the world around them to their evolving musical technique, vocabularies, and artistic ideas. There are increasing numbers of investigations directed at examining the relationships between musical perception, organization, application, and the way musical processes compare with ways that science and mathematics organize their concepts, methodologies, and theories.

Process involves a series of occurrences that produce change or development. **Form** involves the shape or appearance of things that make them identifiable to human consciousness. **Content** is the quantity or essence of phenomena contained in something else. The content of the universe involves everything that exists in *actuality* while form only involves our limited perception of *reality*. While exercising musical interaction, reciprocity, synergy, balance, and creativity within the spontaneous compositional process, we can also observe related processes and patterns within the broader universe. Thus we can discover an infinite array of models of viable dynamic systems. We witness a creative process in motion around common dynamic systems such as beehives, where there is a clear sense of unified purpose, organization, direction, individual and collective skill, and continuity, all leading ultimately to the mutually beneficial creation of honey. Clans, villages, and cities also involve dynamic systems of production that involve complex interconnectivity and interaction aimed at mutually beneficial goals. Polarity and duality seem to abound throughout such dynamic systems within the observable universe. Tendencies towards balance, stasis, and motion appear to determine the nature of transformations, proportion, and the formation of sequences in nature.

In music and art, the process of creation involves preparation, planning, and expressive freedom involving an infinite variety of different approaches. **Free association** largely entails the spontaneous and unrestricted expression of thoughts, concepts, and ideas, allowing each one to lead freely to or suggest the next. Thus, to some observers, free association is more closely related to the realm of actuality than empiricism, since it allows us to utilize our objective, subjective, and subconscious realms of consciousness in consort. Music rarely involves strictly free association, however. **Empiricism** is the view that experience (especially that of the physical senses) is the only source of reliable knowledge. Some people believe that facts can only be derived through careful observation, cataloging phenomena, and then extrapolating laws or principles from such observations and records. Perhaps a path involving both approaches is most productive for the curious composer. The combination of spontaneous and premeditated approaches to composition provides an opportunity to investigate music from the blended perspective of both free association and empiricism.

The Evolution of Music

There are countless inhabitants of Earth—including all those that are microscopic, feathered, scaled, and furred. Humans are just one species among many varied forms of life seeking to comprehend and prosper within our environment. What seems to set people apart from others may be our power to think, analyze, understand, and assimilate to an extent that perhaps ultimately extends to greater degrees of personal gratification and pleasure than other species enjoy. Of course we have no means through which to undeniably verify that presumption. An essential derivative of the increased power and heightened expression of thought is the development of the fine arts. As humans evolved, they gradually organized their environment, eventually enabling them to think less of survival and more towards pleasures and enjoyable pastimes. During leisure the arts were nourished and developed into multifarious forms. As a result, musicians and other artists have undergone personal processes of growth, development, and expression. Creative process may generally include:

Extraction—music and art evolve from culture and personal experience.
Production—involves formative years of artistic development.
Distribution—we share our music with the world in various ways.
Consumption—audiences absorb artistic expression and make it their own.
Disposal—old styles give way to new modes of artistic expressions. (Is that which remains classics?)
The Internet now expands the range of relationships between artistic development, distribution, and public absorption.

Music and arts continually develop ever more differentiated control over their content and patterns of expression. Preliterate music evolved a certain brand of control over rhythm, melody, timbre, harmony, and other musical elements. Its ingredients evolved control over aspects of sound production as both musicians and listeners gradually became acclimated to emerging musical representation, vocabulary, and style. With musical literacy musicians gain a different brand of control over music through the application of representative written symbols that developed into harmonic elaboration, melodic invention, and increasingly more complex rhythm. A wide range of forms growing out of this evolution created musical diversity. Symbols are a form of labeling and labels help us organize our world. Musical labels alone cannot replace musical knowledge; nor can verbal or written discussions about music even begin to fully represent the music itself. Within the twentieth century, jazz has followed an evolutionary course beginning an investigation of music through both free association and empiricism. It began with an initial emphasis on melodic and rhythmic elaboration within blues, ragtime, and traditional jazz (New Orleans Jazz). Those early forms gradually added additional harmonic extensions, tonal elaboration, formal control, and general variety by the time swing and bebop emerged. Each new generation of the jazz evolution has involved musicians straining to extend beyond the limits of prevailing traditional boundaries, thus leading to fresh contemporary expression.

Appreciating Art

We understand art by personally identifying with it. Such identification develops through our capacity for metaphor, which is built into the fine structure of our nervous system. Metaphor involves systems of comparison, where we say that one thing is like another. We learn progressively through repetition and metaphor extends and embellishes that approach to knowledge. A work of expressive art serves as a catalyst for combining assorted metaphors, where our brain serves as the physical vehicle that allows our emotions to absorb and define abstract information within our subconscious. Comprehending subconscious messages can be problematic because of the possibility of multiple interpretations, but we still learn best by making associations.

It is easier to grasp that acting and dancing are the projection of the physical body into an aesthetic medium, since the body itself becomes the aesthetic means. We apprehend an actor's or a dancer's performance by interpreting their action through associating their visual and linguistic messages with those of our own physical, emotional, and intellectual reality. We extend our own perceptions to merge and identify with those of actors and dancers in order to understand and respond to the artistic implications involved.

With painting and sculpture the artist and the spectator alike are in similar positions. In a play or a dance all participants (presenters and audience) are subject to a mutual display where they can more easily identify with the bodies and materials they witness in familiar forms and terms. In visual art the objects they see are only representations, but the mechanism of identification still works in a related fashion with most conventional visual and kinetic art forms. Music operates within a realm of abstraction that is quite a bit farther removed from familiar physical representation, despite its having a tremendous impact on our emotions, minds, and bodies.

Music as an Abstraction

When analyzing music we generally talk about its elements (rhythm, melody, harmony, timbre, form, etc). We are particularly used to thinking of rhythm, melody, and harmony as being the chief elements of music. Nonetheless, as with our other fundamental experiences in life, our basic understanding of music is holistic. We can listen to music and easily discuss what we hear without thoroughly dissecting it or applying the use of specific musical terminology. Whether or not anyone calls our attention to what a particular instrument is doing at a given time, people get some sense of a whole aesthetic expression while listening actively or passively to music. We initially get some personal sense of its beauty, value, and meaning strictly in our own personal terms. Our taste is also shaped by the frequency of our exposure to certain types of music. Analyzing a composition by its discrete components may be difficult initially. If listeners eventually learn to discriminate one instrument, melodic line, or to extract other musical elements in a composition, one from another, however, it eventually enables them to understand the music more deeply.

In building a strong basis for appreciating music holistically we don't necessarily need to hear musical elements separately before combining them into a musical whole. It is better to first grasp music as a whole experience before gradually becoming able to simultaneously differentiate individual components distinctly, through practice. Developing our capacity to grasp musical language is akin to learning spoken language. Developmental linguists have discussed the holophrastic utterance of very young people where children use one brief utterance to designate a whole situation without being able to designate smaller aspects of the situation specifically (Dale 619). Such somewhat "poetic" expression can suggest a wide range of interpretation by the listener while maintaining a highly specific meaning for the child expressing the idea. Our basic sense of music, from an inexperienced listener's perspective, can be equally undifferentiated. Only through a long process of musical development, analysis, and evolution, have rhythm, melody, and harmony become increasingly more clearly distinguishable.

We might consider music a personal and collective philosophy and social function that we strive to comprehend through the absorption, appreciation, and manipulation of organized sound. It involves the pursuit of knowledge and wisdom gained through an examination of music's abstract values, predominantly through speculative examination. In the final analysis, composers, performers, theorists, musicologists, and listeners all attempt to explore musical expression, aesthetics, concepts, and the nature of sound through personal journeys involving much more free association than empiricism. Pythagoras ("Music of the Spheres"), Jean-Philippe Rameau (who revolutionized Western music theory with his assertion that harmony derives from the acoustical harmonics present in a vibrating string or tube), John Coltrane (who developed the substitution formula and harmonic sequence known as the Coltrane Matrix that binds and liberates harmonic progression), and Ornette Coleman (creator of a concept of music called "harmolodic," a musical form that he considered equally applicable as a philosophy of life), all used a broad combination of systematic methods to evolve their intuitive understanding of fundamental sonic principles. Even though these people could never substantiate their theories undeniably, they knew music fundamentally in ways that enabled them to view organized sound more holistically.

Coleman's harmolodics moved beyond the limitations of conventional harmonic principles. His tendencies towards a more open musical grounding, one emerging from the interaction between the players that occurs during "free" improvisation, allowed musicians to break away from the confinement of rigid meters, traditional structural expectations, and predictable melodic and harmonic practices. Harmolodics enables musicians to improvise more freely, democratically, and expressively while maintaining a melodic point of reference and continuity factor that directed and determined the general flow, unity, and compositional form, all generated by the collective experience. Spontaneous composition and improvisation can also allow the audience deeper into the midst of the creative process.

Spontaneous Composition

Music mirrors our encounters in life, and jazz, blues, spirituals, as well as other African-American music is a reflection of diverse African-American experiences such as culture, intellect, philosophies, spiritual belief systems, psyche, and social evolution; just as Bach, Mozart, and Beethoven reflect European culture, experience, and psyche.

We expand our memories by increasing our growing collection of associations. Khepera (*pseudonym*), describes himself as "an eclectic blend of independent scholar/historian, artist, engineering designer, and esotericist. He has taught and lectured across the country on topics ranging from the sacred architecture of Nile Valley civilizations, including their sciences, arts and symbolic languages (*Ancient Nilotic Architecture: A Synthesis of Science, Religion and Philosophy*), to discussing the intersection of modern technology and ancient wisdom systems (*Ogun in the 21st Century: The Connection Between Odu and Digital Technology*." I received a recent email message (reprinted in part here with Khepera's permission) in which Khepera expressed that:

> As we use Nature as the source of our knowledge and inspiration, we engage our environment as a memory recognition exercise, and many if not most of our human artifices/tools are based upon some aspect of inculcating memory, drawing on memory and/or revising/ updating archives of memory as the holistic landscape shifts.
>
> I would posit that another layer/thread here is the extent to which content/knowledge/new insights can be woven/conjured/expressed in an evocative mode such that the *jism* in the jazz becomes more than seminal, but rather a soliton wave form—kind of a musical monument, if you will, like Jeez-eh, as they *useta* spell it. . . .

Dispersion and non-linearity can interact to produce permanent and localized soliton wave forms, a self-reinforcing solitary wave packet or pulse that maintains its shape while it travels at a constant speed. A creative idea may travel a related course.

Recollection

To develop assorted seed ideas over time in musical performance, taking each phrase or motive through a wide set of permutations requires active music memory. Spontaneous composition requires that the mind take a journey to a great number of regions while performing complicated sonic calculation, assessment, and indulging spontaneously in creative decision-making. Memory is a mental system that receives, stores, organizes, alters, and recovers information from sensory input (Coon 1997). A great improviser's memory is continually nourished and enhanced through practice. In ancient times Roman orators often developed the art of memory as they took a mental stroll through the rooms of their villas to embed in their memory the various areas of their homes and its specific content as mental images. To form associations, they would correlate the introductory section of their speech with the entrance hall of the villa or relate other points made in the speech to the statues and furnishings located elsewhere. Transitional

Figure 1. Egyptian Musicians

Figure 2. A Personal Perception of Creative Process

Creative Engagement	Assertive Platform	Analytic Platform	Evaluative Platform
Creative Concept	Inspiration and Knowledge	Artistic Decisions and Expression	Effect on the Planet
Life Is a Series of Processes and Surprises	Knowledge, Humor, and Wisdom Help Minimize Suffering	History Is a Retrospective Contemplation of Past Evolutionary Cycles	All Particles and Events Are but Brief Episodes in the Interconnected Fabric of the Universe
Networks	Creation, Development, Distribution, Human Relations	Feedback Is Active Content	Meaning Is Found Through Observation
Programming	Identity, Contrast, and Repetition	Audience Response	Market Analysis
Emergence	Generative Activity, Product Manifestation Marketing	Process	Dialogic
Intersections Between Arts, Science, and Technology	Balance of Law, Order, and Freedom Yields Power	Observing Mutual Causation	Formation of Grammar and Rule-Bound Systems
Self-Organizing Systems	Based upon Catalysts and Equilibrium	Aesthetics, Love, Interpenetration, Coupling	Successful Means to an End Provides Road Maps for the Future
Artistic Identity Formation	Dynamic Systems Formation—Means of Effective Communication	Destiny ("Particle"), Freedom, and Determinism	Self-Reflection; Subconscious, Subjective, and Objective Analysis
Cybernetics	The Replication or Imitation of Biological Control Systems with the Use of Technology	Exploring Emergence, Evolution, and Stability	Observation and Analysis of Paths Toward Goals
Communication	Exchange, Exploration, and Engagement	Lines of Communication	Allowing Audience to Participate, thus Directing the Flow of Creation
Complex Adaptive Systems	Flexibility, Motion, Knowledge of Cyclical Dynamics	Order from Fluctuation, Polarity, and Abstract Balance	Articulating Process of Evolutionary Narrative
Mathematical Dynamics	Placing Data on a Grid for Measurement	Conclusions Based on Systemic Statistical Analysis	Match Mathematical Conclusions with Other Forms of Analysis
Game Theory	Cognition and Rational Choice	Choice Is Intention	Economic Analysis Based upon Market Reaction
Universal Processes	Observing the Microcosm	Observing the Macrocosm	Finding Correlations

sections might be related to a passageway and its pictures, murals, and busts. They would leave the main sections of the speech to match up with various principal rooms of the villa, and so on. When delivering their speeches in the Forum or Senate, they would mentally walk through their villa to find their associate reminders.

The memory and free play involved in spontaneous composing forms many sets of associated scales, intervals, patterns, social references, emotions, and other dynamics of music and life that are matched with other ideas, memories, and images. Depending upon our social and individual musical conditioning, particular scales or chords can evoke feelings of fear, joy, or sadness. Some scientists have attempted to monitor the processes involved in improvising jazz with various technical tools of scientific analysis in attempt to discover the structure of creativity.

> Creativity is a quintessential feature of human behavior, but the neural substrates that give rise to it remain largely unidentified. Spontaneous artistic creativity is often considered one of the most mysterious forms of creative behavior, frequently described as occurring in an altered state of mind beyond conscious awareness or control while its neurophysiological basis remains obscure (Nisenson 1995). Here we use functional neuroimaging methods to examine musical improvisation as a prototypical form of spontaneous creative behavior, with the assumption that the process is neither mysterious nor obscure, but is instead predicated on novel combinations of ordinary mental processes. It has been suggested that the prefrontal cortex is a region of critical importance that enables the creative process, which includes self-reflection and sensory processing as integral components (Dietrich 7). We hypothesized that spontaneous musical improvisation would be associated with discrete changes in prefrontal activity that provide a biological substrate for actions that are characterized by creative self-expression in the absence of conscious self-monitoring. Furthermore, we hypothesized that alterations in prefrontal cortical activity would be associated with top-down changes in other systems, particularly sensorimotor areas needed to organize the on-line execution of musical ideas and behaviors, as well as limbic structures needed to regulate memory and emotional tone (Halpern 697).

Spontaneous composition requires not only focused memory, but also reflects musical self-evolution and personal virtue. In Europe of earlier times the art of memory was ruled by the virtue prudence. Cicero defined virtue as a "habit of mind in harmony with reason and the order of nature," and said: "Virtue has four parts: Justice, Fortitude, Temperance and Prudence" (Yates 20). Prudence is good sense in managing practical matters that requires our memory, intelligence, and foresight. Memory allows the mind to recall what has happened. With brainpower we can ascertain "what is," thus intelligence becomes our primary faculty for survival. Foresight is the faculty by which we anticipate that which will occur before it happens. All of the most essential qualities of consciousness are continually active during the process of composing spontaneously. It involves a special level of transcendence, a portion of which psychologist Ken Wilber examines in his publication, *The Spectrum of Consciousness,* which introduces an extraordinary model synthesizing Eastern and Western approaches of psychology and spirituality. *The Atman Project,* published in 1980, is a developmental model of self-evolution and transcendence.

Wilber defines these levels in ascending order as:
1. *Sensoriphysical*—realms of matter, sensation, and perception.
2. *Phantasmic-emotional*—the emotional-sexual level, the image mind.
3. *Representational mind*—Piaget's preoperational thinking . . . of symbols and concepts.
4. *Rule/role mind*—concrete operational thinking.
5. *Formal/reflexive mind*—formal operational thinking, the reasoning mind.
6. *Vision-logic*—establishing networks of relationships.
7. *Psychic*—transcendental, transpersonal visionary insight.
8. *Subtle*—the seat of archetypes, the realm of illumination and rapture.
9. *Causal*—The unmanifest sources of all the lesser structures . . . being who is in essence one with the Supreme Self.
10. *Ultimate*—the Supermind (Berman 286).

Figure 3. A Model of Self-Evolution and Transcendence

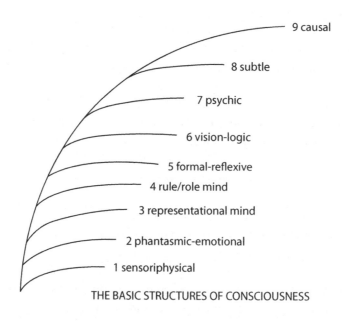

THE BASIC STRUCTURES OF CONSCIOUSNESS

Wilber's model is closely aligned with elements of the oriental chakra model, which reappears in cultures worldwide, throughout the Pacific Basin and from Egypt to

China. Music promotes memory and research has shown memory to be affected by many diverse factors. Music has been found to stimulate parts of the brain and many studies have demonstrated that music enhances the memory of Alzheimer's and dementia patients. Music has also been found to reduce stress, aid relaxation, and alleviate depression (Kirkweg 230). The symbols and ingredients that provide music with meaning need not be in written notation to transform musicians and audiences involved in the process. Such symbols are more than pneumonic aides and tools of cognition. The collective ingredients that create musical experience have a vibratory effect on the total environment, transforming it in ways that no one can fully detect or quantify.

Some Renaissance scholars attempted to escape the prejudices of their era by seeking the "eternal truths" within the hermetic wisdom. During that process they revived daimonic magic as a healing art and as a means of alignment with the cosmic powers. The first such scholar was Marsilio Ficino, who translated the *Hermetica* for the Pope in 1463. One of the most influential of the hermetic scholars of this period was Giordano Bruno. In his *Concerning Shadows of Ideas,* Bruno selected 150 images that were linked to various astrological symbols, planets, houses, signs, and decans (a way of grouping stars or reckoning time that originated in Ancient Egypt) derived from earlier sources. These images come with instructions that guide readers to use them in the art of memory. Bruno's art of memory was also more than a system of mnemonic aides. Its ingredients were designed to effect changes in both the magician (performer) and the world around them (audience and nature) (Walker).

Musical Meaning, Inspiration, and Awareness

Creativity can be defined as the tendency to generate or recognize ideas, possibilities, or alternatives that may be useful in solving problems, communicating with others, and entertaining society (Franken 396). Scientists have evolved theories of human motivation that address questions such as "Why are some people more organized than others?" or "Why do people dream?" In the final analysis, it seems that biology, learning, and cognition may interact with individual talent and differences to produce various assortments of human behavior.

Twentieth-century titans of music such as Duke Ellington, Igor Stravinsky, Art Tatum, Arnold Schoenberg, John Coltrane, Miles Davis, Gustav Holst, Thelonious Monk, Claude Debussy, Charles Mingus, Nusrat Fateh Ali Khan, Mary Lou Williams, Fela Anikulapo Kuti, as well as earlier composers including Saint Yared (born 505 A.D.), Saint Hildegard von Bingen (1098–1179), Johann Sebastian Bach (1685–1750), Antonio Vivaldi (1678–1741), George Frideric Handel (1685–1759) Wolfgang Amadeus Mozart (1756–1791), and Ludwig von Beethoven (1770–1827) were all influential artists who left indelible marks on the mind of humanity that suggest special brands of musical enlightenment. Musical equations of vibration have subsets of underlying mathematics and of physics, but the meaning of music can never be deduced strictly by logic. Its true meaning may be comprehensive universally, but even mathematics cannot contain all of its meaning. Most forms of security rely on encryption, the process of encoding information in such a way that only the one with the special key can decode it. Music is perhaps an encoded time map of the history of human development, but its deeper meaning is encrypted and can never be sufficiently described verbally. It is perhaps encrypted in much the same way that vibrations may conceal and reveal the history of patterning throughout the universe. The rich frequencies of information concealed within every musical note is released upon our ears as composites of radiating sound, much as the flavor of a ripe persimmon releases its rich layers of aroma expressing evolutionary history in the flavor vibrations that excite our sense of smell and taste.

A curt definition of music is "organized sound." It reflects the unity and diversity of universal creation. Music allows us to broaden our visions of existence. Louis Armstrong said, "Jazz is music that's never played the same way once." Ralph Ellison said, "Jazz is an art of individual assertion within and against the group." In 1954 Albert Einstein said:

> A human being is part of the whole called by us universe, a part limited in time and space. We experience ourselves, our thoughts and feelings as something separate from the rest. A kind of optical delusion of consciousness. This delusion is a kind of prison for us, restricting us to our personal desires and to affection for a few persons nearest to us. Our task must be to free ourselves from the prison by widening our circle of compassion to embrace all living creatures and the whole of nature in its beauty. The true value of a human being is determined by the measure and the sense in which they have obtained liberation from the self. We shall require a substantially new manner of thinking if humanity is to survive (Harris 1995).

When Europeans first encountered African music, they mistakenly identified many of Africa's systematic polyrhythm and dissonance as music of random order. They failed to unveil the encryption involved because arrogant dismissal led to misinterpretation. For many Europeans, European colonial architecture serves as the "definitive" model or standard of that which is classic. The problem is the presumption that a Western model is a superior and universal one. Western "classical" music is alternately labeled "serious music" and often considered music appealing to the critical interest of the most developed musical taste worldwide. For example, Bach's music is considered classic to some people because it is said to have flawless construction and timeless appeal. However, Bach's music fell out of public view for almost a century. On March 11, 1829, Felix Mendelssohn conducted the Singakademie in the first complete performance of Johann Sebastian Bach's (1685–1750) *St. Matthew Passion* since the composer's death. The work was a huge success, and the performance marked the beginning of the revival of Bach's works. During its period of its invisibility, was Bach's music timeless?

The point is that the significance of music can never be determined by a single culture. All music has rich information to share that educates, inspires, and elevates humanity. A universal truth or principle is consistently effective universally. No single music qualifies as a universal truth or principle against which all others are measured, but music viewed holistically comes closer to establishing some form of important human reality. The elevation of any music to "superior" stature first requires the reduction of all music to their most essential qualities. Afterwards, music must then test and prove its superiority (by consensus) among people worldwide and the decision must remain equally convincing throughout time. For example, if we isolate, catalog, and assign values to all musical elements such as melody, rhythm, harmony, timbre, texture, dynamics, form, and measure the effects that they have on humankind, then we can begin to "measure" some parameters of musical value with a common standard. A computer program could conceivably weigh each musical sample against a mutual benchmark, then compare and evaluate all musical samples systematically through calculation, and assign a final numerical value to each sample. Even then, however, there would be no guarantee that a reliable stratified list of musical value could ever convincingly isolate a "superior" style that satisfied worldwide scrutiny, and numbers probably would never match the actual effect that music has on listeners. In any case, any result would have to be agreed upon through worldwide agreement. The principles and formulae that enable aircraft flight, or the cure for smallpox, are observable, quantifiable, and verifiable. Bach produced beautiful and superbly crafted musical composition, but his music does not diminish the aesthetic, spiritual, inspirational, therapeutic, and intellectual value of other music worldwide. Just as Occidental conceptions about sexual behavior have no value as criteria that govern worldwide sexual sensuality, Western opinions regarding worldwide musical value cannot meaningfully adjudicate musical value outside its own culture. All music seems potentially powerful when each gesture tends to suggest organic growth, continuity, wisdom, viability, and movement.

Breaking music down into its subunits reveals essential information about its makeup, nonetheless. Dividing anything into its rudimentary elements is usually an important step towards understanding its makeup. Scientists divide particles into their sub-particles to discover basic compositional components enabling them to understand the ways nature organizes and builds life and energy forms. Nuclear fission involves a nuclear reaction in which a massive nucleus splits into smaller nuclei with the simultaneous release of energy. Scientists also collide particles to help understand the origin of existence.

At 4:28 A.M. on September 10, 2008 (Eastern time), scientists sent the beam of protons around the Large Hadron Collider's 17-mile-long racetrack, 300 feet beneath the Swiss-French border, and later sent another beam through again. After 14 years of labor, these scientists at the CERN laboratory outside Geneva successfully activated the world's largest, most powerful particle collider, making this event the most expensive scientific experiment to date (at $8 billion). Future experiments are aimed at enabling scientists to look forward to a new era of understanding about the origins and evolution of the universe. Some scientists have said that this phase of experiments might also provide an opportunity to bring somewhat disparate scientific theories together into a single theory of matter and even "reveal the origins of God." Of course, people grounded in a spiritual orientation would never attempt to reduce God to a physical quantity or dimension. Some things may always remain illusive, and dissecting music does not seem to reveal as much about its effect and meaning as one might expect. Division and collision of particles does seem to maintain that everything has a nucleus—a central phenomenon, idea, or force that governs a given microcosmic or macrocosmic system. Music tends to evolve from the creation and development of a conglomerate of unified systems of sonic phenomena, each extending omni-directionally from some form of central musical core and sonic nexus. Music is a reflection of the people who create it, representing the thought, polarity, harmony, and tension that binds their inner consciousness to the outer world.

Inspiration emerges from exploring, contemplating, and meditating on nuclear ideas. Inspiration does not have to be perfect, precise, quantifiable, or explainable. Its task is purely to produce a meaningful result. What is meaning? Meaning is something that is conveyed or signified, especially when it inspires a sense of significance. How does music reveal its subtle meaning as it expresses joy, anger, anxiety, excitement, pride, concentration, grief, relief, fright, fear, and much more? Does the movement and organization of music attempt to reflect qualities of the physical movement of molecular existence? Can manipulation of the elements of music emulate the dynamics extant in an ocean or rainforest, or suggest the abstract balance and proportions of any other healthy ecosystem. An *ecosystem* is a specific area of size in which climate, landscape, animals, and plants are constantly interacting. A musical composition is a sonic environment (ecosystem) in which a wide range of dynamic musical elements, aesthetic landscapes, performer interaction, and listener absorption are constantly intermingling.

The particular styles, phrases, patterns, and assortment of nuances that we create and perform during musical transmission reflect our individual and collective consciousness, as well as aspects of the environment in which music and people are nurtured. **Deductive reasoning,** sometimes referred to as a "top-down" approach, proceeds from the more general to the more specific. It may begin with a *theory* (musical idea) about a topic of interest that eventually becomes a specific *hypothesis* (motive, theme, or melody) that can then be tested as *observations* collected to support or confirm original theories with specific supporting data (theory and analysis of compositions). **Inductive reasoning** ("bottom up" approach) works the other way around, advancing from specific observations to broader generalizations and theories. In inductive reasoning, we activate the process with specific observations and measures, detect patterns and regularities, create tentative hypotheses to explore, and gradually and systematically evolve general conclusions or theories.

In music, we can presumably approach potential meaning deductively by improvising consciously upon conventional musical ideas. Generally speaking, some musicians reflect **induction**—a tendency to take known quantities in the musical world (observation of existing tunes and traditional structures) and proceed to explore and embellish those fixed and familiar basic ideas and qualities. Such musicians tend to be improvisers with a variety of novel interpretations, embellishments, and approaches. Other musical approaches begin equipped with a theory alone, suggesting the application of **deduction**—advancing from unknown territory and using few preconceived musical guidelines, templates, or references, allowing them to explore general fundamental elements of music more flexibly. Such musicians tend to be **spontaneous composers.** At times we apply induction to produce interdisciplinary art spontaneously, involving assorted collectives of artists. Spontaneous composition occurs when musicians or other artists evolve art from raw ideas, eventually bringing them to a logical and ultimate conclusion that is novel. Both spontaneous composition and other forms of improvisation involve the systematic and imaginative manipulation of sonic information, using instantaneous musical computation and subconscious data processing to achieve the desired outcome.

The custom of borrowing systems of organization from outside the realm of music was firmly established when humankind first imitated the sounds of the natural world. For many centuries composers have experimented with mathematical concepts in relation to music. The concept of "music of the spheres," dating back to Pythagoras, asserted that the perfect proportions of the natural universe governed humankind. Mathematical order was the basis for the choice of musical intervals and the systematic organization used by the ancient Greeks. The term "algorithm" is adopted from the fields of computer science and information science. In contemporary mathematics, computing, linguistics, music, and related disciplines, an **algorithm** is a sequence of instructions, often used for calculation and data processing. An algorithm's instructions establish procedures for solving a problem, usually with the requirement that the procedure terminate at some point. During the 20th century certain composers applied a technique that established new ways of ordering pitches within the context of traditional musical forms. "Algorithmic composition involves procedures and requires provisions that govern parameters of musical composition in ways that have been informally employed since antiquity. In a related fashion, the mind of the spontaneous composer can contain flexible algorithms based upon wide-ranging systematic methodology, instructions, processes, and cumulative knowledge that manifest as both concrete and abstract symbols."

Music heals like medicine, disciplines the mind like meditation, operates within the physical forces of nature like physics, and serves as food for the soul like spirituality. Aaron Copland said, "The whole problem can be stated quite simply by asking, 'Is there a meaning to music?' My answer would be, 'Yes.' And 'Can you state in so many words what the meaning is?' My answer to that would be, 'No'" (Moncur 2008). Meaning in music is always speculative since no one can define or quantify it definitively. The word music was born out of the Egyptian term "muse" that means messenger. If musicians are cultural messengers, many cultures have produced principal leaders and masters in the development of aesthetic knowledge and cultural advancement.

Who ultimately decides what music means? Music applies its own abstract "scientific method" to sound while exploring musical questions and answers. Oral/ aural tradition, written notation, or any other attempt to capture the essence of music concretely remains capable only of outlining its basic ingredients, aspects, and concepts. Musical vibration is of pure essence and any descriptions of music must stand only as forms of deviation from the definitive sonic model. Discussing the friction created between music and its various forms of interpretive deviations results in the creation of interesting theories. Still a score cannot be produced that captures all the subtle nuances of its sounds. The "musical laws" that may satisfy people in a particular culture or epoch of time will certainly find opposition elsewhere during the evolution of world culture.

Like other world music, African oral/aural tradition based its melodic development on the natural tendencies of the overtone series. The dominant seventh chord is the first four-note tertian sonority to unfold intact within that harmonic sequence. The laws governing blues-based African-American music guide a holistic set of flexible harmonic relationships that bind basic major, minor, and dominant chords with their diminished, augmented, and other harmonic alterations, extensions, poly-chords, and substitutions. This forms a unified set of interactive, interconnected, and interrelated harmonic relatives that support free and systematic, melodic and harmonic, logical exploration. The blues matrix thus combines all basic harmonic sonorities into a single unified whole. "Jazz" musicians explore the various relationships and permutations suggested by this matrix.

Figure 4. The Basic Blues Matrix Minus its Additional Arrays of Closely Related Tritone Substitutions, Diminished and Augmented Chords, Poly-chords, and other Extensions and Substitutions

Ab maj7	Ab 7	Ab min7	Bmaj7	B7	Bmin7	Dmaj7	D7	Dmin7	Fmaj7	F7	Fmin7
C#maj7	C#7	C#min7	Emaj7	E7	Emin7	Gmaj7	G7	Gmin7	Bb maj7	Bb 7	Bb min7
F#maj7	F#7	F#min7	Amaj7	A7	Amin7	Cmaj7	C7	Cmin7	Eb maj7	Eb 7	Eb min7
Bmaj7	B7	Bmin7	Dmaj7	D7	Dmin7	Fmaj7	F7	Fmin7	Ab maj7	Ab 7	Ab min7
Emaj7	E7	Emin7	Gmaj7	G7	Gmin7	Bb maj7	Bb 7	Bb min7	Db maj7	Db 7	Db min7
Amaj7	A7	Amin7	Cmaj7	C7	Cmin7	Eb maj7	Eb 7	Eb min7	F#maj7	F#7	F#min7
Dmaj7	D7	Dmin7	Fmaj7	F7	Fmin7	Abmaj7	Ab 7	Ab min7	Bmaj7	B7	Bmin7
Gmaj7	G7	Gmin7	Bb maj7	Bb 7	Bb min7	Db maj7	Db 7	Db min7	Emaj7	E7	Emin7
Cmaj7	C7	Cmin7	Eb maj7	Eb 7	Eb min7	Gb maj7	Gb 7	Gb min7	Amaj7	A7	Amin7
Fmaj7	F7	Fmin7	Ab maj7	Ab 7	Ab min7	Bmaj7	B7	Bmin7	Dmaj7	D7	Dmin7
Bb maj7	Bb 7	Bb min7	Db maj7	Db 7	Db min7	Emaj7	E7	Emin7	Gmaj7	G7	Gmin7

The blues demonstrates the flexibility of a dominant progression that predominantly involves a series of various seventh chords, all of which are located no more than one accidental away from becoming a dominant seventh chord. The basic harmonic framework of the 12-bar blues includes a progression I7/IV7/V7 as its harmonic structural ingredients (e.g., D7/G7/A7). There is a close relationship between the minor seventh chord and the dominant seventh chord, with all chord tones held in common except the third (minor third in the min7 and major third in the dom7); as well as between the major seventh chord and the dominant seventh chord, with all chord tones held in common except the seventh (minor seventh in the min7 and major seventh in the dom7). Therefore, the typical iimin7/ V7/I7 (e.g., Dmin7/G7/C7) is closely related to the unfolding of dominant seventh chords around the circle of fifths (e.g., D7/G7/C7 . . .). Thus there is a great deal of suppleness in navigating through a blues harmonic series where these closely related seventh chords are involved.

Body, Mind, and Spirit

Music, and the universe in general, seem to experiment with transformation, transition, proportion, polarity, contrast, similarity, abstraction, spirit energy, the creative process, motion, and dynamic expression. People worldwide have always adopted musical systems that fit their needs. Significant listener exposure to a set of musical stylistic characteristics and features molds people's aesthetic dispositions and preferences. The musical, ideological, and socio-cultural circumstances that produced African-American music also brought conventional orality, aurality, and literacy paradigms into collision during the transition from Africa to the Americas that gradually lead to the creation of new artistic paradigms. African oral history was transmitted through music from generation to generation over many thousands of years. The African *griot's* and *jeli's* oral and aural transmission of music, in their tremendously diverse spectrum of traditional societies, contributed to a growing body of music knowledge and cultural history. Just as some African hunters believe that most objects around them have a spiritual dimension, many Africans believe that music and words are infused with spiritual properties. *Griot* is a word that the French adopted to replace the original term *"jeli"* [JEH-lee]. The jeli are a class of people in West Africa who traditionally maintained the history of their ancestors through music. *Jeliya* [JEH-lee-yah] is the art of skillfully harnessing the intangible and abstract spiritual forces in the world. Humankind emerged in Africa and the ancients were the first to link nature with spirituality, and ultimately the Creator to creativity.

A *jeli* of Mande origins is a professional musician whose calling in life has been determined by birth. Only members of a limited number of families have the right to play certain instruments and sing about certain aspects of society. Because of their bloodlines, *jeliw* (plural for jeli) have both the right and the duty to perform certain kinds of music. They become highly trained musicians through years of apprenticeship.

The art of the jeli, known as *jeliya*, involves the skillful harnessing of the spiritual power of words and music. A male jeli is called a *jelike* and may sing, play a musical instrument, or function as an orator. A female jeli (known as *jelimuso*) primarily sings, although many young females are now also learning to play instruments these days. In Mali, three instruments in particular are closely associated with jeliya: the *kora*, the *balafon*, and the *ngoni*. For most jeli the kora is not just an instrument, it is also the spiritual accompaniment to the deepest and most introspective thoughts on life, religion, politics, history, and culture.

The meaning of music is intimately intertwined with the power of sound vibration, order, and motion. Our mind, as the governor of our development, is capable of influencing our personal health and destiny. Because many people worldwide believe that our spirit, thoughts, and emotions can profoundly impact our mental, physical, and spiritual health, music is considered the healing force of the universe. It accesses our emotions and psyche in ways that words alone cannot accomplish. Dr. Candace Pert, an internationally recognized psychopharmacologist and author of *Molecules of Emotion,* suggests:

> The neuropeptides and receptors, the biochemicals of emotion, are the messengers carrying information to link the major systems of the body into one unit that we can call the body-mind. We can no longer think of the emotions as having less validity than the physical, material substance, but instead must see them as cellular signals that are involved in the process of translating information into physical reality, literally transforming mind into matter (Pert 36).

Dr. Pert further suggests that, "Because the molecules of emotion are involved in the process of a virus entering a cell, it seems logical to assume that the state of our emotions will affect whether or not we succumb to viral infections." She explains ". . . the chronic suppression of emotions results in a massive disturbance of the psychosomatic network." Thus, "The key is to express it and then let it go, so that it doesn't fester or build, or escalate out of control" (40). Pert is best known for her opiate receptor, endorphin and peptide research. Her work is based on how the body and mind functions as a single psychosomatic network of information molecules that control our health and physiological makeup. Musicians also translate and express emotions through physical manipulation of musical instruments in a seamless psychosomatic network transporting musical information.

Pert's newest book, *Everything You Need to Know to Feel Go(o)d,* examines how mind, body, and spirit are inseparable. We can sense the relationship between our critical thoughts and corresponding tightness in your chest or stomach. When we are happy, excited, or thinking positive thoughts, our whole body feels relaxed. Pert says that between 12,000 and 50,000 thoughts occur in the mind of an average person per day and suggests that thoughts can have profound effects on our psychophysiology. Like light (which quantum physics reveals has a dual energetic and particulate nature), Pert explains, our emotions exist both as energy and matter, in the vibrating receptors on every cell in the body.

> Thousands of years ago, the Buddha pointed out that our thoughts determine our experience of the world. He was the original cognitive therapist, explaining that our beliefs had the power to enslave us or enlighten us. The ancient Indian medical system of Ayurveda also teaches that our biography helps create our biology. (51)

We can project our understanding of the interconnectedness between all systems that make us function as whole beings to the interconnectedness throughout existence. The wholeness of existence exists whether or not we recognize it. Likewise, personal realization and self-awareness are valid to the recipient whether or not there is mutual acceptance or recognition of a particular revelation or experience. No one will ever see the entire picture of the universe, but every piece we observe adds to our understanding of the puzzle and brings us a little closer to a fuller realization. Whatever we think, sense, and experience helps to create our reality, and music colors and enhances our physical, psychic, and spiritual understanding of the world.

The miraculous order and construction of the evolving world provides a bottomless well of motivation and inspiration for artists. Composers realize that it takes knowledge, flexibility, and adaptability to spontaneously create beautiful ideas and expression. We may wonder, "How can our own creative approaches align with various qualities of universal expression?" Musical process and knowledge are important elements of creative expression, and new creative options ultimately change and expand our sets of creative possibilities. Change is inevitable and perennial, and a dynamic stream of imagination, inspired by the world around us, can help us navigate through processes of creative production. Society, nature, new technology, and fellow artists influence each other and increase our inspirational resources. The more openness that artists bring to their creative process the greater the range of possibilities.

Each highly effective artist inevitably becomes an excellent communicator through his or her work. Spontaneous composition, ancestral legacy, empirical knowledge, and logic fortify our intuitive capacity to process sound. Engaging paradoxical ideas and exploring the unknown are common during an artistic exploration. Innovation challenges conventional wisdom, continually creates new theories, and develops synthetic ways of tying new sets of musical elements together. If artistic expression results in meaningful and significant impact on audiences, it does not matter if its ingredients or features used to achieve that level of competence align with prevailing theoretical expectations, speculation, or analysis. For many spontaneous composers, the ultimate goal is to understand the dynamics, interconnectivity, and interdependence of the creative materials, problems and forces within their project.

An investigation of creativity can involve a dual process including deconstruction of a concept on one hand and constructive methodology that explores rebuilding new compositional paradigms, on the other. Jacques Derrida coined the term "deconstruction" in the 1960s. Deconstruction may not seem to necessitate the same degree of tactical analysis, systematic thought, and philosophical continuity that constructive methodology demands. Most often deconstruction seems only to strip a subject to its core. Nonetheless, the concept of deconstruction helps to provide a counterbalance to constructive methodology and traditional conventions.

Titles of Compositions as Nuclei

As a matter of survival, people have always needed to solve problems creatively and this has resulted in the discovery of various forms of novel, varied, and complex solutions. Artists and other people also have a desire to communicate their knowledge, wisdom, feelings, ideas, and values to others. The investigation of the creative process is often influenced or guided in part by various interpretations of cosmology, Taoism, Afrocentrism, myth, and other forms of spiritual development. John Coltrane was amidst the few seminal titans among jazz innovators. Jazz titans are those who change musical style significantly, not just for those who play their particular instrument, but also for everyone among both the full compliment of musicians and audience. The intensely devotional and spiritual aspect of the work of composers is most often avoided. Musicians and researchers often analyze Coltrane's music intellectually and technically, recognizing the impact that he had on twentieth-century music; but theorists and musicologists tend to steer clear of the most distinguished aspect of contribution that his titles often suggest. Since a composer's ideas are often the nucleus of his or her music, at times titles must be seriously considered.

Jazz introduced a particular brand of musical freedom to the world that, ironically, surfaced from a community of people denied access to both their personal freedom and their ancient cultural traditions for centuries. The paradoxical cross-fertilization that occurred between unprecedented degrees of musical freedom blended with an intense desire to retain any possible memory or other aspects of African tradition that could be managed under oppressive and debilitating socio-cultural conditions, led to the production of variegated forms of personal expression and styles reflective of such intense human dynamics. Such circumstances necessitated constant improvisation and the music appropriately replicates extreme and passionate human conditions. There are other situations that produce associated socio-cultural effects, just as Indian music emerged from related degrees of social tension that arose from conflict between traditional conventions and tremendous social upheaval.

John Coltrane's Titles

Between 1957 and 1964, Coltrane became interested in West African music and the music of India. Though raised a Christian, Coltrane later began reading books about Hinduism, Islam, science, astrology, yoga, and African history. When released from the Miles Davis Quintet in 1956, as a result of his drinking, smoking, and destructive drug habit, Coltrane entered a brief period of depression. He eventually emerged from his melancholy state and entered a prolonged period of meditation and prayer that led to what he considered his "spiritual awakening." In the spring of 1957 Coltrane returned to a highly influential, but relatively brief, creative period of work with Thelonious Monk. He later rejoined Miles to collaborate on the classic *Kind of Blue* album and began a change of musical direction that would both summarize his harmonic evolution (culminating in his album *Giant Steps*), and experiment with the quasi-modal and famous "sheets of sound" approaches that became hallmarks of his mature style. This new direction was evident on his recording, *My Favorite Things* and many others. Coltrane's composition *A Love Supreme*, which he recorded with his quartet in December of 1964, was the zenith of this restlessly explorative period that involved elements of both his personal life and music. Some musicians and listeners consider *A Love Supreme* one of the most significant works of art dedicated to God since Michelangelo painted the Sistine Chapel. His later work reflects his interest in planetary archetypes and their mystical qualities.

In the liner notes to *A Love Supreme*, Coltrane relates that he began to have dreams in which it seemed that God revealed various musical ideas and concepts to him. Coltrane said that *A Love Supreme* was revealed to him in its entirety through such a dream in the winter of 1964. The movements of the suite include "Acknowledgment" (after a brief invocation featuring Jimmy Garrison's bass), "Resolution," "Pursuance," and "Psalm." During the latter movement Coltrane leads the ensemble with declamatory statements that seem to function within the ensemble as a call and responsorial-like sermon with the other musicians responding as would an African-American Southern Baptist congregation. In discussing *A Love Supreme* Ashley Kahn concludes:

> What Coltrane called "exploring all the avenues" was essentially the quest to exhaust every possibility for his horn in the course of a song. He devoted himself to rapid runs in which individual notes were virtually indistinguishable, a style quickly labeled "sheets of sound." As Martin Williams puts it in *Saturday Review,* Coltrane "seemed prepared to gush out every conceivable note, run his way a step at a time through every complex chord, every extension, and every substitution, and go beyond that by reaching for sounds that no tenor saxophone had ever uttered before him." Needless to say, this music was not easily understood—critics were quick to find fault with its length and monotony—but it represented an evolution that was welcomed not only by jazz performers, but by composers and even rock musicians as well (Johnson 16).

In a 1966 interview, Coltrane discussed religion and spirituality relating that, "I've always felt that even though a man was not a Christian, he still has to know the truth some way or another. Or if he *was* a Christian, he could know the truth." He continued, "The truth itself doesn't have any name on it to me. And each man has to find this for himself, I think" (Kahn 12). Coltrane's composition "Interstellar Space" may be his final attempt to dissect a portion of the universe, from the fixed position of his musical consciousness, through an exploration of patterns, ideas, dynamic tension and release, gathered over his lifetime through an inductive process reflective of nature's own poetic progression. Titles of composers' works can supply a catalog of their evolving concepts, ideas, and perspectives.

Titles of Coltrane Compositions

1959–1960
"Like Sonny"
"Giant Steps"
"Naima" (his Wife)
"Countdown"
"Cousin Mary"
"Like Sonny" (saxophonist Sonny Rollins)
"My Shining Hour"
"Exotica" *
"One And Four"
"Simple Like"
"Liberia"
"Equinox"

1961–1963
"Dahomey Dance"
"Village Sunrise"
"Impressions"
"Mr. P.C." (bassist Paul Chambers)
"Impressions"
"Spiritual"
"India"
"Big Nick" (saxophonist Nick Nicholas)
"Soul Eyes"
"Tunji" (drummer Michael Olatunji Babatunde)
"Out Of This World"
"My Little Brown Book"
"AFRICA/BRASS"
"Dedicated To You"
"The Promise"

"Lonnie's Lament" (pianist Lonnie Liston Smith)
"Alabama" (for the little girls killed in bombing)
"After The Rain"
"Dear Old Stockholm"

1964
"Crescent"
"Wise One"
"The Drum Thing"
"Bessie's Blues" (vocalist Bessie Smith)
"A LOVE SUPREME"
"Acknowledgement"
"Resolution" (recorded Oct. 8, 1963)
"Pursuance"
"Psalm"
"Nature Boy"

1965
"Brazilia"
"One Down, One Up"
"Song Of Praise"
"Living Space"
"Vigil"
"Ascension"
"Attaining"
"Dearly Beloved"
"Ascent"
"Amen"
"FIRST MEDITATIONS"
"Consequences"

"Love"
"Compassion"
"Serenity"
"Joy" "Evolution"
"Om"
"Kulu Se Mama"
"The Father And The Son And The Holy Ghost"

1966
"Manifestation"
"Reverend King"
"Meditations"
"Leo"
"Peace On Earth"

1967
"Seraphic Light"
"Sun Star"
"Stellar Regions"
"Offering"
"Configuration"
"Jimmy's Mode" (bassist Jimmy Garrison)
"Tranesonic"
"INTERSTELLAR SPACE" (duet with Rashied Ali)
"Mars"
"Venus"
"Jupiter"
"Saturn"
"Expression"
"Ogunde"
"To Be"

Many European composers also expressed interest in spiritual, metaphysical, mystical, and related systems of philosophical thought through their music. The sustainability of the universe is a result of its perpetual motion, continuity, composition, and interactivity, producing an infinite array of interrelationships. Premeditative and spontaneous composers often contemplate and investigate such things in nature through various means, and then strive to reflect universal qualities in their artistic vision.

Gustav Holst—*The Planets Op. 32*

Gustav Holst had a childhood intrigue with theosophy and discovered a book in his library called, *The Art of Synthesis*, by Alan Leo. Leo was an astrologer and Theosophist who published various books on astrology. Leo divided his book into chapters based on the qualities of each planet. The chapters of *The Art of Synthesis* are labeled with headings that described the astrological characteristics of the planets in our solar system, offering Holst a precursor to the structure of one of his own compositions. Holst called his composition *The Planets*, "a series of mood pictures." "Neptune, the Mystic," is given the same title in both Leo's book and Holst's suite. *The Planets Op. 32* (1914–16) thus follows a topical structure closely related to *The Art of Synthesis*:

- —Mars, the Bringer of War
- —Venus, the Bringer of Peace
- —Mercury, the Winged Messenger
- —Jupiter, the Bringer of Jollity
- —Saturn, the Bringer of Old Age
- —Uranus, the Magician
- —Neptune, the Mystic

Igor Stravinsky—*Le Sacre du Printemps*

Composers who were investigating related topics during that era of the early twentieth century influenced Holst's thinking. Before Holst started to compose *The Planets*, both Arnold Schoenberg and Igor Stravinsky traveled to England. Schoenberg came to England and conducted his *Five Orchestral Pieces Op. 18*. Holst most likely attended that concert and became impressed, since he initially labeled the preliminary sketches of *The Planets* "Seven Orchestral Pieces." When Stravinsky came to England around the same time, to conduct his *Le Sacre du Printemps*, Holst must have appreciated Stravinsky's unconventional use of the orchestra. In the first movement of *The Planets*, "Mars," the conspicuous dissonance and unconventional meter seems reflective of Stravinsky's influence.

Stravinsky's work was also full of social commentary and the composition's scandalous passion and violence aligned well with the general disposition of its era. Nationalistic frenzies drove Europe to the brink of World War I, as the continent was plagued by widespread depression; and the European intelligentsia of that period questioned basic Western social values. Stravinsky's suggestive titles also make clear the music's ancient connects to myth and ritual.

Le Sacre du Printemps: Introduction 3:23
Le Sacre du Printemps: The Augurs of Spring
(Dances of the Young Girls) 2:48
Le Sacre du Printemps: Ritual of Abduction 1:15
Le Sacre du Printemps: Spring Khorovod (Round Dance) 3:47
Le Sacre du Printemps: Ritual of the Rival Tribes 1:40
Le Sacre du Printemps: Procession of the Sage 0:36
Le Sacre du Printemps: Adoration of the Earth (The Sage) 0:16
Le Sacre du Printemps: Dance of the Earth 1:10
Le Sacre du Printemps: Introduction 4:14
Le Sacre du Printemps: Mystic Circles of the Young Girls 2:58
Le Sacre du Printemps: Glorification of the Chosen One 1:29
Le Sacre du Printemps: Evocation of the Ancestors 0:40
Le Sacre du Printemps: Ritual Action of the Ancestors 3:28
Le Sacre du Printemps: Sacrificial Dance (The Chosen One)

Arnold Schoenberg—*Five Orchestral Pieces Op. 18*

Like Coltrane, Schoenberg also composed some of his most influential or pivotal work at times of intense personal and artistic crisis. Schoenberg's *Five Orchestral Pieces Op. 18* came at such a time and develops further his contribution to the evolving notion of "total chromaticism." Just as with *Le Sacre du Printemps*, *Five Orchestral Pieces* reflects the tensions and violence of an environment and epoch of related temperament. The stress and strain of the period is reflected in the tension and extreme violence that emerges periodically within Schoenberg's score. The music is unsettling and disturbing just as the expressionistic movement of the time reflected preoccupation with the distressed subconscious and burgeoning societal madness.

Summary

In the pages that follow I explore music with a general personal assumption in mind regarding vibration, spirit, and the nature of existence. Music provides a key to understanding the relationship between the physical and ethereal aspects of the cosmos.

Everything in the vibrating universe is interconnected and nothing is ever entirely destroyed. Our consciousness develops in accordance with evolving levels of awareness, and if we do not develop subconscious contact with dimensions that extend beyond the molecular universe during this brief incarnation, in addition to our cognitive development—activating and integrating body, mind, and spirit to a reasonable degree—then perhaps we will not possess the spiritual readiness to sense or appreciate the more ethereal realms once our spirit leaves its present physical temple. One thing is certain, as science discovered somewhat with sensing dark matter, there is much that lies outside our consciousness, our subconscious awareness, and far beyond the perceivable molecular universe. Likewise, music extends exponentially beyond both the capacity of intuitive comprehension and far beyond the reaches of our even more limited empiricism. Much exists, whether or not we acknowledge, catalog, or sense its presence.

"Musicians don't retire; they stop when there's no more music in them."

—Louis Armstrong

References

Berman, Morris *The Reenchantment of the World.* Ithaca: Cornell University Press. 1981.

Coon, Dennis L. (1997). *Essentials of Psychology.* New York: Brooks/Cole Publishing.

Dale, P. S., Dionne, G., Eley, T. C., and Plomin, R. 2000. "Lexical and Grammatical Development: A Behavioral Genetic Perspective." *Journal of Child Language,* 27/3, pp. 619–642.

Dietrich, Arne. *The Cognitive Neuroscience of Creativity. Psychon Bull Rev.* 2004; 11:1011–1026. http://www.pubmedcentral.nih.gov/articlerender.fcgi?artid=2244806

Franken, Robert E. *Human Motivation,* Thomson Brooks/Cole 3rd ed.

Halpern, A. R; Zatorre, R. J. When that Tune Runs through Your Head: A PET Investigation of Auditory Imagery for Familiar Melodies. *Cereb Cortex.* 1999; 9: 697–704. http://www.pubmedcentral.nih.gov/articlerender.fcgi?artid=2244806

Harris, Kevin. As cited in "Collected Quotes from Albert Einstein" Copyright: Kevin Harris 1995 (may be freely distributed with this acknowledgment) http://rescomp.stanford.edu/~cheshire/EinsteinQuotes.html

Johnson, Anne Janette. *John Coltrane Biography* Musician Guide. January 2009 http:// www.musicianguide.com/biographies/1608000790/John-Coltrane.html

Kahn, Ashley. Essay prepared for *Morning Edition* for the new edition of the Coltrane album, *A Love Supreme* (a double CD). It is a result of research for Kahn's new book *A Love Supreme: The Story of John Coltrane's Signature Album.* As cited on http://www.npr.org/templates/story/story.php?storyId=855350 December 2008.

Kirkweg, Sara B. The Effects of Music on Memory. Copyright 2008 Missouri Western State University. http://clearinghouse.missouriwestern.edu/manuscripts/230.asp

Moncur, Michael. *The Quotation Page.* "Aaron Copland (1900–1990)." http://www.quotationspage.com/quotes/Aaron_Copland/ May 2008.

Nisenson, E. New York: Da Capo Press; 1995. *Ascension: John Coltrane and His Quest.*

Pert, Candace, Ph.D. and Nancy Marriott. *Everything You Need to Know to Feel Go(o)d,* Carlsbad, California: Hay House, Inc. September 2006.

Walker, D. P. *Spiritual and Daimonic Magic from Ficino to Campanella,* U. Notre Dame Press, 1975. Ideas here are generally drawn from this source; it gives a good analysis of Renaissance high magic.

Yates, Frances A. *The Art of Memory,* New York: Penguin Books, 1969.

Chapter Two
Outlining Particles of Poly-Dimensional Harmony: In Search of Music's URAM

Ultimate Reality and Meaning (URAM): Music is a multifarious discipline that requires the employment of all our senses, wisdom, and levels of consciousness. This study attempts to introduce conceptual ideas on various levels of musical inspiration, analysis, and meaning:

1. This is a book of selected etudes, scales, and patterns designed to help musicians enhance their technical and cognitive facility on their instrument while allowing an opportunity to explore a range of appurtenant ideas that relate to creativity, human expression, universal order, and imagination.
2. We will consider assorted approaches to human organization, communication, perspectives, and Nature's patterns of design.
3. It introduces a cursory exploration of musical theory.
4. There are personal, spiritual, and an eclectic range of philosophical notions as well as examinations of various empirical perspectives on music and the universe.
5. It is a general exploration of spontaneous and premeditated composition.

1. Universal Creativity

Early seekers of wisdom aspired to comprehend the forces affecting their existence to better harmonize their life patterns with those of the universe. The effort required patient observation, analysis, and careful scrutiny of a wide range of natural events, patterns, and forces. Throughout time, the most inquisitive minds have refused to limit such investigation to either strictly scholastic or spiritual methodology and perspective. Ancient discoveries of Nature's interconnectedness and design eventually gave rise to calendars, clocks, music, science, and mathematics. We are the beneficiaries of that cumulative knowledge as reflected in numerous practical and theoretical manifestations from aviation and architecture to the arts and string theory (NRC 5). Our perception of consonance, dissonance, order, logic, and time are all related to ancestral observations and conclusions drawn from Nature. Humanity must continue to investigate reality from all perspectives if it is to fathom the secrets of universal creativity.

1.1 *Universal Ingredients for Creative Composition*

How can an understanding of the universe aid in composing and improving music and art? Society constantly demands that its members think, behave, and conform to myopic formulae ostensibly aimed at achieving greater clarity. Normalizing restrictions are often conspicuously aimed at promoting various brands of control and uniformity. An approach that focuses on what can be called "universal creativity," one based on considering the patterns, motions, and physical forces that bind and govern solar systems and galaxies, is much more liberated, abstracted, durable , flexible, penetrating, and ultimate in its approach than any rigid systems of intellectual order. The tendencies expressed within organized energy systems and structures could serve as models for guiding compositional direction, concepts, and structure. Perhaps, then, ultimate Nature might serve as our primary source of creative inspiration (Bindon 17).

Examining music through widely disparate forces and phenomena extant throughout the universe demands extrapolation from a broad range of sources. The inquirer can then place his/her findings under simple categories such as time, polarity, source, nucleus, harmony, motion, gravity, tension and release, consonance and dissonance, and the like. Further designing methodology for correlating disparate concepts and experiences is especially difficult when distilling them into a form suitable to motivate and inspire artistic expression.

Universal creativity and harmony offer keys to contemplating the unimaginable size, order, and diversity of the universe. Imagining that abstract patterns and cycles of universal organization exist is also personally compelling. It grants us a means of wrapping our finite minds around the concept of infinity while attempting to recognize cosmic order in the play of the universe. Not only can exploring natural genealogy be scientifically useful, but it can inspire and liberate our creativity.

The core of music in general can likewise be explored to reveal fundamental elements of sound. A person's desire to gain knowledge of any subject is reflected in their commitment to engage it as closely as possible. This principle is likely true whether one is studying weather patterns, gorillas, viruses, astronomy, the speed of light, or music. If everything has a beginning, middle, and end to its cycle, then repeated discernment of this natural pattern will influence our musical compositions, procedures, and courses of study, and accordingly shape various forms of storytelling. Likewise, if each life form is perceived as part of a continuum, then the interconnectedness of all living things will also be reflected in the prevalent approaches to research in the sciences and humanities, social interaction, and artistic production. Looking more broadly, those things that we consider non-living are nonetheless very much part of natural life cycles as well. Patterns such as nucleation, polarity, dynamic range, rhythmicity, and organizational harmony may reveal inherent purpose in all forms and lead us to discover revealing relationships between many universal systems.

1.2 *Factors in the Consideration of Ultimacy*

The central perspectives discussed herein are based on the assumption that each individual form of expression is, to some small degree, a microcosm of the universe. To gain perspective on **Ultimate Reality and Meaning (URAM)** through the lens of music, we must consider and inspect diverse notions spanning inspiration, creativity, composition, science, and society, as well as spirituality, cosmology, and cultural influence. This purview leads to at least five factors that might serve to elucidate the URAM of music.

1.2.1 Identification of the Structural Center of a Phenomenon

Finding the nucleus, or seed, of any process or phenomenon enables one to understand how the components of a nascent system evolve from and radiate around a central source or fundamental core. Genealogy is the history of families and the evolutionary line of descent that extends from ancestors. In dealing with primary influences on African-, European-, or Asian-derived music, for example, the genealogy of that musical form can be systematically traced to its structural core. The source of African-American musical expression is African culture (Nature), but infinite influences (nurture) inform its contemporary development. The fundamental tone of any overtone (and undertone) series is the seed of each musical sound, yet a systematic array of overtones completes its total expression. A musical sound's fundamental tone, in turn, connects with all other tones within the infinite unfolding of universal harmony. Tension and release in music and art are akin to the oscillations of duality and polarity that may be observed throughout Nature as she propels creativity, growth, and development.

1.2.2 Recognition of the Interdisciplinary Nature of Music

Sight, sound, and movement provide maps to musical inspiration in diverse ways. All of the physical, intellectual, emotional, and transcendent forces impinging on the creative individual affect musical vibration. We can also gain insight into musical composition by reviewing those things that have inspired the music of composers throughout time and across cultures.

1.2.3 Observation of the Universal Order and Fluidity of the Universe

Everything within the universe vibrates, producing interference patterns that yield a systematic abstract order. Like a stone hitting water, multiple dimensions extend omnidirectionally from any given point, involving dynamic quantitative and qualitative features that permeate each point (Duff 261–2). Observation of universal order can provide models for thinking about compositional structure, process, and procedure in music.

1.2.4 Universal Relativity and Meaning

Finding all the rippling effects that a single musical tone has on all other vibrations is impossible. Like the chaotic effect of the flap of a butterfly's wing on the distant weather, the relationships between actions and consequences are often complex and unpredictable. Ultimately everything within existence conveys meaning. In music, every tone affects other tones in its environment. The listener can hear music move from its beginning, through its middle, to its end. Musical events in space (harmonic, melodic, aspects of timbre, etc.) and time (rhythmic, cyclical, linear structure) can be used to help track various ordered physical systems that have the musical analogue of gravitational centers. Structure arises from recognition of mutual relativity and dependency of organizational patterns in a composition.

1.2.5 Universal Tension and Release

Polarity and duality abound throughout the universe. Balance appears to propel and guide motion, proportion, and sequence in Nature. In music, harmony, phrasing, meter, and other structural elements of composition involve identifying related components that form systems of symbiotic agreement, fulfill expectation, and provide a sense of unity. The resulting patterns can provide moments of familiarity and surprise, or create tension and musical (emotional) conflict. Compositions of music and art seek a sense of abstract balance in all their elements.

2. The Seed of Ultimacy in Music

A living seed possesses signature DNA reflective of its progeny's potential history and its own primary purpose and basic composition. The seed idea for a musical composition can contain similar generative potency. In observing Nature's creativity, periodic cycles involving seed germination (nascence), time (development), and harvest (maturity) are revealed. A *nucleus* or seed takes time to evolve and *produce* offspring. Time may be a nonlinear or circular construct, though we tend to think of it as linear. Plato observed in *The Republic*, "Not only for plants that grow in the earth, but also for all creatures that move thereon, there are seasons of fruitfulness and unfruitfulness for soul and body alike, which come whenever a certain cycle is completed" (269). The temporal expanse to which Plato referred is the gestational period, at the conclusion of which the seed ("soul and body") of the living entity either comes successfully to birth or germination, or miscarries. Time as a whole encompasses the period from a seed's gestation to its development during its *journey* or *process*. Harvest is the ultimate *manifestation* of the seeds purpose, where the desired expression reaches completion and is *released* (fruit born). Nothing can be meaningfully attained without undergoing a complete process of development. All processes have opposing forces of *tension* that affect goals within their system of checks and balances. Parasitic, conflicting, or destructive elements are perhaps only counterbalancing forces required to complete a process of seed, time, and harvest.

The lessons that we learn from Nature enable us to evolve our knowledge and understanding of music, kinetics, visual arts, science, and all other important aspects of human life and development. Music, like DNA, is perhaps comprised of a fixed number of frequencies capable of infinite combination. Composers and musicians have evolved tone and rhythm management systems over the ages that launch musicians' notes of choice into motion. Music affects us at the neurological level and all animals may create their own forms of music to enhance the effectiveness of their communication and self-expression. Since the vastness and complexity of the universe extends beyond reduction to any simple formulas, the ultimate reality and meaning of existence may indeed be a perennial series of questions. We certainly have not found conclusive answers to questions such as, "What is life force?" or even, "What is music?" We do learn by simply observing the things around us, through discovering the interconnectedness between such phenomena, and by recognizing correspondences between related forces, structures, events, and dynamics.

Transferring features of Nature's creative processes to the creative development of musical composition requires forming personal style and artistic skill. Rhythm musically contextualizes the rendering of the evolution time. Some consider time a dimension of the fundamental structure of the universe where events unfold in measurable sequences relative to the observer (Hawking 22–5). The attuned observer might also form musical categories of time (rhythmic motion), space (melodic motion), and number (harmonic motion). These categories sequence events into patterns, quantifying the intervals between phenomena (distances between and durations of individual events), and finally enabling a comparison of the motions of sonic objects (musical tones, harmonic progressions, and rhythmic phrases) through analysis. Thus, time becomes a substantial entity that flows (having continuity) as sonic particles move through various containers (forming structures and patterns) to create discernible and complete artistic events (compositions).

Musical compositions can exist simply as ideas written in musical notation or as any number of other acoustic events, including live performances and recordings. Spontaneous composition is immediately realized and cannot exist simply as recorded symbols for a theoretical concept. It involves composing extemporaneously during the ongoing performance. Improvisation requires assembling and applying musical concepts and elements in response to all the musical factors of the moment, based upon a cumulative storehouse of premeditated musical knowledge. All composers use sound, silence, visual elements, and other factors to communicate their creative message, engage the senses, and elicit intellectual, physical, emotional, and subconscious responses from fellow performers and the listening audience. Nature's compositions can involve infinitely more layers of complexity.

3. The Ultimacy of Universal Improvisation

Compositional method can never have a singular pedagogy because creative objectives, aesthetics, and visions vary greatly. We can only make an overarching examination of the process of creation, considering the general techniques involved in organic creation and growth. When compositional pedagogy involves examining processes of universal creativity, "paint by number" methodologies and other such prescriptive tool kits hold only limited value. Life processes involve a rich mixture of awareness, patience, adaptation, flexibility, readiness, interaction, growth, and perpetual improvisation. As Patricia Ryan Madson wrote in her book *Improv Wisdom: Don't Prepare, Just Show Up*, "Life is an improvisation, and if we are lucky, a long one. It may end unexpectedly, and for some, too soon. I won't be the first author to remind readers to seize the day, to live each precious moment fully and with gusto" (15).

Since everything vibrates, music potentially represents a sonic prototype of the interconnectedness of other aspects of existence. The interdependency of every tone (and its envelope of appurtenant overtones) in the universe of sound also reminds us that diversified and stratified functions within other communities of relationship or activity do not diminish the individual importance and necessity of each contributing factor. Thus, the cultivation or destruction of any portion of an ecosystem affects the whole process. Jazz improvisation requires constant vigilance and responsiveness on the part of each ensemble member. Every note produced is an integral segment of the sonic whole.

Challenge is an inevitable feature of life. Biological creation involves a constant struggle with oppositional forces. The process of tension and release becomes detrimental to a life form when levels of tension get too far out of proportion. Struggle motivates evolution. Originally existing as nocturnal creatures due to the dominance of dinosaur species, the mammals' hearing allowed them to develop superior brainpower and evolve into creatures in control over their physical environment. Early mammals were very small and vulnerable. They had to improvise constantly to maintain survival, and were forced to be flexible, analytical, and resourceful. As Madson notes, "Long before there was planning there was improvising. For millennia humans functioned naturally *only* by thinking on their feet, problem-solving in the here and now. I wake up. I look around carefully. I hunt for food. I share it with fellow primates. We find a warm, dry place to sleep. We have a few laughs" (Madson 21).

Nature's improvisation is a basis for understanding the intimacy of musical improvisation. Nature and spontaneous composition both use improvisation as a primary vehicle for their evolution, and creativity (not duplication) is the most important ingredient of the process. Although the process of creativity is difficult to characterize, it involves a balance between harmonizing with a predictable, known outcome, and the constant negotiation with unexpected environmental circumstances that arise. In music, the first step in developing and expressing creativity is to master the language of the artistic idiom. Once basic knowledge is digested, then inspiration can flow through our basic skills. Once grounded in its basic elements, creativity becomes the most important aspect of improvisational production, flexibility, development, and maturity. Eventually, levels of artistic craftsmanship distinguish master artists from neophytes.

Improvisation allows performers and listeners to form a symbiotic partnership, involving transmission and reception, where music is created and absorbed in the moment in pursuit of beauty, expression, balance, and order. Creating music spontaneously also allows an opportunity to combine conception, emotion, and theory with discipline and practice. Theory without practice is barren, and practice devoid of theory is sightless or imprudent. Spontaneous composition affords opportunities to direct a reservoir of knowledge, wisdom, and experience towards self-created problems in an effort to discover new paths towards artistic solutions requiring balanced degrees of concrete structure and abstract freedom. We often learn sets of language vocabulary and phrases by rote that later apply to the expression of an infinite array of ideas. Similarly, the musical resources that we gather through study, meditation, and practice allow for the cultivation of a fertile and unlimited range of personal and collective invention.

4. Ultimacy and Culture: The Afrocentric Nucleus of Jazz Evolution

Just as the character of Nature's particular forces is evident in the music of the ancient Mbuti of the Ituri Forest, the ancient people of the Kalahari Desert, and other ethnic groups with long traditions, the sound of African-American music reflects the original sociocultural environment in which a particular people evolved over millennia. Jazz history reflects the chronological development of African-American music (Pfleiderer 39). It has increasingly become a tool through which the global community can communicate and express its voice. The earliest forms of improvisational music that African Americans produced functioned in a wide variety of ways, as had their ancestral music on the African continent.

Music served as a catalyst for physical, psychological, and cultural survival as African people adapted and evolved in foreign environments. Humans develop assorted cultural folkways and coping mechanisms, and may take a variety of approaches to survival. Africans existed in their homeland for thousands of years before some were abducted and transported to foreign lands. The transition required an extraordinary level of responsiveness to assure both daily and long-term survival (Hurston 127). Thus the nucleus of jazz involves ancient African musical and cultural traditions reflected most clearly in blues.

If, as discussed above, everything in event formation has a nucleus, and if we must consider generative and ontological factors such as seed, time, harvest, duality, and polarity in exploring the ways things evolve, then a summation of oppressed and oppressor forces motivating the course of jazz evolution must reveal its imprint on the music. The debilitating obstacles, personal fortitude, and inventive genius that led to the development of African-American work songs, field hollers, and early blues, eventually gave rise to the many colors of jazz, reflect the evolutionary struggle of these positive and beautiful art forms. Acknowledging these oppressive forces (like recognizing dissonance and tension in music) highlights the powerful and miraculous nature of the development (blossoming, consonance, and resolution) of African-American music, revealing the tenacious cultural elements that were codified into the "Africanisms" that gradually shaped contemporary culture worldwide (Samuel 102–3). That process of struggle and resolution is akin to the mammalian movement from an initial position of physical inferiority and insecurity as prey to that of modern *Homo sapiens*, who have evolved the highly adaptive mental capabilities that led to the establishment of culture, language, poetry, fiction, art, music, sports, drama, comedy, philosophy, and political institutions.

African-American music was influenced by contact with a wide range of traditional African spiritual and metaphysical belief systems such as Islam, Christianity, and other religious and philosophical exposures. Cultural traditions usually remain intact with impacts from the outside, although the ways they are practiced change. When Africans came to the Americas, they retained principles that were part of their native cultures and adapted those principles to their new environments. Denied the opportunity to openly celebrate African religions of their own tradition or choice, spirituality became not only a physical and psychological survival tool, but a direct individual link to the Creator as well. Spiritual themes provided symbols celebrating love—(expressed in Coltrane's "A Love Supreme" [Kofsky 211]); hope—(the Negro Spiritual "When the Saints Go Marching In"), and the indistinguishable cycles of life—(Charles Mingus' "Reincarnation of a Lovebird"). Spirituality, like myth, intuition, and human passion, is a difficult force to quantify, but for countless generations humanity has acknowledged its presence and necessity.

5. Ultimacy in Myth and Ritual

In considering **URAM** from a composer's perspective, one must also look at spirituality, myth, and ritual. The sublime experiences Nature provides are often those awe-inspiring memories that artists seek to emulate. Seeking understanding of the sublime directs us towards the higher frequencies of actuality. Myth presents points of departure for investigative journeys into uncommon realms that frequently replicate microcosms of universal themes—balance, polarity, struggle, revelation, and resolution. Elements of music enhance and heighten the overall effectiveness of ritual.

The purpose of ritual is to create a dramatic and emotional climate within which symbolism, emotions, and abstract ideas become more meaningful and vibrant. Through music, color, movement, and imagination, ritual elements take on enhanced existence. Techniques applied to the genesis of characters, expression (emotion), and interpersonal relationships explored in myth can also serve as archetypes for organizing musical systems. In spontaneous composition, each tonic, tonal center, and set of intervals can potentially gain new conceptual meaning and strategic significance when each entity is assigned specific dramatic and emotional meaning through symbolism. Musical families could be organized, and stylized emotions could emerge, through categorizing musical qualities (harmonic, intervallic, rhythmic, melodic, dynamic, timbral, textural, etc.) and assigning them each specific values and meaning. In the classic European repertoire, Mozart, Wagner, Berg, and other composers used intervals, motives, and phrases in related ways to represent operatic personalities and interpersonal and situational characteristics in their operas and musical works.

Rituals often encourage freedom of psychological, physical, and emotional expression, frequently inspire interdisciplinary communication, and can provide opportunities for communal interaction (Lateef 19). Too much freedom, however, may be considered chaos. Rituals also provide stimulating context within which emotions are stirred to the point of sublime experience. Myths and rituals are central to traditional African culture. Africans in America maintained close association with their traditional music through spiritual celebrations.

Ancient African ritual elements, such as those contained within Yorùbá spiritual thought and practice, illustrate the connection between myth, ritual, and culture. The term "Yorùbá" describes a number of semi-independent peoples loosely linked by geography, language, history, and religion. The population of Yorùbá within the area of southwestern Nigeria and neighboring Benin and Togo constitutes more than 15 million people. Most inhabitants live within the borders of the tropical forest belt, but the remnants of the powerful Oyo kingdom include groups living at the fringes of the northern savanna grasslands. Archaeological evidence suggests Yorùbá ancestors may have lived in this same general area of Africa since prehistoric times.

During the period 1600 to 1850, Vodun (or Voodoo) was perhaps one of the strongest traditional ethnic spiritual influences on African people in the Americas. It was practiced in New Orleans, Haiti, and other parts of the Americas. On the African continent Vodun was found in Benin, Togo, southeastern Ghana, Burkina Faso, and Senegal. Today it remains widespread across cultural groups in West Africa. Vodun is a name attributed to a traditionally West African spiritual system of faith and ritual practices supported and motivated by African music, dance, and visual art. The core functions of Vodun are to explain the forces of the universe, collaborate with those forces, and in so doing influence human behavior. Vodun's oral tradition of faith, stories and myths, conveys genealogy, history, and fables to succeeding generations.

In most parts of traditional African culture, little conceptual separation existed between the worlds of deceased ancestors and those of the living. Through ritual music, African-American contact with Vodun, Santaria, and Holiness-Pentecostal (or Sanctified) settings allowed participants to blend and intertwine aspects of the mundane secular world with those of the arcane spiritual realm (Ramsey 188; Samuel 20, 63). Similarly, many continental Indian texts suggest that all things are spiritual, music especially so. Music can be conceived as the soul of the universe as it is found in harmonious sound everywhere from the rustling of the trees, to the flowing streams, and in the hypnotic sound of raindrops.

The Sanskrit term "Dharma" represents the underlying order in life and the universe (Frawley 138). Dharma is that which upholds or supports the law and order that makes the cosmos and the harmonious complexity of the natural world possible. Music is a reflection of life, and jazz has enjoyed global syncretism due to its integration of both improvising and composing forces. Music cannot be reduced simply to tonal or atonal domains; analog or digital processes; abstract or concrete perspectives. It involves infinitely varied dynamic systems of interdependent and interrelated dimensions; including those currently known and unknown. Music requires a flexibility, wisdom, and openness to mirror life's poly-dimensionality. The universes that contain humanity, life, matter, and all existence have an infinite supply of examples that exemplify the creative process. In developing musical spontaneity, creativity, and expression, we might ask, "How can contemplating assorted processes of universal creativity enhance our musical understanding of systematic spontaneous composition?"

The Indian Vedas are set to distinctive folk (*margi*) and classical (*desi*) styles of melody that were developed side by side to emulate human agony, desire, ecstasy, sorrow, hope, and other passions expressed in the subtleties of music (Frawley 139). Hindustani and Carnatic are the two main streams of classical Indian music, the basic tenets of which were laid down in numerous ancient texts. These branches of music have similar origins and sources (according to ancient scripts), but distinctive styles. Indian music is propelled by melodic and rhythmic formulae (Khan 152). The term "raga," meaning melody, aims to be a highly scientific and practical means of the classification introduced by Venkatamahi. The raga is fundamental to both Hindustani and Carnatic Indian classical music.

Ideally, ritual of any culture is the locus where objective, subjective, and subconscious streams merge within bodies, minds, and spirits of participants. Ritual can draw our attention away from objective reality and towards higher vibratory features of the unknown. Music associated with ritual settings (such as Vodun ritual) has also been described as chaotic when viewed from the fringe of African culture. Perhaps playing polyrhythms (strongly contrasting rhythms expressed simultaneously) on the family of *bata* drums in certain traditional West African Yorùbá rituals was a musical attempt to represent the poly-dimensional unity of the abstract/concrete and space/time continua

(Bebey 102). The general intensity of the music, dance, and visual elements lead some participants to contrasting relaxed, excited, or trance states that expose the fluid interface extant between parallel states of consciousness. In a related way dreams allow our spirits to roam freely between seemingly infinite and chaotically arranged planes of existence. The multilayered sacred ritual music produced throughout traditional world culture has emulated natural content.

Science often shuns consideration of the spiritual and of a Creator who is an abstract, generative, vibratory, and poly-dimensional composer governing universal order. "Creator" here refers to the omnipotent creative source of existence—or the fundamental vibration—and has no particular religious connotations (Huxley 57; Schaefer 212). Clearly no one will ever be able to define or quantify the fundamental cause of existence, and we will always only observe and speculate about those things that appear to extend from a nucleus of existence. Conceptualizing over the single most indescribable and baffling phenomenon imaginable (the essence of existence) is natural, because we all extend from a long line of fundamental nuclear sources which, in turn, have their own long lines of ancestral sources. In any case, the *Creator* herein aligns conveniently and supportively with the principles of *creativity*.

Are melody and rhythm as inextricably linked and interchangeable as are energy and mass? Energy produces mass and melody produces rhythm. A mythical structure

Figure 1. A "Mythical" Structure of Relationships

NUCLEUS	EXPOSITION	DEVELOPMENT	CONCLUSION
(Substrate)	(Theory)	(Method)	(Assumption)
Creator	Fundamental Cause	Evolutionary Continuity	Everlasting Life
Jazz African-American Music	Socio-Cultural Response, Cosmic Reflection, Legacy of Past Masters, Individual Expression in Communal Settings	Spontaneous Composition, Disciplined Freedom, International Dialect Nature as Inspiration, Holistic Perspective	Interactive Process, Human Struggle, Triumph, Thought, and Spirit Challenge Traditional Notions
Africanisms (Cultural Influences)	Nucleus of Jazz Perpetuation of Ancestral Spirits, Oral/Aural Tradition	Cultural Diffusion, Virtuosity of Expression, Content Driven (Not Form Driven)	Worldwide Influence Through Music, Knowledge of Universal Order Through Ritual
Scientific Method	Ask a Question, Do Background Research, Construct a Hypothesis (Make Assumptions)	Experiments to Test Hypothesis, Analyze Data, Draw Conclusion, Math and Physics	Communicate Results, There Is a Logical Explanation for Everything

of relationships between various aspects of the material universe and music suggest potential associations. Are there qualities or characteristics of sound, musical compositions, subatomic particles, galactic particles, or the universe as a whole that are somehow systematically or abstractly interrelated and interconnected in general ways? If we create a basic outline to facilitate assorting cycles of evolutionary events involving their periods of exposition, development, and conclusion, could such a process enable us to conceptualize facets of music, science, society, and other aspects of our universe through a lens that reveals new ways of viewing interrelated qualities of substances, events, and functions? For example:

6. Vibrations of Spontaneous Composition

Vibration may be an identical means through which all known things can be examined. Just as our ears had to be conditioned gradually over many centuries to accept the higher frequencies of the overtone series in its harmonic progressions, science may have to wait awhile to develop tools and instruments precise enough to register the higher frequencies of universal vibration. Music is an integral and conspicuous part of many existing rituals. Perhaps sound and music may eventually provide new ways of exploring spiritual and empirical correspondences.

Vibrations in our world can potentially be heard, felt, smelled, seen, and tasted. Innovators such as Eric Dolphy, Rahsaan Roland Kirk, and other jazz musicians were interested in the sounds of the natural world, and integrated bird-songs and other wild animal sounds into their compositional and instrumental approaches. Some musicians listen to the flow of their own breath and heartbeat, watch flames burning, or observe the rise and fall of waves on the ocean to get musical gestures to move in similar fashion. Olivier Messiaen's work is unique in its individuality, and has exercised a remarkable influence over composers both in his native France and around the world. His *Catalogue d'oiseaux* of 1959 is derived from bird-song, from "Le chocard des alpes" and "Le loriot" to "Le courlis cendré."

Pierre Schaeffer pioneered musique concrète in the late 1940s and 1950s. "Musique concrète" ("concrete music") is often defined as simply making music out of "real world" sounds, or sounds other than those made by conventional musical instruments. More precisely, it attempts to create a new way of musical production and expression. Musique concrète strives to begin with the concrete sounds of our environment, experiment with them, and incorporate them into abstract musical compositions. The movement was facilitated by new developments in technology, such as microphones and the commercial availability of the magnetic tape recorder (created in 1939). Schaeffer and his colleagues used these new tools to manipulate tapes and tape loops.

Musicians and other artists often find inspiration by simply paying closer attention to quiet forests of pine and redwood or the rolling hills of oak and sage. They may learn to merge and connect musical ingredients organically by observing the flow of rivers, as evidenced in Czech composer Bedrich Smetana's symphonic poem "The Moldau" from "Ma Vlast" (My Country). Artistic reflections on social conformity, rhetoric, dogma, war, and narcissism also become forms of musical expression. Despite the divisiveness of several of these themes, mutual understanding, humility, and compassion help to align our attention with more constructive universal harmony and uncover music's beauty and healing nature.

To understand any particular form of music, therefore, examining it from its foundation and placing it within the context of world music history is important, since all elements of the music "particle" are interrelated. To perform the analysis, we must examine various forms of composition at their core to explore how musical ideas grow in general. A composer receives inspiration, organizes musical ingredients, and shapes tones by utilizing the procedures s/he has developed through continual listening, practice, study, and observation. Did music evolve from the consciousness and emotions of humankind, a grounded source? Or did the "Music of the Spheres" and other cosmic sounds emerging from incessant universal motion inspire ancient people?

The roots of the African-American music some call jazz have a blues matrix at its deceivingly simple core. This particular Jazz structure consists of an external triangle within which nine constituent triangles are contained and merge (See Figure 2: The Hesterian Analysis of African-American Jazz). The human spirit triangle sits at the apex of this external triangle. It is supported by an inverted triangle representing music as the international and universal language. The inversion places its base congruent

Figure 2. Hesterian Analysis of African-American Jazz

with that of the first triangle; and it is flanked by a third triangle on its left and a fourth on its right. The third represents the mirror that allows music to reflect the world around it. The fourth represents the collective history of music. Triangles five, six, seven, eight, and nine form the supporting foundation for the greater triangle poised upon it. Triangle number five reminds us that music is potentially both sacred and secular. The sixth triangle identifies the Afrocentric roots of jazz that have evolved for millennia. Triangle seven represents the effect that jazz continues to have on the music industry in the twentieth and twenty-first centuries. Blues is the eighth triangle, located at the center of the greater triangle's base due to its central importance in the harmonic, melodic, and linguistic dimensions of all African-American music. The ninth and final triangle represents creative musicians and other innovative artists as the world's most influential global ambassadors. Musical knowledge evolves individually and collectively in proportion to the quality of musical experience and time actively devoted to its development.

7. Earth Tones (Seismosonic Music)

For a scientific theory to be valid it must be verified empirically. In art, creative output is measured by its ability to communicate with and move listeners and viewers on intellectual, emotional, and physical levels. Music offers intriguing levels of expression that are often associated with images of magic, suspense, and mystery. Although professionals are capable of tracking precise mathematical increments of pitch, rhythm, timbre, and other musical elements, the most salient features of music's emotional impact and effectiveness are elements not usually tracked in composition. Like the universe itself, music exists on multiple planes that permeate and overlap each other, and involves sonic dimensions that run in contrasting and parallel temporal patterning. Composers learn ways that symbiotic elements and layers of sound support, overlap, and extend each other, enabling them to develop more liberated musical vocabulary and style. The compositional palette gains artistic flexibility and expands its expressive dynamics, and musical knowledge increases its general range when the universe serves as an artistic mentor. Some composers attempt to organize their knowledge of basic musical properties and relationships into catalogs and matrices that serve as guiding maps for their musical voyages and experiments. John Coltrane's mandala, or geometric matrix, reflects the systematic thinking of an influential musician who helped transform the twentieth century's aesthetic (White 1981). Do Nature's sounds produce their own geometric patterns?

Earth never experiences a single moment of stasis, and changes its shape according to many different time scales, ranging from millions of years to milliseconds. Subtle movements within the earth result in mountain uplift or erosion while the motion of huge convection cells causes a continuous rearrangement of plates that often leads to earthquakes. Earth's vibrations generate seismic sounds outside the human audible range. These sounds are continuously recorded by hundreds of seismological observatories around the globe. In seismology, vibrations form waves that are used to obtain information about the structure of the earth and the processes that cause earthquakes. Signals from earthquakes, volcanic eruptions, ocean surf, wind, traffic, and explosions can also be recorded. Most of what is known about the earth's interior comes from exploring its structure mathematically. The seismic signals generated from monitoring also exhibit a visual beauty when recorded graphically.

Using graphs formed by seismic waves, Wolfgang Loos composed and mixed *Inner Earth: A Seismosonic Symphony* at Traumton Digital Studio in Berlin. The results were produced by Loos and Frank Scherbaum and released on CD in September 1999. Loos wanted to know how the earth sounded and to find out if the visual fascination of seismograms had an acoustical equivalence.

The CD produced contained music that was composed completely of natural seismic signals produced by the movement of the earth, recorded and transcribed. In it were the sounds of earthquakes, microseism, and volcanic phenomena transposed to pitch equivalents, based on the assigning of representative pitches to the contour of the seismic wave form. Although the registered sound fragments were rearranged and recomposed, no other instruments were added. This approach is related to the Musica Universalis (universal music or music of the spheres), an ancient philosophical concept that regards proportions in the movements of the sun, moon, planets, and other celestial bodies as a form of harmonic and/or mathematical music (Khan 49).

8. Polarity, Duality, and Gravity

Polarity is a unifying principle. While duality often implies physical separateness of related yet opposite phenomena or modes of phenomena, the term "polarity" pulls such opposing forces into a single synergistic expression. Polarity is an abstract concept that is often used in a metaphysical context. It involves the essence of the underlying *unity* and interdependency of dualistic pairs. The two terms are often used interchangeably since, in the final analysis, polarity and duality are inseparable.

Positive and negative electric charges, the yin/yang relationship, the north and south poles of a magnet, the male and female bioforms, and attractive and repulsive forces are classic examples of polarity. The entire physical universe is based on polarity and duality. Metaphysically speaking, the fundamental substance of the entire universe involves a direct expression of subject and object, mind and matter, tension and release, action and consequence, and other polar configurations. Between the notions of polarity and duality there exists an association that is both readily observable (in the scientific sense) and strictly theoretical (in the metaphysical sense). Every quantity, force, or velocity is made up of components of polar direction and magnitude. The ebb and flow caused by the unity of opposing forces is a progressive force. Opposing forces are in fact unified in purpose.

Time, not just space, is a polarity. It displays a definite preferred direction between two opposite modes of being—past and future. We experience the "flow" of time as an ever changing present, with the past and future as opposite fields from the perspective of the present (Csikzentmihalyi 4). In this example we see an excellent clue as to how a *single* phenomenon with a built-in *two-sided* polarity (time) gives rise to a *three-fold* level of manifestation (past-present-future). In fact, every concrete example we see and experience in the physical world is not only a clue to the nature of higher modes of being, but Stephen Michael Nanninga suggests that it is a *direct expression* of the highest level of polarity in the universe.

In similar fashion, silence and sound create a unified, mutually dependent sonic force. Standing waves can be represented by a directional wave train where each wave contains positive and negative amplitudes and a neutral nodal point. Musicians use tension and release to establish polarity on melodic, harmonic, rhythmic, dynamic, structural, and all other elemental scales. Thinking in terms of polarity helps to maintain a sense of balance in art. As Plato remarked, "Since beauty and ugliness are opposite, they are two things; and consequently each of them is one. . . . Your lovers of sights and sounds delight in beautiful tones and colors and shapes and in all the works of art into which these enter; but they have not the power of thought to behold and to take delight in the nature of Beauty itself" (183). When composers entwine predictability, surprise, and other forms of musical polarity, it propels music forward with a sense of purpose, direction, and control. When conventional musical elements are perceived as entropy, elements of polarity still operate, perhaps subtly within realms of unconventional musical dynamics. Each interval, phrase, movement, and composition has a nucleus that serves as the generative nexus for all polarized or dualistic sets of musical ingredients. Composers express awareness of the inward pointing gravitational forces and polarity used to connect their ideas through their suggestive titles. Mary Lou Williams' *Zodiac Suite,* Gustav Holst's *The Planets Suite,* John Coltrane's *Interstellar Space,* Joe Henderson's *Isotope,* and numerous other composers' compositions have titles that reveal their motivations. Polarity is the creative essence of force in music, physics, and metaphysics (Harrison 10).

9. Language in Music

Language often supports music, and responsiveness to both language and music is a quality universal among humans. Its pervasiveness suggests that musical engagement may be fundamental to our survival as a species. Our ancestral relationship with music is initially evident in the nurturing lullabies that mothers traditionally sing to an infant to create the strong and perennial bond that ultimately develops. Some traces of the bonding and nurturing mother/child musical relationship must remain as offspring mature and transfer aspects of their early experiences to their subsequent socio-cultural development. The mother's language and movement are keys to these early forms of musical communication. Language is the primary catalyst for generating human communication, and parental influence has a profound effect on the development of language in their progeny.

In African music even the drums "talk" with clearly articulated speech inflections. African-American music has maintained some of this emphasis. Mutes were applied to brass instruments to increase their spectrum of mock tonal articulation and color, and many musicians often sing while they play their instruments to augment the melodic lines (the singing of bassists Major Holly and Slam Stewart are examples). Although African language was virtually lost in America over time, some African-American stylistic tendencies reflect ways in which ancestral African griots used linguistic nuances when they performed.

Just as the pull of central tones or tonal areas of various types grounds the continual interaction of tension and release in music, duality and polarity in physics produce gravitational force. Gravity is one of the universal forces of nature. It is an attractive force between all things. Gravity involves the acceleration produced by the mutual attraction of two masses. We can readily see gravity in action when at least one of the objects is very large. Gravitational force is greater when objects' masses are larger and if the objects involved are closer together. The gravitational force between two objects depends on their masses, with a magnitude inversely proportional to the square of the distance between the two centers of mass. Gravity is the natural force of attraction exerted by a celestial body—such as the sun, Earth, and other planets in our solar system—upon objects at or near its surface, tending to draw them towards the center of the body or system.

A "gravitational force" affects the family of orbiting overtones around fundamental tones and around the central fundamental tone at the center of a given pitch collection (Snyder 111). In terms of amplitude, the fundamental tone has the greatest mass (amplitude) compared to its overtones. Musical instruments and other vibrating sources produce unique and specific shades of musical color, based upon the arrangement of their overtones, with each tone forming a unique signature colony or system of related tones. The family of related overtones is the set of frequencies that can be heard resonating with the fundamental tone due to its gravitational relationship. The sound of a gong or cymbals will include overtones that are not harmonics, resulting in a composite sound that does not seem to have a definite fundamental pitch. Nonetheless, the musical analogue to the gravitational force still binds the fundamental and overtones together. A harmonic series can emerge from any fundamental tone; so many different harmonic series exist.

10. Transitional Connections

A fundamental tone in music reflects a greater reality. Belief in a fundamental source of creation (Creator), divine purpose (each component in Nature has a specific purpose individually that is in harmony with every other purpose), and a final goal (that the human being begins existence in an afterlife when the physical journey is completed) are spiritual beliefs that are often inseparable from the music of people who hold them. When related ideas about creation, divine purpose, and a final goal are transferred to musical composition, then each note must move to the next most inevitable note. The cyclical endlessness of such journeys perhaps suggests why jazz compositions continually evolve and are never played the same way twice. Nature does not repeat itself. Through a journey involving a multi-step process (experience, practice, listening, and accumulation of knowledge), each musical seed ultimately realizes its purpose and attains completion. But what happens at the very ends of musical, material, and spiritual journeys? Perhaps transitions at the end of particles' journeys share related features in music, physics, and spirituality.

The notion of an existence in the afterlife at the completion of life's physical journey is anathema to most empiricists. Nonetheless, interesting scientific theories have made assertions regarding the transitions from the finite to the infinite that occur at the event horizon of black holes; and in Phage Lambda, quantum leaps that theoretically take place at the quantum level, as theorized in Judith King's book *The Isis Thesis* (57). King studied the Egyptian Book of the Dead and other ancient funerary texts, then compared their contents with theories of quantum physics. She suggests that, in ancient Egyptian funerary texts, the deceased want to merge with the Sun-god in the afterlife. That desire is mirrored by evolutionary events manifesting at the molecular level, as may have taken place with Phage Lambda, and results in the recombinant species Homo Sapiens Lambda. Viral DNA thus becomes absorbed into a higher or more biologically complex genome.

A number of transitional connections theories from different fields of study involve some aspect of spirit or consciousness separating from the physical form and entering another manner of existence. Whether considering the start of a new composition, entering the Netherworld, being pulled by the intense gravitational force of a black hole, or taking a quantum leap, the transition from the world of consciousness into the unknown realm seems heavily shrouded in mysteries that require metaphysical and logical deciphering.

11. Science, Soul, and the Source

An artist's greatest challenge is creatively representing what people do not commonly see, feel, or otherwise experience with our five physical senses, intellect, and subconscious mind. Love and music are powerful and universal in their ability to communicate intimately. Musicians can perform beautiful music together even when they do not speak a common language. Once we get beyond the mere notes of music, what is the nature of music's magic and more intangible ingredients; those that give it life and render it universally effective as a form of communication? Musicians often speak of music as having power, soul, or spirit.

Most musicians involved in composing spontaneously know that musical expression involves intangible characteristics that can defy explanation. People can study theory and composition thoroughly and still remain incapable of producing music that has a strong and lasting impact on audiences. Music education most often devotes little time to directly exploring the process of creativity or musical expression beyond the cataloging and analysis of notes. The notion of spirituality may be used to simply describe an elusive inherent quality of being that is fundamental to the completion of our human existence and aptitude. If spirit, energy, and soul are indeed part of our basic makeup and if we are each a microcosmic reflection of the universe, then what is the essence of Nature's spirituality? Do musical notes operate in manners related to atomic and subatomic functions within their respective environments and systems? May music's spirit and soul also be related to the elusive functions of non-molecular dark matter and dark energy?

Our inability to precisely define music may be related to our minimal comprehension of the universe in general. The discovery of the meaning and placement of every musical tone or vibration may be akin to finding the position and connotation of every molecule and non-molecular phenomenon in the universe. Most physicists, anthropologists, and other investigators are trained to think critically about ways that our perspective might be conditioned by our socio-cultural egos and how that affects our relationship to the data under investigation. There are also contemporary scientific and social views that place our human-centered traditions at the axis of existence.

Utilizing the latest findings and proposals in astrophysics and cosmology, Joel R. Primack and Nancy Ellen Abrams proposed that humans are indeed central to the universe and suggest what this might mean for humanity culturally and individually. They produced a science-based cosmology that theorizes the universe as a whole and advocate the extraordinary place that people have in it. Abrams, a lawyer, writer, and former Fulbright scholar, has held an interest in the history, philosophy, and politics of science for many years. Primack is a cosmologist and an originator and developer of the theory of cold dark matter, now recognized as the standard theory of the configuration and evolution of the universe. His team of scientists uses some of the world's largest supercomputers to simulate the evolution of the universe and assess the results in accordance with observational information.

Primack and Abrams' book, entitled, *The View from the Center of the Universe,* emerged from a course taught at the University of California, Santa Cruz called "Cosmology and Culture." For the first time in human history, a scientific hypothesis of how the universe operates as a whole is emerging; a theory of what the universe is composed, from where it emerged, and how it is evolving. Elizabeth Debold conducted an interview with Joel R. Primack and Nancy Ellen Abrams entitled, "The View from the Center of the Universe." Debold introduces Joel Primack and Nancy Abrams by presenting an overview of their perspective:

In the last few decades, the cultural conversation about science and religion has become less a scholarly debate and increasingly like a barroom brawl. Atheists and theists are wrangling on the radio, in print, and on every possible bandwidth. The prize is a big one: Who *are* we? Where do we come from? Our core identity as humans is at stake. Are we God's children, or are we random accidents in an indifferent universe? In other words, does our existence matter to something larger than ourselves?

In the midst of this polemical slugfest, something quite remarkable is emerging from a growing chorus of scientists whose love for and appreciation of our creative cosmos may eventually lead beyond this polarization. The Hubble and other space probes have brought us stunningly gorgeous pictures that inspire wonder at what we are a part of: incandescent nebulae that are the cradles of stars and glowing supernovae that forge the elements from which we are formed. The universe is far more vast, explosively creative, eerily beautiful, and more mysterious than anyone could ever have imagined. The scale of what we are in the midst of—the vast dark expanses of space, the infinitesimally small distances traced by subatomic particles, and the stretch of spacetime that extends back for billions of light-years—is nothing less than awesome. As astronomer Carl Sagan once said: "A religion that stressed the magnificence of the universe as revealed by modern science might be able to draw forth reserves of reverence and awe hardly tapped by traditional faiths. Sooner or later, such a religion will emerge." But for such a religion to bind itself to the human heart, it has to tell us how to relate to this overwhelming picture that science shows us. Where do we fit in? Are we merely passive witnesses to the unfolding drama of the distant stars? Most materialist scientists demur at this point, believing, as Sagan did, that although the universe can be central to us, we are not central to it.

Shortly after dark matter materialized in physics, the subsequent term "dark energy" emerged in the late 1990s when astronomers discovered that the universe is not only expanding, but also accelerating outward at an even faster pace than previously imagined. They decided that some hidden anti-gravitational force must have been pushing galaxies apart from each other in this accelerated expansion. Separate theories evolved attempting to solve this mystery and a "Standard Model" was ultimately devised, suggesting that the universe is composed of 4 percent atoms and 21 percent dark matter, and the remaining 75 percent is dark energy. Cosmologists remain perplexed by the notion that they have to accept that they have been observing such a small fraction of actuality. Some scientists believe that there was an extremely dense particle present before the Big Bang that must have been so impenetrable no light could escape from it.

Einstein first introduced a "cosmological constant" as a fudge factor when all the atoms in the universe for which physics could account failed to balance its force of gravity. Although Einstein later called the cosmological constant a great blunder and retracted it, theorists have recently re-employed the concept to explain dark energy, even though that acknowledgment fails to reveal exactly what the force is. Robert Scherrer, a professor of physics at Vanderbilt University, concedes that nobody knows what either dark matter or dark energy is, and he is troubled by the complexity involved in the problem of identifying them. He feels that it is tempting to consider them products of the same unknown phenomenon, agrees that two explanations may be necessary, and concludes in a July 12, 2004 e-mail interview that, "It is somewhat embarrassing to have two different unknown sources for the dominant forms of matter and energy in the universe. . . . On the other hand, that may just be the way things are. We don't get to pick the universe we live in."

Intuition may be our souls' telegraph system through which our storehouse of memories and the wellspring of divine inspiration transmit wisdom. The power of fore-thought (intuition) combines with intellectual knowledge and creative power enabling us to generate that which we imagine. For some people the inner voice (intuition) represents a close relationship with the soul. In his book *Autophysiopsychic Music,* renowned jazz artist Yusef Lateef discusses the soul:

> Many questions have been asked concerning the soul. What is it? Where does it come from? How is it developed? Why is it important? What significance is it?
>
> The soul is the genesis to human life. It is born with the individual and is the gyrating force which determines the thought process of good and evil. It does not descend from the heavens or from any outside place. When a person is born, he/she has all the properties that make an individual whole, includ-ing the soul. As with puberty, when a certain age is reached, human beings become cognizant of their sexual powers. At certain stages of development the musician becomes cognizant of their soul, or that there exists a self: a soul. It is at first hidden and imperceptive, though its essence is contained in the body as a seed within a shell, and as the body is gradually developed, the soul grows along with it and becomes manifest. It is a bright essence. It is latent in the seed as fire is latent on the flint. When this inner light is flashed before the individual he/she becomes consciously aware that within is a force to explore—then the individual sets out to know more about it.
>
> The soul is an entity with extreme importance. If great emphasis is placed on physical and intellectual development and none given to the soul, there is an imbalance in the nature of the human soul. The laws of nature govern all things in life. There are as well laws governing the soul. It stands to reason that soul development plays an intense role in the habits of man, particularly noticeable among the artists. He/she must strive to gain the highest level of consciousness and awareness by developing the mind, body, and soul on an even balance. What follows is pure, individual, creative expression.

All things and beings in the universe are connected with each other, visibly or invisibly and through the vibrations of the soul are the most powerful and far reaching. Soul-vibrations communicate like an electric current from soul to soul. They work through the chord of sympathy existing between man and his/her surroundings and reveal past, present, and sometimes future conditions. When a person speaks, thinks, or feels either harshly or kindly of another, it reaches the spirit of that one, either consciously or unconsciously, by the power of vibration. If we happen to be offended with someone and do not show it in speech or action, it cannot be hidden, for the vibrations of our feelings will reach directly to the person in question and he/she will begin to feel our displeasure, however far away he/she may be. The same is the case with our love and pleasure. However we may try to conceal it, in speech or action, it cannot be hidden. In the activity of all things the seer recognizes the pitch, as a musician knows the key in which any particular music is written. Man's atmosphere tells the grade of the activity to his/her vibrations and these are felt through the soul.

Autophysiopsychic music allows the performer to deliver his/her message or say what he/she has to say musically. With his/her soul attuned to other souls he/she is capable of giving deep and far reaching experiences. If the musician is in harmony with the self and humanity, great spiritual heights may be obtained. Their expressions will be a continuous cycle of the pouring forth of heart and soul (3–6).

Is music an expressive human modality within which ultimate reality resides? Autophysiopsychic, like ritual, seems to be directed at the locus where objective, subjective, and subconscious mindstreams merge within our bodies, minds, and spirits. Perhaps our collective storehouse of memory reflects universal creativity. What resides at the fundamental core of our psychological, spiritual, and physical foundations; guides our evolution as a global village; and influences everything we do individually and collectively?

Composers and improvisers may find useful models for organizing contemporary musical material while searching among scientific models. In 1995 Edward Witten introduced M-theory to the world, initiating what has been called the Second Superstring Revolution. This theory combines the five different string theories into one theory, along with a previously abandoned attempt to unify general relativity and quantum mechanics called eleven-dimensional super-gravity. In a PBS documentary based on Brian Greene's book, *The Elegant Universe*, M-theory's creator (Witten) says that, the "M" in M-theory, "stands for *magic, mystery,* or *matrix,* according to taste." The matrixes produced may serve as useful structural prototypes for composers exploring alternative construction models for new musical matrixes.

Is it plausible to imagine organizing general musical characteristics into a single set of unified and consistent formulations of global musical theory? Future composers might assign their chords, rhythms, or melodies to one of several related fundamental forces. John Coltrane, Eddie Harris, Yusef Lateef, Donald Byrd, Steve Coleman, and other jazz musicians have left written evidence of their interest in unifying music into systems that they could apply broadly to their understanding and approach to music worldwide. Some composers catalog melodies and melodious patterns, while others devise harmonic and rhythmic road maps that allow musicians to take a free choice of routes to any harmonic or intervallic destination. Energy has been categorized into several fundamental areas. M-theory's *strong interaction* is a very strong but extremely short-ranged force. *Electromagnetic force* is long-ranged and causes electric and magnetic effects, such as the repulsion between like electrical charges or the interaction of bar magnets. *Weak force* is responsible for radioactive decay and neutrino interactions, while *gravitational force* is weak, but very long-ranged. Each of these four forces could serve as a prototype for loosely related musical concepts, sets of elements, structure organizations, and stylistic components that could be compiled into useful strings and matrixes.

String theory is a model of fundamental physics whose building blocks are one-dimensional extended objects called strings, rather than the zero-dimensional point particles that form the basis for the standard model of particle physics. The phrase is often used as shorthand for Superstring theory, as well as related theories, such as M-theory. By replacing the point-like particles with strings, an apparently consistent quantum theory of gravity emerges (NRC 51). String theory postulates ten or eleven (in M-theory) space/time dimensions, as opposed to the usual four (three spatial and one temporal) used in relativity theory (Duff). Since string theory claims to be a hypothesis of all things, only one consistent formulation of the theory should exist. Instead there are five. M-theory united a web of relationships between each of the theories called dualities (specifically, S-duality, T-duality, and U-duality). Each of these dualities provides a way of converting one of the string theories into another. Could music devise a unified set of tonal, modal, atonal, and free modulations that distilled such a collection into a meaningful whole?

String theory's ten or eleven space/time dimensions provide a potential model for envisioning a broader range of music's poly-dimensional layers. A matrix that includes music's technical, emotional, psychic, and more ethereal content—elements that virtually reside beyond the four dimensional space of Einstein's relativity (e.g., length, width, height, and time)—must take features akin to a matrix representing M-theory's broader range of overlapping and omni-directional dimensions. When we relate string theory to improvisation, we find that the richest music can elicit multiple omni-directional levels of interconnected musical dimensions. The experienced improviser develops an abundant assortment of knowledge and technique, potentially requiring an appropriate musical matrix that serves as a road map enabling musicians to navigate through wide-ranging dynamic, broad-ranging, and flexible musical possibilities. Therefore, contemplating string theory may eventually enable composers to better conceptualize, organize, and visualize new support structures for interdisciplinary resources. Music and physics share a concern for understanding polarity, gravity, structure, and order in relativistic ways.

Perhaps we can no more understand the true essence of music than we have chance of knowing the essence of every particle in the universe. Music is a chain of sonic events. Music has frequencies that we can never detect due to their extremely high or extremely low position beyond our range of hearing. Apparently our ears continually evolve towards an understanding of the overtone series as we gradually encounter microtones and ever-finer divisions of intervallic relationships.

The intangible aspects of music need not be rendered irrelevant simply because we cannot define or detect their essence. Cosmological and astrophysical experts have discovered that most of the universe is made up of invisible substances that do not emit electromagnetic radiation. We cannot distinguish them directly through telescopes or similar instruments. As scientists look ever-more deeply into the world of the subatomic particle, "missing Higgs" emerge with no detectable mass. The missing Higgs could suggest the existence of other higher dimensions (black holes?).

> A major breakthrough in particle physics came in the 1970s when physicists realized that there are very close ties between two of the four fundamental forces—namely, the weak force and the electromagnetic force. The two forces can be described within the same theory, which forms the basis of the Standard Model. This "unification" implies that electricity, magnetism, light, and some types of radioactivity are all manifestations of a single underlying force called, unsurprisingly, the electroweak force. But in order for this unification to work mathematically, it requires that the force-carrying particles have no mass. We know from experiments that this is not true, so physicists Peter Higgs, Robert Brout, and François Englert came up with a solution to solve this conundrum.
>
> They suggested that all particles had no mass just after the Big Bang. As the Universe cooled and the temperature fell below a critical value, an invisible force field called the "Higgs field" was formed, together with the associated "Higgs boson." The field prevails throughout the cosmos: any particles that interact with it are given a mass via the Higgs boson (CERN).

Jean Jacques Rousseau (1712–1778) once said, "Observe Nature and follow the path she traces for you." Our ultimate charge in life may be to remain in harmonious accord with Nature's dynamic range of substances and circumstances. Nature summons us to a variety of tasks and duties during life that allow our individual and collective consciousness to explore, evolve, and prosper. Spontaneous and premeditated composition involves self-inquiry and self-discovery aimed towards understanding past, current, and future sonic relationships.

12. Conclusion

On rare occasions gifted musicians lose themselves while performing in such meditative conditions that they are said to have become empty vessels through which pure creative inspiration flows. Musicians deal with conventional material instruments that broadly engage our physical, mental, and spiritual faculties. Music also offers the possibility of navigating through our world via an integrated flow of psychic, intellectual, and material forces. In the final analysis, people from different disciplines seem to arrive at related conclusions when the universe is the model in common. Regardless of whether ultimate reality leads us to a Heaven, Phage Lambda, Event Horizon, Nirvana, naturalistic reincarnation, transmigration of the soul, or musical ecstasy, the spiritual, logical, and metaphysical differences between our various theories regarding the ultimate transition of material forms is much more semantic than actual. Although we will never know intimately the pure process of universal creativity and finality, the more that we seek understanding and merge with Nature's abstract order, the better we can creatively navigate universal streams, trails, and plateaus.

References

Bebey, Francis. *African Music: A People's Art.* Brooklyn, NY: Lawrence Hill, 1975.

Bindon, P. "Our Relationship with Nature, Part 1." *Rosicrucian Digest* 83.2: 1–2.

Britt, Robert Roy. "Dark Matter and Dark Energy: One and the Same?" (July 2004). May 2007<http://www.space.com/scienceastronomy/mysterymonday_40712.html>.

Cruz, Samuel, Ph.D. *Masked Africanisms: Puerto Rican Pentecostalism.* Dubuque: Kendall/Hunt Publishing Company, 2005.

Csikszentmihalyi, Mihaly. *Finding Flow: The Psychology of Engagement with Everyday Life.* New York: Basic Books, 1997.

Debold, Elizabeth. "What Is Enlightenment?" *EnlightenNext Magazine* 40 (May–July 2008). July 2008 <www.wie.org>.

Duff, M. J., Liu, J. T. and R. Minasian. "Eleven Dimensional Origin of String/String Duality: A One-Loop Test Center for Theoretical Physics." *Nuclear Physics Yes, Issue B* 452 (1995): 261–82.

Floyd, Samuel, Jr. *The Power of Black Music: Interpreting Its History from Africa to the United States.* New York: Oxford University Press, 1995.

Frawley, D. *From the River of Heaven: Hindu and Vedic Knowledge for the Modern Age.* Delhi: Motilal Banarsidass, 2002.

Harrison, Nelson E. "The Metaphysics of Music: Tuning Up in a Tuned-Out World." Lecture at the Music Center's Recital Hall for the Global African Music and Art Festival/Symposium. University of California, Santa Cruz. 20 April 2003.

Hawking, S. W. *A Brief History of Time.* New York: Bantam Dell Publishing Group, 1993.

Hurston, Zora Neale. "How It Feels to Be Colored Me." *Folklore, Memoirs, and Other Writings.* Ed. Cheryl Wall. New York: Library of America. 1995.

Huxley, A. *The Perennial Philosophy.* New York: Harper Perennial Modern Classics, 2004.

Khan, Hazrat Inayat. *The Mysticism of Sound and Music: The Sufi Teaching of Hazrat Inayat Khan.* Boston: Shambhala, 1996.

King, J. K. *The Isis Thesis*. Gaylord, Michigan: Envision Editions, 2004.

Kofsky, Frank. *John Coltrane and the Jazz Revolution of the 1960s*. New York: Pathfinder, 1998.

Lateef, Y. *Autophysiopsychic Music: Method on How to Perform*. Amherst, MA: Fana Music, 1979.

Madson, Patricia Ryan. *Improv Wisdom: Don't Prepare, Just Show Up*. New York: Bell Tower, 2005.

"Missing Higgs." CERN, the European Organization for Nuclear Research. January 2007 <http://public.web.cern.ch/public/en/Science/Higgs-en.html>.

Pfleiderer, M. "The Study of Rhythm in Popular Music. Approaches and Empirical Results." Demonstration Paper presented at Proceedings of the 5th Triennial ESCOM Conference. Institute for Musicology. Hamburg University, Germany. 8–13 September 2003.

Plato. *The Republic of Plato*. Trans. Francis M. Cornford. New York: Oxford University Press, 1945.

Primack, Joel R. and Nancy Ellen Abrams. *The View from the Center of the Universe: Discovering Our Extraordinary Place in the Cosmos*. New York: Penguin/Riverhead, 2006. July 2007 <http://viewfromthecenter.com/>.

Ramsey, Guthrie P., Jr. *Race Music: Black Cultures from Hip-Hop to Bebop*. Los Angeles: University of California Press, 2004.

Schaefer, H. F., III. "Stephen Hawking, The Big Bang, and God." *Real Issue* (Mar./Apr., 1995). March 2007 <http://www.leaderu.com/offices/schaefer/docs/bigbang. html>.

Snyder, B. *Music and Memory: An Introduction*. Cambridge, MA: MIT Press, 2000.

Tyson, Tyson. *NOVA Online*. July 2003 <http://www.pbs.org/wgbh/nova/elegant/greene. html>.

United States National Research Council (NRC). Committee on Elementary-Particle Physics. *Elementary-Particle Physics: Revealing the Secrets of Energy and Matter*. Washington, DC: National Academy of Sciences, 1998.

White, Andrew. N., III. *Trane 'n Me: A Treatise on the Music of John Coltrane*. Washington, DC: Andrew's Musical Enterprises, 1981.

Chapter Three
Genesis: Twin Pyramids

The Christian HISTORY OF CREATION
In the beginning God created the heavens and the earth. The earth was without form, and void; and darkness was on the face of the deep. And the Spirit of God was hovering over the face of the waters. Then God said, "Let there be light"; and there was light. And God saw the light, that it was good; and God divided the light from the darkness. The Creation of Heaven and Earth according to The First Book of Moses called Genesis (King James Version)

"Om": Sound, the Universe, and the Process of Creation

Creation is the sum total of all existence. If all things vibrate, then perhaps sound is the life-force that animates all things—plants, animals, minerals, antimatter, and all phenomena that fill the universe. Any sound, individual auras, sensations of touch, smell, any frequency of light, and the generation of ideas radiates in a vibratory pattern. Some ideas arise from sensations received from external objects and stimuli, while others evolve from reasoning and internal reflection on those external sensations. Our finite faculties cannot discern or fully comprehend the continuity of infinity; thus humankind relates to the safety of the visible, calculable past and the predictable future to reconcile our fear of the vastness of existence.

All musicians need thorough grounding in traditional music vocabularies before setting off to create their own personal dialects. Artistic development requires communal periods of absorption (in schools, various ensembles, or other conventional or unconventional educational organizations or situations) and intense periods of meditation and individual reflection ("wood-shedding"). The creative individual must undergo a period of relative isolation to develop techniques learned in their course of study and must then apply that knowledge to their artistic vision, skill, and personality. The accumulation of knowledge and wisdom inevitably involves continual and gradual stepping stones that periodically result in giant leaps forward in creative development.

When we often try to take quantum leaps over tradition, in an effort to resist existing cultural patterns or pervasive styles, music can create infant vocabularies that are so unfamiliar structurally and ungrounded conceptually to the practitioner that strong communication cannot take place. If individuals are uncomfortable with their own newly created vocabularies, then it clearly follows that they will experience limited success in using those vocabularies to communicate meaningfully with fellow musicians and audiences. Musical language follows a pattern of development akin to that of spoken languages where, for instance, babies first learn to babble before speaking in complete sentences. Stronger communication of ideas comes much later, only after mastering vocabulary, a process that continues to evolve as new words are learned (along with thorough understanding of their definitions) and gradually incorporated into memory. Some performers want to play "non-idiomatic music" to free themselves of the trappings of older styles and develop an individual style and voice. This desire is understandable, but vocabulary and language must still undergo a cumulative process of organic development that requires an investment of time and patience. Every participant in that particular language must engage in a related vocabulary and process if they want to express musical ideas that are coherent to fellow musicians and listeners. A paradox immediately emerges as non-idiomatic musical styles ultimately create recognizable musical gestures, tendencies, and parameters. The intentional avoidance of European tonal ideas, African-American jazz and blues, melodic and rhythmic tendencies, or any other stylistic approaches are soon replaced by an alternate set of "extended techniques" and other elements of expression that are inherently limited by the extent to which musicians digest a broad range of musical fundamentals to replace those they seek to avoid.

All approaches to music create their own unique sets of relatively limited musical elements. If free improvisation limits itself to constantly doing the unexpected, and avoiding all traditional vocabularies, then such a filtered set of musical parameters will quickly reveal its limitations. Performer and listener always form a relationship similar to that of most transmitter and receiver exchanges. If a sincere interest in forming a partnership on both ends of performer/listener relationships exists, then the result is apt to be more successful than if those where an emphasis in self-indulgence on one end and immediate skepticism on the other are predominant. In any case, a musician's ability to express new ideas and approaches effectively usually involves an understanding of the general elements of music and knowledge of ways to balance those basic ingredients even when operating in new territories.

Vibration is capable of great efficacy as human language. Learning to discipline the mind, its functions, and to rename and refocus our perceptions requires patience. Patience means replacing anxiety with stillness. Anxiety is produced when people demand the future today or attempt to prolong the past. The creative artist keeps current by constantly overcoming old relationships with their past and forming new ones based on possibility. How can we possibly know music's purpose? If we love cooking, then the secrets of cooking may be revealed as we master that art. Mastery requires the time, knowledge, and patience that love often enables us to apply more readily. If our purpose is simply to be, then it may not be necessary to change anything within or around us. If we aspire to be creative, as a reflection of nature's creative process, then our purpose must be to attempt to understand the interconnectedness of all existence within the macrocosm and microcosm. This requires an understanding and wisdom that, at its best, extends beyond intellectual and experiential knowledge.

Music is the flexible equation that expresses our relationship with principles of freedom, knowledge, actuality, love, harmony, and wisdom in the universe. It is the act of a vibrating periodic process of mechanical oscillations about a central equilibrium point. The oscillations may be periodic, such as the motion of a pendulum, or random, such as the movement of various parts of an old automobile engine. Forces that oscillate about some specified reference point are expressed in terms of frequency such as cycles per second (cps), Hertz (Hz), cycles per minute (cpm or rpm), and strokes per minute (spm). In *The Mysticism of Sound and Music: The Sufi Teaching of Hazrat Inayat Khan*, the chapter entitled "The Music of the Spheres" contains the following perspective:

> Music as we know it in our everyday language is only a miniature: that which our intelligence has grasped from that music or harmony of the whole universe which is working behind us. The music of the universe is the background of the little picture which we call music. Our sense of music, our attraction to music, shows that music is in the depth of our being. Music is behind the working of the whole universe. Music is not only life's greatest object, but music is life itself (11).

We are all shaped by our experiences. Everything we do, think, and observe—all of who or what we are—is a result of vibrations. "Everlasting" is a word that describes a continuum, and jazz performances, at their best, reflect this. One performance is the continuation of the last and a prelude to subsequent music. One musician's solo is the continuation of the last and a prelude to subsequent solos. Long after masterful musicians physically die, their music lives on and continues to affect our lives. More than the quantity of notes that a musician plays makes their music memorable. The lasting quality of all subjects well-mastered has lingering effects that benefit society.

Music continues to be vital to human existence. It has evolved and enabled the human species to sustain and renew itself. Reverend Deborah L. Johnson, founding minister of the Inner Light Ministries in Santa Cruz, California, spent the month of August 2006 discussing vitality and its connection to a spiritual life. Her sermons reminded me of the way vitality is conveyed through music. The word "vital" comes from the Latin *vitalis* meaning "of life," as derived from *vita*, which means "life." Something that is vital exists as a manifestation of life; a subset of life "concerned with or necessary to the maintenance of life." According to Webster's Dictionary, a vital organism is, "fundamentally concerned with or affecting life or living beings," and it tends, "to renew or refresh the living." Vitality is the ability of an entity to live, evolve, grow, and thrive in its existence, although it takes more than living and growing to capture the essence of vitality.

Restoration is another aspect of creativity. It allows us to continually sustain and renew ourselves as we navigate along the creative path. Inspiration is oxygen for the soul, and reflection allows us to be creative. Reverend Johnson also reminds her congregation of the former slave owner who received an epiphany later in life that inspired him to write the spiritual "Amazing Grace," to rebuke himself for his old racist ways, and restore his sense of morality. She also told the story of Nelson Mandela writing the constitution for the new South Africa while on break from the hard labor he and his colleagues were forced to do in the rock quarries while held as political prisoners on Robben Island. Mandela became the first president of the New Democratic South Africa after his release from prison, where he had been incarcerated in the same 6-foot by 7-foot cell for fourteen years. During these times of hard labor the political prisoners began to educate themselves and their guards. The prisoners taught each other and unified themselves to fight for their freedom. They restored and inspired each other, inviting even higher levels of creativity.

Recognizing that the Creative Source encompasses infinity is a humbling experience. Realizing that we are inherently creative is empowering and liberating. Aspiring to a high level of creativity forms a covenant with the Creative Source. A spiritual covenant is irrevocable and requires that one subordinate himself with humility to the possibilities that exist outside of what is known.

The Creative Source is realized through our various approaches to spirituality. Spirituality is the intuitive self and subconscious mind translating and decoding the essence of the Creative Source. The highest and most direct spiritual message emerges as dreams and during meditation. The blues taught us that great lessons are learned and great music is often born out of personal trials and suffering. We learn to view the universe from a creative mind and soul as we refine ourselves spiritually; and when our dreams and meditation are interrupted by distractions, this wisdom of the universe is lost.

We are holistic beings, an intricate microcosm of body, mind, and spirit. Music is treated as a holistic phenomenon throughout this study because it reflects our collective holistic expression and existence. The body, mind, and spirit are treated thematically in the chapters. The body is the most obvious vehicle and it must be properly attended to in order for us to get the best physical connection and result from our chosen musical instruments. Our mind manages all of the infinite details that flow through our consciousness, filtering, analyzing, and storing that information selectively to our best advantage. The spirit, our highest portion of ourselves, is the innermost and most elusive "self" that connects with our intuition, inspiration (creativity), and the source of existence, and integrates all three aspects of our being. All three dimensions of ourselves, and the universe in which we are contained, can enhance the way we think about the process of creativity.

Creative music is a combination of techniques, spirituality, science, intellect, and emotion (our intuitive or subconscious link to the Creative Source). People worldwide (individually and collectively), who aspire to combine body, mind, and spirit, participate in the urgent creation of a new and improved paradigm. Rather than succumbing to cynicism or despair after fully realizing the gravity of the frightening implications and impact of global warming, when looking critically at the myriad of problems facing contemporary humanity, some creative thinkers feel confident that humankind has the capacity to overcome these challenges and evolve as nature requires. The presence of significantly abundant global creativity will indeed require an evolutionary leap of living in consciousness; one that will reconnect humanity with itself, hopefully resulting in greater degrees of happiness, promoting peace and sustainability. Aspiring to create such a joyous personal and collective peace and global awakening is why careful analysis of creative expression is important.

Creative music and other forms of artistic expression permeate our soul and transcend logical thought, getting us to a level of consciousness beyond that little chattering voice in our heads. Thus, when our awareness broadens, it can become a heightened level of consciousness. H. G. Wells suggested a century ago that all humankind has experienced thus far on Earth may be but a brief dream (or a preparatory initiation) before the dawn of this New Awakening. Advancements achieved in the realms of science and technology must be just a small fraction of our potential to attain knowledge and wisdom within the realm of spiritual advancement. The smaller self that feeds our mind is obviously much more limited, critical, and repetitive than the creative force that feeds our intuition. As the music innovator Sun Ra once said, "Nature never repeats herself."

We pour our personal convictions into our creative expression. It seems that the infinite power of creativity might be best enhanced through creating love-based forms of expression. Holding a newborn child elicits such emotion while, conversely, contact with the horrors of war clearly shows the nadir polarity of our feelings. From a "Martian's" perspective we might exist as a single human species, where subtle DNA variations display an infinitely greater magnitude between individuals than insignificant or more arbitrary differences between races. Unfortunately, we have devised social constructs based on an array of biased insecurities that stand in the way of developing our intuitive awareness and overall consciousness. The further we move away from nature the less we remember of our innate ancestral tendency to honor and follow all paths that lead to truth. When our body, mind, and spirit are not properly aligned, integrated, and harmonized, this debilitating fragmentation reflects the bankrupted social environments that produce the delusions we construct to our own demise and further the destruction of our natural environment. Survival depends upon the awareness that comes from the consistent evolution of consciousness. Perhaps the hope, wisdom, and joy that we absorb through creating or listening to music provide a key to a New Awakening. New, creative music breaks away from the confines of repetition that forms the virtual stasis between more conspicuous stylistic evolution and movements. Just as that first species out of water felt uncomfortable out of its ocean home, most people resist creative and social change. As an innovative artist, therefore, if there is general consensus that what you are creating is inappropriate, then this must not be a reliable indicator that you are on the wrong track.

Matrices and Vibration

Several principles resound throughout this book. Evolution and the vibratory relationship between all universal phenomena are crucial concepts in the pages that follow. That which is continuous contains all forms and the overtone series contains all of the tones we use in music making. Humanity often tends to separate itself from much of the natural environment that surrounds us, despite the obvious reality that people evolved within it and are completely immersed in nature. Thus, as Goethe proclaimed in *Aphorisms in Nature,* "Nature! We are surrounded by her: powerless to separate ourselves from her, and powerless to penetrate beyond her." If we understand nature's infinite and gradual motion, then we can better assimilate the structure of its motion in our creative process. Artists search for the organic connection between music and vibratory universal phenomena. Knowledge, discipline, and wisdom allow our senses and awareness to discern common origins, similarities, vibratory essences, and accumulating such knowledge enables us to grow. In some cultures people learn through an emphasis on meditation and humility, allowing deities to possess their bodies and speak through the vessels that their bodies provide (e.g., rituals performed in parts of the Caribbean and Africa). As we develop new technology and paradigms to keep pace with the development, modern tools continually extend our vision. Both meditation and logic feed creativity, and by accumulating such knowledge we better understand nature, allowing all aspects of our environment to stimulate our creative processes. Hazrat Inayat Khan said:

> What makes us feel drawn to music is that our whole being is music: our mind, our body, the nature in which we live, the nature that has made us, all that is beneath and around us—it is all music. As we are close to all this music and live and move and have our being in music, it therefore interests us. It attracts our attention and gives us pleasure, for it corresponds with the rhythm and tone which are keeping the mechanisms of our whole being intact. What pleases us in any of our arts, whether drawing, painting, carving, architecture, or sculpture, and what interests us in poetry, is the harmony behind them which is music. It is music that poetry suggests to us: the rhythm in its poetry, or the harmony of ideas and phrases.

Besides this, in painting and in drawing it is our sense of proportion and our sense of harmony which gives us all the pleasure we gain in admiring art. What appeals to us in being near to nature is nature's music, and nature's music is more perfect than that of art. It gives us a sense of exaltation to be standing near the running water which has its rhythm, its tone and its harmony. The swaying of branches in the forest, the rising and falling of the waves—all has its music. Once we contemplate and become one with nature, our hearts open to its music (12).

For the purpose of examining the concept of a musical array and its related harmonic events, a "matrix" is a substrate, a structure upon which other elements may be placed. Of course the term matrix has many other contemporary definitions, each of which is related to a conceptual understanding of systematic organization that relates to our basic definition. The following passage from Wikipedia explains one definition.

> In music, especially folk and popular music, a **matrix** is an element of variations which does not change. The term was derived from use in musical writings and from Arthur Koestler's *The Act of Creation,* which defines creativity as the bisociation of [two] sets of ideas or matrices. Musical matrices may be combined in any number, usually more than two, and may be, and must be for analysis, broken down into smaller ones. They may be intended by the composer and perceived by the listener, or they may not, and they may be purposefully ambiguous. The simplest examples given by van der Merwe are fixed notes, definite intervals, and regular beats, while the most complex given are the Baroque fugue, Classical tonality, and Romantic chromaticism.

This definition of matrices can be applied to the analysis of simple songs, such as "Pop Goes the Weasel," where systematic occurrences of the major mode with its traditional harmonic scheme and perfect cadences; metrical organization in 6/8 time; four-bar melodic phrasing with its climax; regular and predictable rhyme structure; with both halves of the tune ending with the same melodic/harmonic figure; and where three primary triads are implied throughout, might suggest organizational units for a simple matrix.

The application of the term "matrix" to the following analysis of African music refers to a systematic harmonic organization that evolved freely from the overtone series that serves to help define the harmonic tendencies suggested in systematic blues harmony and melody. A two-dimensional blues matrix, such as that above, only suggests a fraction of that multidimensional, omni-directional potential that extends as harmonic extensions of a given chord or pitch collection. The perpetual jazz evolution involves a continuous discovery of this harmonic and melodic potential.

Figure 1. A Matrix of Related Blues Changes

Nucleus 1	2	3	4	5	6	7	8	9	10	11	12
C7 Also (b9, & b12)	C#7 Also (b9, & b13)	D7 Also (b9, & b13)	Eb7 Also (b9, & b13)	E7 Also (b9, & b13)	F7 Also (b9, & b13)	F#7 Also (b9, & b13)	G7 Also (b9, & b13)	Ab7 Also (b9, & b13)	A7 Also (b9, & b13)	Bb7 Also (b9, & b13)	B7 Also (b9, & b13)
F#7 Tritone sub	G7 Tritone sub	Ab7 Tritone sub	A7 Tritone sub	Bb7 Tritone sub	B7 Tritone sub	C7 Tritone sub	C#7 Tritone sub	D7 Tritone sub	Eb7 Tritone sub	E7 Tritone sub	F7 Tritone sub
C-7	C#-7	D-7	Eb-7	E-7	F-7	F#-7	G-7	Ab-7	A-7	Bb-7	B-7
Cmaj7	C#maj7	Dmaj7	Ebmaj7	Emaj7	Fmaj7	F#maj7	Gmaj7	Abmaj7	A7maj	Bbmaj7	Bmaj7
A-7	Bb-7	B-7	C-7	C#-7	D-7	Eb-7	E-7	F-7	F#-7	G-7	Ab-7
G-7	Ab-7	A-7	Bb-7	B-7	C-7	C#-7	D-7	Eb-7	E-7	F-7	F#-7
C#o7	Do7	Ebo7	Eo7	Fo7	F#o7	Go7	Abo7	Ao7	Bbo7	Bo7	Co7
C+7(#11)	C#+7(#11)	D+7(#11)	Eb+7(#11)	E+7(#11)	F+7(#11)	F#+7(#11)	G+7(#11)	Ab+7(#11)	A+7(#11)	Bb+7(#11)	B+7(#11)
E-7(b5)	F-7(b5)	F#-7(b5)	G-7(b5)	Ab-7(b5)	A-7(b5)	Bb-7(b5)	B-7(b5)	C-7(b5)	C#-7(b5)	D-7(b5)	Eb-7(b5)
Csus4	C#sus4	Dsus4	Ebsus4	Esus4	Fsus4	F#sus4	Gsus4	Absus4	Asus4	Bbsus4	Bsus4
A-7(b5)	Bb-7(b5)	B-7(b5)	C-7(b5)	C#-7(b5)	D-7(b5)	Eb-7(b5)	E-7(b5)	F-7(b5)	F-7(b5)	G-7(b5)	Ab-7(b5)
Ebmaj7	Emaj7	Fmaj7	F#maj7	Gmaj7	Abmaj7	A7maj7	Bbmaj7	Bmaj7	Cmaj7	C#maj7	Dmaj7
G+7(#11)	Ab+7(#11)	A+7(#11)	Bb+7(#11)	B+7(#11)	C+7(#11)	C#+7(#11)	D+7(#11)	Eb+7(#11)	E+7(#11)	F+7(#11)	F#+7(#11)

Figure 2. Related Tools for Improvisation

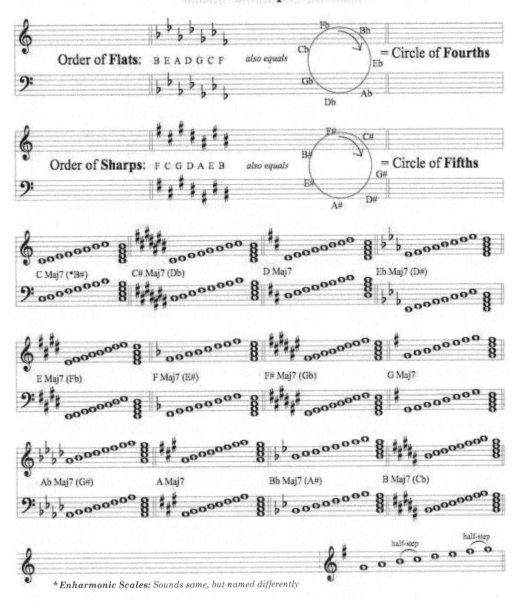

Tools for Improvisation

*Enharmonic Scales: Sounds same, but named differently

John Coltrane's musical legacy suggests an interest in knowing the inter-connectedness of things. Coltrane was interested in spiritual development and, as his composition "India" suggests, the sacred practices of the East had an influence on his music and mystical expansion. Tibet has one of the most spiritual populations on Earth and mandalas are one of many spiritual tools frequently found in that region of the world. The Tibetan perspective is that suffering is inevitable and that death is something that we bring with us into the world at our conception. Although death is with us during every step of our lives, in the religious traditions of Tibet, death is said to provide a unique opportunity for spiritual growth and the ultimate aim of Tibetan religious practice is the transformation of death into an immortal state of benefit to others. The wisdom of the Tibetan Books of the Dead stands at the forefront of Tibet's esoteric teachings that address the art and science of compassionate death.

In Tibetan Buddhism, a mandala is an imaginary palace contemplated during meditation as a representation of universal balance and forces. Every object in the palace is significant and represents some aspect of wisdom or represents a guiding principle. A variety of mandalas represent the life force and each reveals different lessons. The sand mandala holds many characteristics in common with the use of a flexible and ephemeral blues matrix that John Coltrane's spiritual mindset and mandalas suggest.

There is an opening ceremony in which the Tibetan monks begin the mandala sand painting with a series of chants, music, and mantra recitation to bless the site, making it conducive to creating the mandala. The monks then begin to draw the line design for the mandala, an exacting process based on sacred geometry as presented in the ancient scriptures. When the mandala is complete, the monks conclude their creation of the Sand Mandala with a consecration ceremony to request the continuous blessings of the invoked deities of the mandala. After many long hours of tedious and concentrated work to create the mandala, the monks dismantle the mandala in a closing ceremony, sweeping up the colored sands to symbolize the impermanence of all existence. The mixed-colored sand is then given to the audience as blessings for personal health and healing. Coltrane's "blues matrixes" seem to provide a framework for the mandalas that guided his various routes, experiences, and detours during his various approaches to spontaneous composition.

If all universal vibratory phenomena are interrelated, then perhaps love is a unifying factor that reminds us of this connection and helps us overcome our sense of separation. John Coltrane was one of the twentieth century's most influential musicians. Although the significance of his contribution to musical evolution is yet to be fully realized, musicians and listeners who follow his work intimately realize his value immediately. David Baker is one of the many musicians who analyzed some of Coltrane's pivotal compositions. Baker said:

John Coltrane was one of the handful of jazz geniuses of whom it can honestly be said, "He transformed the esthetic." It is almost impossible to find a young player of any merit in jazz today who doesn't owe a demonstrable debt to Coltrane. Whether it's the use of 16th notes as the basic unit of the jazz chorus, ingenious substitutions, "sheets of sound," wide variety of scale colors (particularly the diminished and pentatonic scales), or countless other more subtle things, Trane's presence manifests itself.

Shortly after his death in 1967, *Down Beat* magazine interviewed a number of Coltrane's colleagues and fans. The consistently high esteem in which renowned jazz artists held Coltrane is significant. Many of the musicians interviewed were innovators in their own rite and had worked intimately with Coltrane.

ELVIN JONES: I've never known a person of such even disposition. I never knew him to be anything but a beautiful person. I think he had a great deal to do with my efforts to expand myself musically. He was always encouraging and helpful. I thought, and still think, that he is one of the rare musical geniuses. Although the person is gone, his spirit will live on in the hearts and minds of those who knew him. The whole world will miss this man.

JIMMY GARRISON: I don't think we've suffered any greater loss. The greatest impact he had on me was as a warm and profound human being. His music affected people the way his person affected me. There was nothing hidden in his music. I think all of us are richer by far for having known him.

DIZZY GILLESPIE: We'll let the man's music speak for itself, because it speaks much more eloquently than we can.

EDDIE HARRIS: Trane was one of the few dedicated artists; he played what he believed. He lived like he played. The real tragedy of his death was that he took it upon himself to get so many new musicians exposed—those who would have had to wait years longer for recognition—because he allowed them to play with him. Now the young musicians have no champion for their cause.

RICHARD ABRAMS: Trane was a light to most of the musicians who are cognizant of the musical events of the sixties, especially the younger musicians. He took bebop as far as it could go, bordering on freedom. His tone set a feeling in the air—an approach to sound that seemed to be an extension of the quality of Charlie Parker—plus he was the innovator of the use of eastern scales in jazz. He was always enlightening the younger players.

Throughout his career, Coltrane gradually evolved a musical approach that provided a glance at the systematic methodology that he employed in search of the connection between the physical, cognitive, and ethereal spirit of music. The Coltrane matrix suggests his understanding of the mathematical connections between scales, chords, and intervals of music. This understanding enabled him to pivot logically from any conceivable harmonic or melodic position towards a new musical goal. Thus, the music of Coltrane's late period suggests an evolution towards more trans-harmonic, pan-tonal, and polyrhythmic-based approaches to spontaneous composition. His choice of Elvin Jones for his "classic quartet," at the apex of his career, suggests that his polyrhythmic predisposition was always a part of his evolving musical emphasis, and his later use of two drummers with two bass players suggested a preference for increased rhythmic density and melodic stratification towards which he later aspired.

His matrix enabled Coltrane to pivot omni-directionally from any given scale, chordal construct, or intervallic configuration of a melodic journey. Following his innovative quasi-modal work with Miles Davis, and after his ground-breaking summary of tonal jazz harmony in his "Giant Steps" (1959), by the mid-1960s Coltrane was moving away from former harmonic constraints and towards a more motivically derived and rhythmically based approach to spontaneous composition. Perhaps he also had an related theory of rhythm (or an evolving theory of poly-rhythm) that accounts for the emphasis on rhythmic concerns in his later musical exchanges with Rashied Ali during all four movements of "Interstellar Space." Nonetheless, Coltrane left no matrixes or graphs suggesting related theories of rhythm; and his recordings demonstrate his movement towards greater incorporation of polyrhythm as he gravitated towards greater freedom and away from his earlier self-imposed harmonic constraints. One of Coltrane's final compositions, "Interstellar Space," provides an example of ways in which he reconciled and synthesized disparate harmonic theories during his final compositional phase.

One of the most intriguing theoretical documents that Coltrane left as evidence of his musical thinking was his mandalas or matrixes. In discussing Coltrane's graphs, the terms matrix and mandala are interlinked. Like the beautiful, ritually created, and ephemeral Tibetan sand mandalas, these Coltrane matrixes provided related symbolic tools for his spontaneous composition, involving a combination of mathematical logic, flexibility, and impermanence. If we also consider Coltrane's oft-spoken implications that spirituality supported his music, then thinking generally about the spiral mandala is useful.

From a mystical perspective, we can represent the great spiral of life through an examination of the fractal geometry of spirals from galaxies to atoms, or by generating a musical mandala using the overtone series as its basis. A mandala represents the universe and everything in it, and is Sanskrit for "whole world" or "healing circle." The Tibetan word for "mandala" is "Khyil-khor," which means the center of the Universe in which a fully enlightened being resides. Circles and eggs represent wholeness, unity, the womb, completion, and eternity. Circles are universally associated with meditation, healing, and prayer, and a spiral is a continuously evolving circle.

The delicate balance between mathematical logic and intuitive imagination is closely related to notions of balance that many artists seek in their work. The strength, beauty, and grandeur of clouds; ancient redwood trees; impervious mountain ranges; snow-flakes' geometrical designs; or sand on beaches can serve as archetypes of universal design that can motivate creative expression. Laws capable of withstanding the test of time must remain flexible.

Coltrane's mandalas seem to have evolved from a process of musical self-exploration. Within Tibetan Buddhist culture we find that the process of creating a mandala is as important as the finished product. It takes years of preparation and training to gain the skill and knowledge required to paint. When ready, a Buddhist meditates for three days before a brush can be put to canvas. Coltrane likewise put many years of intensely focused musical preparation and experience in place before summarizing his theories in his compositions, performances, and mandalas. Once carefully trained and prepared, an artist can channel multifaceted arcane information and ideas into their work. Tibetan Buddhist monks create sand mandalas with intricate patterns that reflect multiple levels of understanding. The design is prepared over a period of days, and then blown away to represent the impermanence of life. Tibetans believe that sand mandalas contain the wisdom and knowledge required to achieve enlightenment in this lifetime.

Coltrane's mandalas resemble wheels or circles. A tradition of healing circles in Native American traditions involves sand paintings, medicine wheels, and shields. The powerful symbolism of the medicine wheel represents the universe, change, life, death, birth, and the process of acquiring knowledge. The great circle is the lodge of our bodies, our minds, and our hearts. Although many parallels to the Tibetan mandala exist, Native Americans do not use the word "mandala" to describe their sacred circles. Although Hermetic mandalas are generally linear in Europe, they may also be circular. In Alchemy, the Kabbalah, geometry and numerology play an important role in man-dala design and creation. Carl Jung became interested in them while studying Eastern religion. Jung considered the circular images his clients visualized or experienced as containers or "vessels" into which we project our psyche that returns to us as a means of restoration.

The mystical tradition known as Kabbalah involves the "received teachings" handed down by Jewish Rabbis since the time of Abraham. The Kabbalah is a sophisticated concept involving the forces of nature, and how they interrelate, based on the idea that God created the Universe by speaking in Hebrew. The sound of these words creates all living creatures and sustains them. Various forms of ancient Egyptian arcane symbols, and the Alchemical and Hermetic symbols that evolved from them have contained, preserved, and concealed the deeper meaning of mystical knowledge for thousands of years. They continue to appear throughout contemporary society and affect the ways in which humankind organizes, contemplates upon, and measures existence. Often the principles that govern musical organization are reflective of this eidetic wisdom.

Coltrane's musical matrix suggested the interconnectedness between chords that form the blues' "Tree of Life." In nature, slower vibrations that we can feel by touch ex-tend upward towards progressively faster (and gradually more imperceptible) frequen-cies of sound, electromagnetic radio waves, infrared, ultraviolet light, x-ray, gamma and cosmic rays, etc. Coltrane's matrix seems to consider the ever-quickening higher range frequencies of the overtone series as related systematic possibilities.

Coltrane is among the most systematic composers in the twentieth century. His formative musical training began with his early eclectic educational experiences at his father's church; in elementary, junior high, high school bands; private study at the Philadelphia conservatories; and in his performances with the Navy band. Coltrane's formative years extended into his first musical period, beginning with his R&B days with Big Maybelle, Eddie Cleanhead Vincent, and Earl Bostic. These professional experiences later reached a high point while performing and recording bebop with Dizzy Gillespie and hard bop with Miles Davis, and while developing extended solos with Thelonious Monk. Like his mentors, Coltrane made it clear that the legacy of African-American music extends continually from its ancient African origins and largely involves the evolution of the blues. This exposure to innovations explored among masters of the jazz evolution gradually evolved into his own personal and broad-based harmonic, quasi-modal, and "free" approaches that defined his inimitable mature style. The traditional African music that best reflects nature today (!Kung or Mbuti music, for example) does so because of its intimate proximity to nature. Coltrane's music evolved within an "urban jungle," but aimed to take the traditional music of his formative years, digest it, then personalize it through continually striving to better comprehend the synergy between musical connections. He said:

> I tell you, I believe that men ought to grow themselves into the fullest, the best that they can be. At least this is what I want to do, this is my belief—that I am supposed to grow to be the best good that I can get to. As I'm going there, becoming this, if I ever become, this will just come out of the horn. So whatever that's going to be—I don't know. I just know that good can only bring good (Kofsky 156).

When Coltrane was once asked if he was interested in twelve-tone music he replied that his music already systematically applied all twelve tones. During his final years of development, Coltrane took a closer look at mathematical symmetry and began discussing African music with master percussionist Michael Olatunje Baba-tunde. His interest in musical freedom, African polyrhythms, harmonic extensions, and the application of a greater range of timbre flexibility may explain Coltrane expanding his ensemble to include multiple winds, two bassists, and two drummers.

Any single musical label intended to contain a wide range of creative output inevitably falls short of defining a style. The most innovative masters of African-American music absorbed and assimilated an astounding range of musical ideas and influences prior to personalizing their music through a final "fission-ary" process. The most influential practitioners of jazz, regardless of style, seem convinced that the underlying principles of music remain linked to an evolutionary process that is invariably connected to all music, while grounding itself in the blues matrix that binds African-American musical tradition.

When I discovered John Coltrane's Geometric Drawing in 1982, I learned that Yusef Lateef received the drawings as a gift from Coltrane in 1960. Lateef used the drawings as the opening element (after the title page) in his *Repository of Scales and Melodic Patterns.* Earlier I discovered Coltrane's keen interest in Nicolas Slonimsky's *Thesaurus of Scales and Melodic Patterns.* Since its publication in 1947, Arnold Schoenberg, Freddie Hubbard, Virgil Thomson, and many other great musicians and composers of all genres expressed interest in Slonimsky's exhaustive repository of melodic patterns for its valued use in their compositions and improvisations. A relationship exists between Coltrane's, Lateef's, and Slonimsky's theories of cyclical patterning, melodic devices and development, and intervallic and motivic exploitation. Lateef is recognized as a philosophical-minded jazz pioneer and demonstrates the humility, inventiveness, and individuality that mark all truly great musicians. In 1964, in a "Blindfold Test" for *Down Beat* magazine, jazz critic Leonard Feather said:

> Yusef Lateef in several respects is a setter of precedents among jazz musicians. His was the first combo to make extensive use of exotic sounds and to reflect the impact of extra-American cultures through the use of Oriental-influenced compositions and of unusual instruments. He was also among the first to record as a modern jazz soloist on oboe.
>
> For all his experiments with the flute, argol, tambourine, and the like, he has a background of extensive experience as a name-band musician. Born in Chattanooga, Tenn., reared in Detroit, Mich., he played tenor saxophone with the bands of Lucky Millinder and Dizzy Gillespie as well as others in the late 1940s.
>
> Last February, having quit the Cannonball Adderley Sextet, Lateef formed his own quintet. He has been recording for several years as a leader on Prestige and other labels. His recent Impulse LP, *Jazz Around the World,* provided the idea for the Blindfold Test. All the records played either were recorded overseas or reflect the influence of a foreign musical culture on contemporary jazzmen (29).

Lateef was unique in his approach to this event as well when he "said he preferred to pass on rating the records, so the customary one-to-five-star system was omitted."

Between 1993 and 2003, discussions with Donald Byrd regarding his application of various mathematical concepts to composition revealed that Byrd recognized connections between Coltrane's circular drawings and theories and related approaches applied by other African-American innovators. He felt that Thelonious Monk, Herbie Hancock (listen to the mathematic emphasis in compositions recorded on Hancock's album *Inventions and Dimensions,* for instance), Cecil Taylor, Eddie Harris ("Freedom Jazz Dance," his theory book, etc.), Ornette Coleman (Harmolodic approach), Yusef Lateef (especially conspicuous in his method books), and a few other jazz artists all seemed headed in the general direction of symmetry and harmonic relationship suggested by Coltrane's matrix.

Coltrane recorded his ground breaking tour de force "Giant Steps" in May 1959. The harmonic design in "Giant Steps" involves a substitute harmonic progression popularized by Coltrane's title track composition. A remarkable aspect of this composition was Coltrane's avoidance of emphasis on the traditional supertonic (ii) to dominant (V) chord patterns within his long chain of fast paced harmonic movement. This is most conspicuous throughout the first segment of the piece. Instead of more common supertonic (or subdominant), dominant, and tonic harmonic progression, chords, and root movement involve less conventional harmonic movements in intervals of thirds, fourths, and fifths until the penultimate chord leading to the final cadence (then leading to the recapitulation). In other words, the progression results in a pattern of chord substitutions for the ii-V7-I progression (supertonic-dominant-tonic), creating an unusual root movement by major thirds (as opposed to the usual minor or major seconds, thus the title "Giant Steps"). This progression of Coltrane changes exemplifies an application of the Coltrane matrix. The harmonic progression was later similarly employed in Coltrane's composition "Countdown" (a re-harmonization of Miles Davis's "Tune Up").

Of course, the broad-ranged web of chord substitutions allows ample room for a variety of theoretical interpretations. David Baker discussed his analytical approach to the unconventional chord substitutions in Coltrane's composition in a *Down Beat* article entitled, "John Coltrane's 'Giant Steps' Solo and Composition Transcribed and Annotated."

> Among the more obvious tangible innovations is Trane's subtle use of substitutions. One particular set is usually referred to simply as Giant Steps changes or "Coltrane changes." This technique refers to Trane's manner of converting a simple ii-V-I progression into something very exciting. The Coltrane substitutions can be used whenever a ii-V-I progression extends over four measures. It is converted in this manner:

D mi	G	G		CM		CM
D mi E	AM B	AM B		EM G		CM
II	V resolve	I	V resolve	I	B resolve	I
1/2 step	m3	m3				

Some examples of this technique may be heard on Trane's version of "But Not For Me" and "Tune Up" on the album from which this solo was taken.

Even though Coltrane had something else in mind when he named "Giant Steps," the title has proved apocalyptic for a number of other reasons. In the years since his untimely death, John Coltrane has emerged as one of the two or three most influential figures in jazz since Charlie Parker. His musical steps across the jazz world were truly Giant Steps, the strides of a colossus.

In another sense the title is also apt. For those like myself who are involved in jazz pedagogy, Coltrane's playing on this composition is an improvising lesson. It has been said that for the budding orchestrator, Ravel's *Daphnis and Chloe,* is a virtual textbook. It would not be too much of an oversimplification to say that "Giant Steps" stands in much the same position to the improviser. In my own teaching, I find the playing of John Coltrane on "Giant Steps" the paradigm of sound jazz improvisation (35–40).

"Giant Steps" indeed launched Coltrane's music into new unique directions reflected in the compositions that lead into his mature period. Nevertheless, the full set of

Figure 3a. "Giant Steps"

Figure 3b. "A Love Supreme"

Figure 3c. Musical Material in "A Love Supreme"

(Figures 3a–c duplicated from Hester, K. *The Melodic and Polyrhythmic Development of John Coltrane's Spontaneous Composition in a Racist Society.* Lewiston, NY: Edwin Mellen Press, 1997).

implications produced by Coltrane's design was to come after "A Love Supreme," and other compositions of his later period of development.

Although he referred to the latter portion of this composition as "minor blues," Coltrane's structural organization around quartal melodic and harmonic emphasis in "A Love Supreme" (recorded December 1964) underscored his continual expansion towards less conventional harmonic and intervallic concepts that he explored during the 1950s, and stretched to their limits in "Giant Steps." Other compositions from his late period displayed an interest in quasi-modality. In "Ascension" (recorded in June 1965), for instance, he uses Aeolian, D Phrygian, F Phrygian, etc. This diversity of approach makes it difficult to generalize with any sense of certainty about the direction and meaning of the Coltrane matrix. In any case, closer examination of his music renders certain aspects of his approach increasingly clear:

1. Coltrane was extremely methodical and systematic in his approach to spontaneous composition. His tonal thinking appeared to culminate in "Giant Steps" and then, due in part to the influence of some of the younger musicians around him, he makes a decisive move towards a more ecumenical and free style in the 1960s.
2. He knew that the blues matrix bridged the gap between all his musical concepts. Thus he recognized the correlation between elements of his compositions in tonal, modal, and free musical styles, and continued to present compositions in a wide variety of styles during his performances. His compositions and interpretation of music such as "My Favorite Things," "Naima," "Impressions," and other earlier works were continually transformed during concert performances as his matrix of musical concepts evolved.
3. The music of Africa, India, and other non-Western cultures became increasingly more influential on his work as he moved away from song forms explored during the 1950s.
4. Spirituality was the paramount force during the final decade of Coltrane's life and he spoke out about its influence. Coltrane said, "During the year 1957, I experienced, by the grace of God, a spiritual awakening, which was to lead me to a richer, fuller, more productive life. At that time, in gratitude, I humbly asked to be given the means and privilege to make others happy through music. I feel that this has been granted through His music. ALL PRAISE TO GOD." The titles of many of his compositions between 1957 and 1967 reflect the intensified affect of spiritual and metaphysical influences on his music.

Analyzing Coltrane's matrix reveals some of his ideas about harmonic structure. The matrix he gave Yusef Lateef was in two parts, a background drawing and a complete matrix (reproduced here as Figures 4a and 4c). I have added three more drawings (Figures 4b, 4d, and 4e) to facilitate analysis. The matrixes are like road maps (some more detailed than others) that allow travelers to choose routes and destinations freely as long as they continually have a set of clear goals in mind. Voyagers can travel by foot among a scenic set of pathways; travel more rapidly by car or train; or jump from region to region by airplane or helicopter. Eventually the terrestrial matrixes prepare us for the matrixes of space flight to remote solar systems and galaxies (*Interstellar Space*).

Figure 4a: His first drawing provides background for the second and involves two concentric circles as an organizational structure. The circular paths that they create are divided into twelve sections positioned like the signs of the Zodiac or the twelve hours on a clock. Each cell has three adjacent chromatic pitches that form a triangle. Adjacent triangles are positioned in inverse relationships; in one the apex is up, in the other (inverted triangle) it is down. Tones at the apex of each set throughout the progression are the interval of a perfect fifth from the others on either side (these tones are placed in squares around the circular path). Notes from adjacent triangles that are in closest proximity to each other are situated three half-steps (or a minor third) apart, while notes in adjacent cells located farthest apart are also separated by the interval of a perfect fifth. These landmark tones expose a systematic trajectory of major and minor third relationships and perfect fourth and fifth patterning. Some notes are written directly on the circular path, while others are outside it; but, in both instances, the notes on the path represent tones from either of the two whole-tone scales (one whole-tone's pitch set is on the path and the other outside). The notes that extend from the apex of any given triangle are four half-steps away from the closest note in its orbit from the next triangle. Coltrane encircles each of the pairs of chromatic upper and lower chromatic neighbor-tone that surround the boxed apex tones.

If we now look at the melodic and harmonic construction of "Giant Steps" again, this time with Coltrane's matrix in mind, we see his emerging interest in symmetrical arrangement. The melody's pattern involves four descending thirds (measures 1—2 and 5—6) in the two opening four-measure phrases, and outline the chords G-maj7 and E-half-dim7. These seventh chords have roots a minor third apart. Each pair of chords in measures 1—2 and 5—6 ascends a minor third. For example: measures 1—2 = B—D7, G—B$^\flat$7 and 5—6 = G—B$^\flat$, and E$^\flat$—G$^\flat$7 (the latter chord enharmonic with F$^\sharp$7). The second half of the melody focuses on two measure phrases consisting of four three-note motives that ascend with minor thirds between the outer notes of the diads: measures 8—9 = G (f) B$^\flat$; measures 10—11 = B (a) D; measures 12—13 = D$^\sharp$ (d$^\sharp$) F$^\sharp$; measures 14—15 G (g) B$^\flat$; and the penultimate note (B$^\flat$) then descends a major third for the return to the beginning = B$^\flat$ to G$^\flat$ (F$^\sharp$). The two appearances of major seconds (measures 8 and 10) are embellishments, as measures 12 and 14 confirm. Coltrane's primary matrix may suggest that he was interested in exploring such construction thirds, as both a harmonic substitution for root movement in fourths and fifths and, simultaneously, as a melodic replacement, the more standard vocal-styled emphasis on major and minor seconds. The circled chromatic pairs in Coltrane's primary matrix form major and minor thirds with the first note of the next triangle's tone on either side. For example, C and C$^\sharp$ form major and minor thirds with the neighboring tone E from the next triangle.

Coltrane's quartal melodic construction in "A Love Supreme" perhaps reflects his experiment with the fourths and fifths as suggested in boxed tones of both matrixes. It

Figure 4a. Coltrane Matrix, Example 1 of 2 (Duplicated from the original as found in Lateef, Y. *Repository of Scales and Melodic Patterns.* Amherst, MA: Fana Music, 1981.)

In Figure 4b: I interjected a second drawing, between Coltrane's primary and final matrixes. It includes connecting chromatic dyads that add a new note on either side of each triangle, thus forming one continuous chromatic scale (alternating tones between each of the two orbital paths). A five-pointed star has a number assigned to each point, each identifying the tone (C) in each of the five identical chromatic scale segments.

Figure 4b. Coltrane Matrix—Edited, Example 1 of 3 (Duplicated from the original as found in Lateef, Y. *Repository of Scales and Melodic Patterns.* Amherst, MA: Fana Music, 1981; with editorial additions by Karlton E. Hester.)

In Figure 4c: Lines are drawn through the center of the circle to connect polar opposite pairs of notes that are six half-steps (the interval of a tritone) apart. At the top of the chart these tritone pairs are separated into seven-note pitch sets and upper tones are numbered 7—1, while the lower tones of each tritone pair are numbered 1–7. This seven-note series does not extend all the way around the circle, but just identifies this mirror pattern. The drawing also locates (with arrows) the major thirds that fall on every other tone of each orbit.

Figure 4c. Coltrane Matrix, Example 2 of 2 (Duplicated from the original as found in Lateef, Y. *Repository of Scales and Melodic Patterns.* **Amherst, MA: Fana Music, 1981.)**

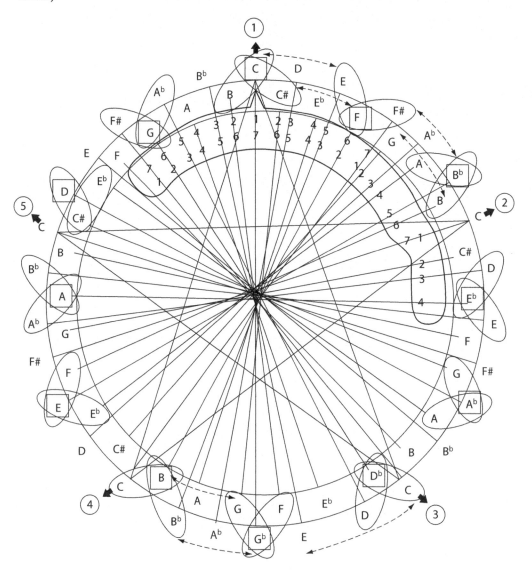

Figure 4d: The next drawing has a sign of the zodiac assigned to each chromatic tone of Coltrane's final matrix. Titles of his latest compositions and album suggest growing interest in cosmic phenomena (*Interstellar Space, Sun Ship, Cosmic Music,* "Mars," "Venus," "Jupiter," "Saturn," *Ascension, Crescent,* "Morning Sunrise," "Leo," etc.). Polar opposite pairs of astrological signs (Aries/Libra, Taurus/Scorpio, Gemini/Sagittarius, Cancer/Capricorn, Leo/Aquarius, Virgo/Pisces) align with Coltrane's polar opposite pairs of tritons around the clock.

Figure 4d. Coltrane Matrix—Edited, Example 2 of 3 (Duplicated from the original as found in Lateef, Y. *Repository of Scales and Melodic Patterns.* **Amherst, MA: Fana Music, 1981; with editorial additions by Karlton E. Hester.)**

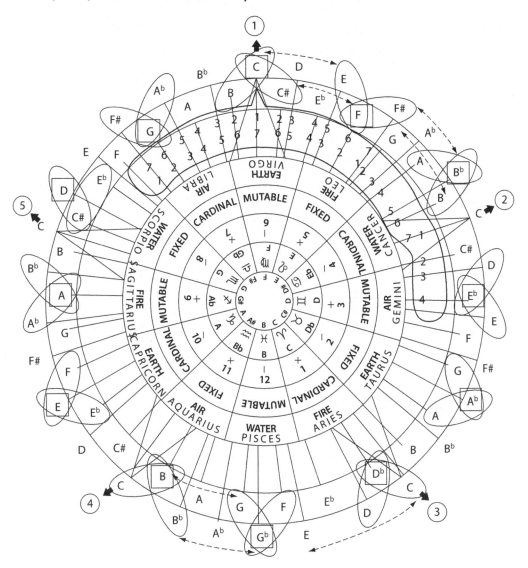

Figure 4e: The final drawing displays another numeric implication of Coltrane's seven-note pairs and identifies the tritone that occurs cyclically on each orbital path (marked with black and white triangles every fourth tone of a whole-tone series).

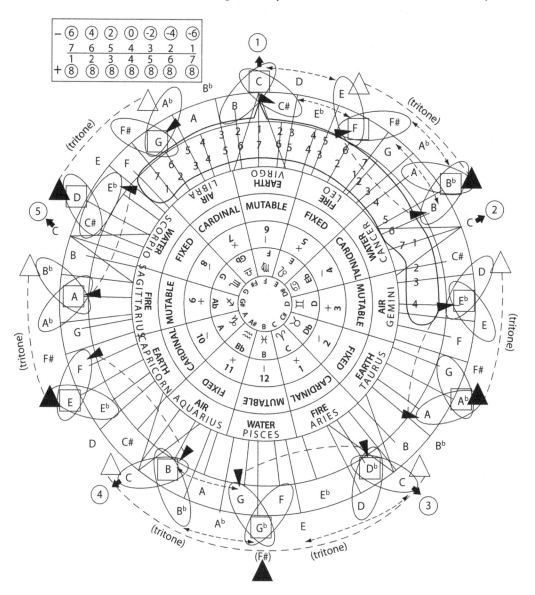

Figure 4e. Coltrane Matrix—Edited, Example 3 of 3 (Duplicated from the original as found in Lateef, Y. *Repository of Scales and Melodic Patterns.* Amherst, MA: Fana Music, 1981; with editorial additions by Karlton E. Hester.)

seems that seconds tend to serve as binding elements for large intervallic concerns in both "Giant Steps" and "A Love Supreme." Fifths and fourths are clearly the subject of his opening melody and the overall structural design of "A Love Supreme." Coltrane does not restrict himself to mechanical use of fourths and fifths throughout this composition, but quartal intervals serve as a continuity factor for the piece. Although "Resolution's" pitch set is entirely quartal (B^b-E^b-A^b-D^b-G^b), Coltrane's basic pitch collection (Fig. 3c), as well as those for the movements "Pursuance" and "Psalms," introduce a slightly broader intervallic mixture.

John Coltrane's final stylistic period marks the culmination of his artistic growth, and stands as a compendium of his total earlier achievements. From 1965 to his death on July 17, 1967, Coltrane developed a progressively more abstract approach to his spontaneous composing, while maintaining connections with his musical past by the continual development of the ideas generated in his earlier periods, and by retaining compositions such as "Naima" and "My Favorite Things" in his performance repertoire to the end of his career. Some scholars feel that his two final recordings, *Expression* and *Interstellar Space*, "exhibit the crystallization of all of the earlier Coltrane traits, although used in an abstract context" (White 53). "Naima" also utilizes perfect fourths, tritones, and major and minor seconds in its harmonic motion. Additionally, in a noticeable departure from the harmonic tendencies of either the song form or blues harmonies of bebop (with the exception of the last four measures that are closely related to the final harmonic sequence in *Slow Dance*, a ballad by Alonzo Levister that Coltrane recorded with The Red Garland Trio in 1957), "Naima" contains implied whole tone scale areas and displays an even greater range of distortion of the original model. Yet it too retains a prominent skeletal structure that unifies and molds each performance throughout Coltrane's later stylistic periods. Although the intervallic emphasis is primarily on thirds, we can also see a little quartal-related motion in the melody of Coltrane's composition "Naima" in measure 1, third beat; measure 10, third beat; and in measure 13, third beat.

NAIMA

John Coltrane

Figure 5. "Naima"

If we locate related patterns within any Coltrane matrix, we begin to outline prospective pathways that can easily establish potential systematic sets of harmonic and melodic structures. We can also explore the harmonic and melodic content of other Coltrane compositions by mapping the harmonic, motivic, and melodic elements in similar fashion to reveal the implications of such patterns. Coltrane's musical style was always changing, and his matrixes may have provided a nucleus from which his melodic and harmonic ideas could evolve methodically. Coltrane applied quite a bit of

Figure 6. "Interstellar Space"—Structural Outline

The loosely structured, formal skeleton is articulated by a carefully applied and skillfully conceived spontaneous arrangement defined by balancing of contrasting musical colors and textures, sonic events, and levels of dynamic intensity. Tracing such musical events demonstrates the tremendous variety, continuity, flexibility, and control that is maintained throughout the suite.

MARS (fast): inaugurates a new departure
Bells—Drum solo (dense, intensity maintained throughout)
Key and pulse obscured
Intervals and "sheets" unify [during]
Intro-wave "sheets"—lyrical—descending "sheets"—lyrical
Drum solo—Bells

VENUS (more relaxed): implies a stage of evaluation and Love
Bells—Drum solo (spacious, translucent textures throughout)
Mode related to D major (long chromatic ascent) serves as center
Rhythmic organization implies pulse at times [during]
Intro-ballad-wave "sheets"—lyrical-wave "sheets"—descending "sheets"
Bells

JUPITER (fast, brief): yields purposefulness
Bells
Clear motivic development throughout [while]
Motive—elements from earlier movements developed—motive
Bells

SATURN (more relaxed): is the stage of establishment
Drum solo (free-flowing)
Strong metrical scheme and key (E♭ minor)
Mode and meter are opposed by Coltrane; always implied by Ali [while]
Blues—elements from earlier movements further developed—blues

poetic license to all of his music, realizing that everything in the Universe is in constant motion and the zodiac is no exception. The equinoxes and other features of cosmic relationships are in constant flux. All such realizations must have had some measure of influence on Coltrane's systematic yet mercurial musical evolution. Coltrane's spontaneous composition, "Interstellar Space," is a good example of him bringing all his various theories together during the final year of his life. At that point, he abandoned strict conventional adherence to the blues matrix in favor of more fluid structural organization that gave access to all musical knowledge (blues, song form, sheets of sound, quasi-modal, motivic, symmetry, etc.) gained throughout his career.

Figure 7a. Signs of the Zodiac

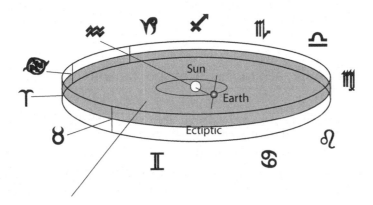

Figure 7b. The Periodic Changes of the Spring Equinox: Change Is Inevitable

In the relatively near future the spring equinox will be in Aquarius.
2,000 years ago the spring equinox was in Pisces.
6,000 years ago the spring equinox was in Taurus.
As the Earth orbits the Sun the line from the Earth to
  the Sun draws the Ecliptic Planes.

Coltrane's approach to spontaneous composition involved a search for aesthetic balance, emotional expression, and appropriate placement of notes that seems akin to the Feng Shui (literally "wind-water"), a component of an ancient Chinese philosophy of nature. Feng Shui is the ancient Chinese practice of placing and arranging space to achieve harmony with the environment. Feng Shui is often identified as a form of geomancy, divination by geographic features; but it is mainly concerned with understanding the relationships between nature and ourselves so that we might live in harmony within our environment. (Geomancy is a form of divination by throwing dirt on the ground and interpreting the result. Other forms of geomancy use geographic features or lines. This type of divination seems to be a form of pareidolia, and, like all divination, involves magical thinking.) Proponents claim that Feng Shui has an effect on health, wealth, and personal relationships. In ancient times, as well as today, Feng Shui (pronounced in English "fung shway") was known as "Kan-Yu," which means "The Law of Heaven and Earth." Feng Shui is a discipline with guidelines compatible with many techniques of agricultural planning as well as internal furniture arrangements. Feng Shui is related to the notion that living *with,* rather than *against,* nature benefits both humans and their environment, and that our lives are deeply affected by our physical and emotional environs. If we surround ourselves with symbols of death, contempt, and indifference towards life and nature, with noise and various forms of ugliness, we will corrupt ourselves in the process. If we surround ourselves with beauty, gentleness, kindness, sympathy, music, and various expressions of the sweetness of life, we ennoble ourselves as well as our environment. A glance at the titles of John Coltrane's compositions reveals many commonalities with Feng Shui philosophy.

A Holistic Approach to Theory of Spontaneous Composition

Music and mathematics measure portions of human experience in the universe. While math assigns numbers to describe various aspects of our environment, music infuses its numbers with musical patterns and symbols. We can analyze music mathematically, but its true intrinsic nature still remains unapproachable. Thinking in terms of "tension" and "release" provides performers with basic technical and conceptual tools. Experienced composers and performers develop a reservoir of musical resources applicable to diverse melodic, harmonic, rhythmic, and dynamic concerns. The application of those resources creates a sense of musical tension or release, motion or repose, and poetically applies a dynamic range of sonic color that renders musical inventions creatively expressive, rather than mechanically predictable.

In Western harmonic practice, we have grown accustomed to certain standard applications of harmonic tension and release. Oscillating between Major, Minor, Minor 7, Augmented, Dominant 7, and Diminished 7 and their corresponding scales or modes is one way to provide modulating colors. Every chord has a corresponding scale from which it is derived. Playing scale tones that are not in a given basic chord causes "tension" that needs resolution in certain contexts of tonal harmony and jazz. Resolving a "tension" tone provides "release" and guides voice-leading decisions in composing. In jazz, tension tones are *non-chord tones* that have a tendency to move towards resolution to chord tones, and for this reason are known as "active" scale-steps. "Active" scale-steps eventually move to "inactive" scale-steps (chord tones) that are called *target notes* because they are the notes that release harmonic tension. Tension tones fall into two categories: 1) "diatonic scale degrees," the "tension" tones that are found "inside" the chord's corresponding scale; and 2) "altered scale degrees," the "tension" tones that are "outside" both the given chord and its corresponding scale. Thus, creating and releasing harmonic tension requires using active scale-steps that are non-chord tones to create tension and inactive scale-steps that are chord tones to provide a release of tension. This style of interaction suggests musical duality that can also apply more broadly to the grouping of other types of harmonic structures and pitch sets. Nevertheless, attempts to reduce jazz to any small set of musical ingredients, formulas, and descriptions are futile. Spontaneous composition involves voyages of self-discovery executed in the moment with a wide range of creative tools in hand.

Musicians activate physical, emotional, and intellectual expression through sound. Music involves a balance between our intuitive capacities, developing physical and mental tools, and vocabulary that allow us to express the ideas we imagine. We spend many years accumulating vocabulary to increase our power of verbal communication. We learn to express ourselves by reading, memorizing passages and terms, accumulating definitions and labels, and through the rudimentary drills and pedagogical processes used to facilitate communication. Just as we must continually develop our verbal abilities, composers hone their skill by accumulating musical tools, vocabulary, and experience through similar patterns of development. Learning to compose spontaneously involves a process that is related to learning to communicate effectively with spoken language. We are born with an innate ability to problem solve and create; therefore, everyone is creative. The creative process should be natural and similar to most activities that we perform daily. In the final analysis, once presented as musical sound, it matters not whether an effective and powerful composition was conceived through premeditated or spontaneous means. Musical notation is just one of many ways to facilitate creative goals. Evolving a general theory of music that can be effectively applied to premeditated and spontaneous composition is a daunting proposition.

Balance involves a continuum because the universe is always moving and evolving, and everything, to a degree, reflects the Creative Source. Our freewill to express all that we can manage to comprehend (with our body, mind, and spirit) requires knowledge of balancing a variety of situations. Balance is not simply locating manifestations of opposite polarity or disposition, but also involves understanding the interconnectedness and synergistic relationships within existence. Artists who possess an intuitive knowledge of balance are those who often influence and shape our musical world. Synergy is one of the chief ingredients present within an effective jazz ensemble's interaction. This process reflects the synergistic vortex—music resulting from the convergence of language, traditions, religious practices, and a multitude of other cultural dimensions in the formation of various forms of African-American culture. Africa is a huge continent with an enormous number of independent cultures, languages, traditions, and musical styles. Consider the varied mixtures of human thought and expression formed when Africans were separated from their respective villages, cultures, families, traditions, and the like, and thrown into arbitrary plantation communities where new social constructs were forged under debilitating circumstances in foreign lands. This created a rich and abstract mixture of ingredients and influences.

Since the conception and perception of musical ideas is highly important in spontaneous musical production, in addition to technical or theoretical knowledge, considering basic modes of thought is necessary. The cultural attitude that we bring to music is reflected in the ultimate outcome. Continental African tradition often unifies sacred and secular poles, where at times there may be little or no distinction between "real" and "supernatural" realms of African consciousness. The African perspective is holistic; where there is openness to the unexpected and the unknown, and discovery often takes place through empathizing and identifying broadly with elements within the environment. The !Kung in the Kalahari Desert may become a snake in their song about a mamba. When asked about their drum, a West African drummer speaks of *"gembe"* rather than "the *gembe,"* just as they might refer to a human companion by name. The distinction between spirituals, blues, soul, funk, and jazz is nebulous and somewhat arbitrary, since both secular and sacred African-American styles of music share related melodic, harmonic, and rhythmic elements. Similarly, since traditional African societies perceive no significant distinction between the objective and spiritual worlds, deceased ancestors can remain attached to the objective reality of certain villages for as long as the names of the deceased are kept alive. Once names are forgotten, deceased villagers join the spiritual realm. Nevertheless, the African spiritual world continues to function in parallel to the objective reality of village life—as part of its subjective and subconscious domains. Thus continental Africans, and Africans throughout the Americas, often consciously combine sacred and secular realms of their existence into their musical approach. Consequently, most African-American music is "soul" music. The soul is an aspect of one's self that is separate from the body and mind, and this more elusive aspect inspires our creative thoughts, actions, and serves as the primary catalyst for musical inspiration for some artists.

African-American musicians, like the traditional African *griot* and *jali* before them, often become a liaison to magic and the sacred realms where the bodies, minds, and spirits of participant listeners are simultaneously engaged. This *experiential mindset* is more prone to merging with and experiencing phenomena than with observing and analyzing it from a distance. This is clear in the presentation of most African-American music, where audiences are traditionally actively involved on multiple levels (physically, mentally, and spiritually), rather than passively witnessing an event with an *analytical mindset*. This is not to say that experiential and analytical mindsets are mutually exclusive, but rather to distinguish between different degrees of emphasis that cultures place upon certain types of experience. In his article, "Raven's Appearance: The Language of Prophecy," Peter Kingsley discusses the differences between sacred models and the general Western perspective. Kingsley thinks that:

> There is the profane way of talking, which is to talk *about* things. And if you care to notice, you will see that in the modern Western world we always talk *about* something. There is the word; then there is the point of reference for the word, which is always separate from the word itself. And this, of course, is the basis for all modern linguistics.
>
> But according to people, such as Parmenides, there is another way of talking. This other way is that instead of talking *about,* you talk *from.* If you sense oneness you talk from oneness; and that oneness is communicated through the magic of word in a way that our minds find incomprehensible but that, even so, fascinates and endlessly obsesses them. For these people were magicians. The founders of logic and science in the West were sorcerers. They knew what they were doing even if, now, no one knows what they did.
>
> And the question of talk is also related to the question of how we discover. In the modern West we are governed, dominated, by the assumption that we discover things through time. By searching, by experimenting, we will eventually uncover the nature of reality bit by bit. This profane model of discovery was already established in the West very many centuries ago. And it has given rise to a catastrophic sense of estrangement from ourselves and everything else. We spend our whole lives searching for solutions and only uncovering more problems; searching for ourselves but never finding; looking for answers in the places where we assume and expect them to be while neglecting the wisdom communicated to us from every direction (Ibid. 12).

The sacred model is based on an altogether different principle than Western models. With the Afrocentric model, there is no principle involving the discovery and consequent ownership of things that already exist before your arrival. It is all there to begin with because everything is given. Everything we ever need to know is automatically provided to us at the very moment when we need to know it. There is only one requirement for entering into a living relationship with this sacred model: the ability to be open to the unexpected and the unknown (Kingsley 13).

Exploring the brain, consciousness, and how the mind processes thought can help artists understand the various ways that music and art are conceived by their creators and received by audiences. John Coltrane and Yusef Lateef are jazz musicians from a long legacy of innovators who exemplify those artists who make consciousness shifts from their mundane states of awareness to heightened states during active creative engagement. Such artists suggest that they seek contact with contemplative and spiritual disciplines for guidance and to enhance their creative capacity. Spontaneous composition focuses the mind in ways that enhance mental clarity and foster the integration of mind, body, and spirit. Ensemble interaction couples individual transcendence with group dynamics that quicken the performers' minds and helps each participant develop musical compassion, empathy, and pattern recognition, and promotes unification with and awareness of performance and expanded environments. The freedom of expression that jazz musicians often experience, as a consequence of such performance rituals, sharpens their intuition and insight. Experience at that level of spontaneous composition often leads to eidetic musical knowledge, a sense of tranquility, heightened self-awareness, and joy.

Since the 1970s, psychologist Mihalyi Csziksentmihalyi has dedicated much of his research to finding the link between creativity and productivity. Musical experiences that result in a sense of well-being are akin to what Csziksentmihalyi calls "finding flow" (Csziksentmihalyi). The flow experience comes with mastery of basketball, expert skiing, playing inspired jazz, or anything that demands all of your concentration and skill to enjoy the satisfaction of achieving something masterful in the moment. Some people consider Csziksentmihalyi's work "unscientific," but anyone who attempts to assess the illusions that manifest from the magic of flow have to consider tools of intuitive investigation when working outside the confining realms of molecular analysis.

Wisdom traditions worldwide are intended to lead practitioners towards consciousness that transcends the physical environment and leads into a realm of empiricism mediated by our individual and collective experiences, cultural influences, readiness, and individual and collective expectations. Since ritual experience aspires to transcend normal states of human consciousness, some psychologists and artists look to the function of music and art in ritual for ontological clues that will help them understand our various levels of consciousness.

Dr. Nelson Harrison is a clinical psychologist, educator, composer, arranger, trombonist, clinician, inventor, and veteran of the Count Basie Orchestra (197881). He has played and recorded with Kenny Clarke, Billy Eckstine, Earl "Fatha" Hines, Jay McShann, Slide Hampton, Walt Harper, Nathan Davis, and Andy Bey. His composer credits consist of over 400 compositions, including movie scores and soundtracks. He invented a unique ten-inch long, five-pound brass instrument he calls the "Trombetto" on which he can play six octaves chromatically.

Harrison is particularly interested in music's cross-disciplinary links to psychology, neuroscience, anthropology, philosophy, cultural studies, and mysticism. His research suggests that African-American music, and other creative art worldwide, often broaches the realm of human consciousness, extending beyond electro-chemical processes; thus such art remains irreducible to any strictly physical substrate. African tonal language and the sound of Nature intertwined in ancient Africa and became the models for its vocal and instrumental music. Considering the fundamental linguistic influences and range of environmental sounds that generate the Global African musical vocabulary that served as the foundation for African-American music, it is useful to explore music's epistemological aspects as a catalyst for understanding the transcendent and contemplative nature of ritual.

During a lecture at the University of California, Santa Cruz in April 2002, Dr. Harrison asked students in my Survey of African Music class, "What is the most important thing to do in life?" Students responded by suggesting that they should "love," "grow," "pursue happiness," and contributed a wide variety of other thoughtful replies. However, Dr. Harrison's answer was that all people have to do is "to be." (As in Shakespeare's "To be or not to be, that is the question.") Harrison's point reflects more than simply an existential philosophical position. In thinking about this again years later, I realize that the veiled directness, sophistication, and profundity of this notion also applies to a composer's ontology. Music has no fixed rules that, if digested thoroughly, guarantee creative success. "To be" helps us realize that the Universe provides us ample opportunity each day to honor the privilege of being alive and to appreciate the value of creative self-expression.

Many of us would enjoy a world in which all people could exercise their creativity and discover ways to find time for personal fulfillment, love, and happiness. If the most important thing we have to do in life is "to be" then perhaps the notion that, "I am, therefore I think," is more properly worded for that philosophical position. Individual self-expression, the hallmark of jazz, and the understanding and attitude that it displays, thus becomes an essential and vital priority of human existence. Musical instruments merely amplify the communicative emotions that we aspire to express through sound. Samite Mulondo (Ugandan flutist, vocalist, and *mbira* player) once told me that he always tried to find the particular song that lay dormant within each new flute he made or discovered. Melody can reflect humankind's psychological and emotional reaction to our internal and external environments. Harmony most often grows out of melody. Rhythm helps to organize, ground, and structure musical elements within the passage of multifaceted musical time. The level of freedom and responsibility that the creative process engenders makes jazz and spontaneous composition successful as a contemporary, global, cultural influence. Seeking to master music solely through the display of technique alone, without learning the subtle art of musical expression, limits the ability to communicate ideas meaningfully and most effectively. Likewise, learning to imitate even the most eloquent, powerful, and beautiful speeches of powerful communicators does not necessarily lead to an ability to communicate original thoughts and ideas effectively.

Although no fixed rules or parameters exist, the most successful spontaneous composition requires an awareness of all musical factors involved in a musical setting while engaging elements of melodic, harmonic, rhythmic, dynamic, timbre, and musical structure during real time performance. Despite the levels of freedom involved, spontaneous composition still requires that each musical tone evolve convincingly to the next most inevitable tone. As each musician manipulates the musical vocabulary to express personal ideas, they converse logically and sensitively with fellow musicians. This requires the coordination and merging of multiple ideas and modes of expression. While tension and release, consonance and dissonance, agreement and disagreement, and other musical factors stimulate and propel ensemble conversations, navigating with a common voice, vision, and flexibility align collective awareness towards mutual musical goals. All musicians residing within the same creative environment must speak a mutual musical language and realize that all participants involved are painting a mutual sonic canvas. Ultimately, the musical portrait must evolve as though it flows from a single set of hands.

Nelson Harrison also posited that creative thought develops in the "analogue-prone" right brain where the intuition rules over processed thought and spiritual inspiration. The left brain deals with labels, spoken languages, and more digitally oriented information. Harrison feels that those who first send their music through the left brain functions (reading or analyzing music initially through their eyes) take an infinitely longer route to creative manifestation than those who process musical information directly through their ears. Harrison said that it was easy for him to calm one of his autistic relatives through jazz and other Global African music, because certain music functions on a related unfiltered poly-dimensional plane, just as an autistic mind does.

Autism is a developmental disability of the brain that is not a form of mental retardation. Autistic people are frequently quite intelligent, but tend to have unusual sensory experiences. Such experiences may involve hypersensitivity, less sensitivity than normal, and/or difficulty interpreting a sense ("agnosia"). Autistic individuals have sensory experience based on actual experiences (not hallucinations), but the experience may feel or sound different than it does with average ("normal") people, or an autistic person may have difficulty interpreting certain experiences. No two autistic people appear to have the exact same pattern of sensory problems.

LEFT (Analytic) Successive Hemispheric Style	RIGHT (Global) Simultaneous Hemispheric Style
1. Verbal	1. Visual
2. Responds to word meaning	2. Responds to tone of voice
3. Sequential	3. Random
4. Processes information linearly	4. Processes information in varied order
5. Responds to logic	5. Responds to emotion
6. Plans ahead	6. Impulsive
7. Recalls people's names	7. Recalls people's faces
8. Speaks with few gestures	8. Gestures when speaking

9. Punctual	9. Less punctual
10. Prefers formal study design background while studying	10. Prefers sound/music
11. Prefers bright lights while studying	11. Prefers frequent mobility while studying

Harrison said that an autistic person takes in multiple levels of information simultaneously, over more extended periods of time than most people are accustomed to sustaining, rather than zooming in on isolated experiences and events (such as individual conversations, single task, single elements on a computer screen, etc.). Abnormal brain functions often involve an imbalance between its hemispheres. Dyslexia, mental retardation, schizophrenia, and attention deficit disorder are other developmental disabilities. Schizophrenics cannot control the passage of information from left brain to right brain, for example. Those stuck within the domain of the left brain virtually build a mental wall between that region and their right brain hemispheres. They may rarely allow their conscious minds access to the intuition except in dream-state, when the subconscious mind is in charge. Regarding the hemispheres of the brain, mathematician Ellen Freedmand says:

> An important factor in understanding learning styles is understanding brain functioning. Both sides of the brain can reason, but by different strategies, and one side may be dominant. The left brain is considered analytic in approach while the right is described as holistic or global. A *successive processor* (left brain) prefers to learn in a step-by-step sequential format, beginning with details leading to a conceptual understanding of a skill. A *simultaneous processor* (right brain) prefers to learning beginning with the general concept and then going on to specifics.
>
> People think and learn in different ways. In any group there will always be evidence of different learning characteristics, but different cultural groups may emphasize one cognitive style over another. A. Hilliard describes "learning style" as the sum of the patterns of how individuals develop habitual ways of responding to experience and distinguishes learning styles by considering the holistic versus the analytic learner.

Akin to the duality of the brain, the dual nature of existence is also clear in the nature of polarity. Regarding the typically proposed contrast that exists between masculine and feminine qualities, I once stumbled across a woman filmmaker on a televised program who said that the feminine quality reflects women's patience because women (in a male-dominated society) always have to wait. She felt that, since women have to exercise patience during all phases of childbearing, they are closer aligned to the gradual process of "becoming" and, generally speaking, more intuitive (over the analytical), and less conditioned towards absolute pragmatism and reliance upon formulate conclusions. African-American musicians have also learned to wait patiently in an oppressive Western society. The resultant music reflects related emphasis on process, spontaneity, intuition, and a preference towards kinesthetic perception and flexibility in artistic expression, rather than absolute reliance upon stability, prescriptive analysis, fixed musical forms, and emphasis on arriving at finite conclusions.

My most intense learning experiences, such as several years of study with master musician Joe Henderson, involved primarily right-brain approaches to learning. Joe Henderson taught everything through direct contact with musical sound itself. Those who prefer a learning process that places greater emphasis upon visual symbols and fixed theories may develop an ability to interpret musical notation efficiently, but might fail to fully develop the more elusive ability to understand spontaneous creation primarily through their ears and intuitive faculties.

Music Leaves Its Indelible Imprint on the Brain

Music and sound leave an indelible imprint on the brain. Years after we initially experience hearing music, emotions often resurface when we again hear or remember a composition associated with that initial experience return. Although we don't know how or why music evolved to become such an important and influential human activity, the

Figure 8. Left Brain/Right Brain Characteristics

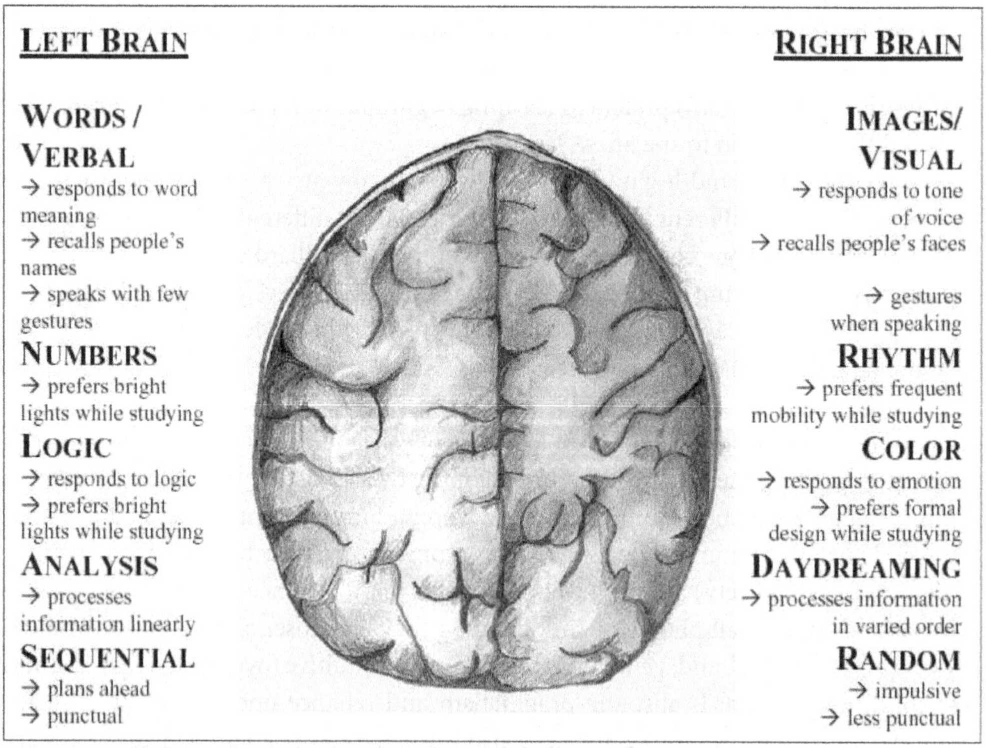

LEFT BRAIN	RIGHT BRAIN
WORDS / VERBAL → responds to word meaning → recalls people's names → speaks with few gestures	**IMAGES/ VISUAL** → responds to tone of voice → recalls people's faces → gestures when speaking
NUMBERS → prefers bright lights while studying	**RHYTHM** → prefers frequent mobility while studying
LOGIC → responds to logic → prefers bright lights while studying	**COLOR** → responds to emotion → prefers formal design while studying
ANALYSIS → processes information linearly	**DAYDREAMING** → processes information in varied order
SEQUENTIAL → plans ahead → punctual	**RANDOM** → impulsive → less punctual

[Based on an illustration given to the author by Dr. Nelson E. Harrison and information from http://www.mathpower.com/brain.htm - 03/15/2004]

elements of music have had a profound effect on people since the first primitive human ancestor carved a flute from a bone or piece of wood more than 50,000 years ago. Music and sound have always stirred emotions of every human culture throughout the history of the world. The intimate and interactive dynamic that exists between music and brain function results in measurable and immeasurable effects on human behavior. Research has shown the shift in perception stimulated by the power of sound. Filmmakers are intensely aware of this fact and composers apply music to their films accordingly. Our minds grow in accordance with the quantity and quality of our musical experiences. In an article published on December 13, 2002 in the *LA Times* entitled "Music Leaves Its Mark on the Brain" staff writer Robert Lee Hotz reported that, "If it's pleasing to the ears, it's tied to rewired circuits that find notes harmonious, study says." Hotz continues:

> From Mozart to Miles Davis, the harmonies of Western music rewire the brain, creating patterns of neural activity at the confluence of emotion and memory that strengthen with each new melody, research made public shows.
> . . .
> "Music is not necessary for human survival, yet something inside us craves it," said Dartmouth music psychologist Petr Janata, who led the global research team. "Our minds have internalized the music."
> Whatever the reason, the effect on the individual brain is measurable.
> Among expert musicians, certain areas of the cortex are up to 5 percent larger than in people with little or no musical training, recent research shows. In musicians who started their training in early childhood, the neural bridge that links the brain's hemispheres, called the corpus callosum, is up to 15 percent larger. A professional musician's auditory cortex—the part of the brain associated with hearing—contains 130 percent more gray matter than that of non-musicians.
> The new study, published Thursday in *Science,* shows for the first time that the abstract knowledge about the harmonic relationships in music inscribes itself on the human cortex, guiding expectations of how musical notes should relate to one another as they are played. Through constant exposure, synapses are trained to respond like a series of tuning forks to the tones characteristic of Western music, several experts said. So far, no one has tested the music of other cultures, but researchers speculate that all music should have the same effect (Hotz).

The pattern in the music literally becomes a pattern in the brain. "It shows this link between music theory and perception and brain function," said Frances H. Rauscher, an expert in music cognition at the University of Wisconsin at Oshkosh. "No one had looked before. The Dartmouth group scanned eight people with a functional magnetic resonance imager as they listened to an eight-minute melody especially composed to move continuously through all twenty-four major and minor musical keys. The volunteers, who each had about twelve years of musical training, performed several music-related tasks while they listened in the scanner. People can hear the same music at various periods in their life and it can have varying effects on them physically each time." Petr Janata went on to say that, "We think it might explain why when you hear a piece of music one time, it might move you to dance. . . . When you hear it another time, you might instead remember the party or the feelings you had there." Robert Lee Hotz adds:

> Within this brain region, however, a melody creates a slightly different pattern of neural activity every time it is heard, as if the laser reading the digital pattern of a compact disc recording varied the pattern slightly each time the music was played.
>
> This dynamic map may be the key to understanding why a piece of music might elicit a certain behavior one time, such as dancing, and something different another time, such as smiling when remembering a dance, the researchers said.

Some types of music are more universally appealing than others. What does this tell us about the qualities of sound and composition? "Music is really popular, but what does it do for the brain?" Janata asks. "Why is it we have the emotional responses we do to music? Why is it that melodies run spontaneously through our heads?" Whatever the answer may be, we all know that our brains are actively engaged in absorbing and appreciating music in diverse ways. Researchers on this area of study have discovered that everyone had just one area in common that tracked and processed melodies, despite the fact that music activated many parts of the brain in general. The region of the brain that deals with melody is the rostromedial prefrontal cortex near the center of the forehead. It is the same region that links to short- and long-term memory and emotions. That area is apparently also involved in more basic sound processing.

David Huron, head of the cognitive and systematic musicology laboratory at Ohio State University, proposed that, since tracing the path of a car allows us to infer the underlying map of a city's streets, the path traced by cortex may allow researchers to see the underlying structure of music (Huron). Although many researchers in this area of music often point to European "classical" music as the flagship for music with the propensity for brain enhancement, Gordon Shaw and Mark Bodner, brain experts at the Music Intelligence Neural Development Institute in Irvine, made it clear that there is nothing special about the effect that Western music has as far as brain anatomy and neural networks are concerned. The distinctive musical circuits in the cortex are just as easily stimulated by exposure to jazz, the music of the Aborigine didgeridoo, Tuvan throat-singing, or Japanese court *gagaku*.

The degree to which music influences our brains depends upon the quality of our exposure to it and the degree to which we engage in it actively. Some people feel that perfect pitch is inherited, but lost if not reinforced by practice. Others conclude that at four months of age, babies already prefer the more consonant intervals of major and minor thirds to the more dissonant sounds of minor seconds. Of course this all depends on cultural exposure, and debates over intervallic preference and notions about what qualities of melody are more musical than others has gone on for centuries. Children's game songs throughout the Global African Diaspora tend to involve the falling minor third, for example. At one time only the "perfect intervals" were considered consonant and all major and minor intervals were labeled dissonant in the West. These cultural attitudes changed over time as the ear gradually experienced a wider range of musical choices that included a variety of sounds and musical intervals.

Africanisms in African-American Music

Music is a mirror that reflects our total experience through physical, emotional, intellectual, and sonic events, as well as through individual and collective musical expression. It reflects elements of an era, culture, and society wherever it occurs. Through music and language we can trace ideas, emotions, and events traversing and chronicling the history of human development. It exposes the way a given people walk, talk, joke, think, strategize, love, and approach survival. In general, musical Africanisms include many traditional African belief systems, customs, linguistic characteristics, and other cultural traits. The African-American approach to spontaneous composition involves the creation of music in the moment. Premeditated composition is typically driven by linear oscillations between elements of musical moments past and present. The distinctive approaches to various features of a culture's music reflect inherent social dynamics. Many such reflections became Afrocentric retentions of traditional African culture retained throughout the African Diaspora. Francis Bebey suggests that:

> It is clear that African music goes far beyond the realm of art. And yet in these modern times, it manages to retain intact those of its former functions that have given African society throughout the ages its own particular character. This is a real capital, which is all the more precious because it is immutable. The formal elements of the music may change in order to keep abreast of the times and various new influences, and although there may be some grounds for pessimism about the future of "authentic African music," its basic functions and deep significance are reassuringly stable (Bebey 142–45).

Africanisms in African-American music evolved as black musicians struggled externally against racism inflicted by European-American society, and internally against prescriptive definitions of racial authenticity spread by African-American listeners who criticized various innovative musical approaches. African-American music is a rich mixture and archive of the Africans' movement from their native land, through the horrors of Middle Passage, and their ultimate adaptation to a new land. The emotional results of listening to the personalized delivery of an African-American spiritual or gospel hymn are tangible. We can track certain musical factors theoretically, but some of that music's most distinguishing factors involve a brand of abstract ingredients that defies analysis.

Thus, we must track features of traditional African music and culture while examining Africanisms in African-American music to understand their root connections. "Afrocentricity" is a term coined by Molefi Asante to describe a modern and controversial branch of philosophy that originated in the late nineteenth century through the work of W. E. B. DuBois and his contemporaries. Asante's perspective suggests that aesthetics often determine the patterns that bind culture in a society, and that they emerge as symbols, colors, rhythms, styles, and forms that function as artistic tools, instruments, and cultural histories. In African and African-American societies music serves as a repository for cultural information. Asante suggests that the African aesthetic is visible in all stylistic domains, from the popular cultural expressions to the classical ones. Therefore, cultural information manifests in all art forms, from fashion to body adornment. Guthrie P. Ramsey, Jr. believes that Afrocentricity is a reflection of a uniquely black experience:

> While African Americans certainly share a great many of the same attributes and sensibilities as other Americans, their collective "American experience" has also been a specific one, producing subjective cultural memories that have reciprocal and powerful relationships with cultural forms such as black music. As Floyd argues, "All black music making is driven by and permeated with the memory of things from the cultural past and that recognition of the viability of such memory should play a role in the perception and criticism of works and performances of black music (Ramsey 33).

As is clear in the freer forms of jazz, musical content dictates form in African and African-American music. The free flow of ideas is either poured into traditional musical forms or led to create new structures generated by innovative musical content. On their native continent, some African music was inclined towards reflection of the multidimensional tendencies in nature through syncopation, a rich array of musical timbre, cross-rhythmic patterning, and polyrhythm. Musical instruments (particularly winds) were also designed to utilize the inherent tendencies and flexibility of the natural overtone series. Overblowing the fundamental tones, and then manipulating those primary notes, formed the foundation for much of the melodic and harmonic tendencies of African music that later, in turn, became the melodic and harmonic basis for early African-American sacred and secular music. The free flow of ideas leads to the creation of structures in which to contain them. Nelson Harrison wrote that, "In the African worldview mythology is more important than history. It follows that in a culture of myths—there's room for all the different perspectives. Science itself becomes a myth, i.e., one way to look at things." Harrison's work acknowledges the spiritual horizons of jazz musicians and the inner mechanics of transcendent experience through psychological and metaphysical explorations of human creativity and consciousness.

While African music is indeed very rhythmic, the drum is not the primary force behind it. Traditional African music has a linguistic foundation that infuses the communicative nature of African-American vocal and instrumental music. Languages of traditional African regions generated the syncopated phonetic structure that defined rhythmic patterns of West African talking drums. Song lyrics determined the rhythmic and tonal elements of African music. Thus, in African and African-American communities, vocal or instrumental music devoid of communicative qualities fails to be fully appreciated by members of the community. If a musician is "just playing notes," people will quickly tell you the music is not saying anything.

African languages are tonal and African Americans transferred some of that tonal tendency to features of their own vernacular English and stylized musical features. Consequently, the rhythmic and tonal pattern of speech determined the rhythmic, harmonic, melodic, and responsorial framework for early African-American vocal and instrumental music. Rich mixtures of vocal devices are used to infuse all African-American music stylistically, augmented with additional instrumental, expressive, and emotional dimension and devices. African vocal and instrumental expression includes: 1) the indefinite pitch used in African-American music to approximate speech—vocal effects that include screams, shouts, moans, and groans; 2) falsetto and falsetto break, where the male head voice is used, or where the alternating between head and chest voices occurs; 3) text is substantially extended through a variety of vocalization techniques, including lyric improvisation where free interpretation and expansion upon the prevailing words to a song takes place; 4) and free melodic and rhythmic embellishment of an original fixed melody rendering flexible traditionally rigid structures, such as repetitive strophic form. African-American brass players were the first to use a variety of mutes to emulate the flexible sounds of conversation.

Global African drums speak in polyrhythms reflective of Nature, while winds and strings perform in polytonal and pan-tonal harmonic languages (pitch bending, microtones, superimposition of "major and minor" sonorities, etc.). The history of African-American oral tradition, literature, and song involves firm grounding in the understanding of multiple meanings (such as the subtle double entendre). In traditional African society, the tendency towards communal interaction within its social traditions is reflected in the interconnection of its interdisciplinary art forms, religion (spirituality), and the team-oriented functions of Global African music.

Musical, sociological, and psychological elements and phonetic structure were transferred into the blues through the African oral and aural tradition that laid the foundation for early African-American culture. Early children's game songs, syllabic and sometimes melismatic field hollers, and the musical cries of nineteenth-century African-American street vendors heard around the United States in cities such as New Orleans, as well as the African-American riverboat men's work cries heard along the Mississippi River were common musical occurrences in daily community life. Varied qualities of singing styles made their way into African-American instrumental music, as players used mutes, bottles, growls, glissandi, and other techniques to modulate their personal sound and develop expressive instrumental modes of verbalization.

Griots and *jalis* are traditional African historians/musicians responsible for chronicling the short-term and long-term histories (memories) of a village and culture. The musical traditions of *griots* and *jalis* usually involve solo narratives (sang to the accompaniment of a string or other musical instrument), or situations where a responding audience supports a soloist. The call and response patterns (sang by alternating soloist and chorus) of African grinding songs often incorporated stories with complex literary symbolism heard during evenings by small audiences of adults and children. On other occasions many *griots* and *jalis* sang songs of mockery and denunciation to call attention to unacceptable social behavior. The music produced for social functions by *griots* and *jalis* (or *jelis*) in West Africa resembles the descendent music of itinerant African-American rural blues musicians. The content of such songs is often derived from personal relationships, daily functions and concerns, and typical human complaints that arise when living in a cruel oppressive environment. The "difference between the lyrics of the blues and most African and New World songs or derision . . . [is] that most blues are sung in *first person*. Their messages are delivered from a first-person viewpoint and their emotional dimension is defined by performers as a 'worried feeling caused by problems in life'" (Kubik 26–27).

Some modern and contemporary jazz forms (especially free jazz of the 1960s) use a wide range of musical approaches, and musical elements are sometimes abstracted to such a point that original melodies, rhythms, harmony, and structure may be difficult to discern. In most cases, extemporization, progressive development, and transmutation become standard procedures that shape Global African stylistic expression. Clarity is maintained in a variety of ways, despite levels of technical difficulty attached to many stylistic forms through a variety of repetitive devices; thus embellishment and modifications are applied without annihilating basic melodic content and unifying structures. Earl Stewart asserts that rhythmic plexuses group themselves into two fundamental opposing forces: "1) those that are designed to *merge* (form the *concresent* aspect of the plexus), and 2) those designed to *contend* (form the *conflicting* aspect of the plexus)." The most enduring practitioners of free jazz grounded themselves thoroughly in an existing improvisational vocabulary before extending that basic knowledge into the development of their own personal dialects. Thorough understanding of an existing vocabulary renders communication in newly evolving styles more successful, and voice-leading tendencies, the merging and contending aspects of rhythm, and other compositional devices can be easily transferred between old and new styles.

Africanisms abound in gospel music, born from spirituals sung by Africans in America during the slave era. Thomas Dorsey of Georgia coined the term "gospel" at the time of the National Baptist Convention in 1921. Dorsey wrote "Precious Lord" and other popular church songs and became known as the father of gospel music. Spirituals served as songs of hope prior to the Emancipation Proclamation, but blues developed afterwards when it became clear that the Civil War did not bring the expected degrees of freedom, equality, and prosperity to Africans in America. Both gospel and blues share conspicuous stylistic features.

Jazz was a direct result of the growing numbers of African-American musicians pursuing careers in the arts following the American Civil War. African Americans had learned relatively few European cultural traditions during the slave era, but with gaining freedom African Americans quickly changed music and dance throughout the United States, and eventually worldwide. At the end of the 1900s, blues and ragtime initiated a musical and cultural revolution in America that launched the twentieth-century jazz evolution and fostered an evolving sense of musical freedom. Freedom involves risk-taking and, due to hostile and oppressive social conditions, African-American music transcended both the traditional cultural patterns of its native Africa and the prevailing Eurocentric musical styles found in America.

African-American music creates intriguing paradoxes. The blues is a pervasive musical system and its lyrical, harmonic, and melodic conventions have become influential music powers in many styles of modern and contemporary music. Blue notes are easily discernable embellishments, common to both instrumental and vocal music. They provide examples of ways that simple musical elements (such as basic scales, chords, and rhythms) can multiply their musical meaning and potential with the addition of carefully chosen notes that enhance basic musical resources in flexible ways. David Evans suggested that blues musicians "proceed from an awareness of flexible pitch areas" (24). In reference to the erroneous and now obsolete notion that the blue notes were "neutral thirds" just halfway between E and E$^\flat$ and B and B$^\flat$, Evans wrote:

> In fact, "neutral" probably would best represent an area between major and minor where notes can be sung, rather than any specific point between them. Blues singers often waiver at the third or seventh or glide from a lower to a slightly higher pitch. The lower part of the third and seventh areas tends to serve as a leading tone respectively to the tonic and fifth below, the upper part as a leading tone to the fifth and tonic above.

The application of blue notes to a simple pentatonic pitch set, for instance, augments the fundamental pitch set and its harmonic implications. Even a basic four-note dominant chord becomes an expansive and innovative pitch set when basic blue notes are applied, forming one of a number of possible "blues scales."

The addition of a lower leading tone to each note of the C7 chord below creates a blues scale. Blues Africanisms, although based upon traditional African sonorities, introduced a melodic and harmonic orientation based on a new Afrocentric attitude regarding tonal resolution. Later, bebop masters explored extended harmonic implications inherent in older blues forms. For example, the addition of an upper leading tone to the root tone creates the C7-flat-nine sonority.

Figure 9.

African-American music was analyzed more rigorously after the historical significance of black music was realized. While some African-American musicians focused upon the technical and theoretical elements of their innovations, others placed the

Blues Scale

C dominant chord with Blue Notes

music into social, cultural, political, and economic contexts, expressing their views more publicly during the second half of the twentieth century. Musicologist Samuel Floyd, Jr. suggests that the spirit of the Negro Renaissance in Harlem was anticipated by the efforts of early twentieth-century black composers such as Scott Joplin, Will Marion Cook, and Harry T. Burleigh to develop vernacular black art into extended musical forms (Floyd 100–107). Witnessing vibrant live performances of African-American music enabled Zora Neale Hurston to express her reaction to Africanisms colorfully (Porter 15). In 1938 Hurston said that the moment that she felt most "colored" was when she attended a particular jazz performance:

> This orchestra grows rambunctious, rears on its hind legs and attacks the tonal veil with primitive fury, rending it, clawing it until it breaks through the jungle beyond. I follow those heathen—follow them exultingly. I dance wildly inside myself (828–829).

Humor often pervades black music, art, language, and culture. The use of double-entendre lyrics in early field hollers, spirituals, the blues, and other African-American musical forms all reveal this tendency towards dual meaning and *symbolism*. In the Negro Spiritual "Swing Low Sweet Chariot," for example, there are both the conspicuous biblical references and a more cryptic symbolism embedded within. The latter information was often intended to inform African Americans in captivity that some representative from the Underground Railroad was nearby and ready to help someone escape that night. Such subtle use of symbolism required both insider cultural awareness of African-American community secrets, and fluency over a variety of elements of musical communication, including the musical context, rhythmic cadences, timing, inflection, mode of delivery (storytelling), application of emotional drama, histrionics, gesturing, facial expressions, and body language.

Traditional African music presentations are interdisciplinary (with aural, visual, and kinetic dimensions), and include interaction between performers and audience members. African-American music retained much of this predisposition. Africanisms have also influenced other modern and contemporary world music, diminishing their cultures' former degrees of separation between audiences and presenters at performances.

Because all early African-based musical traditions share common origins, African-American music too retains certain essential features from its early influences. Traditionally, African musicians lived close to Nature, listening to the natural sounds of their surroundings. Because the patterns of Nature's forces are omni-directional, African music evolved poly-dimensional characteristics as it reflected its environment. Likewise, John Coltrane and some other jazz innovators consider creative music a reflection of the poly-dimensional and omnipotent nature of the Creative Source. Spiritual inspiration was also firmly rooted in traditional music from other regions of the African Diaspora. In the Caribbean, African musical retentions have remained in Jamaica throughout its history, with the strongest influence of African rhythms emerging in the development of reggae, Jamaica's own musical style. African retention of musical traditions may not be as conspicuous in Jamaica as in Trinidad, but such influence remains conspicuous throughout the region to varying degrees.

The retention of African rhythms survived plantation life particularly because they were used in Obeah and Myal spiritual practices. The mixture ("creolization") of Christian beliefs and their combination with African spiritual practices also incorporated these same African rhythms and dances. Later, Revivalism kept African sounds alive both in music and in Jamaica's culture. The Pentecostal faith, for example, retained some African elements. Inspiration in music connected with spiritual practice most often occurs when sustained stimulation of our subconscious reaches the point where readiness, creativity, and opportunity intersect to produce something artistically useful. The Koran says:

> It is He who sends down water from the sky with which we bring forth the buds of every plant. From these we bring forth green foliage and close-growing grain, palm-trees laden with clusters of dates, vineyards and olive groves, and pomegranates alike and different. Behold their fruits when they ripen. Surely in these there are an indication of the majesty and dominance of God, but it has also been provided for the use of humanity (Chapter 6, verse 99).

In South Africa, people often refer to *Ubuntu*. Loosely translated, this is an African traditional idea, concept, and philosophy that emphasizes how all people are a part of each other and unified as one human family and community. *Ubuntu* is central to African culture and life. They place a high premium on sharing, showing respect for elders, and for the care of children. The traditional sense of unity and group consciousness in traditional African culture was systematically severed in the New World. When communal drumming was forbidden in the United States, individual drummers tried to emulate the communal quality of polyrhythmic African interaction on the jazz trap set. The demonstration of respect for elders, so central in African culture, was transferred to a mentoring system extant during the earlier periods of jazz, where techniques and knowledge were passed on from one generation to the next.

Despite the overwhelming influence of the blues on African-American music, it certainly is not the sole signifier of black musical authenticity. African-American musicians have always drawn inspiration from everything within their grasp and transformed information absorbed into something new and personal. Since African-American culture grew out of convergence of a wide assortment of African people, cultural information, and social settings, the range of diversity is reflected in the Africanisms that evolved and transmigrated. Regional styles also developed in North America over time, so that artists developing in the southern regions of the United States displayed contrasting musical styles of expression to those who evolved stylistic traits along the East or West Coast of America. Africanisms in African-American music involve: 1) the absorption and processing of everything within its reach, 2) retaining elements of traditional African music while radically redefining those same traditions and those newly encountered, and 3) the application of innovative and personalized forms of musical expression.

Africanisms infuse rap music, a strong cultural element within the larger social hip-hop movement. Tricia Rose was born and raised in New York City. She spent her childhood in Harlem and the Bronx. She graduated from Yale University where she received a B.A. in Sociology and then received her Ph.D. from Brown University in the field of American Studies. She is most renowned for her groundbreaking book on the emergence of hip hop culture: *Black Noise: Rap Music and Black Culture in Contemporary America,* published in 1994 by Wesleyan Press. Rose argues that what some consider "non-progressive" elements of rap and hiphop have always been characteristics of jazz, the blues, and R&B, as well other non-black cultural forms. Moreover, Rose feels that some of the more controversial elements are generally central to hip-hop and other popular cultural styles. Many historians consider rap an extension of African-American oral, poetic, folklore, and protest traditions, to which it is certainly indebted, and recognize the bridge between those traditions and rap's boasting, signifying, and preaching. Rose calls for, "broadening the scope of investigations in our search for black women's voices," to include rap; but also asserts that, "women rappers are vocal and respected members of the Hip Hop community, and they have quite a handle on what they are doing."

Conclusion: Towards a Truly Unified Music

A divided culture cannot produce a unified music. People have to live together to intimately share a common form of cultural expression. The degrees to which aspects of culture are united or divided are expressed clearly in the art produced. Such unions cannot be realistically fabricated or misappropriated, although we may delude ourselves into thinking otherwise. Through a desire to express uplifting music, the global population will hopefully learn to forget its differences, take full advantage of things we hold in common, and allow individuals and cultures to maintain both individual distinction and unified consciousness. Jazz and other improvised music has the potential to model such behavior. Like the tension and release between discipline and freedom inherent in great art, fluidity of thought can cyclically replace periods of dogmatic bigotry.

Because artistic expression belongs to the audiences of the world, we cannot arbitrarily define music to suit our political aspirations. If music is indeed a mirror of the world it reflects, then culture becomes the chief ingredient that defines the myriad subtleties that provide a culture's distinguishing features. Africans arrived in America with a psychological urge to maintain as many aspects as possible of the traditional African culture they were forced to leave behind. They transferred their new voice into the instruments they found in the New World that resembled the various flutes, fiddles, trumpets, thumb pianos, mallet instruments, drums, double reeds, and other traditional African instruments. They combined disparate African cultures and traditions and forged them into a new African-American cultural expression. The harsh social environment transformed multifunctional traditional African music into a catalyst for survival in the Americas. Racism remains the most severe problem in the development of African-American music. For African-American artists, its influence continues to affect the economic, historical, and pedagogical dimensions of their musical evolution. Nonetheless, artistic expression cannot be confined within a single sector of world society, and soon African-American music belonged to the world.

Thus the modern blues matrix is like a yantra, its harmonic, rhythmic, and melodic implications extend omni-directionally from a given nucleus (fundamental tone, tonal center, etc.). In Hinduism, it literally means "loom"; and in practice a yantra is a symbolic representation of aspects of divinity (usually the Mother Goddess or Durga). Durga, a form of Devi, is the supreme goddess. It is an interlocking matrix of geometric figures, circles, triangles, and floral patterns that form fractal patterns of elegance and beauty. A yantra is supposed to represent a three-dimensional sacred object. The yantra is primarily a meditation tool for serious spiritual seekers as well as sculptors in Hindi classical tradition. The composition of a rose, tree, solar system, or molecule involves a range of dynamic elemental factors, gravitational forces, and natural laws. The mystical yantras are believed to reveal the structural basis of forms and shapes abounding in the universe and they function as revelatory symbols of cosmic truths.

"Your success and happiness lie in you."

—Helen Keller

References

Baker, Davis. "John Coltrane's 'Giant Steps' Solo and Composition Transcribed and Annotated." *Down Beat* (22 July 1971): 35–40.

Dorje, Gyurme. "A Brief Literary History of the *Tibetan Book of the Dead*." (Penguin Classics Deluxe Edition, 2007). Translated by Gyurme Dorje.

Dusek, Val. *The Holistic Inspirations of Physics: The Underground History of Electromagnetic Theory*. New Jersey: Rutgers University Press (August 1999).

Feather, Leonard. "Blindfold Test." *Down Beat* 31/23 (1964): 29.

Freedmand, Ellen. "Right-Brain Left-Brain Learning Styles." http://mathpower.com/brain.htm (March 2008).

George, Patrick A. "Yantra: Hindu Tantric Diagrams." http://ccat.sas.upenn.edu/george/yantra.html (January 2007).

Hotz, Robert Lee. "Music Leaves Its Mark on the Brain." *LA Times*. 13 December 2002, Los Angeles: A1.

Huron, David. *Sweet Anticipation: Music and the Psychology of Expectation*. Cambridge, MA: MIT.

Khan, Hazrat Inayat. *Mysticism of Sound and Music*. Boston: Shambhala Publications, Inc. (September 1996).

Kingsley, Peter. "Raven's Appearance: The Language of Prophesy." *Rosicrucian Digest* 83 (2005): 13.

Kubik, Gerhard. *Africa and the Blues*. Jackson: University Press of Mississippi: 1999. McGarva, David Jung. "Writing Blocks." http://todayiwrite.com/writers-block-and-the-zone-part-2-of-several.html (September 2007).

Merriam-Webster Online http://www.m-w.com/.

Porter, Eric. *What Is this Thing Called Jazz?: African-American Musicians as Artists, Critics and Activists*. Berkeley: University of California Press, 2002.

Robert T. Carroll. *Skeptic's Dictionary*. "Geomancy." http://skepdic.com/geomancy.html. 2009.

Rose, Tricia. "Never Trust a Big Butt and a Smile." *Camera Obscura* 23 (1991): 108–31.

Rose, Tricia. "One Queen, One Tribe, One Destiny." *Village Voice Rock and Roll Quarterly* Spring (1990): 10–11, 16–19.

Sang, Larry. "Feng Shui." American Feng Shui Institute, 1991. http://www.amfengshui.com/ashop/catalogue.php?exp=5|&cat=5.

Sardesi, Milind, Christopher Figge, Mark Bodner, Meridith Crosby, Jill Hansen, Jorge A. Quillfeldt, Sudan Landau, Annette Ostling, Sydni Vuongand Gordon L. Shaw. "Reliable Short-term Memory in the Trion Model: Toward a Cortical Language and Grammar." *Biological Cybernetics* 84 (2001): 173–182.

"Tributes to John Coltrane." *Down Beat* (September 7, 1967) 16–17.

Chapter Four
Impressions: Organic Continuity and Structure

The **UNIVERSE** (the Harmonic Series departs from, revolves around, and returns to a fundamental).

All the matter came into being from energy continuously expanding and changing form. Ultimately the expansion will stop and it will start contracting, ending into nothingness with a "big-crunch." What is before big-bang or after big-crunch, the theory doesn't know (Surya Siddhanta).

"Pursuance": Cultivating Musical Perception

Musical understanding involves perception, cognition, and memory. We seek to organize features of the world into recognizable units that give us a sense of order. Despite our inclinations towards order, however, the power of freedom is universal and cannot be underestimated. This principle has inspired creativity throughout time. Michael O. Eze, a professor of chemistry at the University of Winnipeg, concludes:

> *Maintenance of Order Requires Input of Free Energy:* Since any increase in the entropy or increased disorder of the universe is consistent with a spontaneous reaction, disorder is the more likely process for systems not at equilibrium. So, order in any system makes it very unstable. To maintain order in a system, free energy has to be invested. Stanley Salthe's systems philosophy supports this: "form facilitates entropy production increase locally, by way of catalyzing the degradation of energy gradients" (Salthe 3).

Salthe concludes that, "The presence of form in the universe can be explained as a result of entertainment of the second law of thermodynamics." The second law of thermodynamics is a general principle that constrains the direction of heat transfer and the attainable efficiencies of heat engines. Replacing the word "heat" with "music" reveals a related principle. Freedom is the hallmark of African-American music, where content often dictates form, rendering controlling structures less confining. The law of musical freedom places constraint upon the direction of musical transfer and the attainable efficiencies of music processes. In other words, the direction of musical transfer is under the influence of the overtone series, informing and influencing various formal structures along with other governing laws and principles of sonic dynamics and patterning, as well as traditional social conventions and expectations. Freedom is the catalyst that allows jazz and other African-American styles to absorb and incorporate the diverse musical elements that cross its path. Spontaneity, coupled with preparation, allows performers to adapt freely to musical situations.

What elements allow composers to shape and control their musical expression effectively? Whether we subscribe to conventional or innovative approaches to musical composition, basic qualities can serve as a lens through which all music can be examined. Perhaps we can begin by taking a general look at each element of music.

1. **Form:** What architectural parameters and ingredients provide structural containers that give solid framework and meaningful boundaries capable of supporting abundant internal musical details?
2. **Timbre:** How is musical color and detail introduced, developed, combined, and blended through the use of all elements of music and sound, ranging from all voice registers and qualities; an endless array of traditional instruments from around the world; the ever-expanding palette of sonic qualities introduced by emerging technology; the colorful sounds of animals and insects; and other reverberation in the universe?
3. **Harmony:** How can simultaneous sound form systems of vertical movement and harmonic structures that produce chords and their successive use produce chord progressions? Since people have always held different ideas as to what kinds of harmony are acceptable or pleasing, what universal laws that govern the universe may provide composers and artists with conceptual models for harmonic arrangement, order, and polarity?
4. **Melody:** How do patterns, repetition, contrast, and memory work together to create musical meaning on the horizontal plane?
5. **Rhythm:** How do we measure the placement of musical sound and silence within the context of space and time, and how does rhythmic motion enhance other elements of sound?
6. **Texture:** How are melodies, harmonies, and other sounds stratified to create sonic density, expanded range of color, musical design, and degrees of tension and release?
7. **Dynamics:** In what ways can contrasting or sustained musical dynamics help shape musical meaning?

Spirituality, mysticism, and a quest for musical freedom also influence many composers. The concept of musical freedom, initially introduced and developed in the United States through various forms of jazz and other African-American music, now encompasses a broad spectrum of interdisciplinary, cross-cultural, and multimedia approaches. Contemporary musical ideas range from multiethnic fusion to various forms and blends of digital musical and artistic conceptions. Freedom in compositional conception, on the performance stage, and in virtual performances and presentations is constantly expanding.

Scientists, spiritualists, mystics, and religious followers all attempt to organize their understanding of life and universal order around seemingly consistent principles. Although we have entertained the notion that music reflects universal organization, we cannot prove the overtone series reflects order. We can look for general ways that the organization of sound vibrations and the music humans generate relate to other vibratory and cyclical patterns in the universe. In the early twentieth century, two opposing theories about the origin of the universe emerged. The Steady State Theory proposed that the universe was never born, never dies, and will always essentially be as it is. The Big Bang theory said that the universe began with a point of energy exploding in a "big bang." This theory asserted that all matter came into being from energy continuously expanding and changing form, and ultimately the expansion will stop and the universe will start contracting, ending in nothingness with a "big crunch."

Perhaps, if the universe is infinite, both the big bang and big crunch theories are true and overlap. Some scientists and spiritualists call the duration between the big bang and big crunch one Kalpa (cosmos) or Brahma Diwas (eternal day). Spiritualists believe that one eternal day is preceded and succeeded by an equal period during which matter exists in a dormant, inert state that they call a Brahma Ratri (a divine night "for the nature that sleeps"). Thus, the spiritualists conclude, all souls remain in a dormant state of hibernation during this period. In turn, each evolution of the cosmos from a dormant state may be called a "creation" or "srishti," and its involution back into an inert state is called dissolution (pralaya). Spiritualists use the analogy of days and nights to reflect their theory of the cosmos and divine nights in this eternal sinusoidal cycle of evolutions and involutions.

Does a new artistic style—or an individual spontaneous composition—evolve from a "big bang" of fresh inspiration that is a part of an expanding evolution; or is each new form of expression simply another highlighted moment, cell, or element within a fixed set of sonic possibilities that have always existed and that will always exist in the future? Do we inadvertently reflect these theories in the way we construct compositions?

We also oscillate between periods of relative motion and stasis in music. We use balanced mixtures of sound and silence within musical rhythmic, melodic, and harmonic phrases that continually expand and contract in both predictable and surprising ways. In music, as in life, self-mastery is a prerequisite step towards freedom, success, wisdom, and self-satisfaction. Achieving true power within ensemble performance necessarily follows musical self-realization, individual and collective musical development, and the accumulation of personal and collective knowledge. Measurement of musical growth is calibrated by the degree to which individual musicians measure up to their potential and affect the listener's heart, mind, and soul. Periods of growth and musical plateaus exist along that journey. Sometimes we experience a sense of closure at the end of a composition, while other endings leave us expecting things to come.

When we connect the soul, body, and cognition to musical experience, we enter the interactive realm of physical reality, our emotions, and logic. Emotions play an important role in our lives. Our emotional reactions are diverse and seemingly automatic; and despite our effort to control them, emotions seem to be somewhat beyond our domination. Scientists have found that our autonomic nervous system activity distinguishes emotions. Composers are often interested in human emotion and in the way our brain interprets the world, because such information provides clues as to how people may perceive music. Some people may allow logic to govern their minds and analysis, and some may feel that people who believe in the existence of a soul simply lack an understanding of how the brain works. Others may firmly believe that the aspects of existence that extend beyond our molecular reality leave room for intangible and unquantifiable phenomena. Music may reside within and between all such realms of belief.

Music has no scientific predictive theory, just as there is no predictive theory in biology. We gain knowledge of music and science from the gradual accumulation of information, experience, and historical perspective. However, thus far we know little about the essence of life and we cannot create life forms from neutrinos, the fundamental particles of the universe. Musicians who master fundamental musical building blocks, such as scales, chords, music theory, and other basic ingredients of music, do not automatically become composers who can bring musical notes to life. Some logicians feel that the human brain is not an amazing computer and suggest that our brains are pretty inept at processing the overwhelming quantity of stratified data that enters it. The process of creating and digesting music remains in a category of its own, nonetheless, and its emotional and intellectual impact still exists beyond the reach of logical explanation. Modern electronic tools can register emotional reactions to stimuli by monitoring brainwaves as we listen to music, yet the complex levels of multifaceted meaning that people assign to listening experiences are more extensive than laboratory graphs or other test results can capture.

John Coltrane's mandala demonstrated how a blues matrix can combine tonal, modal, and symmetrical musical systems into a singular unified and flexible road map. Contemporary blues introduces pan-tonal freedom expressed clearly in the harmonically liberating modern bass approach that I call the "twelve-tone walk." Rather than the bass reinforcing only dominant relationships, or a few close-related tonal keys, this contemporary bass approach moves through a never-ending series of patterns that suggest a constant shift in key areas or intervallic sets. Ron Carter is an expert at driving that approach.

The twelve-tone walk involves creating patterns of fundamental tones systematically within a bass line that leave maximum freedom for the soloist. Tritones, minor seconds and fourths (and their inversions), occur frequently when constructing bass rows based upon the twelve-tone walk. These intervals allow for multiple possibilities of resolutions, and the wide intervals and ample supply of leading tones produced distances the ear from more conventional tendencies towards perfect fifths, fourths, and other usual stepwise intervals of triadic tonal harmony. The approach evolves out of the more conventional walking bass line where the dominant seventh chord and a lower leading tone (blue note) to each chord tone forms its distinctive fundamental pitch set. Listening to bassist Ron Carter in the 1960s version of the Miles Davis Quintet, with Miles Davis (trumpet), Wayne Shorter (saxophone), Herbie Hancock (piano), and Tony William (drums), provides vivid examples of this approach in a variety of contexts. (Listen to the box CD set to Davis' *Live at the Plugged Nickel* for examples.)

Music can potentially combine metaphysical, mathematical, and aesthetic qualities into a single experience. Miles Davis (a.k.a. "the Dark Prince"[1]) was one of the most significant and innovative musicians of the twentieth century. As a trumpeter, Davis was at the forefront of virtually every major stylistic innovation in jazz since swing. His work influenced generations and most jazz musicians today still regularly perform his music, attesting his continuing musical prowess. Davis was also a visual artist whose paintings, drawings, and wardrobe reflected his musical personality.

We have intuitive and emotional responses to the highly subtle nature of musical and spiritual experiences. Describing our emotional responses to musical and spiritual stimuli and experiences in words is limited in clarity and effectiveness. During meditative states of consciousness, the subconscious mind seems to neutralize musical complexities rendering them more accessible. That may also account for greater openness to a variety of music during the 1960s when a large number of youth experimented with mind-altering drugs. Those chemicals may have merely artificially increased the listener's meditative or contemplative sensitivity and receptivity.

The musical process is very effective when it is experiential. Hearing or performing music is more important than simply explaining or describing music's theoretical phenomena. As with religion, music evolved as humankind became conscious of the distinction between the external world and personal experiences, emotions, and perspective. Music potentially allows people opportunities to simultaneously activate subconscious, subjective, and objective levels of consciousness.

Music History, Tradition, and Holistic Learning

Twentieth-century music stands on the shoulders of a wide variety of musicians, innovative artists, and thinkers from ancient times forward. During ancient times in Europe (from perhaps around the ninth century), unison and octave singing in Ambrosian and Gregorian chant, and the typical harmonic motion of organum involving parallel fifths and fourths, had early European composers experimenting with the lower partials of the overtone series ("perfect" intervals). As listeners' ears evolved to accept intervals higher up the overtone series, triadic music (from around 1400) developed a propensity

---

1   A nickname that Wayne Shorter assigned Miles.

towards stacking major and minor thirds systematically into triads. Around 1600, larger combinations of thirds were stacked to form the chordal seventh (e.g., C, E, G, B♭) and by 1750, the chordal ninth (e.g., C, E, G, B♭, D). By 1880, the Western musical ear had evolved to accept the fourth partial of the overtone series, where chordal extension to six note sonority, such as the C7 (♯11) (e.g., C, E, G, B♭, D, F♯) established harmonic structures with significant portions of a whole-tone scale (e.g., C - D - E - F♯ - G♯ - A♯ - C). Subsequently, music in the West expanded to include the Pantonal harmonic functions of total chromaticism (beginning with the fifth partial) and the systems that twelve-tone approaches ushered in.

As the twentieth century progressed, composers also experimented with microtones (sixth partial). In other regions of world, ancient traditional music already incorporated quartertones and other higher frequencies of the overtone series into their musical compositions, such as the systematic use of quartertones primarily as melody embellishments (ornaments) in Indian music. Together with Egypt, Mesopotamia, and China, inhabitants of India's northern region constitute one of the oldest civilizations of the world. The oldest book (written in India around 2000 B.C.) describes mantras chanted to honor gods that were based on one, two or three notes and gradually transformed into a heptatonic scale. A seven-note scale emerged by 350 B.C. and was written as sa, re, ga, ma, pa, dha, ni. That scale remained in this form up until now. The Indian scale was also enriched with quartertones, intermediate notes between semitones, giving twenty-two quartertones (shrutis) within one octave.

The harmonic principals underlying contemporary blues, Indian music, and other musical approaches throughout the world are also grounded in the natural harmonic patterns of the overtone series. If the overtone series reflects a natural pattern of vibration, then perhaps it is more akin to our bodies' vibratory frequencies. Ashwin Batish is an extraordinary sitarist and tabla player who has shared related ideas with the author. He received training in the North Indian classical tradition from his father S. D. Batish and later created his own unique fusion of Indian classical sitar with pop, rock, jazz, and calypso funk hybrid forms. Batish feels that natural temperament helps us align our personal bio-frequencies.

Although some modern improvisers (such as Ashwin Batish) use a process of fusion, where existing styles are combined in new and innovative ways, the titans of the twentieth century preferred processes involving musical fission. This fission involves the act or process of splitting musical elements into parts before creating personalized and innovative musical approaches. This is just as all individualist thinkers divide learned vocabulary, philosophy, and other forms of acquired thought into their own new ideas. The artistic progenitors and innovators poured traditional musical legacies into a mutual thermonuclear musical reactor to produce recombinant musical DNA complete with their unique artistic signatures. This required confidence and knowledge combined with an intuitive, technical, and empirical understanding of how the musical universe and the universe-at-large relate through patterns of systematic vibration.

Nonetheless, with both fusion and fission artists, the basic creative factors for spontaneous composition are related.

Figure 1. Creative Factors

ARTISTS AS CREATORS
Emphasis: FORM -------- CONTEXT --------- PURPOSE
Concerns: ETHEREAL ---- CONCEPTUAL ---- TECHNICAL
Problems: mutual vocabulary, time, funding, institutional, opportunity, dynamics of interpersonal interaction
Process: performers prepared, machines, acoustical environment, leadership
Effect: audience reception, composer's (artist's) intent achieved, perpetuation of artistic continuum
Composition Ingredients: melody, rhythm, harmony form, dynamics, interpretation, texture, timbre, emotional content, silence, interdisciplinary interaction, technology, nature, etc.
Motivation: intellectual, emotional, representational, abstract, political, social, economic, spiritual, therapeutic, reactionary, etc.

Like all music and art, spontaneous composition requires an active and relentless process of transmission and reception. The consumer and musicologist examine, measure, classify, and analyze artistic success as receivers. Transmitters of music use music theory and music history to fortify their structural and intuitive understanding of and control over the creative process. Without some grounding in traditional theory, formal presentation, and self-reflection, artists can lack depth, continuity, or expression.

Musical Connections and Communicative Device

The communicative power of blues is not easily analyzed. Its basic form is readily recognizable, but other factors of expression remain more elusive. Nonetheless, while various levels of musical structure are equally important to the whole, the expressive provide deeper levels of meaning to its vitality. This is true of music in general. Bob Snyder concludes that:

> This gives rise to a distinction between *structure* and *expression*. Musical *structure* consists of patterns of events that constitute a musical *syntax*, a sequence of patterns compared over time for similarities and differences. For a syntax to function within the limits of short-term memory, the musical elements of the syntax must be reduced to a relatively small number of discrete

categories. These are usually stabilized in a musical culture in the form of tuning systems, metrical systems, and the like, which form the basic vocabulary of categories a culture uses to create musical patterns. Musical *expression,* on the other hand, consists of the varying nuances that exist within these categories. The relative importance of structure versus expression can vary across different musical cultures.

The patterns of rhythm, melodies, and so on that we are able to remember from music consist of sequences of musical categories. Each occurrence of a category, however, is shaded in a particular way by its nuances, which constitute the expressive aspects of the music. Unlike categories, which are discrete, expressive nuances are *continuous* variations in the pitch or rhythm of a musical event.

An important aspect of nuances is that, under normal circumstances, they cannot be easily remembered by listeners. Because category structure is a basic feature of explicit long-term memory, nuanced information which bypasses this type of memory, is difficult to remember: it is "ineffable."[2] This is probably the major reason why recordings, which freeze the details of particular musical performances, can be listened to many times and continue to seem vital and interesting (Snyder 87–88).

In order to create high quality musical syntax and expression, spontaneous composers must remain fully conscious of the total musical environment throughout a performance. They must acquire a storehouse of options that extends from any given musical position to instantaneously respond to all contributions made by other members of the ensemble. As musical information is absorbed, performers make decisions by selecting an appropriate creative solution from an array of choices. Through musical training and practice, musicians prepare themselves physically, intellectually, and spiritually through concentration drills, diligent routines, meditation, contemplation, and prolonged study. The goal is to elevate musical consciousness to a state of technical preparation and intuitive readiness that provides access to the requisite proactive creative processes.

Studying connections helps us understand the compositional process. Most composers think about the connection between words and music. Although children are incapable of understanding the precise meaning of words at birth, they can sing pitches and melodies, produce simple rhythms, and respond actively to music before their spoken language develops. Spoken language cannot directly express sense impressions and emotions at the level that music does more readily. Generally, as children learn to communicate verbally, words are more frequently used to label things in the physical environment, rather than to define or clarify emotions and sense impressions conveyed to our consciousness. Subtle and nuanced impressions created in the mind by concepts expressed through language consequently yield only vague and marginal descriptions

---

2   Ineffable means incapable of being expressed in words.

for an infinite array of inexpressible internal phenomena. Although music cannot precisely express many impressions impacting our senses and emotions, the musical language often seems a more direct path to emotional communication. Vocal music's close association with language is central to musical expression. In describing art music in the East, Hazrat Inayat Khan relates:

> Vocal music is considered to be the highest, for it is natural; the effect produced by an instrument which is merely a machine cannot be compared with that of the human voice. However perfect strings may be, they cannot make the same impression on the listener as the voice which comes direct from the soul as breath, and has been brought to the surface through the medium of the mind and the vocal organs of the body. When the soul desires to express itself in voice, it first causes an activity in the mind, by means of thought, and projects finer vibrations in the mental plane. These in due course develop and run as breath through the regions of the abdomen, lungs, mouth, throat and nasal organs, causing air to vibrate all through, until they manifest on the surface as voice. The voice therefore naturally expresses the attitude of mind: whether true or false, sincere or insincere (Khan 163).

When words are combined, the levels of subtlety involved send vibratory transmissions deep into the minds, bodies, and spirits of listeners. Merging music with words helps broker the relationship between abstract aesthetic expression and emotions. Understanding the connection between physical and material realms is also important in some cultures, and this perspective carries over into music production. In traditional African culture, the nexus between the physical and spiritual aspects of individuality, and between ancestors and contemporary culture, can extend into the ways people envision connections in music.

> Each person is regarded as both a physical and spiritual being in Yoruba religion. The physical body of the person is known as *ara.* The spiritual aspect is described first as *emi,* or "breath," and second as *ori,* or "head." *Emi* is that power that gives life to the body. The human body would be incapable of thought and be unable to communicate with the world of religious power without *ori.* The aspect that connects *ori* aspects to the course of life of the individual is one of its most important features. Human identity, fate and life plan is chosen before birth. This identity (identified with an ancestor), has a heavenly origin and serves as an individual's personal guardian. Consequently, people are considered the reincarnation of an ancestor (Lawson 67–68).

Musicians explore the relationships between ancestral music and their own, words and music, form and content, and introspection and communication, in ways that expand their musical knowledge, wisdom, and intuition. The more we learn, the more effective we become at relaying our personal emotions to broader subconscious, subjective, and objective domains of human consciousness. All live performance involves improvisation to some extent, since even notated music changes each time at the nuance level. People tend to focus on patterns, rather than every nuance or detail involved, because the infinite variation that inevitably occurs in nature would constantly overload our memory capabilities. Free Jazz and some contemporary approaches to improvised music emphasizes nuance by producing unfamiliar musical events that cannot easily be assembled into syntax. When artists produce work that resides outside conventional rules and practice, they may leave their audiences in a quandary. When composers abandon constructing music that conforms to traditional memorable structure, they have to create new structures and wait for listeners to group their new sounds into patterns and syntax. Jazz (blues) introduced a new cosmopolitan mixture of sounds that gradually shaped novel patterns and nuances into new syntax.

The Language of Twenty-First Century Composition

The twenty-first century composer inherits an exciting musical world in which direct access to an unprecedented amount of interesting and varied ancient, traditional, and new music is readily available worldwide. Trumpet master Clark Terry has told young musicians who attend his clinics that they must first "imitate in order to assimilate, before they can innovate." As many other jazz masters remind students, the only thorough and effective process for mastering music is straightforward, demanding, and requires an enormous investment of time. The conscientious musician then systematically assimilates and processes acquired knowledge before galvanizing their personal styles and methods. Styles of global music grow increasingly closer, often blending disparate vocabularies into new and unique fusions. If we take Terry's words of wisdom to heart, then examining conventional structures is important before forging our own.

Think Melody: By focusing upon melody, the interdependence of all other musical elements becomes immediately clear. A melody involves:

A. Rhythmic and metric elements
B. Appurtenant harmonic relations as well as other accompaniment and support
C. Formal structure and organizational concerns
D. Carefully conceived and sculpted melodic contours
E. Thoughtfully crafted beginning, climax, and ending
F. Continuity, contrast, and developmental factors
G. Nuances, moods, ideas, historical context, and musical purposes

Composing strong melodies requires understanding basic musical materials (scales, chords, rhythm, etc.), internal and external structural design, a sense of aesthetic balance and proportion, and an ability finding creative solutions to musical problems. The best melodies depend on the spaces that surround notes, allowing the phrases of music to breathe, and allowing portions of the accompanying music to seep through to the surface. Space must exist in music in much the same way that punctuation, flexibility, and silence shape speech.

Tracking the ascending and descending horizontal movements of melodic intervals creates what is metaphorically referred to as melodic contour. With certain styles of twentieth-century music, the contour of principal and supporting lines is the most memorable characteristic. The rise and fall of notes takes listeners on a musical journey. When melodies grow out of selected tones of a pitch set, and when a hierarchical schematic structure is involved, emphasis on particular pitches contributes to a redundancy that is useful to a listener's musical memory. Tonality imposes a set of predetermined rules and limitations, social conditioning (as a result of centuries of common use and expectations), and other formulaic constraints to which we become accustomed. Tonality dictates how notes are centralized and the frequency of their occurrence, factors that ultimately determine the pitch's relative importance. Therefore, in tonality, the placement of a pitch determines its function. The most central pitch forms a relationship with the other members of its pitch set that establishes a hierarchical arrangement that produces a range of categories. The expectation of certain pitch behavior within tonality makes it predictable. For those who grow up hearing tonal music, this predictability enables memory to readily grasp musical ideas. Melodies constructed with no central pitch have no automatic reference points to serve as memory aids. Remembering more abstract features of non-tonal melodies thus often relies upon other factors of musical organization. Melodic contour can also become an important pneumonic aid in less familiar instances.

Analyzing Repetition, Patterns, and Symmetry in Charlie Parker

Repetition is found in most music throughout the world. Great artists know how to use predictability and surprise to weave convincing patterns and phrases. The most memorable composers use repetition masterfully. Some theorists constantly identify such factors of tonal coherence without placing repetition within the total set of architectural components that provide context for each musical gesture. Barry Kernfeld often tracks the number of repetitions that occur with solos by Miles Davis, John Coltrane, Charlie Parker, and others without placing his examples within the important musical information supplied by the rhythm section in each instance. When the accompaniment is rich and varied, a repeated phrase can create tremendous tension, drama, and contrast. In his chapter on "Improvisation" in *What to Listen for in Jazz,* Kernfeld's analysis of Charlie Parker's recording of "Koko" focuses upon what he considers a fairly "limited" repertoire of phrases that Parker reportedly links and repeats with incredible speed, creativity, and facility. Music as rich as Parker's cannot be so easily minimized.

Charlie Parker's economy of means investigation is most effective in a harmonically active compositional environment. The melody and improvisation in his composition "Koko" involved a re-harmonization of the bridge to Ray Noble's classic 1938 tune, "Cherokee." The 16-bar bridge can be divided into four separate 4-bar phrases in a variety of ways. The first three phrases all used versions of ii-7 / V7 / I Maj7 chord progressions. The sequence in the last phrase involves a harmonic quickening of ii-7 / V7 chords, which leads back to the original key.

This progression's harmonically challenging nature is due to the tempo at which the chords have to be negotiated in the bebop style. The basic harmonic voyage moves in descending whole-steps (B-A-G-F) from the implied key of B major to the Key of F major, a tritone away in Parker's approach. The symmetry of this harmonic motion is offset by the unpredictable and asymmetrical nature of Parker's rhythmic and melodic phrasing. Over the course of just sixteen bars, Parker creates cadences in four different keys. This modulating background of chords is ripe with the poetic repetition that he employs so masterfully, and that generations of musicians have adopted.

The "Koko" tempo is incredibly fast and Parker composes flawless melodies spontaneously, with the only repeated phrase occurring during the bridge.

Figure 2. Cherokee Chords: Original Words and Music by Ray Noble, 1938

Verse:

| A | E7+ D7-5 | A(V) | A7/6(V) |

| Dalt | D | Dm+7 | Dm6 |

| A | C♯m7-5 Cdim | Cdim(IV) | B7 |

| Bm7-5 | Edim | Bm7-5 | E7 E7+ |

Bridge:

| D9 | F7 | A | F♯m |

| D9 | F7 | A | A |

| D9 | F7 | A | F♯m |

| E7 | Edim | D9 | E7 E7+ |

Figure 3. Charlie Parker's Re-Harmonization of the Bridge of "Cherokee" in "Koko"

Key of B:	ii-7 (Measure 1)	V7 (Measure 2)	I Maj7 (Measure 3)	I Maj7 (Measure 4)
Key of A :	ii-7 (Measure 5)	V7 (Measure 6)	I Maj7 (Measure 7)	I Maj7 (Measure 8)
Key of G :	ii-7 (Measure 9)	V7 (Measure 10)	I Maj7 (Measure 11)	I Maj7 (Measure 12)
Key of F :	ii-7 (Measure 13)	V7 (Measure 14)	Bb: ii-7 (Measure 15)	V7 (Measure 16)
Repeat second half of verse				

Parker created musical ideas rich in melodic content, and the integrity of those ideas were just as profound when played at slower tempi. Kernfeld's book attempts to be specific about how jazz works while missing the nuances that render each repetition significantly different while maintaining their structural function as continuity devices. Tracking obvious repetition is easier than it is to discover the rich craftsmanship and subtle nuances that renders Parker's music so enduring for so many listeners worldwide. The economy of means employed in Parker's spontaneous solo on "Embraceable You" also demonstrates the integral purpose of repetition in some of the most beautiful art that we produce as a species. Parker's "limited" repertoire demonstrates his understanding of how each idea is redefined according to its new environments. Even recurring rhythms, for example, are invariably placed in varying contexts to provide new meaning.

Although the rhythm of the first two beats of the two measures below are identical, the pitch material and context is different each time **(Figure 4)**.

Figure 4.

The constant shifting of pitch material and context allows that same rhythmic content to be used frequently without the listener ever feeling a four eighth-note repetition. In **Figure 5** the repeated rhythm is linked directly, yet the altered pitch material and context renders it surprising.

Figure 5.

Variations of the rhythms of Figure 4 and Figure 5 can then be recombined and re-formed into refreshingly new rhythmic permutations, each within new pitch material and context that most listeners would not anticipate.

Figure 6.

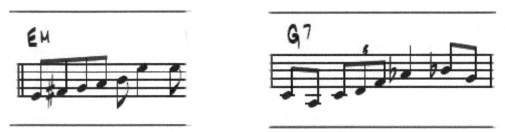

Charlie Parker and other composers use basic units of construction similar to those in nature. The basic ideas involved in using patterns and symmetry in music are akin to those used elsewhere in the universe. Whether examining nature or art, pattern formation relies upon three characteristics: a unit, repetition, and a system of organization. Although mathematicians may treat symmetry as an ideal, it is imperfect in nature. The approximation of symmetry, rather than its precision, interests the mind and yields abstract satisfaction.

Symmetry is also a fundamental organizing principle in nature, art, and culture. Parker and other great musicians and artists understand the functions of symmetry in the use and distribution of patterns. A motif may be asymmetrical or symmetrical. Understanding symmetry allows us to discern the pattern, and sets a standard for determining stability and change to a model. The thoughtful variation of factors within patterns where symmetry is expected transforms predictable and repetitive patterns into great works of art. Although asymmetry involves the absence of symmetry, it may rely upon asymmetry as its fundamental basis. At times, in analyzing symmetry, a fundamental asymmetrical region is identified before finding the smallest element within that domain required to explain the pattern-forming repetition. The fundamental region, repeated to form a pattern, consists of a design, or portion thereof, and the surrounding area that defines it. One quality that viruses, electromagnetism, oriental carpets, and music all have in common is their reliance upon symmetry and symmetry breaking for their durability and vitality. Symmetry breaking is playfulness creating anticipation of symmetry, but that expectation is not met, resulting in surprising and intriguing patterns.

The possibilities for variation in design composition are limitless because of an infinite array of choices. However, the possibilities for the repetition of a particular design, whether symmetrical or asymmetrical, are limited by the laws of pattern formation and are subject to the constraints of symmetry. In music, and all patterns, four basic symmetry operations may be performed upon a fundamental region, or motif. These variations involve exact retrograde inversion. Visual patterns can serve as examples of the musical reflection, rotation, and pivoting that these basic variations involve. In the creation of Oriental rugs, counting and repeating sequences of knots form a pattern. The basic symmetries in carpets are thus affected knot by knot. Below, the letter F is used to demonstrate the four basic symmetry operations or rigid motions:

Figure 7. Symmetry Operations

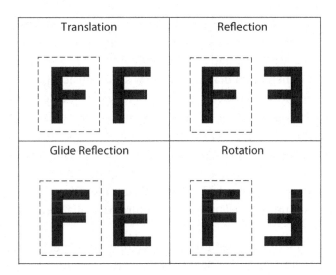

Charlie Parker's musical genius and sense of poetry is clear in his blues composition "Relaxin' at Camarillo." His economy of means, unpredictable phrases, organic and inventive melodic construction, varied phrase lengths, and lyrical rhythmic complexity are all demonstrated within twelve measures.

The tune's bittersweet irony surfaces in stressful conditions from which the composition emerged. Parker wrote "Relaxin' at Camarillo" during the six months that he spent at Camarillo State Hospital in Ventura County, California. While in Camarillo, Parker played saxophone in the hospital band on Saturday nights and tended a lettuce patch. His third wife, Doris Sydnor, moved to California to visit him three times a week, taking a job as a waitress to support herself.[3]

Figure 8 suggests some examples of the harmonic and rhythmic pacing in Charlie Parker's "Relaxin' at Camarillo." The three sets of harmonic changes supporting the melody below serve as a reminder that the actual harmonic context of most jazz melodies (especially the blues) is flexible, since performers can alter chords according to their interpretation of the melody and the large complex of possible substitute harmonies within the blues matrix. The chords written in the example below are but a few of the infinite number of possible harmonic interpretations that could support this melody.

Joe Henderson as Mentor and His Lesson on "Relaxin' at Camarillo"

Joe Henderson was a composer, performer, teacher, and stylist who continually displayed the highest level of musicianship, artistic integrity, and imagination. Between 1979 and 1982 I always looked forward to those special phone calls from Joe letting me know he was in town and asking if I wanted to come over for a lesson. Lessons with Joe always lasted at least several hours. I might arrive at Joe's home on Los Palmos in San Francisco at 3 P.M. and begin warming up on flute. The lessons could end as late as 9 P.M., with Joe taking long breaks to answer phone calls or to answer his door when Eddie Henderson or other guests arrived. Surprisingly, he always rushed back into his studio once he heard that I had worked out a musical problem he introduced before leaving. He would then immediately add a new set of musical problems to solve. Playing was non-stop, so I learned the real meaning of focusing and developing musical stamina. I knew each lesson would be unique, rich in Zen-like musical presentation and content, extremely focused in pace, and unrelenting in its meticulous attention to detail. Joe's profound knowledge and skill supported his remarkably unassuming and easygoing approach, much in keeping with the African griot's tendency towards oral/aural transmission of knowledge and history. Henderson was an incredibly gifted and highly sensitive African-American *jeli* or *griot*. Branford Marsalis said:

> Joe Henderson is one of the most influential saxophone players of the 20th century. I learned all the solos on *Made For Joe* and the records he did with McCoy Tyner, a lot of the stuff he's on, like *The Prisoner*. He was one of the few saxophone players who could really play what I call the modern music, that really came from the bebop tradition but extended the harmonic tradition further. There's a small group of guys in that pantheon: Coltrane, Wayne Shorter, Warne Marsh, Lucky Thompson, Sonny, and Ornette, and Joe Hen. He's an amazing musician. I'm really jaded. I don't really go to the clubs

---

3   Camarillo State Hospital closed in July 1997. The campus of California State University, Channel Islands now occupies the site (thanks, Victor—San Diego, CA).

Figure 8. Head to "Relaxin' at Camarillo" (Charlie Parker)

anymore. There's not really anything I want to hear—except when Joe's in town. And when Joe's in town, I'm there every night! (Bourne 19)

Reducing the musical knowledge gained from study with Joe Henderson to descriptive words is impossible. Sharing some of the music produced during lessons with Joe later in this chapter provides, to some degree, a glance at the depth of musical content gained from that period of intense study, but it still fails to present anything close to the impact and magnitude of that experience.

Spontaneous composition requires complete self-discipline. From Joe (as well as from his cousin, Dr. Donald Byrd), I learned the high level of contemplation, meditation, focus, and concentration required to compose and perform simultaneously. Henderson transmitted his lessons through musical notes he played at the piano, and rarely through words or written notation. The phrases produced over hours of playing gradually revealed the depth, importance, logic, and flexibility of the blues matrix. Each idea introduced during the lesson, presented in cogent increments, revealed lines that were fresh, potent, and exposed esoteric knowledge of the aesthetics, history, and theoretical foundation of the continued evolution of African-American music. Renee Rosnes, the pianist with Henderson's quartet in 1992, felt that:

> What's amazing about all the times I've played with him is that Joe never has a bad night, never has a bad *minute.* He's a great improviser. Every solo has a beginning, a middle, an end. He'll play a motif and develop it, and later on you'll have forgotten it, but he'll come back to it. He can take anything and take it to the limit. That's true of all my favorite players—that they don't have any limitations. Joe inspires me to always reach for the depths of every tune (Bourne 18).

Joe Henderson taught me to go beyond just my breath, hands, tongue, and throat, and to articulate with my "inner being." He made it clear that music was never simply based on memorized formulaic devices. It is a matter of self-expression grounded in a firm and thorough musical foundation. There is absolutely no substitution for hours of concentrated practice and study in pursuit of the absolute precision, imagination, and flexibility of mind that spontaneous composing requires. Buddy Collette and Donald Byrd were other mentors who made clear the unity that exists between all great music and the interdependence of all musical elements: melody, harmony, rhythm, timbre, dynamics, form, expression, and texture. The warmth, sensitivity, and empathy of Joe's personality transferred to his musical output. It also made me understand why the depth contained within the expression of the most provocative music makes listeners reach deep within their own souls. Joe never spoke of these ideas or concepts overtly; rather, he demonstrated them musically as I followed attentively on my flute.

After my formal study at Joe's house, my informal learning continued each time that I heard him perform live or on recordings. On rare occasions, I heard Joe sit in on piano at a small club in North Beach (San Francisco), with James Lewis on bass, working harmonic ideas out in real time as he provided an opportunity for younger artists to gain exposure. Soon after I moved from the West Coast to New York (in 1984), I heard Joe play a series of concerts at the Village Vanguard with his trio in a series of special live recording sessions. Listening to Joe work with bassist Ron Carter and drummer Al Foster (without a piano) for a week on this gig (which was preserved on a two-record set [The *State of the Tenor* in the mid-1980s]) was yet another level of semi-private lesson. When Joe Henderson later performed with my Lab Ensembles at Cornell University in April 1993, he received full standing ovations before a sold-out Ithaca audience—a testimony to his ability to thrill any audience.[4] I saw Joe work similar magic on audiences wherever I heard him perform. His performances were presented in a casual fashion similar to his private teaching style; he said little or nothing verbally to his audiences during performances. He always said everything that was necessary on stage (and in his music studio at home) through his saxophone's humility, wisdom, and beautiful music. Michael Bourne wrote in his *Down Beat* article, "The Sound That Launched a Thousand Horns":

> There's no "typical" Joe Henderson album, and every solo is, like the soloist, original and unusual, thoughtful, and always from the heart.
>
> "I think playing the saxophone is what I'm supposed to be doing on this planet," says Joe Henderson. "We all have to do *something*. I play the saxophone. It's the best way I know that I can make the largest number of people happy and get for myself that largest amount of happiness" (Ibid. 16).

The blues is arguably the most complex, poetic, flexible, universally assessable, and direct system of music in contemporary society. It cannot be reduced to a simple set of scale tones or chords and, from a jazz master's perspective, could never simply involve the memorization of Charlie Parker's "licks." Instead, jazz study is a matter of doing "as" Parker does (with regards to originality and imaginative skill) rather than simply doing "what" he did (by memorizing Parker's solos). Joe Henderson's lesson (choruses), interpreting "Relaxin' at Camarillo," explores bebop implications and demonstrates both the richness of the harmonic matrix and bebop's fluid melodic process of tension and release. The solo improvisation developed for "Relaxin' at Camarillo" below, also demonstrates the inseparability of melody and harmony. Analyzing the principal melody (in **Figure 8** above) and the improvised solo studies on "Relaxin' at Camarillo" reveals: 1) the variety of scales and chords employed; 2) its balanced mixture of conjunct and disjunct motion; 3) assorted phrase lengths; 4) the superbly crafted rhythmic phrasing; 5) motivic and melodic development; 6) general mixtures of tension and release; 7) its well-timed climaxes; and 8) the balance between predictability and surprise throughout.

Examine the harmonic and rhythmic pacing of the head and chord changes to Charlie Parker's "Relaxin' at Camarillo." Since no single set of chords or chord voicing supports a given jazz composition, musicians vary harmony continually as they vary their solos and accompaniments according to the matrix of harmonic possibilities. In particular, analyze melodic tones in accordance with the variety of possible chord

---

4   This occurred during my decade-long Cornell appointment as the Herbert Gussman Director of "Jazz" studies.

changes (again, that by no means represents a complete set of possibilities) that support the melody below. Look for musical extensions, elisions, suspensions, contradictions, and elements of predictability and surprise that display the infinite possibilities inherent within the blues matrix and expose the futility of rigid rules in jazz.

Figure 9. Hester's "Relaxin' at Camarillo" Lesson with Joe Henderson

Relaxin' At Camarillo Changes

Karlton Hester

The Importance of Repetition as a Melodic Device

Repetition is an important aspect of melodic, rhythmic, harmonic, dynamic, and formal construction. We need musical ideas repeated cyclically to keep them present long enough to establish and file them in our memory for future associations. Repetition is an important unifying principle used to enhance melodic construction in music worldwide. Varieties of repetition include octave displacement, sequence, extension, truncation, fragmentation, change of mode, tonal shift, retrograde, inversion, retrograde inversion, and juxtaposition.

Proximity is a very powerful factor that reinforces the way we remember musical events. Musical motion is metaphorical because our image of notes moving sequentially in physical steps on the overtone series is implied. No actual physical steps rise or fall. A spontaneous composer must think in terms of intervallic, motivic, and melodic grouping in shaping solos organically. The distances between notes and the general direction of a melody help to define the boundaries of such groupings. Sequences of pitches have to be shaped into cells according to their construction, similarity of their position within phrase structures, and harmonic function.

Exact repetition of musical ideas produces monotony and boredom that soon results in loss of effectiveness because bored audiences no longer listen actively. Within the many varieties of repetitions, *octave displacement* is one of the easiest techniques used to avoid exact repetition of a melody or motive in simple melodic construction. A less predictable and more flexible technique is *sequence*. Sequence involves transposing a section of a theme or melody by any interval other than an octave. This is a useful device that works with the trans-tonal concept of constant modulation, in dealing consort with varied vertical harmonic structures, or in modal situations. Even with rich harmonic variety, repetition can still become tiresome when sequences involve more than two or three adjacent patterns. Making slight changes to strains of sequences can make them more interesting and durable. Such modifications can be rhythmic (while maintaining the same pitch content) or harmonic (making chromatic alterations to modify the intervallic relationships between notes of the original model of a sequential group).

Figure 10. Sequence and Extension

Compositions involve melodic manipulation and developing an assortment of sequence types. Melodic or motivic sequences contribute certain elements of predictability and cohesiveness to compositions. Each recurring statement of a melody or motive may begin at a different pitch level, but often follows closely (or exactly) the original model's intervallic contour, the expressive dynamics of the basic idea, and its structural integrity.

In sequential patterns, subsequent repetitions of a thematic model are often extended to make them more fascinating. In compositions with slow harmonic pacing, extension may occur along with other alterations over a great span of measures. The opposite approach, *truncation,* is also effective over slower harmonic progressions and occurs when a note or series of notes is removed from the end of a melody or phrase, shortening the subsequent musical statement. This may be a gradual process that unfolds over an extended span of time. Although both devices are used freely in a variety of musical situations, the effects of extension and truncation are most conspicuous when used consecutively. Thelonious Monk's "Straight No Chaser" uses both extension and truncation. Monk also used *fragmentation* in developing some of his compositions. Fragmenting a phrase or melody scatters fragments of thematic material carefully throughout a composition.

Figure 11. "Straight, No Chaser"

Change of mode results in changing the scale color of a theme or phrase within a mutual context. For example, this brand of melodic modulation occurs when changing from the major mode to the parallel ascending melodic minor mode (from C Ionian to C harmonic minor mode). A related technique places a melodic theme (or section of a theme) in a new and contrasting harmonic context. *Tonal shifts* of this brand are a technique practiced by modern players such as Sonny Rollins, Ornette

Coleman, John Coltrane, Joe Henderson, and Herbie Hancock. It is especially effective in adding harmonic and melodic tension and motion to modal compositions. It usually finds the soloist moving obliquely against the prevailing harmony in ascending or descending sequences, often removing motion by chromatic half-step, whole-step, or major or minor thirds. For example, a short C Mixolydian phrase constructed on a C7 chord is subsequently transposed to E♭7, then to D7, and on to D♭7 while sustaining the initial C7 chord as harmonic support. Such themes often execute tonal shifts while maintaining the original intervallic construction (C-E-B♭-G, E♭-G-D♭-B♭, D-F♯-C-A, D♭-F-C♭-A♭).

Figure 12. Change of Mode

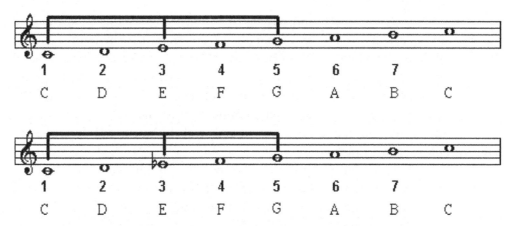

Melodic construction also involves other types of variations and permutations of a melodic idea. *Retrograde* is simply the reverse statement of the melody (a theme played backward), while *retrograde inversion* presents an inversion[5] of a melody backward. In other words, retrograde inversion is the technique of combining retrograde and inverted motion; thus the original phrase or melody is rendered both upside down and backward. Inversion requires transforming each ascending interval into the corresponding descending interval and vice versa. Thus, when the prime or original version of a collection of pitches occurs in a specific order, the retrograde form is created by writing the notes in reverse order. The melodic inversion of the original involves those intervals written upside down, changing all interval directions. Writing all the notes of the inversion in reverse order creates the retrograde inversion. Although the melodic contour may appear essentially unchanged, the tones of diatonic inversion adhere to only the notes of the original key, creating new intervallic relationships.

---

5   An inversion presents an interval or sequence of intervals upside down.

Figure 13. Prime (Original), Retrograde, Inversion, Retrograde Inversion

Musicians can alter melodic materials in a variety of other ways to avoid the predictability generally associated with repetition. Artists realize that too strict an application of such devices is unmusical, however, and attempt to always think poetically when constructing all musical components.

Melodies are also enhanced and developed through *augmentation* (lengthening the rhythmic values of phrases) and *diminution* (shortening the rhythmic values of phrases). Additional melodic variation is achieved through the *juxtaposition* of material from one section of a composition with either original or altered material from another. An approach of equal effectiveness involves altering melodies and phrases by simplifying or complicating the lines. Simplification strips an elaborately decorated line to its essential core. Conversely, complication adds embellishment and decoration to basic melodic motives or phrases.

In discussing several basic approaches to jazz improvisation commonly applied during the first half of the twentieth century, David Baker first describes the musical environments in which they arise. In particular, Baker discusses compositions that emphasize vertical or harmonic alignment ("vertical tunes" such as Coltrane's "Tune Up" and "Giant Steps"); those that involve slow moving or few chord changes ("horizontal tunes" such as Miles Davis' "So What" and Herbie Hancock's "Maiden Voyage"); and compositions that combine these two approaches (such as Duke Ellington's "Caravan" and some modern and contemporary blues). Baker gives three examples from a variety of jazz compositions, from early New Orleans style jazz to hard-bop tunes:

> a. A scalar approach, whereby we reduce each chord or series of chords to basic scale colors. This is essentially the direction pointed to in George Russell's *The Lydian Concept of Tonal Organization*. In this approach, we are less concerned with outlining the particular chords than with presenting a scale or mode that would sound the key area implied by the chords.
> b. In the second approach, the player articulates each chord. He might simply use arpeggios and seventh chords in a rhythm of his own choosing, or he might use what I have labeled root-oriented patterns, such as 1212, 1212, or 1231 or 1235, etc. In a progression like Cmin (2 beats) F (2 beats) B (4 beats), they would translate to C D C D, F G F G, B C B C, etc.
> c. A third approach uses patterns either predetermined or spontaneously conceived. This approach is favored by many post bebop players.

The above approaches are by no means mutually exclusive. In fact, most players use all three in the course of a single solo. There are many factors that seem to dictate the use of one as opposed to another at any particular time.

If a tune is extremely vertical, some combination of all three seems to work best, according to the player's point of view. If the player wishes to minimize the vertical aspects of the composition, he might do so by using scales. If he wished to reinforce the vertical aspects, he might choose to articulate each chord by using triads, sevenths, ninths, etc. If he chose to walk a middle ground, he might use scales, patterns, and arpeggios.

If a tune is extremely horizontal, the scalar approach seems imperative. When the harmony is static (when the changes move slowly) some sort of melodic or rhythmic motion must exist. If we run the chord using arpeggios and seventh chords, the material is too sparse to give the song much forward thrust (Baker 35–40).

These three basic jazz approaches are utilized in numerous modern blues, quasi-modal, and song form compositions. As Baker mentions, in modern and contemporary improvisation, the entire vocabulary of these and other approaches can be used interchangeably in developing a performer's solo.

Related Elements in Spontaneous and Premeditated Composition

Cultural and personal aesthetic preferences aside, little difference exists between the most essential requirements for effective, spontaneous, or premeditated music making. One person's clarity and simplicity is another's lack of life and color. Compositions share certain common rhythmic features, thematic dispositions, and melodic structure, and have related strategic requirements in common as well. Some people prefer density, color, and hyperactivity while others consider that same art cluttered and chaotic. The most successful musicians know how to navigate between a wide range of colors, dynamics, moods, and levels of intensity within both shorter and longer compositions.

To set convincing long-range structural goals, compositions of any style require well-grounded harmonic, melodic, and rhythmic architectural plans for successfully designing musical landscapes. Composers often used clear, short, and memorable musical germ material to generate and sustain gradually evolving themes, melodies, harmonies, and rhythms. Simple melodic, harmonic, and rhythmic seeds embedded in the infrastructure of a composition become structural goals that guide its general flow and direction, while assorted embellishments, variations, assorted expressive detail, and various modes of contrast promote musical vitality, sustain interest, and provide meaning. Similar features and structural requirements apply to shorter compositions as well.

Harmonic and rhythmic constructs govern melodic and motivic unfolding, and vice versa. Thus voice-leading principles on the horizontal plane of musical construction also reflect vertical dynamics of harmonic construction. Melodic, rhythmic, and harmonic motion are carefully arranged to oscillate between contrasting poles of tension and release for both the small and large phrase grouping. Composers that avoid tonality or other conventional stylistic approaches still find other effective ways to create balanced color, sublime moments, pleasing proportion, and generate excitement using a broad spectrum of sound combinations. Symmetrical scales (such as chromatic, whole-tone, and octatonic scales), arbitrary sequences, and altered scales can provide a broad array of resources for creating non-tonal vocabulary.

Jazz and blues musicians often incorporated elements of the European tonal system and premeditated composition into African-American music (Scott Joplin, W. C. Handy, James Reese Europe, Art Tatum, Dorothy Donegan, Anthony Davis, et al.), and many European composers experimented with African-American ragtime, blues, and other stylistic elements (Antonin Dvorak, Alban Berg, Paul Hindemith, Igor Stravinsky, Darius Milhaud, Claude Debussy, etc.).[6] When attempting to abandon, blend, extend, or revise tonality. Just as the music of John Coltrane, Mary Lou Williams, and Yusef Lateef was heavily influenced by their spiritual and mystical studies and beliefs, many composers of premeditated composition in the European tradition were also similarly inclined.

The Theosophical connections within the music of Dane Rudhyar are well known among composers. Rudhyar was born Daniel Chennevière in Paris in 1895, and changed his name when he immigrated to America in 1916. Rudhyar's music is little-known today because it was not a major influence on other twentieth-century composers. His spiritual and mystical inclinations did have quite a significant impact on better-known composers. During the 1920s, Rudhyar was a central figure in the Halcyon Theosophical community in Southern California. Among those influenced by the community was Henry Cowell, who later became John Cage's mentor. After 1934, Rudhyar stopped composing and became a leading advocate of astrology. In 1976, Rudhyar returned to composing, and his late output included two string quartets.

Henry Cowell was an important innovator of European American music in the early part of the twentieth century. In Cowell's *Symphony No. 11* (*Seven Rituals of Music*), his "Seven Rituals of Music" are ritual musical episodes that accompany "the life of man from birth to death." It starts with "music for a child asleep" and ends with "music of the ritual of death." Pierre Boulez combined the techniques of twelve-tone composers with the mystical qualities of his mentor, Olivier Messiaen. Messiaen was an influential French composer, organist, and teacher known for his use of mystical and religious themes. His highly personal style is noted for its rhythmic complexity, rich tonal color, and unique harmonic language.

Armenian composer Alan Hovhaness was an important twentieth-century American composer whose music anticipated many future trends and aesthetic values

---

6   European composers relatively quickly abandoned systematic exploration of the upper extensions of the harmonic series (9ths, 11ths, 13ths, etc.) to pursue atonal and serial exploration.

in European-American music. His significance remains overlooked by musical academia due in part to his avoidance of the vogues of Americana, serialism and atonality. Instead Hovhaness was one of the earliest premeditated composers to integrate Western musical idioms with Eastern ones before the term "World Music" was coined. His aleatoric counterpoint from 1944, and employment of incantatory melodies over static harmonies, occurred decades before the European avant-garde engaged related concepts. The visionary and mystical nature of his work, at times with overtones of gypsy music, rank him as the progenitor of New Age music and the Spiritual Minimalism developed by later composers, such as Arvo Pärt and John Tavener. Estonian composer Arvo Pärt composed some of his music in a minimalist style, but much of his music is bound up with sacred texts. Pärt's meditative mystical music has devotional quality, at times, that underscores his use of neo-Renaissance harmony, medieval melodic techniques, and Gregorian chant. As the musical world gradually became more connected globally, artists and thinkers worldwide began to view the creative possibilities more holistically and flexibly. Twentieth-century science also explored less rigid theories of the molecular universe.

Before his mental breakdown in 1918, Albert Einstein's cosmology paper and his self-critical comments regarding Lambda (1917) opened a wide range of cosmology debates. Einstein's theory of relativity came under fire after World War I when physicists, who began to test the general implications of general relativity, attacked Einstein's static model from the theoretical angle (Healey). At the same time, astronomers, who sought mystical truth without equations, attacked from the opposite side while contemplating whether our galaxy is unique or merely one among a multitude of systems. Cory Powell talks about Alexander Friedmann's expansion of Einstein's theory, which explored more flexible applications. Friedmann not only destabilized Einstein's belief in stability, but he also showed that curved space did not automatically imply a finite universe. Friedmann concluded that a concave universe (the shape that corresponds to Einstein's unbounded cosmos of limited extent) would fold in on itself; while a flat and convex universe could be infinite in dimension (Powell 88–89). Scientists too, became a little more comfortable with factoring a Creative Source into their theoretical equations metaphorically. Powell said:

> In Friedmann's hands, the corrected equations of relativity allowed an extraordinary array of possible cosmologies, every single one of them alive with motion: expanding universes, detracting universes, even oscillating universes that grow and shrink as if they were the exhalations and inhalations of a cosmic Creator. Each of his solutions corresponded to a different geometry of space, a particular warping of the four-dimensional analogue of a distorted rubber sheet. An oscillating universe would be concave, or bowl shaped, as in Einstein's initial cosmological mode. A contracting universe would also have this shape, but a depressingly limited life span. Expanding universes might be convex, shaped somewhat like a riding saddle, in which case they would

expand forever; or flat, in which case the force of gravity would exactly balance the expansion (Powell 88–89).

Music is also alive with motion that cannot be contained within the realm of a single culture or theoretical canon. Musicians have perhaps always bounced around the possibilities of sound as exhalations and inhalations of a cosmic Creator. Today the evolution of thought exists along increasingly diversified lines as contemporary technology provides ever-expanding means of sound production. Musicians have also wondered about the ways that music impacts the mind and the molecular universe. Composers have a vested interest in knowing how the minds of listeners interact with their music.

Memory, Repetition, and Musical Form

Rhythm is a fundamental element that measures the passage of time in music. Rhythm contributes enormously to our feeling of motion within the space and time of musical expression, creating a sense of regularity and differentiation. Rhythm often involves regular cycles of repetition, but irregular temporal sequences of events are just as defining. Nonetheless, rhythmic ideas are also more easily remembered through *rhythmic grouping*, where events are grouped by their rhythmic similarity. Rhythmic groupings are defined by the time interval between events and their accentuation. Accents and metrical patterns help organize rhythmic events into smaller units that can be remembered more easily. Meter involves the measurement of musical time through regular or irregular patterns of fixed temporal units called beats. Meter establishes a basic temporal tension pattern, where the arrangements of weaker beats create anticipation of the stronger ones. Expectation allows the listener's mind to organize rhythmic patterns into structural units that keep them oriented time-wise throughout a performance. Rhythmic tension often occurs at points immediately before and immediately after metrical markers. This is especially true with syncopated rhythmic passages. The growing expectation that builds as listeners approach metrical markers creates a need for relief following downbeats.

The mind thrives on tracking similarities and differences, and successful composers know how to develop the music in ways that take advantage of this tendency. Controlling elements of similarity and contrast help composers navigate between variegated recognizable or memorable patterns, transitional material, and contrasting musical material. Listeners track musical patterns as they gradually begin to resemble a model or cease being similar to one another. This enables composers to plan the range and timing of musical similarities, transformations, and variation in ways that help maintain structural control of musical architecture. The closer together that two patterns appear within a piece of music, the easier it is for the mind to recognize their similarity. Therefore, when two musical ideas are in close proximity, the greater the degree of variation there can be between two musical ideas without distorting their similarity. The mind continually and systematically organizes features of our listening experiences into forms that can be effectively classified and catalogued in our memory for future use. In his book, *Music and Memory: An Introduction*, Bob Snyder considers the following concepts:

(1) *Objective set,* grouping effects established in and unique to a particular piece of music, which are learned during the course of listening to a particular piece, and which have to do with expectations unique to and established *during that piece,* such as recognizing a musical theme and its transformations.

(2) *Subjective set,* grouping effects that are part of a *style,* which are learned during the course of listening to *many* pieces, and which involve expectations established across many pieces that are *similar* in some way. Knowing that a particular kind of section is about to happen in a particular kind of piece would be an example of subjective set (Snyder 45).

Formal structure is important to control and provide context for large-scale events occurring over time spans that exceed the limitations of short-term memory. When greater distances of time between related musical ideas are involved, more conspicuous structural markers are used as reminders of the original model. The structural or formal levels of musical organization usually involve entire sections of music. A ternary form, for instance, involves an initial group or set of recognizable melodic and rhythmic material (A), followed by an alternating set of contrasting musical material (B), then the recurrence of the original set of material (A). In addition to contributing contrast, the distance between periods of repetition (B) helps to bind the similar music together by creating structural borders and boundaries.

The boundaries that form various parameters of music help shape its functions in a variety of ways. The principle of similarity can simply involve the recurrence of a pitch central to a tonality. If that nuclear note is not highlighted by frequent emphasis, placement at a strategic location, and other significant points of reference, it must rely strictly upon a listener's long-term memory to recall that particular musical event. In Gestalt psychology, consistent or continuous movement in a particular direction tends to perpetuate itself in that same direction. A related principle of continuity applies when a series of musical events establish groupings that move systematically, consistently, and continuously in similar direction or by similar intervallic size. A group of tones moving in the same direction and occurring in intervals of similar size tend to form a melodic grouping.

Thus, composers can anticipate some of our memory's tendencies and experiment with satisfying or denying certain expectations among listeners. Most people can identify the central pitch of a passage of any music with a tonal center. People can also remember recurring phrases of music if there is not too great a distance between similar phrases or musical events. Through repetition, the more our memory practices certain behaviors the better we digest them. Taste, sight, sound, and other human behavior develops as our memories are trained through exposure to various features of repetition and contrast.

Echoic memory is an aspect of early sensory information processing by which a sensory impression persists long enough so that it can be encoded into basic features and bound together into events. According to several recent theories, what is formed at this point are basic perceptual representations of the world and the things in it. These representations are thought to exist as "images," not necessarily specific visual images, but image-like (i.e., perceptual—it is possible to have a sound or smell or taste image) abstractions that form a basic "picture" of the world. The representations may also constitute a basic form in which many long-term memories are encoded. Existing prior to language and linguistic processing (perhaps also in animal species that do not use language), they may form a kind of pre-linguistic syntax of mental representation. Some of these perceptual representations may be difficult to capture in verbal language. Indeed, some of the meaning music conveys may take the form of such representations, which might explain why some aspects of musical meaning seem to resist concise verbal explanation (Snyder 23).

Of course, understanding memory involves a much more complex investigative process than simply tracking the distances between events implies. Certain music stays in our minds because of our personal attraction to certain features, even when melodies and rhythms are highly abstracted or thoroughly composed. Our mind absorbs, prioritizes, and retains information in different ways. Cognitive psychology has studied the rate at which we forget things learned, and Steven J. Lynn, Kevin M. McConkey, and Harry P. Bahrick are among researchers who have studied memory from various angles. Theorists often want to know: How accurate is memory? Are there important differences in how and what we remember across the life span? What is the prevalence of "repressed memory" for traumatic events? Studies show that very long-term memory (VLTM) retains particular types of information more readily. For instance, Bahrick's study of long-term memory found that the duration of memories of the faces of high school classmates is very long, and are rarely forgotten once recognition cues have been given. Similar results were found regarding the retention of personal names.

In music this suggests sounds that we consider more attractive or personal may linger longer in our memory than those for which our minds and feeling remain less attracted or inspired. Nevertheless, organization of phenomena in the world is based upon our memory capacity. Memory involves the processing capability of the human nervous system and has evolved over time. Thus, we learn to organize sound through recognizing ordered sonic events and then correlating individual and series of sound events into memorable patterns. We also learn to shift our focus towards specific sonic details within the otherwise overwhelming simultaneous layers of sound that potentially covers the entire frequency range in our environment. Snyder reminds us that, even at its most basic level, the filtering process of selective hearing is very involved.

One of the main problems the auditory system has to solve is how to take the single continuous variation in air pressure present at each ear and, from this, form a representation of all the separate sound sources present. This is a truly remarkable achievement. We hear many levels of organized patterns in speech, music, and environmental sounds that are not obvious in the physical sound waves themselves. Rather than hearing completely isolated sounds or an undifferentiated continuum, we hear phonemes, words, sentences, melodies, rhythms, and phrases, all consisting of parts that seem related despite their taking place at different frequencies and at different times. We can also hear the wind blowing, a bird singing, an automobile engine starting, and someone speaking as four separate sounds, even if they are all occurring simultaneously. If this were not the case, all we would ever hear would be a single sound, consisting of the sum of all sounds present at a given moment. These levels of organization are the result of certain aspects of our own perception, cognition, and memory (Snyder 31).

The nuances of music or sound provide the majority of its meaning. Our general auditory capacity organizes such representations of all the separate sound sources present automatically, at any given moment, into distinct filtered messages that allow us to create and discern the distinct strands of sonic information within our multi-stratified listening experiences.

Building intensity is an important expressive technique in music, and juxtaposing phrase groupings is a useful process in heightening tension. Generally speaking, heightened intensity changes stimulus and causes increased neural activity (Tenny 33–41). All music elements can intensify. Increases in amplitude, elevating sounds in pitch, producing harmonically more dissonant sonorities, brighter timbres, faster tempos, denser temporal distribution, and all other sonic modulations can render music more intense and causes heightened neural activity. In cinema it is clear that spoken drama lacks the emotional intensification of music when scenes with and without music are compared. Intensification of amplitude and tempo in music parallel and thus assist physiological and psychological excitement, leading to emotional elevation and discharge. The intensification of music and art combine to create synergy and motivation where each discipline's range of expression is imbued with heightened enhancement and inspiration from the other. If a dancer is mesmerizing alone, the dynamic range of her movement increases with a steady intensification of music.

We can achieve *intensification* at the phrase level or larger when several factors used to establish a grouping boundary happen simultaneously. For example, if a sequence of ascending phrases or motives occurs simultaneously with an opposing sequence of descending phrases, tension is increased. When several layers of independent phases or melodic grouping are aligned vertically, it intensifies to a higher magnitude than that produced with individual grouping boundaries alone. Intensification can also produce related higher-level grouping when melodic or phrase events are aligned horizontally into *parallel groupings*. In other words, when related groupings of events are aligned horizontally, grouping boundaries emphasize and connect their similarities, thus intensifying their collective statement.

In considering ways to form the musical correspondences and elements that provide organic continuity, remember that sounds perceived as similar tend to be grouped together. Groups formed by the *principle of similarity* occur on both vertical (groupings of simultaneous sounds) and horizontal dimensions of music. Pitches moving in similar intervals tend to group together, for example. As similar groups are formed into sequential patterns, modifications to their melodic contour will cause further melodic segmentation into additional sub-groupings. Events with similar temporal or acoustical qualities (such as timbre, dynamics, rhythm, and articulation), also tend to be grouped according to related characteristics. Orchestration can offer additional layers of variety or similarity through manipulating a wide range of timbral devices. Instrumental clusters heard as related are also grouped together. Consequently, using contrasting sets of instruments to create periods of similarity and contrast can promote memory retention of musical events and enhance the expressive dynamics of a composition.

Large and Small Conclusions

All distinguishable musical elements (on both microcosmic and macrocosmic scales) need a sense of closure to determine their function and to fix their parameters of identity definitively. Closure in larger groups (such as movements and phrases) has more feeling of finality than the smaller grouping boundaries of motives or sequential patterns. Factors of closure can imply either continuity or separation between all structural elements when involving relationships between sequential patterns, phrases, melodies, etc. Because short-term memory retains chunks of general information (or music) closure can guide the minds of listeners. Closure determines the relationship between individual phrases in ways which shape the larger aspects of musical motion, expression, and meaning. In most musical styles, traditions of theoretical rules and learned behavioral patterns determine expectations of closure in our minds. Over time, such individual and collective memories evolve into a culture's musical syntax.

A musical culture evolves from situations, concepts, and practices involving a group of people's commonly shared music-related schemas. These circumstances form a mutual context for the perception and understanding of music, that consists of a plethora of emotional, intellectual, psychological, spiritual, and social factors that are experienced and tacitly agreed upon without a formal cultural contract. Although musical schemas are part of a shared musical culture, cultural participants still learn them through varied individual and collective experiences. Everything that we hear, from a mother's serenade for her infant to the assorted forms of formal musical study contribute to our schemas; but the schemas that form a musical culture do not exist as explicit knowledge (Snyder 102).

All life processes have closure. Because closure shapes all musical elements, a number of factors contribute to closure. Sometimes partial closure occurs melodically or harmonically while suspended or delayed within the realms of separate and independent rhythmic, dynamic, or formal closure. This enables a composer to establish diverse multiple layers of intensity, each with its own musical agenda, purpose, and goal. Silence often establishes closure. When the majority of stratified parameters experience closure simultaneously, a more intense sense of closure occurs at the structural level. The factors of proximity and similarity that apply to other forms of musical grouping apply to closure as well. The interaction and relationship between factors of closure, proximity, and similarity produce aspects of predictability and surprise that propel musical ideas forward in interesting ways, keeping listeners engaged throughout a composition. Thus, repetition of previously introduced music generally is more successful at suggesting closure ("returning home" or to the point of departure) than the introduction of new musical material.

The most innovative and influential artists tend to gather bits of information from a variety of past traditions along the path to developing their own personal approach. Pioneers of modern European electronic music were influenced by a multiplicity of earlier musical pioneers and stylistic precursors. Lejaren Hiller began to use computers to explore ways to increase musical frequency range, timbre, and compositional freedom. Increased freedom often includes a broadening of harmonic, timbral, melodic, rhythmic, structural parameters, and expanded degrees of chance or improvisation. Hiller collaborated with John Cage and his 1956 "Illiac Suite" which was the first substantial piece of music composed on a computer. Hiller collaborated with Leonard Isaacson to write programs for the Illiac computer. Their work resulted in innovative approaches to composing that involved style simulation. Other European and European-American composers used chance (John Cage) and mathematical models (Iannis Xenakis), such as probability laws, stochastics (a mathematical theory that develops predictability from laws of probability), game theory, and Markov chains to explore new avenues to musical freedom. Xenakis's "GENDY3" is a stochastic work entirely produced by a computer program written in 1991 by the composer himself at CEMAMu. The work "GENDY3" is the continuation of the series of stochastic music works that Xenakis inaugurated in 1955 with Metastasis. Xenakis also mixed an intuitive approach to composition with his various algorithmic computer programs (Cope 9–10). Cope discusses the European pioneers of virtual music:

> One of the first formal types of algorithms in music history, and another good example of virtual music, is the eighteenth-century *Musikalisches Würfelspiel*, or musical dice game. The idea behind this musically sophisticated game involved composing a series of measures of music that could be recombined in many different ways and still be stylistically viable—virtual music. Following this process, even a very simple piece becomes a source of innumerable new works. A typical *Würfelspiel* of sixteen measures, for example, yields 11^{16},

or roughly forty-six quadrillion works, with each work, although varying in aesthetic quality, being stylistically correct (Cope 1996). Composers of *Musikalisches Würfelspiele* included Johann Philipp Kirnberger, C. P. E. Bach, Franz Josef Haydn, Wolfgang Amadeus Mozart, Maximilian Stadler, Antonio Callegari, and Pasquale Ricci, among others (4–5).

In the final analysis, whether using more conventional approaches to premeditated composition, chance, algorithms, spontaneous approaches, or any combination of methods, the variations, permutations, and economy of means essentially boil down to recombinant music. Surpassing nature's own organic methods is hard.

Analysis of W. A. Mozart, Symphony in E-flat (K. 543)

Now that we have looked at repetition, closure, proximity, and similarity in a variety of ways, we can examine methods employed by composers to discover how such factors occur within various stylistic approaches. Let us briefly examine W. A. Mozart's *Symphony in E-flat* (K. 543) to discover how some of his musical elements are assembled. In particular, Mozart uses spontaneity, repetition, rhythm, orchestral timbre, and harmonic structure to frame his ideas and promote their development.

Mozart is well known for the speed at which he composed flawless masterworks. As with Bach, this close proximity between the conception of musical ideas and their ultimate fixation in written scores, places Mozart's premeditated output very close to the process of spontaneous composition. Mozart's *E-flat Major Symphony* (K. 543) was the first of his last three symphonies, all of which were written in the summer of 1788. The *E-flat Major* was completed on June 26, 1788; the *G Minor* (K. 550) on July 25; and the *C Major* (K. 551) on August 10. Mozart's career ebbed during the summer these three symphonies were composed. His faith that his musicianship would win him a secure position in the affection of Vienna, enabling him to live without dependence on his patronage, completely diminished. Though *Figaro* had been extremely successful at Vienna in 1786, it was kept off the stage the following season. *Don Giovanni* had to be produced at Prague and was a resounding success, but it failed in Vienna. The death of Gluck left a post for which he was qualified, but he only received a position at Kammermusicus, where he wrote dance music for balls at the Redoutensaal.

Though these three summer symphonies are often referred to as "symphonic triptych," Mozart didn't necessarily intend for them to be performed together (however, because of the contrast between them, they may be performed with success on the same program). The *E-flat Major Symphony* is the lyrical, the *G Minor* the dramatic, and the *C Major* the ceremonial. Usually works such as the "symphonic triptych" were written with the same special purpose or event in mind, but the purpose or event that called for these symphonies has never been discovered, nor is there record of their performance during Mozart's lifetime. The tragic circumstances of Mozart's life took

Figure 14. Analysis of W. A. Mozart, *Symphony in E-flat* **(K. 543)**

EXPOSITION

Section	Introduction			PT				
Measures	1	9	18	26	1 2 3	44	1 2 3	54 trans → Elide
Phrase Structure & Motives								
Harmony	Eb:1 vii*	V pedal	unusual use of dissonance (C; Db); dim. 4th & 7th	Eb				
Rhythm								
Melody	Repeated notes; scale figures in violins (descending, p.)	Fragmented in flute; ascending low string scale figures	Melody in canon	Violin PT; Hns. & Bns. Echo		Low Str. Counter Statement of theme; fl. & cl. Echo		Trans. the me
Texture	Full orchestra, f. Many tutti figures (repeated chords)	Primarily p. No thematic development	Subito f Thin (p) strings	Scale figures for dynamic contrast (occasionally)		Subito f		Full orchestra

Section	ST						
Measures	72	90	98	106 Ext	114	135	142
Phrase Structure & Motives			4 4	Ext			
Harmony	Elide	Eb V/V	Bb	(Derived from Second ph. Gr.)		(Some new cad. Material)	Bb
Rhythm	f		p				
Melody	Scale fig. Descending End transition violins - desc. Sequence	Begin wist. End w/w.w.	Extension; winds w/2nd pharse group of ST. begins in Cl & ends w/flute	Extended by figurative sequences		soft	
Texture	Full full		thin (p)	(Cadence figures in sequence)			

DEVELOPMENT

Measures	143	147		180
Phrase	Moves abruptly between keys			
Harmony	g	Ab highly unstable; chromatic alterations dim. Chords frequently	g	V7/Eb
Melody	from trans. material Winds enter with e.x pattern. Th. 2 va.	motives treated sequentially derived from Expo. thematic material	Pause	Brief 4 measure link to recap.
	p f p / 2 2 2 / % % % (contrast)			
Texture	Full			

RECAPITULATION

Section	PT			ST	
Measures	185	1 2 3	212	1 2 3 trans → Elision	255 (etc.)
Harmony	Eb Eb				Eb
Rhythm	All material heard in regular order (as exposition). Also a relatively brief recapitulation. Theme return in same voices essentially unchanged				
Melody	All usual transpositions to tonic key made (i.e. second theme)		f		
Texture	p				

CODA

Measures	303
	Eb - with scale figures and material from exposition closing (last figure heard prior to cadence). Ends with figures (final) ... before cadential

> **W.A. Mozar**
> **E-flat Maj. Symphony**
> **KV 543 # 39**
> **Analysis by K.E. Hester**

their toll on the man, but they apparently had no visible negative effect on his artistic output. Undoubtedly, nonetheless, the circumstances in his personal life reflect in his music.

The orchestra clearly reflects Mozart's personal voice in these works. Orchestral sound is as important to this composer as individual (personal) sound is to the spontaneous composer. The orchestra varies its color (just as an improvising artist modulates his or her individual sound on each note or phrase) with various combinations of instrumental sounds to create different moods and effects. The *E-flat* symphony is the lyrical symphony that reflects joy. It is scored for one flute (no oboes), two clarinets, two bassoons, two horns, two trumpets, drums, and strings. The clarinets replace the more traditional two oboes. European clarinets existed for a hundred years before this work was composed, but it slowly made its way to the concert hall. The *E-flat Major Symphony* was the first symphony by an important composer in which the clarinet was assigned a leading orchestral role. In replacing the oboe, it became the principle melodic voice of the symphonic orchestra after the violin (Mozart disliked the flute because of its problems with intonation during this period of European musical development).

Reoccurring ideas in music help establish structural boundaries in composition. Modified repetition of various musical fragments helps maintain compositional continuity. Thus melodic fragments and motives reoccur throughout the movement in a variety of positions and forms. The repetition of principle themes articulates the long-term structural events (macrocosm), while shorter fragments work on shorter-range internal goals (microcosm). These elements, along with introductions and conclusions that typically surround principle thematic sections, articulate compositional structure.

The *E-flat Major Symphony* begins with twenty-five measures of introduction constructed from rhythmic patterns of repeated notes and chords sounded throughout the orchestra. Ascending rapid scale figures in the upper strings are used to connect these simple patterns. These scalar figures occur in measures nine through fourteen above a dominant pedal. The events all accompany the fragmented melody of the flute and they lead to unusual dissonance intervals and chords (such as the C against the D-flat in measure eighteen, the diminished seventh chords in measure twenty-one, and the diminished seventh and fourths intervals of measures twenty-two and twenty-three). The sudden forte dynamic level that accompanies them makes the dissonant chords and intervals, considered audacious for eighteenth-century European ears, even more noticeable. This is a long introduction for Mozart, but this is not unusual for the period. Haydn frequently used long introductions.

The principle theme is heard at the beginning of the Allegro (3/4) in the first violin and is echoed by the horns and bassoons. The movement is difficult to perform because of the many dramatic contrasts within a single tempo. The first subject seems too fast if taken at a tempo that suits the energetic sequel in the transition to the second subject (which should not sound too hurried). The full orchestra then produces the transition to the second theme.

The second subject begins in measure ninety-eight in the violins and is completed in the winds in measure one hundred. Though new cadential material appears in the closing of the exposition, it ends in B-flat Major.

Attention to proportion is important in spontaneous and premeditated composition. Since Mozart used a long introduction as an opener, he must compensate accordingly elsewhere to maintain aesthetic balance. Both the development and the recapitulation are relatively short (the development being unstable and moving through G Minor and A-flat Major) and the usual transpositions are found in the recapitulation. The coda again makes use of the descending scales of the introduction.

Just as we move around the blues matrix smoothly by traveling to close-related harmonic zones (those that reside one accidental away are most closely related), the same holds true for European classical compositions. Harmonic stress and surprises are supplied by voyages into more distant harmonic domains. The second movement (Andante con moto) is in A-flat Major, a key rarely used by Mozart and one never before used by him as the primary tonality for a large-scale work. This relatively simple movement is very skillfully worked out, with a transitional figure in F minor emerging into a complex polyphonic form that moves as far to the sharp side of the key matrix as B Major. In all cases, however, each harmonic motion relates to succeeding ones (B Major has a enharmonic third relation to A-flat Major, for example).

Compositions, of either the spontaneous or premeditated variety, often have two, three, or four distinct primary sections to their compositional structures. The exposition (point of departure), development (travel to farthest distance from home), and recapitulation (return) divisions of one style become the head, bridge, and repeated section of music (ABA) of another approach, culture, or stylistic region. The third movement (Minuet) is a well-known theme that has been arranged to exploit almost every possible instrument combination. It is a very straightforward minuet without thematic development and with a trio primarily for flute and two clarinets with string accompaniment. At the trio, the second clarinet is heard playing an arpeggiated figure in the low register against the lyrical melody of the first clarinet. Mozart used this device frequently. Bringing the clarinet forward in this fashion is significant to its new orchestral role. Though it has been said that Mozart often delights in his finale, where he seems interested in seeing how many different thematic ideas he can manipulate effectively and still maintain unity, this movement (finale) is an exception. The finale is based upon the first nine notes of the opening theme (stated initially in the violins). There is a transition, which consists of figurative ideas, and a second theme appears; but this theme is actually a variant of the first. The exposition concludes with the first five notes of the theme sounding in various sections of the orchestra, ending with a cadence in B-flat.

In the development section, the B-flat harmonic region is followed by chord progression to the dominant of C Major, which is cut short with a pause before reaching the tonic that brings back the theme in A-flat major. A short recapitulation is followed by an extended coda that, again, uses the monothematic material. Recombinant features of Mozart's approach allow us to compare this work to the work of other composers. The finale resembles Haydn's monothematic treatment of a movement. At the same time, a full sonata form is successfully executed while achieving masterful variety of a single idea. The ability to use an economy of means to achieve maximum gains is a goal towards which all composers should strive.

Mozart's movement provides fine examples of musical balance, proportion, and contrast. Such models and structures should remain in the minds of spontaneous composers as they shape their musical material in real time. Consciousness of a number of ways to use shape, articulate, and control large-scale formal structure, and the smaller components of various internal repetition, will add greater coherence to musical production when applied skillfully and creatively.

Form and Content

All phenomena have form determined by the boundaries that contain its aspects. In some musical approaches, form is determined in advance of other musical details. Other approaches, at the opposite end of the spectrum, may evolve content first from a variety of musical elements and operations and determine form in retrospect. Regardless of the procedure used to develop a particular composition, form and content—like the interrelationship between melody, rhythm, timbre, dynamics, texture, and harmony—are inseparable.

Form is articulated by a wide variety of approaches to repetition and contrast, but dynamics, timbre, texture, and other expressive musical elements are equally effective as structural markers. Throughout global cultures people demonstrate an innate ability to intuitively distill the logic of music without complex technical analysis. Basic formal structures used in many jazz compositions include binary, ternary, song, strophic, rondo, through-composed, and other conventional musical forms because the most important emphasis on expressive features remains at the nuance levels.

Strophic form, where a single melody is repeated (with only words changing with each verse), is another type of "song form." Spirituals and blues songs are often strophic structurally, although the high degree of embellishment and freely interpreted approaches to melodies and rhythm challenges this definition. Many blues singers embellish melodies in strophic form to such an extent that interpretations render strophic songs akin to theme and variation form.

Many compositions begin with a melody followed by a contrasting melody. This is *binary form.* Compositions also involve multiple sections and strategically positioned key changes that combine to create the overall form of a piece. *Song form* is a term often used to label for AABA formal structure where, as with binary form, each new letter defines either a contrasting musical thought or the repetition of the original section of melody. The B is sometimes called the *bridge,* or *channel,* and may traditionally involve modulation to a new key. This form is closely related to *ternary form* (ABA), since the only difference involves a repetition of the initial A section. Some Swing-era musicians referred to the B section of a song with the expression *George Washington.* A third section of contrasting melody would be labeled C.

Ragtime composers frequently used a modified rondo form as the main structure of their compositions. Scott Joplin's "Maple Leaf Rag" uses a repetition pattern related to the rondo form. Its formal structure includes a recurring theme (A) surrounded by several contrasting themes labeled B, C, and D (e.g., ABACA-DA). Other ragtime composers use structures closely related to marches and other Eurocentric compositional structures based upon ABACA rondo form.

After the initial evolution of the metrically elastic country blues forms, classic and urban blues forms standardized as twelve and sixteen-bar formal structures. Country (or rural) blues musicians most often performed alone. This style of presentation allowed them greater freedom than is typically possible within ensemble performance. Later, New Orleans-style and other early jazz compositions began using the predictable four- or eight-measure repetitive phrase structures of many Eurocentric musical styles. Jelly Roll Morton and Duke Ellington were among the first jazz composers to deviate from those predictable phrase structures. Later, free jazz and other contemporary jazz compositions often used a form more closely related to *through-composed* style, completely avoiding predictable repetition of primary themes.

Composition and improvisation require an intimate understanding of form and long-term structure. Inductive reasoning, the process of deriving general principles from facts or instances, supports styles where content evolves strictly from musical content. Deductive reasoning infers details from general principles; thus beginning with premeditated structures seems a good fit for that approach. Afrocentric jazz and spontaneous compositional style as well as Eurocentric "classical" and premeditated approaches to composition are grounded in the overtone series and recombinant composition. But certain elements of culture are reflected in the subtle details of distinguishing musical characteristics. Afrocentric and Eurocentric styles seem to diverge formally and stylistically along deductive and inductive lines, however, just as Egyptian and Babylonian mathematics diverged along algebraic (scholastic) and geometric (natural), theoretical, and philosophical lines.

"Love the moment, and the energy of that moment will spread beyond all boundaries."

—Corita Kent

References

Bahrick, Harry P. and Lynda K. Hall. "The Importance of Retrieval Failures to Long-term Retention: A Metacognitive Explanation of the Spacing Effect." Department of Psychology, Ohio Wesleyan University. Delaware, OH. 2 March 2005. 9 Jan. 2009 <http://www.sciencedirect.com/science?_ob=ArticleURL&_udi=B6WK4-4FM0NWF-2&_user=4428&_rdoc=1&_fmt=&_orig=search&_sort=d&view=c&_acct=C000059601&_version=1&_urlVersion=0&_userid=4428&md5=09dec074ae fb9b5e899539cef51c8d3f>.

Baker, Davis. "John Coltrane's 'Giant Steps' Solo and Composition Transcribed and Annotated." *Down Beat* (22 July 1971): 35–40.

Bourne, Michael. "The Sound that Launched a Thousand Horns." *Down Beat* (Mar. 1992): 18–19.

Cope, D. *Virtual Music—Computer Synthesis of Musical Style.* Cambridge, MA: MIT Press, 2001.

Ekman, P., R. W. Levenson, and W. V. Friesen. "Autonomic Nervous System Activity Distinguishes Among Emotions." Plenum, New York (1981): 1208–1210.

Healey, Richard. "Change Without Change, and How to Observe it in General Relativity." *Synthese* 141 (September 2004): 1–35. (Excerpted at <http://www.springerlink. com/content/h12u5r4522754468/>).

Khan, Hazrat Inayat. *The Mysticism of Sound and Music: The Sufi Teaching of Hazrat Inayat Khan.* Boston: Shambhala, 1996.

Maniktala, Rakesh. "Spiritualism, Modern Science and Ancient History." *Ancient Science.* July 21, 2006 <http://www.geocities.com/ancientscience/beliefs.htm>.

Powell, Cory S. *God in the Equation: How Einstein Became the Prophet of the New Religious Era.* New York: The Free Press, 2002.

Salthe, Stanley N. "Theoretical Biology as an Anticipatory Text: The Relevance of Uexküll to Current Issues in Evolutionary Systems." *Semiotica* 134 (2001): 359–380.

Snyder, Bob. *Music and Memory: An Introduction.* Cambridge, MA: The MIT Press, 2000.

Tenny, C. L. "The Aspectual Interface Hypothesis: The Connection Between Syntax and Lexical Semantics." *Lexicon Project Working Papers* 24. Cambridge, MA: Center for Cognitive Science at MIT, 1988.

"The Four Basic Symmetries." *Symmetry and Patterns: The Art of Oriental Carpets.* 2005. The Textile Museum and Math Forum @ Drexel. Philadelphia. July 2007 <http://mathforum.org/geometry/rugs/symmetry/basic.html>.

Thomas, Lawson, E. and Robert N. McCauley, *Bringing Ritual to Mind: Psychological Foundations of Cultural Forms.* Cambridge, MA: Cambridge University Press, 2002.

"Time Line of Albert Einstein's Life." *Einstein's Big Idea.* Nova Science Programming, PBS. June 2005. April 2007 <http://www.pbs.org/wgbh/nova/einstein/timeline/>.

Chapter Five
International Language: Expression

The EARTH (The Matrix of Musical Life)

All planets prior to their formation are part of their parent stars, like the nine planets of our solar system were part of the Sun. After parting from the Sun, it took millions of years for our Earth to cool and become solid. The Earth is hollow inside, with a tiny white-dwarf "sun" at its center. Most of the other planets in this universe are hollow inside. And most of the planets are inhabited too, because the basic purpose of planets is to support life—as that of stars is to support planets, according to Ramayana and Puranas.

"Attaining": Self-Exploration, Symbolism, and the Tao

To see more of existence we need to look at the universe without the limitations of our preconceptions. If we are not restricted by search for carbon-based life forms much like ourselves, then we may miss the 90 percent or more of those forms that (or who) may reside within the realm of Dark Matter. Likewise, musicians and other artists prepare themselves within established artistic traditions; but the most creative artists then find other creative dimensions in route to discovering their own unique voice.

Miles Davis was a musical master of poetic clarity, dynamic diversity (in both the music and creative personnel he chose for his bands), and musical metaphor. His comments and his visual artwork align with other quietly explosive, expressive, and unique aspects of his personality and music. In 1959 Davis said:

> I wanted the music this new group would play to be freer, more modal, more African or Eastern, and less Western. I wanted them to go beyond themselves. . . . I've always told the musicians in my band to play what they know and then play above that. Because then anything can happen, and that's where great art and music happen.

Throughout the twentieth century, many African-American musicians have had reservations about converting their thoughts on music into words in print. Many great innovators of jazz never publicly applied verbal descriptions to their music or musical theories. Having been systematically exploited throughout their careers, many did not want to give away trade secrets in a racist society with a long legacy of merciless exploitation of African-American labor and production. Louis Armstrong, Duke Ellington, Charles Mingus, Miles Davis, and other masters wrote interesting autobiographies, but they did not reveal the technical or theoretical ingredients that formed the rich detail of their musical approaches. Other innovators obviously felt that the poetic nature of their art form required equally poetic, cogent, or arcane descriptions. A few innovators prefer expressing their musical concepts through symbols. Anthony Braxton labels his compositions with personally designed symbols. John Coltrane was a systematic and spiritual innovator who seemed to discover the intimate essence of the connections between his body, mind, and spirit through creating music.

The Coltrane matrix or mandala suggests his exploration of the mathematical and metaphysical connections between scales, chords, and intervals, and then eventually found a way to ground that realization in his life-long spiritual quest. This flexible approach enabled him to pivot in any direction of melodic movement, chord progression, or intervallic configuration. "Interstellar Space" may be the clearest example of how his mind ultimately brought all such theories together in real time during his final period. Coltrane also seemed to have a related theory of rhythm (or an emerging theory involving polyrhythm). This freedom of movement provides insight into reasons why he was moving away from harmonic constraints towards a less restrictive approach to spontaneous composition. His choice of Elvin Jones for his "classic quartet" suggests that a polyrhythmic predisposition was always a part of his basic musical conception; and when he began working with two drummers (adding drummer Rashied Ali) and two basses we get a glimpse at how his music evolved as he matured. Meditation upon harmony, unity, balance, and beauty can transfix an artist's mind.

Balance within the individual is essential to Taoism (pronounced "Dow-ism"), which believes all things have a basic harmony. The mystical and traditional teachings of Taoism began to evolve with the Chinese sage Lao-Tse (or Lao Tzu, a contemporary of Confucius, born in 604 B.C.) and Chuang-Tzu (in the fourth century B.C.). Taoism was founded in China by Lao-Tse's book, the *Tao-te-Ching*, the sacred text for Taoists. Taoism began as a process of psychology and philosophy. It was adopted as China's state religion in 440 A.D., well after Lao-Tse's death in 531 B.C. Taoism is based on the practice of striving to become one with the "Tao," or the force that flows through all animate and inanimate things—the force that balances the universe. Taoists believe that peace may only be conceived through the development of virtue. All followers of the Tao should seek to attain the Three Jewels—compassion, moderation, and humility. Taoists can attain the Three Jewels by nurturing their "Ch'i," or their life force, through living a moderate lifestyle in a balanced and carefully planned manner. This is achieved by weighing the consequences and reciprocations of each action taken, and by remaining compassionate to all other living beings. Thus, it is characterized by its grounding in the idea of the essential unity of humanity with nature and the fundamental harmony of all things through balancing of yin and yang energies. Over the last two-and-a-half thousand years, Taoism has explored the idea of a human connection and interaction with nature. Chuang-Tzu proposed that:

> In the great beginning there was non-being. It has neither being nor name. The One originates from it; it has oneness but not yet physical form. That which is formless is divided into yin and yang, and . . . through movement and rest it produces all things. When things are produced in accordance with the principle of life, there is physical form. When the physical form embodies and preserves the spirit so that all activities follow their specific principles, that is nature (Bindon 19).

A spontaneous composer has the opportunity to explore balance, harmony, structure, and the source of creative power that inherently resides within each of us and ultimately connects us to the greater universe. This conception of balance and harmony is illustrated by the Taoist "Yin Yang" symbol. The two polar opposite shapes are in a swirling pattern to illustrate change, which is considered the only constant factor in the universe. The dark side, or the "Yin," represents the mundane Earth, while the arcane light side, the "Yang," represents the sky, or the heavens. Taoism understands that nothing in nature is purely light or dark, good or evil. To represent this fact, there is a small dot of the opposite color on both sides of the symbol. Since no external God exists in Taoism, life's vicissitudes are worked out internally through meditation and observation. The *Tao Te Ching* (*The Book of the Way*) expresses the potential power of the spontaneous composer to use an economy of means to generate living music in its forty-second verse:

> The Tao gives birth to One.
> One gives birth to Two.
> Two gives birth to Three.
> Three gives birth to all things.
>
> All things have their backs to the female
> and stand facing the male.
> When male and female combine,
> all things achieve harmony.
>
> Ordinary men hate solitude.
> But the Master makes use of it,
> embracing his aloneness, realizing
> he is one with the whole universe.

People often conclude that spirituality cannot be factored into musical analysis because it cannot be measured in any type of galvanometer, with a slide rule, or by application of other physical scientific tools. There are, however, phenomena that impact upon our intuition, intellect, and subconscious minds that cannot be measured quantitatively with absolute certainty—our specific thought processes, for example. In his book *Mathematical Philosophy,* C. J. Keyser wrote, "Absolute certainty is a privilege of uneducated minds—and fanatics. It is for scientific folk an unattainable ideal" (120). We should remember that at one time an atom was a nonentity, before later becoming an indivisible unit of matter for material scientists. The properties of those manufactured products made from atoms, in the molecular aspects of the universe, depend on how those atoms are arranged. Rearranging the atoms in coal makes diamonds. In the future, nanotechnology may enable people to arrange the fundamental building blocks of nature easily and inexpensively within the laws of physics. This will result in the fabrication of a new generation of cleaner, stronger, lighter, and more precise products which will enable us to look farther and deeper into the macro and micro realms of the universe. But the molecular universe is but a small portion of existence. Empirical analysis concluded that ether was motionless. Nonetheless, in time, the Bohr atom, the quantum theory, and relativity upset those empirical certainties of earlier science.

The patterns and generative structures that govern the growth of trees and other plants; the formation of clouds and mountain ranges; and the forces that guide solar and planetary motion are not entirely reducible to the laws that theorists can apply to the analysis of music. We certainly know some things are true based upon the qualitative impact they have on our minds and hearts. Thus, with qualitative certainty (not quantitative empirical certainty), we can appreciate the music we love without validating our intuitive judgment through scientific means. Creations in nature are flexible and enduring, and the universe operates with qualitative certainty in manufacturing some of its mysteries.

The process of building a composition, or its composer, also involves an assortment of quantitative and qualitative means. Reviewing the evolution of Coltrane's musical development demonstrates the progressive phases of his stylistic development: from his formative years; subsequent study at Philadelphia conservatories and his period with the Navy band; his R&B days with Big Maybelle, Eddie Cleanhead Vincent, and Earl Bostic; his emergence during bebop with Dizzy Gillespie; adventurous hard-bop and quasi-modal musical journeys with Miles Davis; and learning the iconoclast Monk perspective from Thelonious Monk, until he finally formulated the personal expanded-harmonic (with polytonal implications), quasi-modal, and "free jazz" approaches of his own inimitable "late period" style. The pan-tonal implications of Coltrane's late music codified his musical evolution. When Coltrane was asked if he was interested in twelve-tone music, he replied that his music already utilized all twelve tones. Coltrane consistently increased his range of musical freedom. The power of freedom and spontaneity cannot be underestimated. Freedom is not only a fundamental element in creative music, but is also a universal principle that has inspired creativity throughout time.

Improvisation and spontaneous composition require freedom to respond to the transfer of information that takes place constantly in performances by musical ensembles. Those transfers are governed by the musical rules upon which all musicians involved in the ensemble have agreed. That tacit, mutual agreement is what defines and unifies the ensemble's identity. With musical freedom comes universal laws of system dynamics and artistic responsibilities.

The concept of freedom is the hallmark of African-American music. In spontaneous composition that particular trademark is given expanded poetic license. Freedom is the catalyst that allows jazz and other African-American stylistic forms to absorb any worldwide musical elements that cross their paths, and after the conversion of such ingredients, to utilize its influence in expressing something fresh and universal. Spontaneity allows performers to adapt to any given musical situation freely, and without relinquishing the wealthy backlogs of musical knowledge and resources within their core. The beauty, strength, and wisdom of such a musical nucleus ultimately lead to global appreciation and confluence. The numerous satellite approaches that emerged from African-American music in recent years account for the subsequent emergence of bluegrass, rock and roll, "improvised music," various forms of fusion, and many of the countless other eclectic musical activities, styles, and concepts that emerged during the twentieth and twenty-first centuries. Thus African-American music gradually launched new musical paradigms that influenced creativity globally and, in turn, ultimately produced blended art forms reflective of contemporary culture worldwide.

Creativity's Intimate Relationships with Harmony, Proportion, and Magic

Creative thinking and the creative process lack proximity in traditional Western music education. Creativity involves the ability to produce new manifestations in art, mechanics, or other aspects of life that enable us to solve problems by new or novel means. It is the ability to create or invent through imaginative skill in music, as in most other art forms. Whether acquired skill, knowledge, creativity, and improvisation are applied by doctors working in the emergency room, chefs cooking in a kitchen, or performing musicians, both interpreters and inventors (transmitters and receivers) must be involved in the process. Unfortunately, Western music institutions are most often geared towards producing interpreters rather than inventors, and towards teaching analysis of art rather than "creative problem solving" (Feinberg 54). Some Western university music students or conservatory graduates find it difficult to spontaneously create a melody and develop that melody convincingly through their own creative intuition, musical imaginations, knowledge, and artistic judgment. Master jazz musicians are capable of spontaneously creating music from basic musical seeds and structural outlines that is innovative, virtuosic, and compositionally sound. With regards to music and sound, Lateef says:

The autophysiopsychic performer of music must endeavor to understand the nature of sound in that it is sound that he/she is producing. Sound gives to the consciousness an evidence of its existence, although it is in fact the active part of consciousness itself that turns into sound. The consciousness bears witness to its own voice. It is this realization that sound appeals to man. Tone has either a warm or cold effect according to its element, since all elements are made of different degrees of vibrations. Therefore, sound can produce an agreeable or disagreeable effect upon man's mind and body. Every person has a sound that is particularly unique; the musician should be aware of his/her own sound.

Thoughts, too, are important in that they are as alive as physical germs. They work for one's advantage or disadvantage according to their nature. The sensitive musician creates, fashions, and controls them for he/she realizes that the effect of the personal expression upon the listener depends upon the thoughts that are imbedded in his/ her sound. The thoughts proceeding from the mind reach far. They extend from mind to mind. The vibrations of mind are much stronger than those of words. The earnest feelings of one heart can pierce the heart of another. They can even speak in the silence, spreading into the sphere, so that the very atmosphere of a person's presence proclaims his/ her thoughts and emotions. Sound has an effect on each atom of the body, for each atom resounds; on all glands, on the circulation of the blood and on pulsation, sound has an effect. With music, attraction is a natural effect of sound. Music, in one sense, is the shortest, the most direct way to self realization, but one must know what music and how to use it. Man's state of mind can be read by his/her music; For however great and expert he/she may be, he/ she cannot produce by mere skill without a developed feeling within himself the grace and beauty which appeals to his/her heart (5).

How does the impact of sound affect our emotions and physical senses? Scientists estimate that the range of human hearing extends from 16–20,000 hertz (referred to as the "sonic range"). Countless inaudible, subsonic frequencies exist below that range and an ultra-sonic spectrum that extends above. Human hearing is measured in decibels and the Occupational Safety and Health Administration in the United States generally estimates that the maximum sound intensity to which humans can be exposed for extended periods of time (over an eight-hour period) without incurring hearing loss is 75 decibels (dbA). General levels of street noise in large urban areas often average 80 decibels and the volume at "heavy metal" rock concerts often exceeds 90 dbA. Certain heavily amplified jazz concerts, and orchestral performances of more dramatic and powerful compositions, may also exceed 85 dbA. So we are gradually losing our hearing.

Some researchers theorize that certain rhythmic patterns in music have a draining or weakening effect on the human organism that could potentially result in loss of symmetry between the two cerebral hemispheres of the brain. They claim that this may result in perceptual disorientation and manifestations of stress. We know that rhythm has the ability to elevate us to a new level of sensory awareness. Rhythm can move us from various states of ecstasy to feelings of unity, liberating those emotions that lead the human body towards a state of anxiety or alarm. Other sounds that conflict with the rate of our body vibration and those of various other incoming frequencies can also cause physical or emotional discomfort. The body cells generally seem to vibrate at more than 1,000 cycles per second. Consequently, the human body functions as a vibratory transformer that must filter all other incoming frequencies daily. We are familiar with the television commercial where a singer shatters glass. Frequencies produced by some household appliances, or the incessant sound of television hum that can vibrate at frequencies of at least 15,750 cycles per second, usually permeate the entire home environment, producing a draining effect on living organisms as well as fragile inanimate objects.

In sharp contrast to the earlier viewpoint that creativity is a quality reserved only for the gifted few, today it is considered a quality that all individuals possess in varying degrees and that developing this innate quality satisfies a psychological need. Creativity comes in many shapes, styles, and forms. Many creative people do not tolerate simple distractions easily. Experimentation indicates creativity is accompanied by a heightened sensitivity to the environment. Creative artists tend to amplify sights, sounds, and textures—the stimuli around them.

The psychoanalytic explanation of creativity poses two kinds of thought processes. "Primitive" or primary-process thinking belongs to the realms of dreams, transcendence, free associations, fantasies, drug highs, and mystical trances. This process is primary because it is the basic thought of the intuitive or unconscious realm. The contrasting secondary process is logical, analytic, and reality-oriented. Creative inspiration seems to evolve from the ability to regress to primary thought. Our intuitive mind may be labeled "primitive" because it is the most basic requirement for our survival. But actually, as our superior mode of processed thought, creativity is connected to our subconscious mind, and that realm provides the driving force for our autonomic nervous system, intuition, and other vital aspects of our personal existence.

Creativity allows us to express not only our personal experiences, observations, joy, and suffering, it enables us to elevate and amplify our perspective to resonate with the thoughts, feelings, and experiences of a cross-section of humanity. Michelangelo Buonarroti was born in the sixteenth century, and became an accomplished artist, sculptor, architect, and poet who demonstrated his knowledge and skill by creating a large number of amazing works. Michelangelo's skill with capturing the human anatomy allowed him to express the feelings and emotions characteristic of his time. He was the workaholic genius who painted the ceiling of the Sistine Chapel. He also wrote poems revealing his inner feelings about universal themes such as love, death, and redemption. The torment and horror we see in his frescos are perhaps an indication of the hardships Michelangelo encountered during his life (Oremland 370).

Creative and intellectual ability requires two different thought processes. Some researchers believe that the right hemisphere of the brain is responsible for the primary, creative thought and the left controls secondary, logical reasoning. With creative individuals both hemispheres are equally active. When a person is closer to a meditative state they produce higher levels of alpha waves. A meditative state involves clearing internal chatter and allowing the subconscious creative juices to flow. Through measuring the degree of cortical arousal with electroencephalograms, scientists found that, generally, the more aroused a person is, the fewer alpha waves he or she produces. Most people produce alpha waves when they are relaxing and increase alpha when they are working on an imaginative problem. The best rational work is done at medium levels of arousal (secondary thought). If brain wave frequency is too high, then concentrating on a task at hand is hard. If it is too low, one's mind floats off in daydream. Primary thought occurs with both very high and very low levels of arousal (from dream states at one end to emotional highs at the other). Performers can reach degrees of cognition where creative intellect seems to run faster than the technical power required for interpreting such information as sound. Such a condition is not fully conducive to creative thinking in music, and can produce a sense of frustration, because the body is not yet capable of reproducing physically the musical ideas created in the head. Creative music learning should be both pleasurable and demanding, requiring hard work to bring forth greater creative pleasure.

The spiritual domain is at once the most intimate and most elusive aspect of human experience. For some artists, the Creator inspires their creativity. Creativity is a quality that all living things possess. It is the evolutionary characteristic that enables the inhabitants of the universe to make the adaptations necessary for survival. Those who discover their creative potential apply intuitive imagination to whatever they choose to accomplish. Games (chess, basketball, billiards, etc.), culinary arts, architecture, gardening, parenting, or the successful execution of any other human endeavors are enhanced by creative imagination. Innovators often merge processed thought with unusually high levels of intellectual analysis and motor skill to reach their most demanding levels of creative production.

Some psychologists suggest that creative people gravitate towards designs that are complex, asymmetric, ambiguous, and odd over the simpler, orderly, and familiar designs that less actively creative people prefer. Despite empirical research and observation, defining creativity is extremely difficult, if not impossible. Many artists feel that the product of humankind's creative ability cannot be explained so much as revealed—nor comprehended so much as apprehended. Hence, the science of aesthetics must always be intriguingly inexact. Marion Brown (jazz composer and performing artist) feels that "music emerging from the Black experience is a distinct musical idiom with its own tradition and performance techniques. Academically it can stand objective scrutiny, yet its inclusion into any curriculum exceeds the purely musical" (Heath 139).

We need music education that can make learning experiences more expressively dynamic, directly relevant to our quality of life, and more proactively creative. We need an approach to music that not only enables the student to interpret the music, but also encourages him/her to respond intellectually and intuitively to the creative process that produced it. Such an approach, that resides close to both the creative process and the created product (in this case the music), involves creative problem solving—an approach that can do more than merely teach the history and analysis of musical content. While a student is learning the fundamentals and interpretation of music, they can also cultivate knowledge, behaviors, and ways of thinking and listening that promote a pattern of continuous and simultaneous growth in technical awareness, aesthetic appreciation, and creativity.

Developing a Personal Musical Style

People have searched perpetually for patterns that would help them organize their lives as individuals and as social communities. Ancient mathematicians and astronomers used their naked eyes to examine physical relationships between cycles produced by the earth, sun, and moon. Based upon cyclical, numerical, and geometrical patterns that our ancestors discovered, people established the patterns of numbers used to devise calendars, lengths of measurement, and other computing devices. Their discoveries also created myths that reflected their ancient observations, suspicions, and desire for order in their lives. All organisms on Earth respond to the solar and lunar influence as they occur in the cycles of the synodic month (lunation cycle or lunar phases) and the year. The repetition of astral cycles such as full moons, eclipses, and planetary conjunctions revealed a cosmology to ancient astronomers that was both numerical and spatial. It seemed that mathematics imbued creation with order and meaning. People realized that they could count the phenomena in their environment and form those numbers into various organized groups. Geometry eventually arose as the field of knowledge dealing with spatial relationships, thus emerging as one of the two fields of pre-modern mathematics (the other being the systematic investigation of numbers). They concluded that "God is a geometer," and the Delphic adage "as above, so below" suggest that cosmic patterns in early life became a source of revelatory information. In Egypt, the Great Pyramid (of 2480 B.C.) epitomizes this approach. Precisely constructed to the points of the compass, the pyramid's "passageways aligned to stars, its base and height fit the 'squared circle' of Earth and Moon" (Heath 139). Beyond humankind's fascination for understanding and measuring the universe, however, stands the inherent desire to know and express oneself.

In spontaneous composition we have an opportunity to use self-inquiry, cognition, and intuition to develop tools of self-discovery. Just as the Egyptian pyramids attest to the presence of a special brand of esoteric wisdom that produced knowledge of a general and abstract nature, the worldwide music legacies of great composers and innovators are the accomplishments they left for humankind. Our ultimate task may simply be to express ourselves sincerely and obtain self-mastery in accordance to the harmony of nature. Often we are guided towards careers according to social or parental dictates. A path suggested by external advice may not be the path for which we may be destined. Jean Jacques Rousseau felt that nature summons us to the essential duties of human life. He said, "Observe nature and follow the path she traces for you."

If we reside in a universe governed by interconnectivity and relativity, it then seems that: 1) everything has a nucleus, including life itself; 2) time is our most precious commodity; and 3) it is important to appreciate life in all its forms. If seeds, atoms, cells, fundamental frequencies, or soul personalities serve as different forms of nuclei, then everything within "infinity" (the sum total of Creation, whether we consider that whole God, Goddess, the Cosmic, or the like) radiates around a primordial nucleus that binds all things. Thus each composition can reflect this fundamental organic arrangement in its organization.

In 1976, I introduced the term "Musicism" to suggest the strong relationship that I felt between mysticism and music. Both mysticism and music are fluid in design. Meditation enhances concentration and spontaneous composition requires an ability to focus keenly on each musical moment to enable the musical consciousness to navigate and oscillate continually between cognition and creative inspiration. In the arts, new vistas continually inspire the creative mind towards self-discovery, expansive modes of thought, and perpetual motion. Artistic expression is a powerful force capable of affecting human thought and behavior.

Creative inspiration should not be taken for granted, as it reflects that which drives and defines other cosmic operations. Robert Fludd's Mosaical Philosophy posits that "the eternal wisdom" is the unity or beginning of all things and that all things emanate from this fundamental source. Thus this wisdom expresses both unity and infinity. In music, the fundamental tone from which its related overtone and undertone series emanate infinitely and omni-directionally form a parallel configuration and process of eternal wisdom. Just as the light from an exploded star can be seen billions of miles and years afterwards, sound vibrations travel in a related fashion, if at a more deliberate pace. St. Paul considered this eternal wisdom the eternal One, "the Father of all, who is above all, and over all, and in all." Hermes referred to God as "an intellectual circle, whose center is all that which existeth and whose circumference is without and beyond all things." Solomon felt that divine Wisdom "is the holy spirit of discipline, which is the vapor of the virtue or power of God, and a certain flowing forth or emanation of the brightness of the Almighty, the beauty or clearness of his eternal light, and an immaculate mirror of the majesty of God" (Kepler 123).

Content is the primary focus for some artists, and focus upon form grabs the attention of others, but balanced elemental ingredients will capture the imagination of audiences. The aesthetically pleasing balance of a spruce tree and dramatic appearance of approaching thunderclouds during an intensely colorful sunrise both maintain constant motion and are intriguing, enlivening, and generative. Nature is never perfectly symmetrical but her approach to balance is life producing and resilient. Perfect mathematical balance and symmetry are inherently static by definition. Despite a static condition's theoretical existence (and of course knowledge could not be accumulated under stasis), absolute stasis can never produce life. Does matter generate the intangible factors that form the core of our inner personalities? Can music become self-generation without a composer's inspiration? Even with algorithmic music, a combination of human intuition and a computer's mechanical mathematic formulation is required to generate music's dynamic motion. Music is the accumulation of knowledge and wisdom, enabling us to reflect the nature of abstract balance to varying degrees. The artist learns to take the most basic idea, shape it thoughtfully and with imagination, then communicate the results with their heart, soul, and mind to a broad range of listeners.

For personal styles to be effective, composers must possess the ability to communicate broadly. Communication requires cultivating language. To create new languages, or extend older traditional ones, existing languages need to be digested thoroughly and analyzed intellectually and intuitively. Few people create entirely new vocabularies, but a few of the most powerful innovators extend existing vocabularies dramatically to create their own dialect. We can express ourselves, reason, and problem-solve regardless of the particular spoken or musical language we grow up learning. Any time-tested language learned diligently and thoroughly empowers the learner. In music, the broader the range of experiential knowledge, the greater our potential becomes for developing a musical style that will communicate universally.

Styles are recognized according to the distinctive patterns and nuances used to form a musical language. Although composers often obscure their signature patterns through a variety of melodic, rhythmic, and harmonic variations; through the utilization of timbre or voice exchange; and by amassing a large quantity of preferred phrases, certain characteristics of an artist's style can readily be distilled. We can gather important information about the characteristics of a composer's style by analyzing the nature of patterns in their compositions, looking at the subtle continuity and unification factors that bind their compositions, exploring the means through which fundamental musical ideas are embellished, and through dissecting compositions in a variety of ways to examine their fragments.

Joseph Schillinger was a professor of both mathematics and music at Columbia State University in the 1920s. His theory of composition proposed that all great works of music were constructed according to precise mathematical principles. Schillinger reduced musical composition to mathematical formulas and showed that tracing the fluctuations of a *New York Times* business curve on graph paper, and then translating the units of the resultant graph into proportionate melodic and harmonic intervals could manufacture compositions similar to Bach's own. George Gershwin was among his students, and Schillinger's mathematical system of composition reportedly figured prominently in Gershwin's famous opera, *Porgy and Bess* (Hammel and Kahn 107).

Nonetheless, not all people agree that convincing music can be distilled through a system of style replication based upon splicing together existing musical fragments of a composer's work from a fixed reservoir of musical ideas. Experts have resisted the notion that the human creativity that produces music composition can be reduced to simple formulas that produce "recombinant music." Regardless of the arguments for and against recombinant music, organic compositions and improvisation involve skillfully lacing together related intervals, motives, sequences, and melodic phrases. Tritones (diminished fifth or augmented fourths), semitones (or half-steps), and sixths (and their enharmonic[11] equivalents) are prominent as building blocks in the composition below (Figures 1 and 2).

Regardless of whether musicians are practicing alone in a room, rehearsing with an ensemble, or performing before a huge audience in a formal concert, creative musicians strive to make everything played technically, expressively, and logistically sound. Most musicians want their music to be aesthetically beautiful and meaningful at all times. As planets in a solar system surround their nucleus (the sun) in a precise order, so is harmony governed by the order prescribed by the overtone series guide melodic and harmonic voice-leading, movement, and construction. The gravitational force of fundamental tones establishes the governing nuclei and orbiting system of overtones of each musical system.

Figure 1.

Think harmony: melody, rhythm, and harmony are inseparable. If we consider creating a composition beginning with harmony, however, the system of tension and release suggested by various qualities of contrasting chords in a harmonic progression determine essential elements of our musical design. The pacing and flow of chord progressions determine important aspects of the mood and color, and shape the prevailing sound environment. Harmonic permutations produce variety through assorted combinations of intervallic construction and their related inversions and arpeggiations. Harmonic construction is shaped and evolved through the application of rhythm and melodic patterning. No magical formulas exist, but composers master harmony through systematic study, drills, and experimentation. As we develop our musical creations, therefore, we should consider:

---

[1]   In modern music, an enharmonic is a note (or key signature) that is the equivalent of some other note (or key signature), but is spelled differently. For example, the notes C♯ (C sharp) and D♭ (D flat) are *enharmonically equivalent* because they are identical in pitch, although they have different names and diatonic functionality.

Figure 2. "The Aquarian"—Excerpt (from the *Hesterian Cycles***)**

A. Do the particular chord colors and harmonic pacing of the music make people dance, think, or feel the way we intend?

B. Do you know where you are within the harmonic matrix at all times when composing or performing?

C. Does your approach to harmony involve an understanding of interconnected relationships between all chord families?

D. Are you comfortable and confident expressing yourself within the harmonic language you are developing?

E. Are you in technical control of your instrument so that you can effectively express your musical ideas?

F. Do you thoroughly understand the harmonic theory and structure of underlying your musical materials?

Contemporary Debate over the Geometry of Music

Symbols for music are all conceptual, so a variety of systematic visual representations can form the basis of musical approaches. The idea of foreground, background, and middle-ground planes enables the mind to visualize and separate dimensions of sound and musical elements. Often, once certain middle-ground and background compositional elemental features are established (rhythmic, harmonic, formal, etc.), spontaneous composers can create a more complex foreground within that context, adding melodic or thematic detail and embellishment. Musical motion (tones, rhythms, harmonies, etc.) can also find readily available visual motion to model and support as well. Kinetic elements of filmmaking, choreography, and an array of ritualistic environments have made good use of musical motion, and those powerful endeavors inspire composers.

A tendency towards creating virtual music has existed throughout time. A listener's focus is often directed towards internal and external repetition. To limit levels of predictability and monotony, periods of repetition are laced together with various transitional figures, scales, and patterns that help prolong principal melodic and harmonic statements. The assemblage of linked and interwoven musical ingredients can lead to formulaic approaches and experiments based upon probability in composition. In his book *Virtual Music—Computer Synthesis of Musical Style,* composer David Cope points out that the overwhelming access to and supply of musical information, and the ability to manipulate information that came with the advent of computers, has increased the capability to explore virtual music exponentially (Cope 88–89). Computers are, therefore, perfectly equipped to splice together a composer's signature rhythmic, melodic, harmonic, and textural stylistic tendencies, with features of a composer's tendencies towards certain permutations, to create compositions reflective of their stylistic approach. The subtle and expressive nuances of jazz and other improvised music may be less readily reproduced, but some subtleties and embellishments can be detected and reproduced by computers to a certain degree. Practitioners of experiments in musical intelligence are tackling related compositional concepts.

Most composers are aware of mathematical influence on music's multifaceted organizational and essential domains (proportions and calibrations of time, pitch, rhythm, harmonic, etc.) and, thus, often factor mathematical patterns into their musical thinking and processes. Serial composition recognizes the geometry of music, and some computer generated compositional approaches are more successful than dodecaphonic music at avoiding arbitrary genesis and, since the mind recognizes logical organization, computer-generated music is gaining greater success among a broad listening audience.

Musical style is a signature of musical intelligence and individual personality. David Cope writes programs and algorithms that can analyze existing music and create new compositions in the style of an original musical style. His primary area of research investigates the relationship between artificial intelligence and music. Cope's own work has encompassed a variety of genres and his Experiments in Musical Intelligence software has produced compositions, from short pieces to full-length operas, in the style of over a hundred composers. Most recently, his original compositions have often been written in collaboration with the computer, based on the input of his earlier works, as his principal creative direction seeks a synergy between a composer's creativity and computer algorithm. Algorithm involves a logical sequential procedure for solving a mathematical problem in a finite number of steps, often by repeating the same basic operation.

Experiments in Musical Intelligence (EMI) create new challenges to the ways that we think about music. If composers and improvisers use and reuse an enormous (but theoretically fixed) catalogue of musical ingredients and formulas, then computers can potentially analyze the stylistic parameters, individual preferences and tendencies, and various distinguishing characteristics of a composer's style and produce computer-generated music that follows their stylistic inclinations. Like the computer, composers too can begin with a fixed set of musical elements, forms, and systematically derived musical content and create "instant" compositions of both premeditated and spontaneous varieties. Because our minds naturally organize most experiences into patterns and because of our natural human tendency towards repetition in virtually all stages of the human learning processes, experienced spontaneous composers will usually create music that reveals a clear sense of individual logic through their patterns and repetitive sequences. Such logical structures in unconventional music may involve stepping outside conventional rules and standard practice. They may replace repetition of rhythms or melodic fragments with repetition of certain expressive, dynamic, or timber schemes. Wolfram applies a related notion to scientific inquiry to demonstrate how the mind tends to find order in what at first may appear chaotic:

> In the past several chapters, we have seen many examples of behavior that simple programs can produce. But while we have discussed a whole range of different kinds of underlying rules, we have for the most part considered only the simplest possible initial conditions—so that for example we have usually started with just a single black cell. . . . My purpose in this chapter is to go to the opposite extreme, and to consider completely random initial conditions, in which, for example, every cell is chosen to be black or white at random.
>
> One might think that starting from such randomness no order would ever emerge. But, in fact, what we will find in this chapter is that many systems spontaneously tend to organize themselves, so that even with completely random initial conditions they end up producing behavior that has many features that are not at all random (223).

Before the age of computers, composers often attempted to complete unfinished works of dead composers with a related analytic and predictive concept and approach. Some people resist the notion of any value of extending recombinant processes to a deceased composer's work. For example, Helene Berg suppressed many primary documents concerning Alban Berg's *Lulu* (1929–1934), including all sketches and manuscripts of the unfinished third act of his masterpiece, perhaps to avoid misrepresentations of Berg's musical intentions. Consequently, from the opera's 1937 premiere until 1979, it had been performed incompletely. Most scholarly analyses of the work had been based upon the notions of Berg's official biographer, Willi Reich, until the availability of the short score in 1963 to George Perle revealed a more complete insight into Berg's true intentions for the work.

Douglas Hofstadter, Director of the Center for Research on Concepts and Cognition and Professor of Cognitive Science at the College of Arts and Sciences at Indiana University Bloomington, is a major figure in the study of creativity. He and some of his colleagues have expressed his distress over the notion that recombinant music can "deceive" listeners with its virtual creative process. He feels that recombinant music merely provides listeners with diluted musical experiences, and believes that machines are entering into a domain where only human composers can truly inspire people. Hofstadter's position was clear when he wrote:

Here, then, is my opening salvo of quatrains in reaction to Cope's characterization of music style as patterns.

Is music a craft,	Might it all be illusion
Or is it an art?	From a practiced riff-boy?
Does it come from mere training,	Does music, like poetry,
Or spring from the heart?	Cry from one's core,
Is music just notes,	Or is it just splicings
Merely patterns combined	Of licks, and no more?
By a cocktail-bar pianist	Do the études by Chopin
With a wandering mind?	Reveal his soul's mood,
Though Fats Waller's ticklin'	Or was Frédéric Chopin
Suggests profound joy,	Just some slick "pattern dude?"
	(Cope 42)

While Hofstadter's whimsical poem may be entertaining, it certainly does not diminish the fact that great composers, of all genres of music understand the importance and necessity of repetition in music, and composers indeed develop signature phrases and sets of recognizable personal tendencies that become their trademark. These stylistic characteristics are traceable with the trained ear or with the aid of any number of electronic tracking devices. This in no way suggests that repetition demonstrates lack of ingenuity or imagination. Nature too uses repetition extensively in its own poetic form. Just as people express unique ideas through the fixed sets of familiar vocabulary, provincial styles of delivery, and the closely related grammatical structures of regional spoken language, composers manage to create delightfully varied musical surprises and distinguished creative work through the economic means of "recombinant music."

Some understand the basic implications of Cope's Experiments in Musical Intelligence. Despite the levels of genius that produce classic compositions, the "Geometry of Music" inevitably produces predictable outcomes. Nature employs recombinant DNA. Princeton music theorist Dmitri Tymoczko suggests that a number of related geometrical representations exist in music. He said, "It's as if we had maps of many small neighborhoods in a city, but we didn't have a sense of how those maps fit together" (Boyle). In trying to link these maps together, Tymoczko turned to a brand of mathematics often applied to the problems of extra-dimensional physics and visualized music as a lattice of points in a folded, symmetrical space known as orbifolds. Orbifolds are familiar to modern string theorists who have used music as a metaphor to represent its fundamental particles for years. Tymoczko uses the mathematics of string theory to probe the secrets of the physical universe and also applied orbifolds to understand the fundamentals of music (Boyle). Tymoczko devised an approach to representing the universe of all possible musical chords in graphic form. In a related article for *Time* magazine (published Friday, Jan. 26, 2007), Michael D. Lemonick discussed *The Geometry of Music*. In discussing Tymoczko's work, Lemonick wrote:

> When you first hear them, a Gregorian chant, a Debussy prelude, and a John Coltrane improvisation might seem to have almost nothing in common—except that they all include chord progressions and something you could plausibly call a melody. But music theorists have long known that there's something else that ties these disparate musical forms together. The composers of these, and virtually every other style of Western music over the past millennium tend to draw from a tiny fraction of the set of all possible chords. And their chord progressions tend to be efficient, changing as few notes, by as little as possible, from one chord to the next.
>
> Exactly how one style relates to another, however, has remained a mystery—except over one brief stretch of musical history. That, says Princeton University composer Dmitri Tymoczko, "is why, no matter where you go to school, you learn almost exclusively about classical music from about 1700 to 1900. It's kind of ridiculous."

Tymoczko feels that showing how compositions (from a range of styles) move through his orbifold spaces enables scholars and educators to understand how different styles of Western music relate to each other and evolve. In a related discussion of Tymoczko theory, Alan Boyle says:

> The same mathematical principles that physicists use in string theory can be applied to analyze a string quartet, a music theorist writes in this week's issue of the journal *Science*. He's devised a new geometrical model that just might serve as a "theory of everything," at least when it comes to Western musical traditions.
>
> The idea of expressing music geometrically goes back centuries. The five-line staffs used in musical notation, for example, can be thought of as grids for plotting the points and curves of a melody. Musicians have looked to the "circle of fifths" as a formula for understanding tonal chord progression since the 1700s. But lots of musical styles lie outside the classical circles, ranging from the chromatic sweep of Wagner to the dissonance of Schönberg to the fusion of Miles Davis.
>
> . . . Could Tymoczko's geometrical scheme open the way to computer-composed music that might surpass Bach and Beethoven?

" That's not going to happen," he said. "This isn't going to take anyone from being a mediocre composer to a brilliant composer. But it might help you get from being a beginning composer to a pretty good composer. . . . We're going to be able to instruct computers to produce musical results. At the very least, we won't ask computers to do impossible things."

Tymoczko's work managed to become the first paper on music theory ever published in the journal *Science*. His cosmology of chords, grouped into the multidimensional orbifolds, turn back on themselves with a twist just as the chords of the blues matrix fold back on each other. Lemonick continues:

> Indeed, the simplest chords, which consist of just two notes, live on an actual Möbius strip. Three-note chords reside in spaces that look like prisms—except that opposing faces connect to each other. And more complex chords inhabit spaces that are as hard to visualize as the multidimensional universes of string theory.
>
> But if you go to Tymoczko's web site (music.princeton.edu/~dmitri) you can see exactly what he's getting at by looking at movies he has created to represent tunes by Chopin and, of all things, Deep Purple. In both cases, as the music progresses, one chord after another lights up in patterns that occupy a surprisingly small stretch of musical real estate. According to Tymoczko, most pieces of chord-based music tend to do the same, although they may live in a different part of the orbifold space. Indeed, any conceivable chord lies somewhere in that space, although most of them would sound screechingly harsh to human ears.
>
> The discovery is useful for at least a couple of reasons, says Tymoczko. "One is that composers have been exploring the geometrical structure of these maps since the beginning of Western music without really knowing what they were doing." It's as though you figured out your way around a city like Boston, for example, without realizing that some of your routes intersect. "If someone then showed you a map," he says, "you might say, 'Wow, I didn't realize the Safeway was close to the disco.' We can now go back and look at hundreds of years of this intuitive musical pathmaking and realize that there are some very simple principles that describe the process."

The patterning of the Tymoczko Orbifolds is akin to the "Symmetries, Lattices, and Tilings" that John Conway suggests when he concludes in *An Introduction to Orbifolds*:

> When looking at an object (like the girl Alice in *Through the Looking Glass*) and its mirror image, you may be unable to distinguish between the original and its reflection. Similarly, a fly crawling on a brick wall knows where it is on its brick, but has no way of telling one brick from the next. The two sides

of the mirror and the different bricks in the wall are indistinguishable, or "symmetric."

Changes we can make that don't affect our observations of an object are called symmetries of the object, and they constitute its symmetry group. For instance, swapping Alice with her reflection is an element of the symmetry group of Alice's universe. By moving from one brick to the next, the fly sees a symmetry of his brick wall.

We are studying the symmetry groups of surfaces. These surfaces may include Kali printouts, the objects displayed by Kaliedo Tile, floors, walls, and furniture.

In the study of orbifolds, we identify ourselves with the image we see behind the looking glass—we stop distinguishing between the two "different" copies of ourselves. The mirror halves the world (if we extend it indefinitely in every direction), equating each point on one side with a point on the other. We only need to understand one half (Burgiel).

Figure 3. Tymoczko Orbifold Sample, with Two-Note Intervals on the Möbius Strip of Unordered Tone Pairs. "t" = 10; "e" = 11; Transposition Is Sideways Motion, etc.

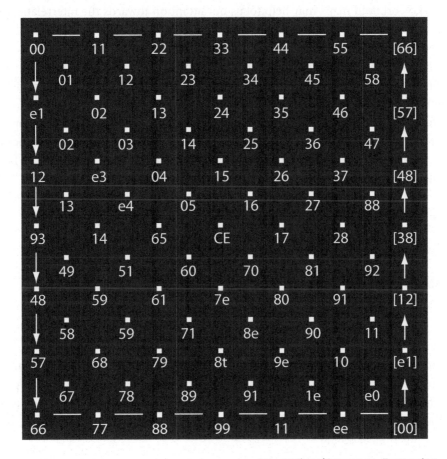

Musicians move between harmonies systematically in a kaleidoscopic matrix of related sonorities. The basic harmony of traditional Western tonality divides the octave into three- or four-part sonorities that promote effective voice leading between closely related chords. The foreground melodic notes on the surface of music may extend or diminish the harmonic implications and conventional patterns that reside in the background, but essentially smooth harmonic motion involves movement to closely related harmonic regions that are just one accidental away. We cannot replace the mind and ear of a great composer by programming a computer with either Cope's Experiments in Musical Intelligence (EMI) or Tymoczko's orbifold maps. Beautiful compositions cannot be created instantaneously. Tymoczko warns, "I don't want to sell these maps as the royal road to composition. They don't substitute for the hard work of learning how to move notes around." Nevertheless, most of the music that we create does have elements in common that are traceable through harmonic patterns derived from the natural order of the harmonic series.

Musical Tools: Interrelationships Between Melody, Harmony, and Rhythm

Tymoczko's orbifold maps may help focus our attention towards the interrelationships and interconnectivity to other elements of music beyond harmony. Music elements worldwide embody complex metrical schemes, syncopation, additive meters, polyrhythm, cross-rhythms, simplicity, and every imaginable permutation of rhythmic phrasing. No two cultures produce music that equally apply or explore melodic, harmonic, rhythmic, or timber possibilities. African music is more inclined towards reflecting the multi-dimensional tendencies in nature as implied by its syncopation, cross-rhythms, and polyrhythm. In North Indian music, when the *Sa* drone is sounded, the overtone series is evoked and many of the tones most closely related to the fundamental are sounded.

Figure 4. North Indian Music—overtones

During the late Renaissance, European composers experimented with unusual meters and polyrhythm as a reaction to the more inflexible nature of earlier polyphonic vocal music. Metrical experimentation was later abandoned during the Renaissance and Baroque eras. Mozart and Haydn composed the majority of their music, which was virtually devoid of earlier levels of syncopation and polyrhythm, in 4/4-time. The level of experimentation with meter experienced in medieval music did not return to Eurocentric music until the twentieth century.

A growing obsession with fixed harmony seems to have arrived just as the tempered scale came into widespread use in Europe during the seventeenth century. European composers moved increasingly more freely through a system of close-related keys to prolong their harmonic and melodic ideas. Beethoven and other European composers later experimented with harmonic extensions, with the rhythm of phrases, and other musical forms, but when emphasis shifted noticeably to melody and harmony concerns, metrical exploration remained essentially unexplored. Lack of attention to complex meter and polyrhythm may be due to a need for rhythmic buttressing as harmony wanders increasingly from tonal centers. When one musical element becomes more complex, others often counter-balance by providing stability through simplification.

Twentieth-century African-American music experienced success because it experimented with a broad spectrum of musical elements. Duke Ellington, Mary Lou Williams, Miles, Ornette Coleman, Coltrane, Cecil Taylor, Charles Mingus, Anthony Braxton, and countless other innovators explored melody, harmony, rhythm, form, timbre, texture, dynamics, and new approaches to cross-fertilized composition. We find related metrical experimentation emerging early in the twentieth century, especially if we carefully consider the patterns of syncopated accentuation of ragtime musicians (such as Scott Joplin and other early jazz composers) as suggestions of metrical complexity. In ragtime style, accents could be easily replaced by metrical shifts (that is clear if you add a bar line each time a strong accent appears) to achieve an intriguing and unpredictable poly-metrical outcome. Jazz fuses together many such overlapping and sophisticated elements of melody, harmony, and rhythm with wisdom that simplifies complex concepts, reducing them to their fundamental core functions. Saxophonist/composer Steve Coleman discusses related elements of cross-fertilization in jazz:

> Third stream is today widely regarded as an aberration, and I, for one, am unable to hear those two words without recalling the Mencken-like critic (and Bix Beiderbecke biographer) Ralph Berton's dismissal of the entire movement as Schuller and Lewis pissing in the same urinal. But third stream's legacy becomes staggering if, in addition to Schuller's variations on Monk's "Criss Cross" and Lewis's concerti grossi for the Modern Jazz Quartet, we stretch the definition backward and forward to include Scott Joplin's *Treemonisha*, James P. Johnson's "Harlem Suite" and "Yamakraw," Ellington's "Harlem" and "The Three Black Kings," Mary Lou Williams's "The Zodiac Suite," Tadd Dameron's "Fontainebleau," Ralph Burns's "Summer Sequence," Bob Graettinger's "City of Glass," George Russell's "All About Rosie," Charles Mingus's "Half Mast Inhibition" and "The Shoes of the Fisherman's Wife," Ornette Coleman's "Forms and Feelings" and *Skies of America*, Hannibal Marvin Peterson's "The Children of the Fire," John Carter's *Castles of Ghana*, Anthony Davis's X, Uri

Caine's Mozart and Mahler adaptations, parts of Carla Bley's *Escalator Over the Hill,* and all of Stan Getz and Eddie Sauter's *Focus,* Miles Davis and Gil Evans's *Miles Ahead* and *Sketches of Spain,* and Wayne Shorter's *Alegria.*

Give me a longer deadline and more column inches and I swear I could name a few hundred more, not even counting comparable works by European jazz composers or curiosities like Bley's "And Now the Queen" (after Stravinsky), Coltrane's "Impressions" (after Ravel, by way of Morton Gould), Art Tatum's finger-busting interpretations of Dvorak's "Humoresque," and Jelly Roll Morton's tip of the cap to Chopin on "Dead Man's Blues." In his autobiography, Miles Davis said one inspiration for *Kind of Blue* was a thumb piano he heard behind an African ballet troupe. But those textures suggest he and Bill Evans were listening to a lot of Debussy. It's easy to hear Sly and James Brown in *Agharta* and *Pangaea;* Miles said Stockhausen was also in the mix. When Wynton Marsalis first burst on the scene as a trumpeter with laurels in both jazz and classical music, he insisted on keeping the two apart, like fleishedik and milchedik. Lately, though, even he's come around, with unorthodox works like *Blood on the Fields* and *All Rise.*

Improvisers have also benefited from an immersion in the classics, even if their references are more difficult to identify. Jimmy Heath once told me that as young men in Philadelphia in the 1940s, he and Coltrane—aware of Charlie Parker's fascination with the European modernists—spent countless hours examining scores in the free library, looking for ideas to elaborate on in their solos. According to the late Roland Hanna, the early boppers were especially keen on Scriabin for his daring with flatted fifths. The bebop era was also when young musicians who already knew their instruments began studying the aesthetics of improvisation and fine points of harmony with private teachers like Lennie Tristano, Dennis Sandole, and Stanford Gold. From this it was a short step to homemade systems of improvisation, like George Russell's Lydian theory, Mary Lou Williams's zoning, Ornette Coleman's harmolodics, and who can keep track of how many others? Playing jazz was no longer just doing what came naturally—as if it ever was. Whereas pianists once swung the classics, today Keith Jarrett and Brad Mehldau often class the jazzers, turning unsuspecting pop tunes into Chopin or Liszt. On a brighter note, Ornette Coleman so loves Mozartian symmetry that he frequently sounds like a Texas bluesman wearing a powdered wig—phrased differently, "Dancing in Your Head" could be a minuet.

Fundamental musical relationships between music of all stylistic genres and musical periods have always been clear to some composers and performers. Regardless of the time or place a composition evolves, the principles of melodic construction and development often depend upon rhythmic, melodic, harmonic, and expressive variation that can provide interesting ways to develop a composition. Altering the shape of melodies and rhythms involves changing the sizes of intervals, length of rhythmic segments and motives, and altering the contours of melodic lines in both spontaneous and premeditated compositions of all genres. Basic determinants in all music include the careful manipulation of tension and release, controlling the direction of musical motion, utilization of dynamic contrast, and the application of a wide range of musical expression. Yusef Lateef understands that rhythm is an essential element of music because of its highly important marriage to musical motion and expression:

> Motion is the significance of life and the law of motion is rhythm. The musician must know that he/she has a sense of rhythm and that their rhythm is uniquely their own. To bring it to the surface they only need to search within themselves.
>
> In autophysiopsychic music [we] vary the rhythm of melodic lines. If the rhythm of melodic lines is not varied the music will sound monotonous and will have a negative effect upon the minds and bodies of the listeners. The whole universe is a single mechanism working by the law of rhythm. There is no heartbeat that does not move with the motion of rhythm.
>
> Another vital aspect in the application of the method of personal expression is the understanding and utilization of the emotions. When the emotions are faced fearlessly and applied they become tools of musical aesthetics. The highly sensitive musician must let their emotions live within each note of his/her musical expression. This is what is meant by the expression "you have got to say something." In other words, the skilled, adept musician must incorporate a proper balance of thinking and feeling. He/She must recognize their emotion as a natural phenomenon and utilize it (6).

Displacement of the rhythm of a given melody creates variety while maintaining melodic continuity. Rhythmic and melodic displacements are techniques that remove a rhythm or melodic phrase from its initial position in a measure or harmonic progression. Melody can be rhythmically displaced through *augmentation* (or elongation) and *diminution* (truncation) for subtle or dramatic contrast. Augmentation uses longer rhythms to express a melody previously articulated with shorter rhythmic values. It usually increases the value of the notes by a constant ratio. A compressed form of rhythmic displacement uses shorter rhythms to express a melody previously articulated with longer rhythmic values and is called diminution. Diminution's process of decreasing the rhythmic values also usually decreases the value of the notes by a constant ratio.

Summary of Basic Spontaneous Compositional Ideas

Chord qualities: The quality of a chord depends on the intervallic relationships between the notes of chords (root, fifth, seventh, etc.). For example, counting up from the root, a major third plus a minor third, plus another minor third forms a dominant seventh chord. Tonal music has basically three harmonic functions: tonic, dominant, and subdominant (and their related substitutes). Thus different qualities of chords with C as a root can fall into three categories of harmonic functions as follows:

Tonic	Dominant	Supertonic (Subdominant)
Cmaj7	C7	Cm7
Cmaj7($\sharp$11)	Cdim7	C7$\flat$5 (half-dim)

Modes: Modal scales can produce the following related chord qualities. Playing on one mode will produce a particular chord quality. A clear set of modal scales are easily derived by using the various white keys of a piano alternately as the roots:

- From C to C is called the *Ionian* mode (half-steps between scale degrees 3 and 4, 7 and 8)
- From D to D is called the *Dorian* mode (half steps between 2 and 3, 6 and 7)
- From E to E is called the *Phrygian* mode (half steps between 1 and 2, 5 and 6)
- From F to F is called the *Lydian* mode (half steps between 4 and 5, 6 and 8)
- From G to G is called the *Mixolydian* mode (half steps between 3 and 4, 6 and 7)
- From A to A is called the *Aeolian* mode (half steps between 2 and 3, 5 and 6)
- From B to B is called the *Locrian* mode (half steps between 1 and 2, 4 and 5)

Chord qualities match modes as follows:

- Cmaj7 - Ionian
- Cm7 - Dorian, Aeolian
- Cmaj7($\sharp$11) - Lydian
- C7 - Mixolydian
- Cm7 ($\flat$5) - Locrian

Cdim7 does not match with a modal scale, but is produced by flat ninths and thirteenths of extended dominant seventh chords. A Cdim7 is composed of the notes C, E$\flat$, G$\flat$, and A. Adding one note a half-step higher to each of those chord tones produces a diminished scale: C (C$\sharp$), E$\flat$ (E), G$\flat$ (G), and B$\flat\flat$ (B$\flat$). These added notes, added to the original set, form two adjacent diminished seventh chords. A related pitch set may be achieved by adding notes a half-step *below* that forms a third diminished seventh chord (B, D, F, and A^).

Substitutions: C7 - F$\sharp$7 and E$\flat$7 - A7 are chords with roots a tritone apart, and can be substituted for each other because of the principal common tones they contain, the common tritones they share. Such substitute chords are closer to the nucleus of a given harmonic matrix than other brands. The more "distant" harmonic substitutions, when systematically incorporated, gradually stretch the harmonic framework to a greater

Figure 5. Dominant Chords and the Shaping of Blues Tonality

extent. The flexibility inherent within a musical system involving chains of tritones and related seventh chords (properly positioned major, minor, diminished, and half-diminished chords can reach each other by changing only a single note, for example) that underlie blues tonality and form just a portion of the basic structure allows connection to an infinite array of harmonic and melodic possibilities.

Figure 6. Dominant Chords Substitutions and the Expansion of Blues Tonality

Tonal improvisations need strong harmonic grounding. Interesting composition and soloing comes from thinking in terms of varied harmonic pacing and skillful voice-leading, reflective of attractive modulating chord qualities. Neither strong composition nor convincing improvisation rely upon arbitrarily altering or adding notes to a chord or simply matching harmonically appropriate scales.

Eastern philosophy sometimes makes symbolic references to music that provide a thoughtful and helpful perspective. The Hindu trinity of Brahma, Vishnu, and Siva provides a metaphor for the triune principal functions of tonal harmony. Accordingly, Brahma, the god of creation, corresponds to the tonic function. Vishnu, the preserver, is the dominant function. And last, but not least, is Siva the destroyer, who is the sub-dominant function. The three functions can be thought of in terms of tension, release, and stasis. The tonic sets a home area (stasis), the dominant preserves the home area by always tending to lead back home, and the subdominant pulls away from the home area. This idea of tension (moving away) and release (returning home) is found throughout all music (not just tonal). And the number three is a very important numeric symbol throughout world society.

Tension and Release

Thinking in terms of "Tension and Release" provides an opportunity for artists to consider a wide range of natural and artistic dimensions. Tension and release, in its innumerable qualities, shapes, and forms, are factors that provide the dynamic qualities needed to provide harmonic, rhythmic, and melodic color and depth to musical ideas. Variety and coherence are basic to all artistic creation. Mixing qualities of the primary chords at the foundation of the traditional Western tonal harmonic system (major, minor, augmented, dominant, and diminished), and creating new chords that perform in related ways offer a wide range of ways to extend musical vocabulary while keeping it fluid, organic, and non-mechanical.

Each chord symbol implies specific scale tones and chord tones. Non-chord tones create dissonance against basic chord tones, even though they are part of the same pitch set that cause harmonic tension. A composer's need to resolve this tension propels the composition forward. Resolving tension, whether arising from passing tones moving between chord tones or by dissonant chords situated between consonant ones, provide melodic and harmonic oscillation. Non-chord tones in motion are referred to as "active" scale tones. Active scale tones aim towards target chord tones. Tension tones that are found outside the diatonic scale tones release additional tension by aiming towards diatonic tones. Nonetheless, final resolution still occurs when any action tones arrive at chord tone positions. Movement towards target notes often involves pairs of surrounding tension tones that can converge on the note of resolution from both above and below.

Composers also create tension and release using a *double chromatic* in a three note unit involving two tension notes that converge on a target tone of resolution from a single direction. *Double chromatic tones* occur when a whole-step exists between the initial tone and the third tone, the target note. The *outside tension tones* are altered scale degrees that resolve chromatically into the target note. In some instances double chromatic movement occurs when two tension tones of a three-note phrase move chromatically in the same direction towards the target note. There are strategies and resources that can aid the development of individual styles.

Developing a Daily Practice Routine

Spontaneous composers must hone their skills through practice. Creative ways in which melodic, harmonic, rhythmic, and dynamic control are developed are infinite. The practice suggestions and concepts outlined below form but a single set of introductory ideas to consider.

I. Developing Basic Tools for Spontaneous Composition (thorough aural conditioning and ear training) is prerequisite to learning to compose music in the moment. This process develops daily routine practice procedures, personal approaches to improvisation, memorization, intonation drills, and basic keyboard orientation. Such training is based upon an understanding of rudimentary scales, rhythms, and chords. Begin improvising over basic accompaniment, such as a simple drone or ostinato pattern. Use that initial musical environment to carefully explore and develop confidence and to foster a basic musical understanding of the chosen sound environment. Examine the implied scales or chords thoroughly before moving ahead to other more complex configurations.

A. Gaining an awareness of exactly how sound, dynamics, attitude, technical facility, etc., impact composition.
   1. Learning basic scales, arpeggios, and interval drills in all keys.
   2. Learning to hear successions of intervals through drills involving playing new and familiar melodies in various keys.
   3. Learning to create balanced melodic phrases through systematically shaping scales and interval patterns into spontaneous melodies while practicing them.
   4. Increasing awareness of ways that articulation, vibrato, stylistic "feel," phrasing, embouchure, timber, proper breathing, etc., enhance expression.
   5. Observing the difference between musical symbols and music/ sound proper, and the importance of creating new contemporary structures, symbols, and concepts to accommodate new musical times, ideas, and means of expression.

B. Exploring the significance of rhythm.
   1. Beginning with rhythm and polyrhythm as the primary basis for explorations of melodic, harmonic, and contrapuntal development.
   2. Giving "life" and expressive vitality to musical ideas through rhythmic exercises.
   3. Maintaining rhythmic consciousness (keeping your place in the measure precisely) even as musical elements increase in levels of complexity.

C. Exploring elements of style.
   1. Listening, mimicry, transcription, and historical/socio-cultural analysis.
   2. Analyzing articulation, rhythm, timbre, pitch manipulation, musical nuances, and other stylistic subtleties.
   3. Developing personal style and gaining control over compositional means through which generating a range of specific moods is possible.
   4. Augmenting, extending, or creating variations on traditional styles.

D. Exercising creativity.
   1. Taking a careful look at the holistic creative process.
   2. Studying movement, balance, contrast, color, and expression in nature.
   3. Communicating specified ideas, emotions, or images effectively.
   4. Maintaining focused consciousness, contemplation, concentration, and musical meditation.

II. Spontaneous composers should consider melody, rhythm, harmony, form, timbre, texture, and other elements of music as endless sets of open-ended tools and possibilities.

III. Stratification of responsibilities within ensembles involved in collective concepts of creations.
A. Develop collective daily exercises in the tonal tradition.
B. Develop collective daily exercises in the blues tradition.
C. Develop collective daily exercises in quasi-modal traditions.
D. Understand collective responsibilities that come with musical freedom.
E. Understand form involving the articulation of structure with flexible sets of musical devices.
F. Observe models of simplicity and complexity in nature and apply concepts discovered collectively.
G. Create evolutionary art that reflects universal dynamics as well as social and moral responsibility.
  1. Unity, balance, and empathy.
  2. Democracy, freedom, and self-expression.
  3. Respect for tradition but not at the expense of individual responsibility to represent one's own contemporary world, with the confidence to suggest (anticipate) the future.
IV. Other Ensemble Drills.
A. Mixing minor functions (harmonic and melodic minor scales, Dorian, half-diminished, etc.).
B. Mixing major (minor/major7, Ionian, relative min6, bebop scale, etc.).
C. Mixing dominant functions (aug7, dim7, octatonic scale, whole-tone scale, etc.).
D. Mixing major, minor, and dominant functions: Western music often uses ii-V-I or IV-V-I harmonic patterns. Explore other chord patterns that imply the initiation of motion (action), maximize tension, then resolve towards stability.
E. Apply all elements learned to developing a "tonal" *solo* performance on changes to "Bye Bye Blackbird." Mixing a variety of major, minor, and dominant chord substitutions to add variety to the basic harmonic.
F. Rule: Try to keep your practice routine an additive process. Keep all past and present lessons current and actively evolving.
V. Create a bass line from the following pitch sets and be prepared to accompany other instruments in your ensemble.
- Diminished (octatonic)—e.g., B♭ diminished: B♭- C♭- D♭- D - E - F - G - A♭ - B♭
- Pentatonic—e.g., A minor pentatonic (same as C major pentatonic):A - C - D - E - G

Intervals of Basic Scales

If you take the sequence of half-steps and whole-steps in the major scale and offset it by starting on subsequent degrees of that sequence, you get a set of adjacent scales (modes) that have ancient European modal music names assigned.

Scale Name	Sequence of Semitones	Associated Chords (in C)
Ionian (Major)	(2 2 1 2 2 2 1)	CΔ
Dorian	(2 1 2 2 2 1 2)	C-7
Phrygian	(1 2 2 2 1 2 2)	C-7
Lydian	(2 2 2 1 2 2 1)	CA7(♯11)
Mixolydian (Dominant)	(2 2 1 2 2 1 2)	C7
Aeolian (Minor)	(2 1 2 2 1 2 2)	C7
Locrian	(1 2 2 1 2 2 2)	CØ7

Note: In shaping melodies spontaneously with the Ionian mode, begin by leaving out the fourth degree. In Lydian mode, try avoiding the fifth degree. Learning a variety of scale and modal resources can help expand musical vocabulary and means.

Minor Chords and Scales

Major chords are more limited in potential melodic and harmonic variety than the primary minor chords (m7, m9, m(Maj7), m11, m6/9, and m6/9(♯11), m7 (♭5), etc.). The most direct relationship between the unaltered minor seventh chord and a corresponding pitch set is the Aeolian mode (natural minor scale). However, the Dorian mode is frequently the preferred corresponding pitch set for the unaltered minor seventh chord. The Aeolian mode has a minor sixth while the Dorian mode has a major sixth, but all other scale tones of both pitch sets are in common.

In typical minor keys that use harmonic progressions involving dominant seventh chords with an unaltered ninth; the minor sixth of the Dorian mode anticipates the altered ninth of the dominant seventh chord. The Aeolian mode functions best as a minor seventh chord precedes a dominant seventh with a flat ninth. The Aeolian is preferred in that harmonic situation because the flat ninth and fifth of the altered dominant chord shares that tritone with the second and sixth degrees of the Aeolian mode.

- *D Dorian:* D - E - F - G - A - B - C - D (raised 6th, compared with Aeolian set of tones, is B);
  - Dominant chord is A7(9): A - B - C♯ - D - E - (F♯) - G - A (tritone between tones C♯ and G)
- *D Aeolian:* D - E - F - G - A - B♭ - C - D (tritone between tones E and B♭);
  - Altered Dominant chord is A7(♭9): A - B♭ - C♯ - D - E - (F♯) - G - A

The raised sixth and the raised seventh of the harmonic and melodic (ascending form) minor scales combine upper and lower tetra-chords from different scales. In using the melodic minor scale the lower tetra-chord is minor and the upper major. When the minor chord includes a minor seventh, it is often best to treat the major seventh as passing tone horizontally. The harmonic minor scale can be an effective choice because the raised seventh is a brief temporary dissonance with a strong goal. The harmonic minor scale can function effectively in harmonic progressions involving ii-minor (Maj7) chords (minor triad with a raised-seventh), when the minor seventh chord serves as a tonic chord of the key, or over a minor ostinato bass pattern.

- *D Harmonic Minor:* D - E - F - G - A - B - C♯ - D (tritone between tones C♯ and G)
- *Melodic Minor* (ascending form): D - E - F - G - A - B - C♯ - D

Blues Tonality

African-American music reflects particular socio-cultural traits, aesthetic preferences, and other stylistic characteristics that are difficult to define or fabricate. A living art form deflects attempts to package its individual elements into homogenized packages and compartments. The blues is so evasive that its microtonal notes, like those of its African ancestors, cannot be realized on the well-tempered keyboard. Blues cannot be reduced to a single pitch set or fixed chord progression, and its rhythms cannot be written accurately with standard Eurocentric musical notation.

Blue Notes and the Target Tones They Surround

Elements of the blues are found within areas of the Sudan, Gold Coast, and various other stylistic regions of Africa. The African musician's tendency towards a process of arpeggiation clarifies African-American harmonic tradition. Tendencies towards heterophony and the parallel harmonic motion do not grow out of European rules of tonal harmony. Blues evolved from retention of African tonal systems that are not uniform. Within the West African regions from where most Africans were abducted, a large variety of tonal frameworks involving tetra-, penta-, hexa-, and heptatonic musical systems existed. Each musical system represents primary target tones, derived from a larger, more fluid set of tones (that include a variety of "blue notes" that embellish principal tones) that display the gravitational intervallic tendencies of target melodic tones in African and African-American music. The tendency towards resolution by semitones appears to be more African American than African. The tonal principles that perpetuate African and African-American harmonic traditions grow out of their melodic tendencies, and not vice versa. Therefore, blues harmony, as well as vertical tendencies towards parallel fourths and thirds in the brass or reed sections of certain 1940s swing bands, grows out of singular and multiple horizontal melodic movements that reflect certain forms of traditional African music.

> But if the blues really has so much in common stylistically with some of the musical cultures of the west central Sudanic belt, as discussed earlier, we should, as a next step, look at the tonal systems used in that region. According to A. M. Jones's "harmony map" and the results of my own field work in some of

these areas, particularly in northern Nigeria, northern and central Cameroon, the Central African Republic, and even the Republic of Sudan, most of this vast region from the Niger Bend to Lake Chad, and beyond to the upper Nile River, is an arc of pentatonic tonal systems. These are combined with unison singing (both in Arabic-Islamic and autochthonous styles), not excluding the occasional presence of rudimentary harmonic patterns in fourths, such as in the *batal* dance of the Chamba. In western Nigeria, the pentatonic area extends as far south as the Òyò Yoruba; in Dahomey (Republique du Benin) and Togo it includes the Fõ, in Cameroon some "grassfield" peoples such as the Bamum, Tikar, Vute, and so on.

In the region outlined, pentatonic tonal systems are in no way uniform, however; they appear in a variety of shapes, mostly anhemitonic, i.e., without semitones and made up of major seconds and minor thirds. Most of them alternate between these two interval types within the octave layout, while others—under the impact of ornamental, melismatic styles from old contact with North Africa—add a microtonal dimension to the pentatonic framework (Kubik 127).

Blue notes are not simply a specific microtonal lowering of the third, fifth, and seventh scale degrees of a major scale. Africans often consider the flatted and raised thirds identical intervals where a particular musical context or circumstance alone dictates the appropriateness of one over the other. The assumption among musicologists is generally that the diverse tonal systems that form African-American music conform to European scales and harmonic patterns. In actuality, Global African music is driven and governed more by horizontal concerns than by harmonic rules and principles.

Harmony Applied to Blues Melody

The banjo may have been the first African-American musical invention based upon West African models. Its construction reflects an evolution towards European influence in its eventual capability to explore Western harmony. The banjo eventually became the primary blues instrument long before the guitar was popularized. Accounts from as early as 1620 describe Africans performing on instruments made of calabash gourds as sounding surfaces stretched with animal skin. These early instruments had between two to six strings and their necks were fretless. Some of the names for the banjo were "banjar," "banjill," "banza," "bangoe," "bangie," "banshaw," and the like (Eyre 52). In the late 1800s the banjo began to evolve into its current round, drum-shaped form.

After the Civil War the blues arose as a distillate of the African music brought over by enslaved Africans and the new field hollers, ballads, church music, and rhythmic dance tunes called jump-ups that African Americans invented in what would soon become the United States of America. The styles joined and evolved into music for solo singers who would engage in African-style call-and-response with the banjo, and eventually on the guitar. Musicians would sing a line, and the banjo or guitar would answer each of their phrases. Thus the emphasis remained on horizontal aspects of music. By the 1890s the blues were sung in many rural areas of the South and the word "blues" was adopted to describe this unique African-American musical tradition. By 1910, the term "blues" was used fairly commonly in Eurocentric society.

African-American music eventually incorporated European-derived tonic, subdominant, and dominant chords to accompany its African melodies. Africans in America apparently gravitated towards revised European harmonic progressions that supported their melodies' needs and that resembled their own traditional harmonic functions. But it added a twist, a continual series of dominant chords (and their closest relatives) that led to a poetic twelve-tone chromatic series. The roots of a very basic blues progression in C are C, F, and G. If we tune the C major scale according to the overtones of C, using also the overtones of the F (a perfect fifth below) and G (a perfect fifth above) we get:

C = (1) C
D = (9/8) C
E = (5/4) C
F = (4/3) C
G = (3/2) C
A = (5/3) C
B = (15/8) C
C' = (2) C

Jazz flexibility is based upon the blues—an extension of African music that evolves from an abundance of tonal systems based on the structure of the natural overtone series. The overtone series does not correspond precisely with the frequencies of the twelve-note Western tempered scale. The of the overtone series is 31 cents flat (969 cents), compared to the tempered of 1,000 cents, and the E (386 cents), is 14 cents lower. The eleventh partial at 551 cents is exactly midway between a European F and an F sharp (Kubik 129). Building three seventh chords on the fundamental roots C, F, and G produces a pitch set reflective of blues melodic tendencies.

Figure 7. Dominant Chords, Secondary Dominants, and the Shaping of Blues Tonality

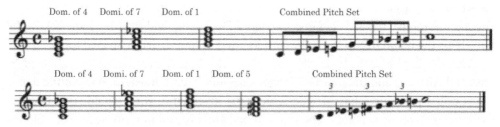

While some regions of Africa produced music with several tonal shifts, others were propelled by harmonic motion that seemed to evolve from a single fundamental of the overtone series with perhaps only a single tonal shift. As a result, the origin of the blues and other early African-American music required the convergence of an overlapping and diverse range of African musical approaches, retention, and cultural blending.

Thus, the blues progression became the remarkable extension of a single string of secondary dominants (and their diminished, augmented, major, and minor substitutions) in accordance with principles of the harmonic series that grounds harmony worldwide. Figures 5–7 above show how blues justified its African melodic tendencies through newly acquired harmonic extensions. The origin of those harmonic tendencies cannot be isolated to a single region of Africa. Africa is a fluid continent where trade and migration have remained continuous. Kubik says: "I am reluctant to associate the remote origins of the blues with those stringed instrument traditions of the western-most parts of Africa (Senegambia, etc.), where up to four tonality shifts can occur within a cycle. Some blues may have incorporated just one such shift, between the basic tonal center and a secondary center, a fifth downward (respectively, a fourth upward)" (130).

Figure 8. Dominant Chord and Its Close Relatives

Seventh chords residing one accidental away from the dominant seventh chord.

The nature of many African melodies usually creates what may seem to be striking contradictions that demonstrate the forced marriage of African and European musical cultures. In fact, however, the occurrence of both major and minor thirds simultaneously or in tangent combinations, and other related musical characteristics of African and African-American music, was neither a theoretical error nor anomaly (See Figure 7). If we divorce blues from its domain of origin and impose arbitrary tonal systems upon it:

> It becomes clear that each vocal line is an integrated, patterned whole, without any particular tones having special status. In spite of their regular use for accompanying the blues and early forms of jazz, the three common Western chords appear to be the real "aliens," although blues and jazz musicians have for two or three generations now internalized them. And yet, musicians in the Deep South and even in many urban areas have never seemed quite comfortable with these chords. Mississippi bluesman Skip James' "Devil Got My Woman" (Paramount 13088, February 1931) is a testimony for a radically different approach, even in the early 1930s (Kubik 118–119).

. . .Western categorizations tend to obscure the integrity of the blues singers' pitch resources and patterns. It is therefore necessary to abstract the vocal
lines from their accompaniment by instruments tuned to the Western scale,
and to look at the vocal lines and their tonal systems in isolation. The question
of what the blue notes actually "are" can be reformulated to discover from
what sort of tonal system the majority of singers in the rural blues proceed,
and where that system originally could have come from (126).

Many musicians and musicologists limit the blues to a simple scale and chord pattern.
Contained within this scale are tones referred to as blue notes in America. A set of blue
notes can be formed at the keyboard when the minor third (-3), the augmented fourth
(+4), and minor seventh (-7) are added to a major seventh chord. The resulting pitch set
gives the blues a unique quality. Playing the following blues scale played against a blues
progression creates a blues effect.

Blues Scale in F:

F (1) - G$^\sharp$ (2) - A (3) - B (4) - C (5) - D (6) - E$^\flat$ (7) - E (8) - F (1)
As mentioned earlier, a more complete set of blue notes is established when a pianist
superimposes one dominant chord over another that is a half-step below the principal
blues chord. In F7, for example, superimposing an F7 chord above an E7 chord creates
another complete blues scale. Thus a leading tone (blue note) is created for each pitch
in the fundamental chord (F7):
E7 (E - G$^\sharp$ - B - D) + F7 (F - A - C - E$^\flat$) = Blues Scale **(F - G$^\sharp$ - A - B - C - D - E$^\flat$ - E - F)**

Simple Blues Progression:

| F7 | C7($^\sharp$11) | F7 | F7($^\sharp$11) | B$^\flat$7 | B$^\flat$7($^\flat$9) | F7 | F7 | C7 | B$^\flat$7 | F7 | F7 |
In reality, the blues never limited itself to the notes of any single blues scale, and certainly
not to the even-tempered tones of the piano. The examination of blues solos throughout
the twentieth century show a full range of chromatic directions and choices available
for a variety of blues composition and improvisation. Bebop and other modern jazz
styles demonstrate a more uniformly evolved style of improvisation that expands the
range of colorful linear blues resources. The "Bebop scale" is just one of many blues-
derived pitch sets common in modern jazz.

Blues is the "double-entendre" taken to a high level of musical sophistication. The
discrepancy between Eurocentric labeling of Afrocentric practice prevailed throughout
the history of African-American music. The notes actually performed in the written
notation of either instrumental or vocal forms never quite coincide with the chord
symbols attached to them. Such symbols represent a set of harmonic and melodic potential and do not stand as a prescription for a limited set of fixed tones. African vocal
music generally does not rely upon fixed-pitch sets. More often seemingly fixed scale

tones represent target melodic tones around which an array of diatonic, chromatic, and microtonal notes orbit. This reflects the African tendency to emulate the flexibility of spoken language and nature's abstract creative freedom. This linguistic approach was transferred to strings, winds, (talking) drums, and most other African instruments. In jazz a chord written C7 in blues tonality implies the possibility of theoretically playing all inversions, extensions, and forms of major, minor, augmented and diminished chords, and altered scales meaningfully above a fundamental tone C. This harmonic flexibility is further extended by adding a fluid microtonal, sliding approach to melodic construction evident throughout African-American musical styles. This was clearly a part of blues styles from its beginning:

> The knowledge of the slider technique, inherited from central Africa, can be traced in the southern United States at least to the early twentieth century. W. C. Handy, who was in large part responsible for popularizing the blues during the early decades of the twentieth century, reports in his autobiography how in around 1903 he came across a musician at Tutwiler, a Mississippi Delta town, who played a guitar using a knife to slide along the strings. Big Joe Williams (b. 1903), another important slide guitar player, has stated that one-stringed zithers built by children in his youth "on the wall with a strand of baling wire, two thread spools for bridges, and a half-pint whiskey bottle for a slider" were definitely the "source of the slide guitar style."
>
> The knowledge of the slider technique may have reached the Deep South from various sources. One possibility is that it reached the area with the bulk of African descendants who were transported there from the eastern seaboard states in the first four decades of the nineteenth century, after the Louisiana Purchase and the Amerindian removal. In any case, some of "the more archaic-sounding" African-American music has been recorded in the delta bottoms of Mississippi, the swamps of Louisiana, and the canebrakes of Texas, "all remote, rural areas settled late in the history of the South," to quote blues researcher Bob Eagle (Kubik 18–20).

Bebop Scale in F:

F (1) - G (2) - A (3) - B♭ (4) - C (5) - D (6) - E♭ (-7) - E (7) - F (1)

Other common scales include (by intervallic construction):

Scale Name	Sequence of Semitones	Associated Chords (in C)
Diminished (Octatonic)	(1 2 1 2 1 2 1 2)	C°7, D♭Ø7, C7(B9)
Whole Tone (Heptatonic)	(2 2 2 2 2 2)	C+7

The symmetrical scales above provide the blues with added flexibility. The combination of assorted blues scales, chord resources, and microtones enable the spontaneous composer to form an infinite variety of sounds. Chords such as the dominant seventh with a sharp-9 (C-E-G-B♭-D♯) reflect the distinct African quality that defied European theory that early musicologists originally tried to impose. (Europeans who first wrote about their experiences could not understand why Africans played or sang both the major and minor thirds together in their chords.) In improvisation, focusing on our musical weaknesses to increase our technical facility, knowledge, and vocabulary is wise. However, some performers over the course of their careers will stay pretty much with a single musical approach or concept, while others will continually move away from their comfort zones to explore new horizons and styles, enabling their imaginations to constantly grow (such as titans Duke Ellington, Mary Lou Williams, Miles, Monk, Mingus, and Coltrane).

Hammel and Kahn feel, "Music is universal, crosses cultural, historical, and intellectual boundaries, and is grounded in mathematics. Mathematics is also universal, crosses cultural, historical, and intellectual boundaries, and is reflected in music" (Hammel and Kahn 5). In spontaneous composition, spirituality meets art and science, merging the ethereal and material planes of existence for some artists. Music ultimately reflects culture, politics, health, cognition, and other aspects of individual and collective reality. African-American sea shanties, field hollers, spirituals, blues, ragtime, New Orleans jazz, swing, rhythm and blues, bebop, cool, hard bop, free jazz, and jazz fusion reflect the times, emotions, and environments in which they evolved. People working on plantations, children playing games, religious practices, language, celebrations, and other aspects of daily life all contribute to the collective consciousness that produced jazz. The contemporary world's progress, ideals, subtleties, and restrictions are reflected in both progressive and "retrospective" music of today. Hammel and Kahn suggest, "And African-American jazz musicians used notes that couldn't actually be played on the piano—because they seemed to slip between the keys into cracks—called blue notes. When we write down the music of other cultures in terms of familiar Western scales, we are to a certain extent approximating and distorting" (44).

The Overtone Series as the Foundation for Blues

Exploring the overtone or harmonic series provides a path to understanding the unfolding of blues intervals, scales, and timbre. At times composers and performers explore the mathematical aspects of the overtone series to discover building blocks for musical structures that support their ideas, sounds, and melodies. Through a long span of experiences and time, Africans on their continent and in America combined an array of basic scale-generating principles. The overtone series was the fundamental source that was resilient enough to justify the musical convergence that occurred as earlier African cultures exchanged ideas, and also as a consequence of forced separation and combination of people and their music during slave era oppression and limitations.

The term "overtone series," the series of tones generated by a vibrating object and extending naturally above its lowest frequency tone, involves a specific set of frequency components. Although the term "harmonic series" is often used interchangeably, it is a related term for a more precisely defined mathematical concept. The term "harmonic series" specifically refers to a set of numbers related by whole number ratios, such as the set of frequencies (in Hz.) 1000, 2000, 3000, 4000, 5000, 6000; or 500, 1000, 1500, 2000, 2500, 3000, etc. The *fundamental* in the lowest component of the first series is 1000 Hz, while 500 Hz is the fundamental of the second series. The other frequency components above the fundamental are called harmonics, overtones, or partials.

We can use the physical model of a plucked string to help understand why a pattern of composite tones extended above the fundamental pitch is actually recognized as a unit. The monochord is a simple device composed of a string fixed at its ends, a moveable bridge, and a resonating body. Theorists have used it since the Middle Ages to investigate the relationship between string length and pitch. The monochord's string vibrates at a rate directly proportional to its length. In addition to vibrating over the entire length of the monochord, a string simultaneously vibrates over all the minute fractional divisions of its length (including 1/2, 1/3, 1/4, 1/5, 1/6, etc.) producing increasingly higher frequencies (overtones) that are inversely proportional (2x, 3x, 4x, 5x, 6x, etc.) to those string length divisions. Fixed ends of strings allow only certain wavelength modes to sound. The frequency of the fundamental mode of C3 (the C below middle C, 131 Hz) produces overtones harmonically related (they are integer multiples of the fundamental). Harmonics 4, 5, and 6 form a major chord. Adding harmonic 7 forms a dominant seventh chord.

Harmonic Frequencies	Hz	Note	Description
1	131	C3	Fundamental
2	262	C4	1 Octave higher
3	393	G4	A Fifth above C4
4	524	C5	2 Octaves above fund, and a fourth above G4
5	655	E5	A Third above C5
6	786	G5	A Fifth above C5
7	917	almost B♭5	

When any string, tube, or reed is excited to periodic vibration, it produces a low primary frequency of vibration (a *fundamental tone*), and a set of *harmonic overtones*. Violinists and flutists often play harmonics by suppressing the fundamental mode of vibration (fingering the fundamental or choosing a string that sounds the desired fundamental tone) and sounding pitches an octave or more higher. Describing how a flutist accomplishes this is more difficult than describing what a violinist does to achieve the same end. A string player uses their finger ever so lightly into the middle of a stopped (or open string) to divide its length in half to produce the node that suppresses the fundamental mode and sounds the octave. An *octave* consists of two pitches whose *frequencies* are in the ratio of 1:2 (fundamental: overtone). The upper pitch acoustically reinforces the lower, being a perfect multiple of the lower. We call such intervals a *consonance*. Modes of vibration are related to the nodes or fixed points of the vibration; that is, excluding the end points that are given. In the fundamental mode, there are no nodes. The entire string arches up and down with the maximum displacement from its position of rest being at the center. The maximum upward outline of the string and the maximum downward outline of the string form what has been labeled its "envelope of vibration." We can continue dividing the string by an increasing number of nodes, thus generating the overtone series for any given pitch.

The natural harmonic series from partial 4 to 11:

Approx. Pitch:	C	E↓	G	B♭↓	C	D	E↓	F♯↓↓
Partial No.:	4	5	6	7	8	9	10	11
Cents:	0	386	702	969	0	204	386	0

Blues involves an array of scalar patterns, some of which conform significantly to those found in regions of Africa outside the west central belt of Sudan. The tritone that results from adding a "flatted fifth" above a given root tone (or the sharp eleventh if displaced by an octave) is reflective of a melodic emphasis shared by continental Africans and found in African-American blues. Partials 4 to 7 introduce the first tritone (E - B♭). Between partial 4 and 11 we find the beginning of a series of tritones (E - B♭, C - F♯), and the number of tritones inherent in an overtone series increase as we continue to ascend the series. The blues begins with a series of dominant seventh chords. By the advent of bebop, the blues begins to incorporate an increasing number of tritones through the addition of chord extensions such as flat-9s, flat-11s, sharp-9s, sharp-11s, and the like. We will continue to discuss the overtone series in greater detail later, because it is the living extension of nature at the nucleus of music.

Nature provides models for building interconnectivity, poly-dimensionality, omni-directional harmony and solidarity, and it ultimately confirms that creativity is more enduring than destruction. Creative power creates levels of harmony that are much more lasting than destructive violence because creativity is inherently about building evolving states of solidarity. It counterbalances polar opposite destructive tendencies and other imbalances. The meanings of music and poetry are thus intimately intertwined. They both involve and engage the collective consciousness directly through the power of sincerity, vibration, order, logic, and motion. Since our minds are the governor of our development, capable of influencing our personal health, imagination, and destiny, music and poetry are among the most influential tools that people have that are capable of permeating our body, mind, and spirit to a greater degree than anything else. Because music's abstract meaning accesses our emotions and psyche in ways that words never can, its power extends far beyond the future, subsequent to the time in which its

Figure 9: Repertoire of Scale for Improvisation

Chord Symbol (5 basic categories)	Scale Name	Construction (in Whole and Half Steps)	Scale in Key of C	Basic Chord in Key of C
C	Major / Ionian	W W H W W W H	C D E F G A B C	C E G B D
C 7	Dominant / Mixolydian	W W H W W W HW	C D E F G A Bb C	C E G Bb D
C min	Minor / Dorian	W H W W W H W	C D Eb F G A Bb C	C Eb G Bb D
C ø	Half Diminished / Locrian	H W H W W W H	C Db Eb F Gb Ab Bb C	C Eb Gb Bb
C dim	Diminished / Octatonic	W H W H W H W H	C D Eb F Gb Ab A B C	C Eb Gb A (Bbb)

Chord	Related Scale	Construction (in Whole and Half Steps)	Scale in Key of C	Chord in Key of C
Major Scale Choices:				
C (+4)	Major (don't emphasize 4th)	W W H W W W H	C D E F G A B C	C E G B D
C (+4)	Lydian (major scale with raised 4th)	W W W H W W H	C D E F# G A B C	C E G B D
C (b6)	Major with flat 6	W W H W W m3 H	C D E F G Ab B C	C E G B D
C (+5,+4)	Lydian Augmented	W W W W H W H	C D E F# G# A B C	C E G# B D
C	Augmented	m3 H m3 H m3 H	C D# E G Ab B C	C E G# B D
C	Diminished (H - W etc.)	H W H W H W H W	C Db Eb E F# G A Bb C	C E D G
C	Blues Scale	m3 H H H m3 W	C Eb F# G Bb C	C E G
Dominant Scale Choices:				
C 7	Dominant / Mixolydian	W W H W W H W	C D E F G A Bb C	C E G Bb D
C 7 (+4)	Lydian - Dominant	W W W H W H W	C D E F# G A Bb C	C E G Bb D
C 7 (b6)	Hindu (one of many)	W W H W H W W	C D E F G Ab Bb C	C E G Bb D
C 7+	Whole Tone	W W W W W W	C D E F# G# Bb C	C E G# Bb D
C 7(b9)	Diminished (H - W etc.)	H W H W H W H W	C Db Eb E F# G A Bb C	D E G Bb Db (D#)
C 7(+9)	Diminished Whole Tone	H W H W W W W	C Db Eb E F# G# Bb C	C E G# D# (Db)
C 7	Blues Scale	m3 H H H m3 W	C Eb E F# G Bb C	C E G Bb D (D#)
Minor Scale Choices:				
C min	Minor / Dorian	W H W W W H W	C D Eb F G A Bb C	C Eb G Bb D F
C min	Pure Minor / Aeolian	W H W W H W W	C D Eb F G Ab Bb C	C Eb G Bb D F
C min (Δ)	Melodic Minor (ascending)	W H W W W W H	C D Eb F G A B C	C Eb G B D F
C min	Blues Scale	m3 W H H m3 W	C Eb F F# G Bb C	C Eb G D (F)
C min (Δ)	Diminished (W - H etc.)	W H W H W H W H	C D Eb F F# G# A B C	C Eb G B D F
C min (Δ)	Harmonic Minor	W H W W H m3 H	C D Eb F G Ab B C	C Eb G B D F
C min	Phrygian	H W W W H W W	C Db Eb F G Ab Bb C	C Eb G Bb
Half Diminished Scale Choices:				
C ø	Half Diminished / Locrian	H W H W W W W	C Db Eb F Gb Ab Bb C	C Eb Gb Bb
C ø	Half Diminished @2 / Locrian @2	W H W H W W W	C D Eb F Gb Ab Bb C	C Eb Gb Bb D
Diminished Scale Choice:				
C dim	Diminished / Octatonic	W H W H W H W H	C D Eb F Gb Ab A B C	C Eb Gb A
Dominant 7th & Suspended 4th:				
C 7 (sus4)	Dominant 7th scale, omit the 3rd	W m3 W W H W	C D F G A Bb C	C F G Bb D

artists originally produce their work. It is the universe that shows us infinite ways to be creative and constructive.

"What is most intimate to life is the evolutionary process, the process of creation, the performance of creative intelligence. When we hear music, we find that the background of sound is maintained and the foreground of sound comes up—some sharp notes on the background of some lull—maintaining the continuity of melody and binding together in harmony the single notes that come up as waves on the silent bed of the ocean. This is precisely the creative process. The wholeness of Being in its eternal silence warms up and produces the background of the music of life, and on the foreground of Being spring up the waves of relativity, waves of life. Each wave has a tendency to rise and fall, and in this rise and fall is the progress of music. The music of life is the rise and fall of the impulses of relativity on the background and foreground of eternal silence of the Absolute. So music reminds us of what one is; it displays the story of life. When one finds what one actually is, one is attracted to it. Whether one is aware of it or not, the reality of life is found in music, and therefore it is natural that music should have a universal attraction."

—Maharishi Mahesh Yogi

"Don't be afraid your life will end; be afraid that it will never begin."

—Grace Hansen

References

Bindon, Peter. "Our Nature with Nature, Part 1." *Rosicrucian Digest* 83.2 (2005): 17–23.

Boyle, Alan. "The Geometry of Music." *Cosmic Log.* December 2006 <http://cosmiclog.msnbc.msn.com/archive/2006/07/07/950.aspx>.

Burgiel, Heidi. "Unfolding Orbifolds." *The Geometry Center.* 7 Dec. 1995. December 2007 <http://www.geom.uiuc.edu/education/math5337/Orbifolds/introduction.html>.

Coleman, Steve. "Melodic Material Generated by Symmetrically Derived Laws of Motion." *M-base.* March 2006 <http://www.m-base.com/cnmat_ucb/Symmetry_Movement.html>.

Cope, David. *Virtual Music—Computer Synthesis of Musical Style.* Cambridge, MA: MIT Press, 2001.

Eyre, Banning. *In Griot Time: An American Guitarist in Mali.* Philadelphia: Temple University Press, 2000.

Feinberg, Saul. "Creative Problem Solving and the Music Listening Experience." *Music Educators Journal* 61.1 (September, 1974): 53–60.

Hammel, T. and C. V. Kahn. *Math and Music—Harmonious Connections.* Palo Alto, CA: Dale Seymour Publications, 1995.

Heath, Robin. *Sun, Moon and Earth.* New York: Walker and Co., 2001.

Kepler, Johannes. "Harmonies of the World." *Great Books of the Modern World 16.* Robert Maynard Hutchins, ed. 60 vols. Chicago: William Benton, 1952.

Lateef, Yusef. *Method on How to Perform Autophysiopsychic Music.* Amherst, MA: Fana Music, 1979.

Lemonick, Michael D. "The Geometry of Music." Jan. 26, 2007. *InsideTime.com.* November 2007 <http://www.time.com/time/magazine/article/0,9171,1582330,00.html>.

Liebert, Robert S. *Michelangelo: A Psychoanalytic Study of His Life and Images.* New Haven and London: Yale University Press. 1983.

Sadie, Stanley, editor. *The Grove Dictionary of Music.* Oxford University Press, Incorporated 2001.

"The Social Foundation of the Music of Black America." *Music Educators Journal* 60.6 (February 1974).

Wolfram, Stephen. *A New Kind of Science.* Champaign, IL: Wolfram Media, Inc. 2002.

Chapter Six
History: *Giant Steps*

LIFE on EARTH (The Progression and Evolution of Harmony)
The Earth was formed in the second manvantar, while the Moon was formed in the third. Continents came out of the oceans in the fourth manvantar. Vegetation was born in the fifth, animals in sixth, and humans at the beginning of the current seventh. So, human life on Earth is roughly 120 million years old (Smriti 26).

At the birth of every cosmos the complete knowledge of God is transmitted in wave-form and spreads out with the expanding universe (RigVeda 132).

"Living Space": Systematic Musical Organization

Existence began with sound vibration. Many of the world's cosmologies associate the beginning of the Universe with a loud, percussive, and unexpected bang or noise. Noise is vibration representing raw sound. Music inherently involves various types of sound production and vibration measurement, dealing with the calculation of pitch, rhythm, amplitude, and the other periodic phenomena. Rhythm involves episodic durations of all tone patterns and, although generally measured in linear time, the stratification of rhythm is omni-directional. Moon cycles, sap rising in the spring, and the pulsing of arteries in the body are examples of rhythms of life. Even before various life forms evolved from Earth's watery environments, gradual advancements in vision soon created an endless competition between predator and prey as both parties could now see who was approaching. The food chain symbolized the systems of polarity, tension and release, motion and stasis, and change extant throughout the expanding Universe as it forces dance for survival. A composition represents elements of this dance.

Rhythm marks the passage of time. Composers' titles often reflect the influence of astrological cycles of life and periodic metaphysical concerns. Prehistoric humans developed various socio-cultural systems and tradition often based upon knowledge of astronomy, astrology and a variety of calendric counters. People in various parts of the world observed the sidereal phases of the day, month, year, and the changing positions of the planets carefully. Astronomical events could be aligned with social history and then be studied and recorded by primitive historical containers and calendric counters, such as markings representing events on a stretched piece of animal hide; engravings or scratching on bones, stone, or other material; totem poles; cave drawings; notches on a tree branch; and various forms of ancient iconography. In time, more sophisticated calendars were used. Ordering cycles in sets of seven (days of the week), twelve (months of the year), and such have musical equivalents (triads, pentatonic pitch sets, seven- and twelve-note scales, etc.) that may be derived from archetypal numbers and are used socially to provide order in the most significant areas of human existence—those involving the passage of time. Eventually, many important cultural events were expressed through poetry and music as myths, legends, and fables, and evolved through metaphorical and allegorical forms.

Our consciousness provides the means through which to determine our own direction in time. As musicians, we demonstrate such choices in the rhythms we choose. This relative freedom of choice results from ages of evolution. Natural law inevitably involves processes and cycles of integration and disintegration. Evolution is predominantly forward-looking by definition, as the past helps to define the direction of the future. In music, as in nature, the creative process involves a systematic progression of events from fundamental cells and motives to larger themes, melodies, and movements. Single cell organisms evolved from their liquid habitat into jellyfish; a collection of cells that tended to move all directions at once. When the early eye evolved, to help distinguish light from darkness, its chosen location gave primitive flatworms a sense of direction, and the world's first brain eventually formed. When round worms later produced the first through-flowing system for the ingestion and excretion of food, all animals that followed developed related systems for their nourishment. Snails were among the first to develop shells (from their mineral waste) that served as armored protection from predators. Composers shape individual tones and musical elements into collections of ideas directed by a sense of evolutionary musical purpose.

The universe seems based upon order. But evolution apparently moves in spirals that involve some modified returns with the three-and-a-half billion years in the seas of life. Dolphins and whales, for instance, are mammals that eventually returned to sea after taking an unimaginably slow and gradual period of time to evolve from the sea onto land. Perhaps this tendency bears some conceptual relationship to the returns of overtones to the fundamental, as tones unfold and return home through sound. Throughout time great thinkers have pondered the relationships that exist between God, the universe, and music. The Stoics considered the notion of the inevitable order of the universe to be fundamentally rational. Their thinking related to that of the Roman author Cicero (106–43), who argued for the existence of God based on order found within the universe, a theory that later became widely used. In Cicero's *On the Nature of the Gods,* he states:

Our master Cleanthes gave four reasons to account for the formation in men's minds of their ideas of the gods, the most potent of these he said was the uniform motion and revolution of the heavens, and the varied groupings and ordered beauty of the sun, moon, and stars, the very sight of which was in itself enough to prove that these things are not the mere effect of chance (19).

All things that people have encountered throughout the history of human development affected the evolution of music. Music is a form of human communication and collective consciousness. After *Australopithecus* emerged through the evolution of mammals, African kingdoms, slave trades, and the Industrial Age eventually sprang into a world dominated by computer technology. But all such ebbs and flows that occur over millions of years operate within their own unified galaxy and are ultimately connected to, and reflective of, the universal "web" filled with interconnected continuity factors and balanced formulae. We have tried to make sense of it all by evaluating our environment through the lens of matter, time, and space. The concept of "Music of the Spheres," the notion that cosmic harmony reflects the bonds of sympathy that exist between macrocosmic and microcosmic elements of the universe, became a central theme expressed in early astrology and related philosophical writings. Those more strictly inclined towards empiricism generally disagreed with such theories. In Aristotle's *On the Heavens,* he disagrees with the speculation pervasive during his time with regards to the theory that the motion of stars, planets, and other heavenly bodies produces sound, all of which must be compatible. (In other words, planetary and stellar sounds were considered concordant just as strings on a piano resonate in harmony.) Aristotle said:

> This theory, in spite of the grace and originality with which it has been stated, is nevertheless untrue. Some thinkers suppose that the motion of bodies of that size must produce noise, since on our Earth the motion of bodies far inferior in size and in speed of movement has that effect. Also, when the Sun and the moon, they say, are moving with so rapid a motion, how should they not produce a sound immensely great? Starting from this argument and from the observation that their speeds, as measured by their distances, are in the same ratios as musical concordances, they assert that the sound given forth by the circular movement of the stars is harmony. Since, however, it appears uncountable that we should hear this music, they explain this by saying that the sound is in our ears from the very moment of birth and is thus indistinguishable from its contrary silence, since sound and silence are discriminated by mutual contrast. What happens to men, then, is just what happens to coppersmiths, who are accustomed to the noise of the smithy that makes no difference to them (19).

Human consciousness is like a mirror that reflects what we perceive with our mind (and from the thoughts of others) and senses. Space and time are arbitrary constructs. Our notions of space often reflect our inability to clearly discern all the poly-dimensional and omni-directional diversity, the range of spectrum, and complex nature of phenomena that exist within existence. Logical thought filters through poly-dimensional actuality to devise a more manageable and filtered reality. Creative right-brain thinkers are more prone towards accepting the complex dimensions that the abstract multiplicity of interconnected actuality represents. The mind oscillates between the poles of logical and creative thought, but research on brain theory reveals why some people are excellent inventors but poor producers, while others are good managers but weak leaders.

As we apply brain dominance theory to the three essential roles of organizations, we see that the manager's role primarily would be left brain and the leader's role right brain. The producer's role would depend upon the nature of the work. If it is verbal, logical, or analytical work, that would be essentially left brain. If it is more intuitive, emotional, or creative work it would be right brain. People who are excellent managers but poor leaders may be extremely well organized and run a tight ship with superior systems, procedures, and detailed job descriptions. But unless they are internally motivated, little gets done because there is no feeling, no heart; everything is too mechanical, too formal, too tight, too protective. A looser organization may work much better even though it may appear to an outside observer to be disorganized and confused. Truly significant accomplishments may result simply because people share a common vision, purpose, or sense of mission (Covey).

The brain is divided into two hemispheres, the left and the right, and each hemisphere specializes in different functions, processes different kinds of information, and deals with different kinds of problems. The left-brain works more with logic and analysis; the right works more with emotions and imagination.

Thus the titans of spontaneous compositions are those capable of balancing logic and creativity. They can create order out of what appears to some as chaos because they are equipped to work on multi-dimensional and interconnected planes. What some may label as "creative chaos" drives creative improvisation because it is governed by guiding structure that can be logically and spiritually motivated. Although the creative environment may appear chaotic to left-brain analysis, the right-brain thinker better understands diverse ways to manage operations; flexible styles of loose-fitting, charismatic, and democratic leadership; and a range of methods through which dynamic strategy and navigational music formulation occur. The key component of jazz is innovation, and the best practices aimed at this aspiration must evolve a systemic approach for discovering strategies that combine a concomitant development of technical facility, musical knowledge, and creative artistic expression. Once such a process is established through practice and experience, creating guiding structure for meaningful musical expression in any musical setting is possible. As musicians work collectively to build strategic alliances that build innovation systems for spontaneous composition, new musical languages evolve. Potentially, many cultures can evolve from the jazz prototype that sustains wide-ranging innovation strategies (for sports teams, business, and other social relationships).

Time is a digital measurement system that serves as a logical extension of the mind in an attempt to measure the limits of consciousness. Therefore, our mind, senses, and their extensions of consciousness provide us with an abstract and logical vision of actuality. The limits of such vision extend as far as our ever-expanding capability to peer beyond horizons into new vistas. As our ears and consciousness evolve, consonants emerge from dissonance and order from chaos, while perhaps the vibratory nature of the overtone series frequencies remains somewhat constant. Our perception of actuality may be as severely distorted as our body's image becomes when cast upon a flawed ("trick") mirror at the circus.

The Importance of Musical Beauty and Pleasure

A beautiful rose or sunset brings pleasure to sensitive beings and living organisms. A rose responds to vibrations of sunlight, moisture, and other physical elements. Pleasure and ecstasy involve immediacy. They exist not only in objective reality but also directly within the minds of people. Music functions as the most immediate of all the arts, and often closely aligns with ecstasy. Why is the music we hear more immediate than the art perceived through other senses? Music's vibrations impact our nervous systems directly, causing our brains to generate pleasure and anticipation through the aural symbols created by melody, harmony, rhythm, dynamics, form, and other musical elements. Emotions stirred in such a fashion provide music with intellectual, emotional, and psychological meaning. Each individual interprets the "meaning" of music differently. The collective audience arrives at a multifarious meaning to music that reflects the poly-dimensional quality that music represents.

Cultural conditioning can also influence our perception of the musical relations our individual ears sense and interpret. Beauty invariably remains "in the ear of the beholder," and certain musical compositions enjoy more universal appeal than others. However, no music either captures or escapes the hearts and minds of everyone. Musical preference is personal and intimate and the music that manages to captivate us enlarges our world internally and externally. It provides depth and order to the sustained beauty of our internal reality. When centered within ourselves we may begin to contemplate music's relationship to universal order and its miniature reflection of the harmony of nature. Hazrat Inayat Khan sums this concept up in this way:

> In a true composition a miniature of nature's music is seen. The effect of thunder, rain, and storm, and the picture of hills and rivers make a real art. Although art is an improvisation on nature, yet it is only genuine when it keeps close to nature.
>
> The music which expresses the nature and character of individuals, nations, or races is still higher. The highest and most ideal form of composition is that which expresses life, character, emotion, and feelings, for this is the

inner world which is only seen by the eye of the mind. A genius uses music as a language to express fully, without the help of words, whatever he may wish to be known; for music, a perfect and universal language, can express feelings more comprehensively than any tongue.

Music loses its freedom by being subject to the laws of technique, but mystics in their sacred music, regardless of the world's praise, free both their composition and improvisations from the limitations of technicality (163).

Freeing music from "the limitations of technicality" requires movement from the logical to the creative realms of cognition. The mind grasps music in the same way it absorbs and learns other aspects of its environment. Part of what makes us perceive music as flowing in organic and convincing ways is the application of similarity. Snyder refers to the *principle of similarity* when he posits that sounds perceived as similar tend to be grouped together. Groups formed by the principle of similarity, occur in both vertical (groupings of simultaneous sounds) and horizontal dimensions of music. As similar groups are formed into sequential patterns, modifications in their melodic contour of pitch tend to cause melodic segmentation into additional separate groupings, where pitches moving in similar intervals tend to group together. Events with similar *temporal* or *acoustical* qualities, such as timbre, dynamics, rhythm, and articulation, also tend to be grouped with those with related characteristics. Composition explores a wide range of principles of similarity as music unfolds with logic and organic continuity. Orchestration can expand the musical palette into additional layers of variety or similarity by including details of timbre. When instrumental clusters intended to be heard as related are grouped together using a particular set of instruments (French horn, flute, clarinet, or other sections of the symphonic band or orchestra) to navigate between elements of similarity and contrast, the results are subtle or dramatic changes in orchestration.

The mind thrives on tracking such similarities, and successful composers know how to guide listeners through a musical journey. Controlling elements of similarity and contrast help differentiate and navigate between the musical application of recognizable or memorable patterns, transitional material, and either subtly or dramatically contrasting music. This also requires knowing when a musical pattern ceases being similar to another. Such elements of musical architecture can be best exploited through developing an awareness of the character, range, and timing of musical similarities, transformations, and variation. Composers must realize that the closer together two patterns appear in a piece of music, the easier it is to recognize their similarity. Therefore, when two musical ideas exist in close proximity, the differences between the musical ideas can be greater while still recognizing their similarity.

The spiritual and mathematical fingerprint that music leaves is its veritable sonic DNA, the parameters of which can only be partially represented with musical symbols. Spontaneous composition requires exploring overlapping musical elements, qualities, and systems. Maintaining the obligatory and perennial musical orientation while improvising—a prerequisite of spontaneous compositions—comes from knowing the harmonic and melodic potential of every note played. In other words, to know where you are situated and exactly where you are going musically depends upon your knowledge of all possibilities inherent within the tonal, rhythmic, and harmonic matrix that binds a given musical environment. For example, an environment involving the C-major scale (Ionian mode) implies a related chain of chords: C-minor (the parallel minor), A-minor (the relative minor key), G-Mixolydian (dominant chord), and a full set of other related chords. Each scale tone is potentially the root of a chord or harmonic series. Chords within a harmonic matrix are first formed from pitch sets comprised of notes with only a single contrasting note from the home key. Distant related chords involve larger numbers of contrasting tones. Musicians must remain conscious of the nucleus of a musical region and all related paths that radiate from that center (C-harmonic minor, A-minor, G-Mixolydian, etc.). The nucleus of a musical matrix, in tonal music, behaves much as the alleged gravitational force of black holes that scientists speculate reside at the center of the Milky Way. The first primary interval to pull back towards the gravitational force of the harmonic nucleus (the root tone) of the overtone series, after the perfect octave frequency, is the perfect fifth, the interval found in the second octave of the overtone series. In tonal harmony, blues, and other harmonic systems structurally grounded in the overtone series, has bass movement that often follows the circle of fifths root patterns:

Circle of Fifths: C - F - B♭ - E♭ - A♭ - D♭ [C♯] - G♭[F♯] - C♭[B] - E - A -D - G

Figure 1. Simple Harmonic Matrix in C

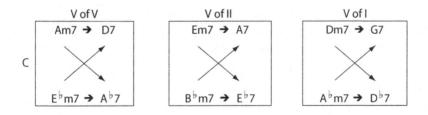

Matrixes and Balance

Good *voice-leading* is a consequence of smooth harmonic motion and vice versa. If Cmaj7 is the tonal center, for instance, then we can develop a series of harmonic road maps that connect closely and distantly related chords and scales:

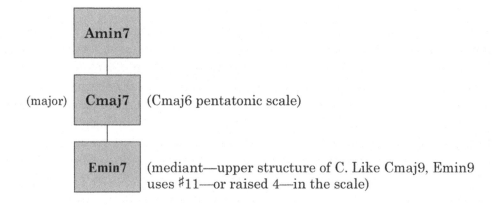

(major) **Cmaj7** (Cmaj6 pentatonic scale)

Amin7

Emin7 (mediant—upper structure of C. Like Cmaj9, Emin9 uses ♯11—or raised 4—in the scale)

Another matrix of harmonic movement:

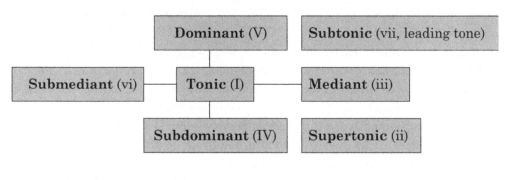

Chord Progressions

Although some early blues and early jazz progressions used variations of the traditional European I-IV-V, the more common sequence throughout the twentieth century in jazz was the basic chord progression, I-VI-II-V. As in traditional European harmony, chords emanate from three primary areas: the tonic, subdominant, and dominant. We can think of tonic as "home," subdominant as "movement away from home," and dominant as "returning home."

Tonic Region: In addition to chord I, the tonic area also includes chord III and occasionally chord VI. Since their roots are a diatonic third away from chord I, three out of the four notes of these chords are shared with chord I. Consequently, diatonic root movement of a third is considered a *weak* progression because a sense of inversion of the tonic chord exists (Cmaj7 to Cmaj6 in third inversion; Cmaj7 to Cmaj9 in first inversion—with no root). This close relationship allows chord III to often substitute for (or form an extension of) chord I.

Subdominant Region: Since the II chord is more common as a subdominant than the IV chord, in jazz chord II is the primary subdominant chord that leads to the dominant V chord. Chord IV is more common as a subdominant in blues chord. Since chord VI substitutes for tonic and subdominant chords, the application of the chord is determined by the particular musical context. Adding the sixth tone of a given major triad (tone A added to the C triad) produces a major sixth chord. The major sixth chord also contains all of the pitch classes for a minor seventh chord, where the notes in a C6 chord are C-E-G-A and Am 7, A-C-E-G.

Dominant Region: This region is governed by chord V and chord VII. The dominant quality of a chord is usually defined by the tritone (flattened fifth) interval that creates what traditional European harmony considered a strong dissonance in need of resolution to a chord that sounds more at rest. This is not usually the case in jazz or blues. Most blues progressions use a series of dominant chords that do not seek such resolution. The VII most often occurs as some type of diminished chord (half- or full-diminished).

Chord substitutions create variety, stability, and surprise. If music is too predictable it soon becomes dull. Substitute chords create unexpected harmonic action that makes music move more in accordance to the colorful, unique, and abstractly systematic patterns of nature. Under optimum circumstances, the tension and release created by chord progressions allows harmony to breathe and propels the music forward towards goals and resting points. If we think of the flow of music as being directed (according to their traditional harmonic functions) by a system of traffic signals, then the progression functions as follows:

- Green light chords: IV and ii—initiating action (leaving home)
- Yellow light chords: V and vii—cadences, halting action (heading home)
- Red light chords: I, vi, and iii—points of temporary or final rest (rest stops, hotel, or home)

Therefore, in the key of C-major, some of the most common chords (based upon diatonic scale degrees) are:

• *ii*	• *d(min7)*	• *Green light*
• V	• G	• Yellow light
• iii	• e	• Red light
• I	• C	• Red light
• vi	• a	• Red light
• ii	• d	• Green light
• IV	• F	• Green light
• vii	• b(dim)	• Yellow light

Jazz musicians tend to move continually through many keys, but the basic principle remains the same. If we extend the stoplight analogy to travel along the harmonic functions of the circle of fifths, we can journey as follows:

Cmaj7	Cmin7	F7		Bbmaj	Bbmin7	Eb7		Abmaj	Etc.
home	leaving home	heading home		home	leaving home	heading home		home	

Map of harmonic goals for a dominant chord:

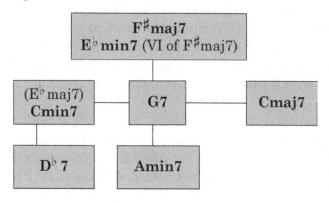

Closure

All elements (microcosmic and macrocosmic) need a sense of closure to determine their range, function, and other defining parameters. Closure in larger groups (such as phrases) usually feels more final than the grouping boundaries of motives or sequential patterns. Factors of closure can imply continuity or separation between all structural elements (such as relationships between sequential patterns, phrases, melodies, etc.). Since short-term memory is limited to retaining chunks (of music in this case), mastery of closure can be a powerful tool for composers. Closure determines the relationship between individual phrases in ways that help shape the overall characteristic of musical orientation, motion, and meaning. In most musical styles, traditional musical rules and learned behavioral patterns fix expectations of closure in our individual and collective minds that eventually evolve into a culture's musical syntax.

A musical culture evolves from shared experiences, situations, concepts, and practices involving music-related schemas and aesthetic values. These circumstances form a mutual context for the perception and understanding of music, that consists of a plethora of emotional, intellectual, psychological, and social factors that are tacitly agreed upon, most often without any formal cultural agreement. Although musical schemas are part of a shared musical culture, cultural participants still learn them through a variety of individual and collective experiences, from a mother's serenade for her infant to various forms of musical study. However, Bob Snyder feels that, "By no means do all the schemas that form a musical culture exist in the form of explicit knowledge" (102).

A number of factors contribute to closure and the specific layers involved in closure may occur at staggered or simultaneous intervals. Sometimes, partial closure occurs melodically or harmonically, while closure remains delayed within rhythm, dynamics, or other elements of music. This enables a composer to establish dynamic flexibility and continuity; to control the ebb and flow of surprise or tension. Closure is often established by silence. When the majority of parameters experience closure simultaneously, a more intense sense of closure occurs at the structural level. Factors of proximity and similarity in grouping apply to closure as well. Balancing the relationship between predictability and surprise helps move musical ideas forward in interesting ways that keep listeners engaged throughout a composition. Thus, repetition of previously introduced music generally is more successful at suggesting closure ("returning home" or to the point of departure) than the introduction of new musical material during musical endings.

Continuity

Composers can use a wide variety of continuity factors to bind a composition together organically. Spontaneous composers need to give all such factors attention when creating music. Flexible boundaries contain various parameters of music and help control musical movement and mixture. The identification and recurrence of a nuclear pitch is central to the concept of tonality. Such musical organization requires long-term memory to track and recall the strategic location of key musical tones. In Gestalt psychology, consistent (continuous) movement in a particular direction tends to perpetuate itself in that same direction. Likewise, in music, the principle of continuity applies when a series of musical events systematically, consistently, and continuously change values, forming cells of musical information operating in the same direction, melodic character, or intervallic size. Thus, relationships between series of musical events form groupings in ways similar to those in which individual tones establish similarity. A group of pitches will tend to form a melodic grouping while moving in the same direction in intervals of similar size. In this the way musical ingredients gradually recombine in the chemistry of music. Intervals with salient features in common (as dominant sevenths, their tritone substitutions, diminished chords, augmented chords, and minor seventh chords share features) also form groups. The resulting series can provide smooth and satisfying harmonic or melodic sequences.

Figure 2. Sample Harmonic or Melodic Sequences

Tritone substitutions—you can replace any dominant with another a tritone away:

Progression:	**Dmin7**	**G7**	**Cmin7**	**F7**	**Bbmin7**	**Eb7**	**etc.**
Substitutions:	Dmin7	D♭7	Cmin7	B7	B♭min7	A7	etc.

(Creating a new descending chromatic bass line: D - D♭ - B - B♭ - A)

The chord D♭7 (D♭, F, A♭, C♭) contains a third (F) and seventh (C♭/B) that render that chord compatible with its tritone substitution, G7 (that contains the same interval, F and B/C♭). Therefore, both chords share the same tritone, the most distinct and salient interval in both dominant chords. The combined elements of the two related chords foster an even closer relationship. For example, if we use the same pair of chords G7 + D♭7, they become even more closely related when we borrow one tone from either chord and add it to the other. Adding the flat-9 to either or both chords gives them more notes in common. In the following example the addition of flat-9 now produces four notes in common (reproduced below as enharmonic equivalents) rather than two:

- G7 and D♭7 become G7(♭9) and D♭ (♭9)
- G7(♭9) = G - [B] - [D] - [F] - [A♭]
- D♭(♭9) = D♭ - [F] - [A♭] - [B] - [D]

Borrowing tones from whole tone scales forms other close-related dominant seventh chords:

- G7 (♯5): G, B, D♯, F (D♯ is ♯5)
- G7 (♯11): G, B, C♯, F (C♯ is ♯11)

Chord Extensions

Compared to predominantly triadic chord formations of early European functional harmony, jazz chords begin with a basic seventh chord and extend them. When basic chords are extended, durable harmonic structures manifest and a greater number of chord combinations becomes possible. Understanding this complex assortment of harmonic possibilities is not difficult if you track these expansions gradually. Generally, two groupings contain most extended chords; there are true extended chords and altered extended chords. Some extended chords (unaltered) follow the natural construction of the original scale structure. Altered chords are those that use tones outside the original pitch set.

All implied chord tones are not always played in a chord. For example, the seventh and third may be sounded in the right hand of the piano while the root is covered in the left hand bass tone. The fifth is not a defining note in most basic chords and is often omitted.

Basic chords are extended to increase their density, flexibility, interest, and harmonic potential. *Tension tones* between chords can be attached to chords, forming new pitch sets. For example, the C9 ($^\sharp$11) chord (C, E, F$^\sharp$, B$^\flat$, D) can be filled in with tension tones (G and A) to complete a pitch set that aligns with the ascending G melodic minor scale (G - A - B$^\flat$ - C - D - E - F$^\sharp$). Chords can be expanded to their full extent to form various types of thirteenth chords. Here are examples of some fully expanded major thirteenth chords with sharp eleventh:

Figure 3. Major Thirteenth Chords with Sharp Eleventh

Root	3rd	5th	7th	9th	11th	13th
C	E	G	B	D	F$^\sharp$	A
D	F$^\sharp$	A	C$^\sharp$	E	G$^\sharp$	B
E	G$^\sharp$	B	D$^\sharp$	F$^\sharp$	A$^\sharp$	C$^\sharp$
F	A	C	E	G	B	D
G	B	D	F$^\sharp$	A	C$^\sharp$	E
A	C$^\sharp$	E	G$^\sharp$	B	D$^\sharp$	F$^\sharp$
B	D$^\sharp$	F$^\sharp$	A$^\sharp$	C$^\sharp$	E$^\sharp$	G$^\sharp$

Suspensions are tension tones that occur when a chord tone neighbor replaces an original chord tone. Tension is often resolved by moving the suspended pitch to a basic chord tone (1, 3, 5) or to a stable position within another acceptable chord. Adding the unaltered eleventh to a C9 chord (the note F one octave higher than the usual fourth position in the scale) generally requires deleting the third of the chord and allows composers an opportunity to create a typical 4 - 3 suspension. In such a suspension, the C11 often resolves to a C7 chord: 4 (F) - 3 (E), moving from a quartal (consider the fourths in the chord (involving notes F-C-G)) to a tertian sonority. The same chord (C11) is also often expressed as C^{sus}7 or, less concisely, using poly-chord nomenclature (Gmi7/C [bass-tone]). The 4 - 3 suspension is one of the most common suspensions in jazz and popular harmony.

The interval of the thirteenth transposes the sixth octave and most often occurs as an extension of dominant chords. This interval is never called a sixth while functioning as part of dominant seventh chords. Frequently the thirteenth functions as a substitute tone for the fifth of a dominant chord—G7(13): 1, 3, 7, 13, for example. The thirteenth chord is also a common case where both the fifth and eleventh are generally omitted.

The harmonic implications discussed above create a set of possibilities that can be arranged into systematic cells or simple Harmonic Matrixes (**Figure 5: Harmonic Matrixes**—see following pages).

Intensification is a musical feature that highlights and differentiates certain musical phrases from melodic or rhythmic groupings, at the phrase level or larger. *Intensification* occurs when several factors that distinguish a grouping boundary happen simultaneously. A multifaceted hierarchy of musical groupings (harmonic, melodic, rhythmic, dynamic, repetition, density, symmetrical features, climatic goals, etc.) is possible because music is multidimensional. The synergism that occurs when several layers of grouping stratification are collectively aligned vertically creates intensification of a higher level of grouping boundary than individual groupings. From a listener's perspective, heightened intensity involves change in stimuli that causes an increase in neural activity (Tenny 33–41). Increases in amplitude, and all other modulations in sound, makes music more intense and causes heightened neural activity. This includes elevations in pitch, becoming harmonically more complex or dissonant, increasing tempi, or through other such means. Other brands of related higher-level grouping factors surface when whole groupings are from horizontal *parallel groupings*. In other words, when related groupings of events are aligned horizontally, grouping boundaries often form in such a way as to connect their similarities. Instances of *parallel groupings* are clear at the ends of formal sections when cadences, phrase groupings, rhythmic endings, and other culminating features occur at ends of common forms (sonata, ternary, strophic, variation, etc.).

Secondary Dominants

In conventional harmony, a secondary dominant is a V7 of V7 chord. Composers use an altered form of the secondary dominant (V7 of V7) progression. For example, in the key of C, the ii7-V7 progression approaches G7 by Dm7. The root of such a harmonic progression in this case is the same as a related dominant progression (D7-G7-C). Because D-minor and D-dominant seventh chords are separated by only one note (f-f#), the chords are readily exchanged. In conventional practice, any chord that is not a tonic chord can be preceded by a secondary dominant. An advantage of changing m7 chords to secondary dominants is that composers have a broader choice of more interesting melodic tones, harmonic extensions, and alterations that are available to dominant seventh chords. A secondary dominant can also have its own secondary dominant. We could take the progression iii7-VI7-ii7-V7 sequence and make all the minor 7 chords a chain of dominants, temporally destroying the sense of a central key.

Figure 4.

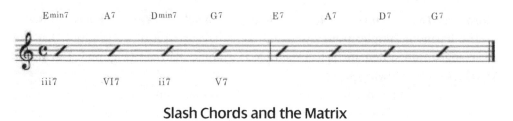

Slash Chords and the Matrix

Composers and arrangers often specify the bass note to be used on particular chords. A composer may want the pianist to play a G7 with the third in the bass. It would be written as G7/B. The "slashed" tone does not have to be a conventional diatonic chord tone. If, for instance, a composer or arranger wanted to hear a C chord with an "A" in the bass s/he would write, C/A.

Figure 5. Harmonic Matrixes

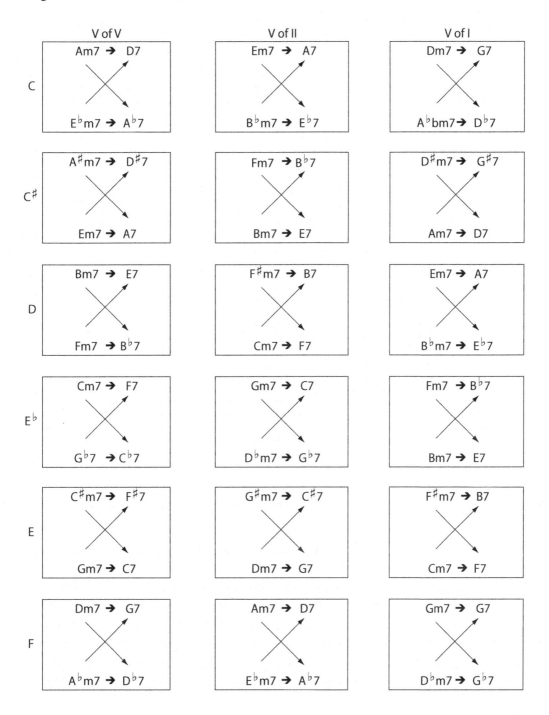

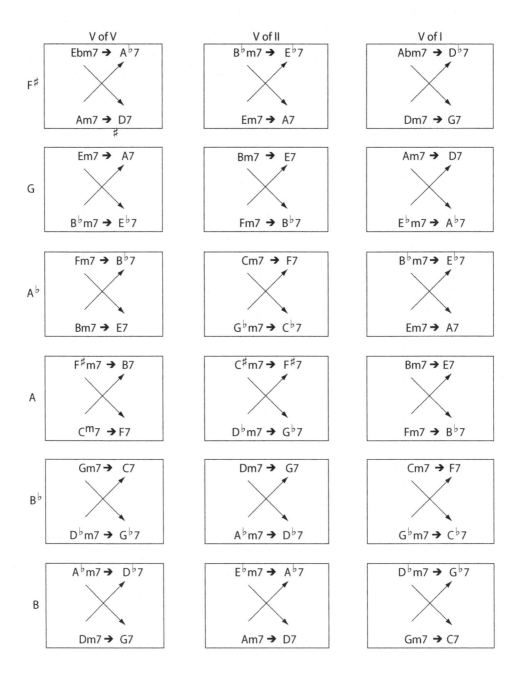

Giving life to musical seed (nucleus) ideas, whether they are on the harmonic, thematic, or melodic level, means devising ways to move, link, and expand sonic events in organic and convincing ways. Creating musical devices that provide continuous progression of tension and release gives life to music through a variety of controlled mechanisms. Musical mixtures involving consonant and dissonant chords direct motion towards and away from focal key areas, rhythmic and metrical development, contrasting dynamics, orchestration, and the application of new technology. On one internal or microcosmic level, connecting and lacing together thematic features or melodic ideas gathers smaller details into larger constructs and propels the musical movement forward. Controlling short-range goals involves first mastering compositional technique through an economy of musical means. Artists cannot develop long-range compositions before mastering smaller forms. The structural level involves the larger framework or aspects of skeletal concerns. Form provides support for musical detail, thus determining how melodies, harmonies, transitions, and musical portions unfold gracefully within a composition. Nonetheless, all levels of musical construction manipulate dynamic contrast, repetition, stasis and motion, and poetic variety. Composers constantly aspire towards clarity of musical direction and purpose as each gesture aspires to carefully distribute musical goals.

The spontaneous composer must cultivate the same set of musical concerns applied to effective premeditated composition. A good or poor melody registers upon the listener's ear regardless of whether a melody is spontaneously or premeditatedly conceived. All composers must balance a range of musical dimensions (amplitude, dramatic expression, rhythmic intensity and relaxation, etc.), a variety of motion (similar, oblique, contrary, etc.) to create powerful beginnings and endings, and other important compositional concerns. Spontaneous composition involves inventing new ideas while exhibiting careful control over each musical gesture, nuance, and movement from every note to the next most inevitable one.

Earlier we discussed the ways African-American music evolved with a tendency to flirt with all musical systems with which it came in contact. Jazz conforms neither to the rules of European musical theory or the strict traditions of African musical practice. Some jazz freely explores aspects of modified tonal harmony and modality, or vaguely suggests twelve-tone principals (such as the "twelve-tone walk" often explored in the progressive jazz bass line). Blues is "twelve-tone poetry" that emanates systematically from a fundamental tone through a matrix of orbiting journeys. Yet jazz is never governed by the styles that it chooses to temporarily examine and utilize.

In mathematics, a matrix is any abstract quantity that can be added and multiplied. Plural matrices involve a rectangular table of elements that may be numbers or symbols used to describe linear equations, keep track of the coefficients of linear transformations, and record data that depend on multiple parameters. Matrices can be added, multiplied, and decomposed in various ways, which also makes them a key concept in the field of linear algebra.

In music, especially folk and popular music, a matrix is commonly considered an element of systematic variations that does not change (van der Merwe 94). The term was derived from use in musical writings and from Arthur Koestler's *The Act of Creation,* which defines creativity as the dual association of two sets of ideas or matrices (143). Musical matrices may be combined in any number, usually more than two, and may be broken down into smaller units. They may be intended by the composer and perceived by the listener, or they may be purposefully ambiguous (van der Merwe 95). The simplest examples involve fixed notes, definite intervals, and regular beats, while the most complex given are the Baroque fugue, Classical tonality, Romantic chromaticism, and the Modern Blues. Blues matrices generally involve systematic arrangements of chords connected only one accidental away. Various matrices can also be networked. Coordinated matrices may possess contrary elements, depending on the degree to which they are interconnected or diverge, respectively, and whether they are easier or more difficult to reconcile. Matrices for African and Indian music feature more rhythmic complexity and contrary elements than European music that more often coincides with metrical beats.

The human mind intuitively recognizes order. The soul perhaps thrives on understanding the abstract and dynamic expression that nature provides. The body's small and gross motor skills are honed to develop technical facility on a given musical instrument, gradually enabling musical ideas to be expressed. The mind is the vessel into which endless musical content is poured, examined, and refined. Spirit may be the inner voice that receives and channels inspiration. Inspiration allows artists to determine general artistic purpose and parameters.

The Universe is an infinite series of omni-directional relationships that can be expressed through matrices. The human body forms its own complex series of interdependent, connective components and chain of events. Terminals located in our feet transmit esoteric vibrations of information to the regulatory pituitary and pineal glands. Transmitters in our hands generate force and information that govern activity of the heart. These systematic networks form a complex matrix that enables acupuncturists to locate and stimulate nerve centers in one part of the body that affect functions in another related sector. Order can form a reliable path to musical freedom. Form and order are not only limits that bind ideas within discernable laws and boundaries; they produce systematic matrixes that can also serve as road maps to infinite (but disciplined) freedom. The blues matrix functions in a similar fashion. Scales and chords in one region are intimately connected to remote harmonic and melodic material in other distant areas. Manipulation of any chord or scale affects its relationship to everything around it. Today's digital rendering capabilities allow us to visualize musical relationships more appropriately in double, three dimensional, spherical helix, and other matrix designs. A musical matrix can display the systematic interconnectedness between musical elements of a system.

All spontaneous composers use matrices to organize their thinking and procedures in ways that can enable them to take seemingly mundane source material and create magical, musical series of sounds. Moving within systems of dynamic interconnectivity (such as the Worldwide Web) seems reflective of the universe's own methods and processes. The endless array of symmetrical and asymmetrical "rows" of musical resources and material stored in the mind of a seasoned musician can weave skillfully into ordered systems. Just as grains of sand form beautiful patterns spontaneously around an invisible nucleus when vibrated upon a sheet of metal (by using a violin bow to vibrate the sheet of metal), or just as planets and moons vibrate and revolve around a sun in solar systems with precision, ordered musical patterning forms complex and beautiful mandallas around fundamental source material.

The blues matrix is a systematic way to unite musical materials organically, and to develop a means of expressive communication through navigating its language. Thus, the blues matrix is like a tree with deep running roots. Each branch, leaf, and root stem is interconnected but unique. Collectively they form a single manifestation with a unified source, grounding, origin, destiny, and purpose. We might think of the roots of a tree as reflective undertones of an overtone series; while the leaves and branches are its overtones, the trunk can represent the "perfect intervals" that join its radiating aspects. A tree just has "to be" a tree.

Societies worldwide seem to land on related ways of ordering and measuring the affairs of human activity. From the ancient prime numbers 1, 2, 3, 5, and 7, mathematicians have structured operations (base 10, base 12, etc.) that correlate with elements of basic musical theoretical organization and the patterning of our daily lives. The numbers 1 (unity), 2 (duality), 3 (trinity), 4 (Zodiac's grouping of Cardinal Signs), etc., provide the structural basis for many basic units of measurements and order that we use daily. Our various chromatic, twelve-tone, quartal, pentatonic, whole-tone, diatonic, octatonic, and other linear and horizontal musical units and patterns fit snugly into the ordering we find throughout the histories of human societies.

More Exercises in Building Melodic and Harmonic Vocabulary

Developing a melodic, harmonic, and rhythmic vocabulary for spontaneous composition requires gradually acquiring an enormous backlog of musical memory. Scales and chord patterns must be practiced diligently in all permutations. Once basic scale and chord patterns are thoroughly absorbed, new and more interesting patterns are formed by combining elements of contrasting scales and chords to create new configurations (combining features of augmented and diminished chords, or recombining upper and lower tetrachords from contrasting scales to find new pitch-sets, for example).

The exercises in the appendix are intended to stimulate thinking along the lines of motivic and melodic development. Rather than thinking of a melody or motive as a one-dimensional unit or fixed set (consisting only of linear features), composers should think of new ways to combine musical qualities to form a new developmental cell (new scales, pitch sets, and chords). Scale and chord qualities, such as diminished, augmented, major, and minor, can be mixed with assorted directional (ascending or descending), qualitative (rounded, balanced, etc.), and other new features. After all examples are thoroughly understood and mastered, your own ways to approach creating binary cells will emerge.

To begin shaping the minds and ears of spontaneous composers, students need talent, opportunity (which includes access to musical resources), practice, and patience (TOPP). Moving to higher levels of development requires expert mentoring, focus upon artistic originality, tenacity, and time (MOTT). Emerging artists have their own set of personal musical problems to solve. Besides a host of artistic problems, finding ways to create ample meditation, contemplation, practice, and study time is a constant challenge for all musicians.

"Manifestation": Music and Language

Music has power to move us emotionally—in battle, in love, in grief—and to communicate with children too young for spoken language. Its power was highly revered, recognized, and explored in the ancient cultures of China, India, Egypt, Kush, Sumer, and Greece. The ancients felt that music governed the heavenly bodies and that its vibrations brought creation into being. Its healing power was greatly respected. The history of the ancient world was preserved in the chants of myth and poetry.

Music, spoken word, non-verbal (gestures, body language, eye contact, etc.), or any other form of communication requires that its particular factors of transmission be agreed upon in meaning by members of a particular community. Conveying meaning and ideas is thus a systematic means of communicating using sounds, conventional symbols, physical motion (including but not limited to sign languages or other gesturing), and other familiar and subtle modes of communicating thoughts and concepts.

Music and language communicate ideas, emotions, and descriptive information through sound vibrations that ultimately serve to chronicle the cultural and social history of human development and the environment in which people live. Reducing music and language to mere displays of mastery of rules, patterns, and the development of technique minimizes their inherent communicative power and influence. Musical expression most often operates in multidimensional forms.

We continually explore the ways music serves as a vehicle through which personal, aesthetic, spiritual, and emotional experience unfolds. Music may reflect humankind's most intimate study and application of vibration. (Verse two of the King James Bible reads, "And the Spirit of God moved upon the face of the water"). Some musicians feel that each cell of musical expression extends in helical patterns that radiate from a fundamental spiritual vibration. Regardless of the source from which music proliferates, its most enduring features tend to leave indelible marks on the heart, body, and memory of listeners. Composers succeed when a specific emotion, purpose, or directive that motivates a given composition achieves its communicative objective. Ellington's composition "Take the 'A' Train" virtually transports the listener onto that perpetual New York City vehicle. The listener's mind supplies the specific physical, intellectual, and emotional details that complete the musical picture.

Spontaneous composers often work in interdisciplinary settings that include other visual arts in actual and virtual space. Music depends heavily upon actual and abstract time. The language of music forms temporal sequences that we attempt to express in written and aural symbols that create artificial temporal relationships between tones and musical images. Poetry comes to life through arbitrary symbols that affect the souls of readers and listeners. Each art form wields a force that combines with space and time to suggest metaphysical and mathematical laws that people learn to comprehend and appreciate over time. Combining multiple artistic languages in interdisciplinary presentations is potentially stimulating and powerful. Managing the merger of disparate artistic forms requires the skillful hands and ears of the artists involved.

Scales and chords have distinct musical characteristics to which people attach particular meanings, moods, and an infinite array of associations. Minor chords, and their corresponding scales (Aeolian, Dorian, minor pentatonic, etc.), create musical patterns that are often connected to more subdued or somber emotions. The particular nature of a performer's tone (whether it sounds relaxed, tense, clear, controlled, flexible, etc.) helps define the impression or meaning of a musical moment. The ability to make musical ideas sing and flow involves experienced ears, compassion, and practice. Just as sole reliance upon a mechanical approach to practicing etudes and scalar patterns potentially leads to mechanical performance of compositions, the opposite can also be true. To avoid rudimentary sounding performances musicians can design daily musical drills that bring scales, arpeggios, and etudes to life, thus transforming scales and modal resources into melody and song through thoughtful phrasing, applying dynamic contrast, and using skillfully mixed articulation to shape and vary otherwise routine patterns and sequences.

Tension and relaxation inherent in African-American musical style is largely a consequence of its syncopated rhythms, or the accents on portions of beats that oppose the prevailing meter. This creates momentary contradiction of the prevailing pulse that is intriguing and stimulating. The temporary transformation of the fundamental character of the meter that occurs, or contradiction of the regular succession of strong and weak beats within a suggested metrical context, does not completely displace the prevailing meter despite the virtual effect of abruptly shifting the bar lines. Avoiding rhythmic monotony helps actively engage the listener.

In constructing syncopated melodies, phrases have a sense of buoyancy as though they oppose a gravitational force (the down beat) and sustain this sense of suspension indefinitely. In shaping syncopated melodies, musicians often start somewhere other than on the beat. For best effect, students can begin a phrase on the "e," the "and," or on the "a" of the beat (anyplace other than on the beat) and end phrases likewise.[11] This approach creates a feeling that phrases continue their train of thought in the musical conversation. Students should examine the rhythms of their melodies to determine if they are interesting, varied, and strong in their effect independent of tone and melodic contour (that is, when divorced of pitch content).

Figure 6. Syncopated Phrasing

---

[1] This refers to the method of subdividing a beat (in duple meter, for instance) into four parts: 1-e-&-a, 2-e-&-a, etc.

Musicians often practice everything at a variety of tempos, dynamic levels, and in various styles while carefully and gradually developing ever more–thematic compositions. Maintaining interest, variety, and intensity at the slow tempos is particularly challenging. Conversely, developing individual style and cogent musical ideas at faster tempos first requires a command over a rich palette of musical resources, and mastery of musical resources at slower paces, before spontaneous solos can acquire and display rich musical integrity. Beginning with simple ideas and gradually adding increasingly more demanding layers of embellishments and musical development is one way to maintain sure-footed musical construction as a spontaneous composition unfolds.

When composing spontaneously as an ensemble, the stratification of various musical levels (foreground, middle-ground, and background) and musical roles (soloist, colorist, accompanist, etc.) ideally remain somewhat flexible and clearly defined. Excessive volume should never force fellow musicians to cut through walls of high-level amplitude because certain instruments are inherently louder or powered by large amplifiers. Applying principles of empathy, balance, and proportion to group spontaneous composition is especially important.

Cecil Taylor

Some artists' work is so unique that it falls between all prevailing stylistic categories. The music of Cecil Taylor is worthy of close analysis for those up to the task of first transcribing it. When he came onto the jazz scene, music like Taylor's did not exist anywhere in the world. His iconoclastic approach to composition is still grounded in musical concerns that support more conventional styles.

Cecil Taylor's music has at its fundamental core the *"mores* and folkways of Negroes," which his self-investigation also reflects. Taylor's application of "African methodological concept" (Figi 31), combined with elements of Western European music, gained especially while attending the New England Conservatory of music in the early fifties, creates a unique blend in his personal style. He could not study composition at the conservatory because "the department head . . . figured that he already had one Negro [composition student], and that was enough" (Spellman 55). Taylor responded proactively to the blatant racism of that academic experience: "That meant that to me that I had to be black if for no other reason than that they thought that black was bad" (Spellman 55). Nevertheless, in the end, his music fell into neither preexisting Afrocentric nor Eurocentric stylistic patterns. Taylor's convictions conspicuously shaped his approach to freedom.

One of the most important things an artist can achieve is to develop his or her own personal style. If developing a unique and individual voice within a rich tradition of musical innovation and experimentation is the primordial criteria for jazz, then Cecil Taylor is summarily qualified to serve as a sample of unique approach and style. Taylor's approach to composing epitomizes making music to fit one's own vision, using an ample application of symmetry as a unifying device. In the 1970 publication of the book *Jazz People* by Valerie Wilmer, the author describes Taylor as, "A genius whose work is the jazz, or black music, equivalent of straight composers like Bartok" (203). One of Taylor's most memorable quotes is: "The thing that makes jazz so interesting is that each man [woman] is his [her] own academy. . . . If he's [she's] really going to be persuasive, he [she] learns about other academies, but the idea is that he [she] must have that special thing. And sometimes you don't even know what it is." Taylor always chooses to view the world strictly through his own eyes. If one listens to anything from Mr. Taylor's discography it is clear that he has always been his own musical personality and his music is always grounded in solid preparation.

Born in Long Island City in 1933, Cecil Taylor's uncle led him to stride pianists such as Fats Waller at an early age. His mother grew up with Sonny Greer (Duke Ellington's Drummer), and Taylor certainly was influenced by such sumptuous domestic circumstances, but his influences are much broader than that. Taylor also graduated from the New England Conservatory of Music in Boston before returning to New York to launch a career at a time when work for pianists in clubs was scarce. Wilmer mentions the bitter irony of the most difficult times when Taylor worked in a restaurant as a dishwasher, while his records were played in the dining room along with those of Ornette Coleman and John Coltrane.

Intense and focused practice quickly led Taylor out of that dire situation into the controversial role of an uncompromising pianist and composer who, along with Ornette Coleman, Albert Ayler, and other innovators, split the international jazz community evenly between those who recognized the significance of their contribution and those who clung to well-worn standards of the past. As with all things of authentic and lasting value, however, each of these artists eventually received just recognition. Ayler did not live long enough to witness the full benefit of such recognition, but both Taylor and Coleman have received the prestigious MacArthur Genius Award and have ever-expanding audiences for their music.

Although the misappropriation of African culture has been charged to racist oppression in America, the appropriation of all musical elements in the surrounding environment is part of African-American tradition, as reflected in the music of Ellington, Art Tatum, Dorothy Donegan, Anthony Braxton, and many other composers. Taylor embraced European influences and readily admitted that, "Bartók showed me what you can do with folk material" (Spellman 27–28). He intentionally absorbed "the energies of the European composers, their technique, consciously, and blend[ing] this with the traditional music of the American Negro . . . to create a new energy" (28). By the time his first album was released in 1955, listeners to Taylor's *Jazz Advance* felt that, "[H]is harmony, though not his rhythm, is already in a world far advanced beyond bop. His soloing consists of one contrast after another: simple dissonances versus tone clusters, wide versus narrow octave ranges, calls versus response" (Litweiler 202). By the time Taylor's 1961 album *Into The Hot* with the Gil Evans Orchestra emerged, bridging his early period with his "mature style," he had abandoned traditional notation and dictated the features of his scores to performers. Archie Shepp performed on the recording and confirms that, "He would play the line, and we would repeat it. That way we got a more natural feeling for the tune and we got to understand what Cecil wanted . . . 'Book Pots,' which a lot of critics have called a masterpiece of modern jazz, was written this way" (Spellman 44).

Direction, purpose, structure, and logic create and support freedom. Spontaneous composition leads to effective innovation when musical ingredients are expertly balanced and controlled. Such improvisation-driven prototypes are inevitably linked to clear structure. Structures bring poetic logic into well-defined matrices or road maps that reveal underlying processes, organizational configuration and construction, and strategic planning. The chords, melodic fragments, rhythms, dynamic gestures, and other musical events that are carefully arranged extemporaneously in jazz are a result of finding the right balance between brilliant flashes of creative insight and structural or gravitational grounding. Free expression becomes chaos to listeners who are inexperienced with absorbing too many riveting concepts at once or with reconciling new approaches contained in musical expression. Too much uncertainty disorients people and may make them feel less comfortable or less secure in their understanding of an experience. Musicians struggle with finding ways to explore new frontiers while grounding their audience in something that feels familiar. The balance of ingredients also requires finding the correct brand of leadership, management, and democracy within an ensemble to render it properly united and synergistic. The progenitors, innovators, and titans of any musical style understand how such things work most effectively.

Taylor's 1966 album *Unit Structures* was the catalyst for displaying his mature approach. Taylor explains in the liner notes to *Unit Structures* that he felt, "Western notation blocks total absorption in the 'action' playing." The next phase of Taylor's approach involved imaginative drummers with colorful and flexible approaches to rhythm, such as the masterful Sonny Murray and Andrew Cyrille. These musicians heavily influenced Taylor's rhythmic orientation from this point forward, making his music more mercurial while suggesting the polyrhythmic implications that jazz musicians had learned to superimpose over simple metrical structures, such as four/four meter. Taylor said in his liner notes to *Unit Structures*:

> It seems to me that the big change we had a large part in precipitating was the dispensing of the *overt* manifestation of four. It became a concept that we no longer felt we had the necessity of stating, but understood that we *experienced* it and that it was, in many ways, the given premise of—or even the motivation of—all that we were going to do. And that what we were going to do now was to investigate the multiples possible, you see, so that the relationship of how Andrew Cyrille uses his high-hat or his large cymbal, how the high-hat divides time, how the cymbal divides time, how the bass pedal divides time, how his sticks on the snare . . . I mean, it becomes infinite (Figi 14).

Taylor's self-penned liner notes to *Unit Structures,* entitled "Sound Structure of Subculture Becoming," distilled his musical structures and metaphysical ideas in poetic language expressed in a non-linear and logical fashion, replicating his musical approach. Many researchers have attempted to analyze Taylor's thoughts as contained in these observations. His notes represent ideas that align with the unity of vision and new socio-cultural Global African consciousness of his artistic contemporaries. Taylor again rejects the Western Art music's intellectual restriction and racist arrogance:

> Time seen not as beats to be measured after academy's podium angle. The classic order, stone churches with pillars poised, daggers ripping skies, castrati robed in fever pitch, stuff the stale sacrament, bloodless meat, for the fastidious eye; "offering" sought the righteous; only found sterility in squares/ never to curl limbs in reaction to soundless bottoms.

As Taylor condemned the hierarchical nature of the Eurocentric "classical" paradigm, and even those such as John Cage, who consider their approach one of rejecting the "classic order," ("Measurement of sound is its silences"), he described a restrictive Eurocentric mindset that pervades its consequent art and culture. In *Four Lives in the Bebop Business,* Taylor again underscores this perspective:

> David Tudor is supposed to be the great pianist of the modern Western music because he's so detached. You're damned right he's detached. He's so detached he ain't even there. Like, he would never get emotionally involved in it; and dig, that's the word, they don't *want* to get involved with music. It's a theory, it's a mental exercise in which the body is there as an attribute to complement that exercise. The body is in no way supposed to get involved in it.
>
> It's like this painter. I said, "Like that painting of yours could have been done by a machine," and he said, "Well, the human body is just a machine." The most exciting level of creativity as expressed to me by these people is like that of a machine. For them, the ultimate kick is to be a machine (Spellman 36).

In "Freedom and Individuality in the Music of Cecil Taylor," Matthew Goodheart takes a close look at Cecil Taylor and his music. In "Part II: The Foundation of Taylor's Music," Goodheart concludes that:

> [Taylor] sees in these artists as a "reactive occult" and accuses them of ultimately embracing the same destructive elements that are the failings of the order they claim to reject. He aligns them with Boulez, Babbitt, and the other serial composers by saying "in action unknowable detached rationalization of inaction and detachment mathematical series, permutation and row-underlying premise = idea precedes experience." As we shall see, Taylor sees

experience, the body, and their integration as fundamental to the making of music which is connected in a profound way to life.

From Goodheart's perspective, Taylor proposes, in what Archie Shepp called "natural music," a music based on the rhythmic structure as it relates to the body and our physical experience: "Physiognomy, inherent matter-calling stretched into sound (layers) in rhythms regular and irregular measuring co-existing bodies of sound" (Spellman 36). Goodheart says that, "He goes to some lengths to separate this corporeal impulse of rhythm from those of the 'classical order,' and the destructiveness of 'academy's' use of time."

> Rhythm-sound energy is found in the amplitude of each time unit. Time measurement as isolated matter abstracted from mind, transformed symbols thru conductor, agent speaking in angles: a movement vacuum death encircling act, defining nothing Pythagorean desert a wasteland lit deafness before ultimate silent arena senses ride naked in souls.
>
> Would then define the pelvis as cathartic region prime undulation, ultimate communion, internal while life is becoming visible physical conversation between all body's limbs: Rhythm is life the space of time danced thru (Taylor).

Taylor's often interdisciplinary approach to performance has included collaboration with dancers and poets. One such performance was presented as an outdoor concert by the Guggenheim Museum in New York with Taylor on piano and dancer/choreographer Min Tanaka (with whom Cecil has worked for many years) on September 17, 1994. The virtuoso pianist also received enthusiastic acclaim for his landmark performance at Lincoln Center that year.

Cecil Taylor's mastery of his own unique musical domain has been recognized throughout the world for several decades, and much of his solo and ensemble music is preserved on audio and visual recordings. Mr. Taylor has taught at the University of Wisconsin, Antioch College in Ohio, and at Glassboro State College in New Jersey. He served as a featured guest artist at Cornell University in the spring of 1995, working and performing with the Experimental Lab Ensemble and presenting his views through his poetry.

The Language of Rhythm

Rhythm is a linear feeling of movement within musical time, most often with a strong implication of regularity and differentiation. It often involves regularity or repetition, but irregular temporal sequences of events are just as rhythmic. Rhythmic ideas are also more easily remembered through *rhythmic grouping*, where events are grouped according to their rhythmic similarity. *Rhythmic* groupings are defined by intrinsic time intervals between events and accentuation. Accents, like metrical patterns, help systematize rhythmic events into smaller groups that can be more easily remembered, applied, and digested. Meter involves the pattern of fixed temporal units called beats by which musical time is measured. Meter establishes a basic temporal tension and release pattern, where the weaker beats create expectation of the stronger beats and vice versa. This framework elicits expectations that allow listeners to organize varied rhythmic patterns into structural units that better orient listeners. Rhythmic events positioned at points immediately before and immediately after metrical markers tend to build greater tension. This is particularly true in syncopated passages. A listener's increased expectation builds as musical development approaches metrical markers, and continues to anticipate relief of tension shortly after the downbeat when rhythmic expectation is not satisfied as anticipated.

The rhythmic complexity of traditional African music often loosely reflects rhythms in the natural environment and other forces within which it emerges. Many Africans believe that to lead a balanced, productive, and good life they must entrain themselves with the universal rhythms of nature. The poly-dimensional development of rhythm is more dominant in Global African music than it is in the music heard in Western cultures. In *Math and Music—Harmonious Connections,* Hammel and Kahn discuss the distinct quality and polarity of rhythmic intensity in African music.

A typical African musical ensemble consists of a large, low drum, up to 12 other drums, and a collection of iron bells, gongs, shawms (similar to oboes), and flutes. The music created by such an ensemble is polyrhythmic, meaning "having many rhythms." There are anywhere from two to six or seven rhythms going on at once. Although there is no dominant rhythm, one musician usually beats a short phrase on a gong or bell that is used as a mutual reference point by all the other musicians.

Anthropologists think that polyrhythmic music exists because of the belief that the presence of both a male and female principle is necessary to reach a state of perfection in any endeavor. In many parts of Africa, three is considered a male number, while two and four are considered female numbers. Therefore, having at least two different rhythms (one with a cycle of three beats, or some multiple of two) fulfills the requirement of having both a male and female element.

Unlike Indian music, where the tabla player creates both rhythms, each drummer in an African ensemble has his own rhythm. A drum master from the Fanti tribe of Africa calls this the "hidden rhythm." The drummer practices this rhythm (usually a simple multiple of two or three) alone until he is good enough, and can keep time well enough, to attempt combining it with everyone else's. And he is not considered a true African drummer until he can keep his rhythm going while listening to two other rhythms at the same time. Mathematically speaking, the polyrhythm created by this ensemble is very complicated. Twos, threes, fours, sixes, and eights beat against each other creating a many-layered pulsating rhythm. The best dancers are those who express all the rhythms—a different one for each body part! Mathematics can be used to analyze the polyrhythms of African music, but there's no conscious effort on the part of the performer to use it.

The music of Bali and Java is also very percussive and rhythmically complicated. The typical ensemble is called a gamelan, and consists mostly of percussion, with maybe a few flutes and strings. There are two of each instrument—a male/female pair whose rhythms echo one another and overlap so subtly that it sounds like a single drum playing. The instruments reverberate with an intense, pulsing energy and weave a tapestry of rhythm that, like the polyrhythms of Africa, defies analysis (17–18).

Indian music also involves complicated rhythmic structures. Tabla players develop an ability to negotiate complicated rhythmic combinations such as cycles of twelve beats against eleven and fifteen beats against thirteen. One of the tabla player's hands performs a rhythm that divides a block of time into twelve or fifteen equal parts, while the other hand simultaneously divides the same time period into eleven or thirteen equal parts. As with African music, rhythm is generally felt viscerally and intuitively rather than analyzed. Each composer, performer, or listener develops a personalized (rather than analytical) relationship with rhythm. The mathematics that support music—logic that implies a more fluid, abstract, and intuitive mathematical discipline counter to the exact science of conventional mathematics—seems to resemble the flexible disposition of nature's mathematics. Many shared or related approaches, concepts, and elements join various forms of music around the world. Music, in turn, is the key to sensing the forces of the Universe. Hazrat Inayat Khan tells us:

> Therefore, for the most illuminated souls who have ever lived in this world—as for the greatest of all prophets of India—their whole life was music. From the miniature music which we understand, they expanded themselves to the whole universe of music, and in that way they were able to inspire. The one who finds the key to the music of the whole working of life—it is he who becomes intuitive; it is he who has inspiration; it is he to whom revelations manifest, for then his language becomes music. Every object we see is revealing. In what form? It tells us its character, nature, and secret. Every person who comes to us tells us his past, present, and future. In what way? Every presence explains to us all that it contains. In what manner? In the form of music—if only we can hear it. There is no other language: its rhythm, it is tone. We hear it but we do not hear it with our ears. A friendly person shows harmony in his voice, his words, his movement and manner. An unfriendly person, in all his movements, in his glance and expression, in his walk, in everything, will show disharmony—if only one can see it (18).

Thus we are all compositions with our own personal rhythms and inherent frequencies. Our consonance and dissonance define who we are as individuals and determine the quality of "particle" that we are.

Relationships Between *Free Composition*, Indian-Based, and African-Based Music

When studying music generated by oral/aural traditions, such as those of African, Indian, Chinese, European, and other world cultures, the most significant inspiration is the love for music making. Music becomes the lens through which artists view, measure, and analyze their world. It can serve as the means through which artists honor and interact with the Creator. Indian musicians believe that through music you can purify your soul and mind, enabling people to love their neighbors, love children, and love oneself. Some African musicians believe that no separation exists between the spiritual realm and all phases of objective reality, and they use music as a vehicle to communicate with those who reside within or between both mundane and arcane domains. The universality of music allows musicians to communicate beyond words and to give more love to the world and all its inhabitants (human and otherwise) (Ali Akbar Khan 4). An abundance of philosophical and spiritual overlapping exists between various world cultures, and those relationships justify the similarities between many traditional musical approaches.

Indian music is concerned with balance, tension, and release, and the evolution of pitch as it travels on a musical journey (and its evolution from a suggested fundamental). It is less concerned with a separate progression of harmony than with the musical representation of nature's expression. Nature is inevitably stratified, unified, and diverse. The Bhagavad Gita tells us that what we call the human body actually is a combination of three bodies:

1. The **Physical body** (Sthula sharira), one which we see and feel with our senses.
2. The **Astral body** (Sukshma sharira), our higher dimension body, which is connected with our physical body by an infinitely extensible "silver cord" at the naval.
3. The **Cause body** (Karana sharira), much subtler than the astral body, plus the waveform record of all our Karma and desires (vasana), good or bad (Bhagavad Gita 167–8).

In European music, Schenker (as well as other theorists and composers) too understood that the tonal system is a balance of opposing forces in which every note (individual), chord, and key area is in some way related to a fundamental tone (whole). Heinrich Schenker (1868–1935) was a music theorist renowned for his approach to musical analysis, now usually called Schenkerian analysis. Following his death, his incomplete theoretical work *Free Composition* (*Der freie Satz*, 1935) was published.

Schenker gradually transformed his thinking from simply an interesting idea into a coherent theory by understanding music not as a series of related chords, but as a stratified linear process with clear goals and direction. This "structural hearing" reduced the primary elements of music to a set of relationships that are closely related to the way a master jazz musician understands the hierarchical matrix and flow of chord changes. Just as jazz musicians realize that melody, melodic interplay, rhythm, harmony, dynamics, and other musical elements are inseparable, Schenker combined his ideas on harmony with a theory of counterpoint. Schenker evolved his theory of tonal music throughout most of his career. During this time he wrote many other essays that discussed a wide range of topics, from close analyses of rhythm and texture to studies of improvisation. Although his analyses were concerned with all the essential parameters of a musical composition, he felt that the key to understanding the structure of tonal music resided within pitch organization. This concern with the mastery of pitch organization binds Schenker's perspective with Indian- and African-based music. These musical approaches have melodic, harmonic, and structural goals that are systematically configured so that background skeletal organization determines the direction of foreground and middle-ground musical detail.

In both Indian- and African-based music, information is passed from one generation to another, orally and aurally, through master musical mentors. Ali Akbar Khan (often referred to as "Sathi," a friend who accompanies you on a journey) is a master of North Indian Classical Music. He came to the United States with a desire to promote and nurture Indian music in every country around the globe. After opening his Ali Akbar Khan College of Music in California (Marin County) he worked to bring new insights into the multidimensional facets of melodic experimentation, rhythmic complexity, improvisation, and ornamentation of Indian music (Ali Akbar Khan 3). Over the years he has also collaborated with jazz artists, such as John Handy, resulting in some interesting fusion-style recording and performance projects. The study of Indian music begins with a process of simplicity and patience. In one of his course manuals, Ali Akbar Khan states,

> I always start with the simple scales and rags, and I always begin with the fixed compositions—like a child who first learns to draw by tracing a picture. Slowly, slowly it helps to learn by following the example of the teacher (4).

North Indian Classical music has its own unique terminology. Just as each note of Global African music must "say something" to achieve melodic, harmonic, and rhythmic success, each note of Indian music must be treated with similar care. Notes become an expression of emotions and ideas and are not simply the exhibition of mastery of scales and arpeggios. Notes are not treated uniformly in either case, but each note has a specific message, power, goal, and purpose. In learning the notes (or Svaras) of the Sargam of North Indian Classical Music, Khan suggests:

> You must learn how to sing pure note, pure pitch. Each note must give the proper effect. Therefore, each time you try to get each note pure, clean, perfect, full of perfection, you have to think of music touching your brain and heart (7).

Scale and melodic formations are culturally specific and intimately related to a social disposition, styles of cultural movement, language, instrument design, and tuning theory. Most Western music derives its basic tones from the even-tempered piano. The "equal tempered scale" is a compromise-tuning scheme developed for keyboard instruments, such as the piano, enabling them to be played with equal ease in all keys. The discovery of a numerical relationship between string length and musical interval is commonly attributed to Pythagoras (c. 500 B.C.). A Pythagorean Tuning of the Diatonic Scale is based on the unbroken line of fifths. "Just tempering" runs into problems (for the piano) in constructing a circle of fifths because the circle does not close. The gap or discrepancy in frequency that appears at twelve consecutive fifths and seven octaves down is known as the Pythagorean Comma. Of course, the measurement of distances between all tones, including smaller intervals (major and minor seconds), is affected by its tuning system.

The various schemes to reconcile the Pythagorean Comma, that is to close the circle of fifths, are called cyclic temperaments. Well or equal tempering is one of them. There have been other schemes to divide the octave not only into twelve parts but also into five, fourteen, sixteen, nineteen, thirty-one, and fifty-three parts. These are all cyclic temperaments. The ancient Greek tuning was not cyclic and is one of the linear temperaments. Various linear temperaments have been used throughout musical history under circumstances where the music was not essentially harmonic but linear; hence there was no need to define intervals of relative consonance and dissonance (Helmholtz Appendix XX).

Figure 7.

Note	Just Scale	Equal Temper.	Difference
C4	261.63	261.63	0.0
C4 ♯	272.54	277.18	+4.64
D4	294.33	293.66	−0.67
E4 ♭	313.96	311.13	−2.84
E4	327.03	329.63	+2.60
F4	348.83	349.23	+0.40
F4 ♯	367.92	369.99	+2.07
G4	392.44	392.00	−0.44
A4 ♭	418.60	415.30	−3.30
A4	436.05	440.00	+3.94
B4 ♭	470.93	466.16	−4.77
B4	490.55	493.8	+3.33
C5	523.25	523.25	0.0

Figure 7. (continued)

Interval	Ratio to Fundamental	Ratio to Fundamental
	Just Scale	*Equal Temperament*
Unison	1.0000	1.0000
Minor Second	25/24 = 1.0417	1.05946
Major Second	9/8 = 1.1250	1.12246
Minor Third	6/5 = 1.2000	1.18921
Major Third	5/4 = 1.2500	1.25992
Fourth	4/3 = 1.3333	1.33483
Diminished Fifth	45/32 = 1.4063	1.41421
Fifth	3/2 = 1.5000	1.49831
Minor Sixth	8/5 = 1.6000	1.58740
Major Sixth	5/3 = 1.6667	1.68179
Minor Seventh	9/5 = 1.8000	1.78180

For tone-producing instrumental systems, such as vibrating strings or air columns, "harmonic tuning" (or the Just Scale) occurs as a natural extension of the overtone series. All the notes in the scale are related by rational numbers. Thus, traditions that use just tuning are more aligned with the natural overtone series and do not use notes that match the even-tempered notes of Western music. The chart below shows the note frequencies (in Hz) for C Major for just and equal temperament, starting on middle C (C4), and for intervallic ratios to fundamentals.

Musical tones in Indian music are organized in an elaborate system based upon just temperament. Aligning music with the natural tuning of the overtone series creates a soothing effect on people. A melody played on an even-tempered instrument (such as the seven [shuddh] notes of the sargam [scale] are: S R G m P D N).

Figure 8.

Names	Pronunciation	Notation	Western Equivalent
1 Sadja	Sa	S	Do
2 Rishaba	Re	R	Re
3 Ghandhara	Ga	G	Mi
4 Madhyama	Ma	m	Fa
5 Panchama	Pa	P	Sol
6 Dhaivata	Dha	D	La
7 Nishada	Ni	N	Ti

We have said that traditional African music is polyrhythmic, polyphonic, poly-harmonic, and poly-dimensional because, as performers reflect their environment, it is a reflection of nature. Most quality music maintains a natural sense of order, flexibility, dynamic expression, variety, predictability, and surprise. Just as African music evolved its tones from the universal order of the overtone series (through over-blowing the fundamental tone of a one- or two-holed African flute, for instance), Indian music has prescribed just-tempered pitch sets, each with various meanings, moods, and functions. Both African and Indian approaches to music often involve high degrees of improvisation based upon firm traditional knowledge and musical law established as music and culture evolved. Vishnu Narayan Bhatkhande (1860–1936) of Bombay developed the ten *thats* classification system. That (pronounced "tot") means skeleton or framework. The ten thats organized ragas into a system of scales. Each scale has all seven tones, the aroh-avroh (ascending–descending pattern) are the same, and includes only one form of a note in each scale pattern. Vishnu Narayan Bhatkhande chose ten from the thirty-two possible basic permutations in altered-note combinations and named them after the particular ragas they resemble. Bhatkhande's ten thats are:

1.	Asawari	S R g m P d n ˜S
2.	Bhairav	S r G m P d N ˜S
3.	Bhairavi	S r g m P d n ˜S
4.	Bilaval	S R G m P D N ˜S
5.	Kafi	S R g m P D n ˜S
6.	Kalyan	S R G M P D N ˜S
7.	Khammaj	S R G m P D n ˜S
8.	Marwa	S r G M P D N ˜S
9.	Purvi	S r G M P d N ˜S
10.	Todi	S r g M P d N ˜S

The mood and purpose suggested by the sound of each pitch set have been assigned a specific function. The thats are one of several systems of classification for ragas in current use. Five of the thats are morning ragas: Asawari, Bhairav, Bhairavi, Bilaval, and Todi. The remaining five are evening ragas: Kafi, Kalyan, Khammaj, Marwa, and Purvi. Two other systems used today are the melkarta system and the parivar or raga-ragini system (Ali Akbar Khan 9).

Tals: The Rhythmic Cycles

If meter is systematic ordering of rhythm through marking off recurring cycles with accents delineating quadruple (| > - - -|> - - - |) or triple (| > - - |> - - |) divisions, then we can follow the grouping of such accents in music around the world to study the formation of metrical cycles. The Western application of visual musical barlines does not always transfer to forms of world music that are orally and aurally transmitted, but accents are heard and felt regardless of whether they are initially written or improvised. In African-based music, polyrhythms often provide constantly shifting accents that create a continual virtual series of superimposed multiple (or changing) meters. Tals refer to the rhythmic cycles of North Indian Classical Music that set up its rhythmic cycle patterns methodically (Ali Akbar Khan 10).

Dhrupad

a. Chautal (2 matras: 2 + 2 + 2 + 2 + 2 + 2) [. . .]
b. Adha Chautal (14 matras: 4 + 2 + 2 + 2 + 2 + 2) [. . .]
c. Dhammar (14 matras: 5 + 2 + 3 + 4) [. . .]
d. Sulfak (10 matras: 2 + 2 + 2 + 2 + 2) [. . .]
e. Teora (7 matras: 3 + 2 + 2) [. . .]

Khyal

a. Tintal (16 matras: 4 + 4 + 4 + 4) [. . .]
b. Ektal (12 matras)
c. Vilambit theka (12 matras: 2 + 2 + 2 + 2 + 2 + 2) [. . .]
d. Jhaptal (10 matras: 2 + 3 + 2 + 3) [. . .]

Light Classical

a. Sitakhani (16 matras: 4 + 4 + 4 + 4) [. . .]
b. Chachar (14 matras: 3 + 4 + 3 + 4) [. . .]
c. Kaharwa (8 matras: 4 + 4) [. . .]
d. Rupak (7 matras: 3 + 2 + 2) [. . .]
e. Dadra (6 matras: 3 + 3) [. . .]

To get beyond simply cataloging facts about Indian music I spoke with a dear friend, who is also a master of the sitar. Ashwan Batish has been a man with a specific mission to make the sitar into a contemporary electric instrument as relevant as the electric guitar. Born in India, he was raised in a house where Indian classical music was the norm. His father, Pandit Shiv Dayal Batish, played the sitar. It was not until the family moved to England in 1962 that he first heard and loved rock and roll. And he moved closer to rock when his father played sitar on the Beatles' "Help!" album. Based in Santa Cruz, California now, Batish has made a number of albums to back up his thesis, showing that the sitar can groove as hard as any other stringed instrument.

The family moved again in 1973, this time farther west, to the U.S. By this time, Batish had become an accomplished sitar player himself, although he never viewed it as a career, focusing instead on aeronautics. However, the economic downturn in the 1970s ended that idea, and Batish turned to accounting, finally earning a master's degree before thinking seriously about music. Even then, he never considered mating his love of rock with Indian music, beginning by recording discs of Indian classical music. In fact, his 1980 debut "Morning Meditations" was actually a collaboration with his father. He gradually ventured further into rock. His most radical move came in 1986, when he put out "Sitar Power" (on his own Batish label, released on Shanachie in 1987, reissued on CD Batish 1994). The sitar was electrified, the rhythm section of bass and drums roared, and he had transformed the instrument into something that mixed the best of East and West, with ragas, reggae, and rock, although all the tunes were based on traditional ragas. Although it received rave reviews at the time, Batish made no attempt to capitalize on it. If anything, he backed away from albums to focus on his family and run his Batish Institute of Music and Fine Arts in Santa Cruz, CA. In fact, it wasn't until 1994 that the follow-up, "Sitar Power #2," was released. By this time, world music had begun to catch up with Batish, although he did follow it up with another live disc, "In Montreal."

Ashwan Batish has been in no rush to explore the field he helped pioneer. He still teaches and performs, but his concentration seems to have returned to Indian classical music. I spoke with Ashwan in July 2009 about North Indian music's relationship to African-American music. He said:

> You also have to remember, that the Northern Indian music is almost the same as jazz—when you had the Blues. That is why Northern Indian music has become so rich. Its heritage and its culture are because we had all these upheavals, all the fighting and all the plundering and the raping, the problems of the war—invaders inhabiting. The nice word for that is "acculturation." But the beautiful part of it now is this intermingling created all the stress and the difficulties had the people's emotions bubbling upwards, and that is what North Indian music is about. Part of it is just a mish mash of people trying to mix things up together, which also became a tradition. And this is why we have all these rags colliding with each other to make a new form. And all of that kind of left the North Indian system in partly in a quandary also, because they didn't know if this was all legal or not. And so to try and legitimize it, they would have conferences and discuss, "This rags is here now, should we make that a rogue that we write in the books or should we just wait until it gets more maturity?" (Laughing) So everybody starts to sing it and then it's worth it now to be in the books.
>
> So it became a hit-and-run kind of issue. Whereas in the South India, those forms were derived out of a very traditional base. And even they had some history of "experimentism," but there were more mathematical formulations being applied instead of just a raw "let's try it and see what happens" sort of deal. So it is a little more organized in the South, but the northern system was all into modern experimenting and playing, that is so rich and diverse. So I would say that what we are talking about: . . . the heart of today's modern

North Indian music . . . is because they literally lost touch with the reigns on information. Not having that, they were on the streets fighting for the dollar (or for the rupi as they say), and so to do that, music was moved into the streets and the red district zones. If you played well, you had rupis dropped in your bucket. So that meant practice, practice, practice! The struggle is almost the same that we notice over here. You see?

And you notice the underground part of it is that the traditional part of it moved underground, some of it got lost because of the burning of libraries, the burning of books. And at the same time that people were burning them, some people thought, "wow this is pretty awesome." They were also hiding the books and taking them with them. So some of our books came back from Persia back into India, or from wherever else . . . the Spanish also. But Persians were the ones who preserved them the most. They destroyed the most, and yet preserved the most. Aesop's fables from Greece, they were all bunched under our tales, but he took them and he said "Well these are also stories" so he wrote all of them in Hindi but he didn't tell everybody where he got them from.

One of the Vedas went to Germany where Hitler took all the Vedas. That was the Vedas in war, you see? And they found them because this guy was tearing pages and selling some channa rice, which is corn—I believe that is where Hitler picked up all his war mongering. . . . There are four Vedas of knowledge, and then we have the sub-Vedas.

"There are only two ways to live your life. One is as though nothing is a miracle. The other is as though everything is a miracle."

—Albert Einstein

References

Covey, Stephen R. *Principle-Centered Leadership.* Audio CD. Free Press, 1992.

Creeley, Robert, ed. *Selected Writings of Charles Olson.* New York: New Directions 1967.

Figi, J. B. "Cecil Taylor: African Code, Black Methodology." *Down Beat* (July, 1975): 13.

Goodheart, Matthew. "Freedom and Individuality in the Music of Cecil Taylor." 1996. Evolving Door Music. August 2007 <http://users.lmi.net/mgheart/thesis/part2.html# anchor62185>.

Griffith, Ralph T. H. *The Rig Veda.* Translation of the Sanskrit text. 1896.

Hammel, T. and C. V. Kahn. *Math and Music—Harmonious Connections.* Palo Alto, CA: Dale Seymour Publications, 1995.

Jois, Rama and M. Justice. *Ancient Indian Law: Eternal Values in Manu Smriti* Delhi: Universal Law Publishing Company, 2007.

Khan, Ali Akbar. *Indian Music.* Course syllabus. Ali Akbar Khan College of Music. San Rafael, CA. 2002.

Khan, Hazrat Inayat. *The Mysticism of Sound and Music: The Sufi Teaching of Hazrat Inayat Khan.* Boston: Shambhala, 1996.

Koestler, Arthur. *The Act of Creation.* London, England: Arkana Publishing, 1990.

Lewis, Ralph. "Our Nature with Nature, Part 1." *Rosicrucian Digest,* 83.2 (2005): 19.

Litweiler, John. *The Freedom Principal: Jazz After 1958.* New York: Da Capo, 1984.

Radano, Ronald M. *New Musical Figurations: Anthony Braxton's Cultural Critique.* Chicago: University of Chicago Press, 1993.

Shepp, Archie. "An Artist Speaks Bluntly." *Down Beat* (Dec. 16, 1965): 11.

Snyder, Bob. *Music and Memory: An Introduction.* Cambridge, MA: The MIT Press, 2000.

Spellman, A. B. *Four Lives in the Bebop Business.* New York: Limelight Edition, 1966, 1992.

Summary of the Bhagavad Gita. 3 By Author Unknown. June 2006. <http://www.bhagavad-gita.us/articles/684/1/Summary-of-the-Bhagavad-Gita/Page1.html>.

Taylor, Cecil. Liner notes. *Unit Structures.* L.P. (1966).

Tenney, James. *A History of Consonance and Dissonance.* New York: Oxford University Press, 1988.

Van der Merwe, Peter. *Origins of the Popular Style: The Antecedents of Twentieth-Century Popular Music.* New York: Oxford University Press, 1989.

Chapter Seven
Ambassadors: Spiritual

SPIRIT (Inspiration and the Voyage of the Individual Spirit)

This "combination" human body is the carrier, the vehicle of our "Atma," the Spirit, the actual "me." During our sleep (unconsciously) and during meditation (consciously) our astral body can leave the physical body. For the astral body being at a much higher vibration level, physical things are no barrier to it. When we "die," only our physical body is destroyed. We, the "spirit," along with the astral body and cause body are born again in another physical body, as directed by our Karmic record. In between the death and rebirth, the spirit, along with the astral body goes to a particular astral plane depending on its level of evolution.

"Compassion": Ensemble Performance and Modern Music

Some listeners find the composition "Compassion" from John Coltrane's 1965 album called *Meditations* somewhat hard to listen to. Human compassion is an appurtenance to the "ultimate reality" and reflective of our most meaningful embodiment of human emotional advancement and maturity. In music the expression of compassion may connect to spiritual expression. Scott Yanow finds that:

> This CD [*Meditations*] reissues what was arguably the finest of the John Coltrane-Pharoah Sanders collaborations. On five diverse but almost consistently intense movements ("The Father and the Son and the Holy Ghost," "Compassion," "Love," "Consequences," and "Serenity"), the two tenor saxophonists, pianist McCoy Tyner, bassist Jimmy Garrison, and both Elvin Jones and Rashied Ali on drums create some powerful, dense, and emotional music. Unlike some of the live jams of 1966, the passionate performances never ramble on too long, and the screams and screeches fit logically into the

spiritual themes. This would be the last recording of Coltrane with Tyner and Jones.

Compassion is the acute consciousness of the interdependence of all things. Many spiritual leaders feel that a person achieves the highest peak and deepest reach in his or her search for self-fulfillment through compassion. His Holiness, the fourteenth Dalai Lama of Tibet said, "The whole purpose of religion is to facilitate love and compassion, patience, tolerance, humility, forgiveness." The Dalai Lama is a Buddhist monk, scholar, and the temporal and religious leader of the Tibetan people who has the respect of the world community. When the Communist Chinese invaded Tibet in 1959, the Dalai Lama was forced into exile. He emerged as an international statesman for peace and was awarded the Nobel Peace Prize in 1989 for his consistent refusal to accept the use of violence in the struggle for peace in Tibet. He is recognized internationally as a champion of human rights, as an environmentalist, and as an advocate for compassion and personal responsibility. Thus compassion is more than simply a sentiment, it also concerns perpetuating justice and doing works of mercy.

Matthew Fox views spirituality as compassion. He argues that humanity's hope for survival rests in completely altering our awareness of the entire fabric of society, using compassion as the touchstone for creating a spiritually centered, ecologically minded feminism that can guide and nurture a world society that values impartiality, sharing, creativity, and stewardship of the Earth. Fox says, "Compassion is not a moral commandment but a flow and overflow of the fullest human and divine energies" (126).

Since music reflects society and the universe in general, examining past or present social, political, and cultural domains, or historical periods, often serves as inspiration and direction for creative artists. Certain historical eras are largely defined by music. During the 1960s many people in America felt that music and enlightenment would stultify aggression, racism, and sexism and "save the world" from impending self-destruction. Soon afterwards, however, a social reaction to the 1960s revolution led many people to identify with retrospective images, more conservative socio-political styles of behavior, and audience-induced concepts in the arts to an uncanny degree. Market packaging seemed to replace creative content and youthful age became a vacuous image and commodity that replaced earlier tendencies towards individuality, social consciousness, and experimentation. Self-centered insecurity brought an "attitude" to replace empathy and kindness. This was all too apparent as jazz marched on for over three decades without a name for the new, definitive style. Music reflected all of this and more.

The 1960s were one of those rare periods in history where a critical mass of young people in the West was looking for higher degrees of personal freedom. This brand of social attitude produced a broad reflection within experimental musical approaches throughout society. A great number of new styles emerged throughout the first three-quarters of the twentieth century. Ragtime, blues, New Orleans jazz, boogie-woogie, swing, bebop, rhythm and blues, cool, hard bop, free jazz, and fusion were among the numerous distinct African-American stylistic developments that blossomed before 1975. Ironically, after this emergence of over a dozen clearly distinguishable and readily identifiable new styles over a period of seven decades, the last quarter of the twentieth century primarily produced only nostalgic and retrospective jazz music. Given today's technology, spontaneous composers have a great range of opportunity to study traditional vocabularies carefully, and to examine the ways that musical vocabularies are formed and evolve. The most effective way to experiment requires composers to problem solve in real time, exercising systematic and responsible musical liberty. The following chart shows assorted compositional parameters and elements to consider during periods of free spontaneous composition.

Figure 1. Matrix for Spontaneous Composition by Karlton E. Hester

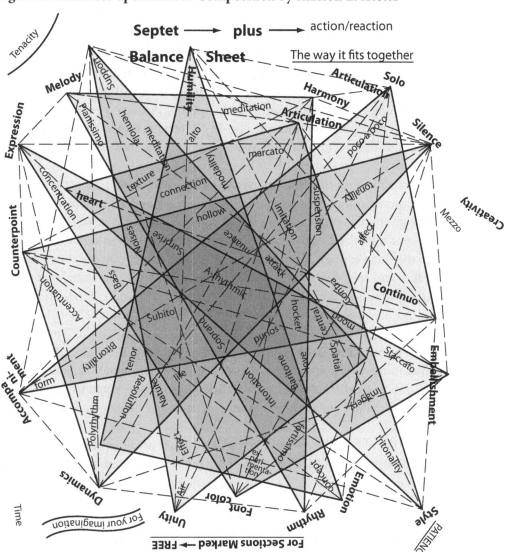

Establishing a new mutual vocabulary requires understanding how established vocabularies work in general. It also demands that the musicians evolving innovative musical lexis listen to each other's musical ideas, direction, and stylistic tendencies. Music is guided by the mind's ability to recognize certain sequences of musical events, retain them, then construct associations with each musical gesture as events unfold. Greater distances of time occurring between musical ideas necessitate larger structural markers as reminders. If composers devise and form musical ideas carefully, then listeners more readily retain them. In turn, digesting key fragments of musical information establishes thematic indicators that listeners and performers can use as markers, tracing the development of a composition's courses. The notion of coherent succession of musical time involves ordering musical events in ways that expose the relationships that clarify the creative objective. The human mind does not reliably remember the sequence in which spontaneous musical events materialize, and different functions of memory behave in accordance with a variety of time levels. Thus the ability to remember the precise order of events in musical time varies with different performance situations. Melodic, harmonic, and rhythmic groupings could not function as coherent patterns—with characteristic contours and distinguished rhythms—if we could not remember their most distinguishing components in an orderly fashion. Primary structural or formal levels consist of entire sections of music. Lucidity of form is important for controlling larger scale events that occur over time spans exceeding the limitations of short-term memory.

The more our memory practices and repeats certain behaviors, the better we learn them. Our sense and comprehension of taste, sight, sound, and other human behaviors develop through training our memories with a combination of repetition and contrast. Bob Snyder concludes that echoic memory involves early sensory information processing that persists long enough to be encoded into basic recognizable features that are joined together into episodes. Other theories propose that basic perceptual representations of our environment are formed as a consequence. Such representations develop images and not necessarily specific visual impressions (for example, touch, sound, smell, or taste image) that give a more conceptual portrait of our world. Theoretically, many long-term memories are encoded illustrations presented to our subconscious and conscious minds as pre-linguistic syntax of cognitive representation. Some of these perceptual symbols are difficult to express verbally or through written language, much as it is difficult to reduce some aspects of musical meaning to terse verbal definitions and conclusions.

Our perception of how the environment and existence are organized is based upon the capacity of our memory. Memory is the human nervous system's processing capability that has evolved over time. We learn to organize sound through recognizing the order of sonic events within the physical world. Individual and series of sound events are then sifted and correlated into memorable patterns. Even at the most fundamental level, Snyder considers this complex process one of the main problems the auditory system has to solve. Knowing how to take the continuous variation in air pressure that impacts our ear and extracting the multiplicity of separate resonant sources present within a conglomerate sound envelope would be quite revealing. Throughout our environment we hear many subtle levels of organized patterns in speech, music, and environmental sounds that are not readily conspicuous in the physical sound waves themselves (Bregman 12–14). Such sounds form composite sounds that we recognize. Instead of hearing only colonies of isolated sounds or an undifferentiated continuum formed by their mixtures, we group composites of sound that may seem related by various associations together, despite their occurring at different frequencies and time intervals. Thus, the wind blowing, a bird singing, an automobile engine starting, the words of human conversation, and such, all maintain their separate identity and distinction even as they occur simultaneously. Due to this particular brand of filtering and cataloging information, therefore, we do not hear everything as a single flow of sound. Human perception, cognition, and memory account for the sounds that occur around us being organized into distinct conceptual packages.

Snyder suggests that events can be grouped in two general ways. He concludes that the structure of the human nervous system evolved in a way that enabled us to understand the surrounding world by developing information absorbed by our conscious and subconscious mind into primitive grouping processes that always function in similar ways. He concludes that we have little control over primitive grouping processes, but can reinterpret their output in light of further memory-related processing at times. "Frequency, amplitude, and our perception of boundaries where events begin and end are detected in the earliest stage of processing, feature extraction, that obtain cues recognized by higher-level processing (long-term memory)" (32). Links of events form when basic features combine to form *simultaneous* grouping processes that are again grouped together to form *sequential* grouping processes. Eventually, such patterns are committed to memory, over time forming *learned grouping processes*. Learned grouping affects long-term memory that ultimately operates at a higher level of processed thought, occurring further along in the nervous system than those to which Snyder refers as primitive grouping effects. He considers:

1. *Objective set,* grouping effects established in and unique to a particular piece of music, which are learned during the course of listening to a particular piece, and which have to do with expectations unique to and established *during that piece,* such as recognizing a musical theme and its transformations.
2. *Subjective set,* grouping effects that are part of a *style,* which are learned during the course of listening to *many* pieces, and which involve expectations established across many pieces that are *similar* in some way. Knowing that a particular kind of section is about to happen in a particular style of piece would be an example of subjective set (45).

Music tells interesting stories when the composer's conceptual and theoretical plans are solidly constructed. When the artist's individual spirit, technical facility, and cumulative knowledge infuse music, the listening audience senses a balance of such ingredients it registers as an exalted quality of music. Inspiration often heightens when a sense of purpose concentrates and propels musical ideas. Self-discipline and concentration shape the foundation over which creativity is applied, exercised, and developed. An artist performs and composes in accordance with their level of training, personality, experience, and lifestyle. Composers do not need to avoid problems involving unconventional instrumentation, experimental approaches, or the application of new musical vocabulary when they learn to conquer associated problems by forming new coherent musical equations. Emphasis on spontaneous composition involves extemporaneous problem solving and must remain at the root of jazz if it is to remain a living art form reflective of nature's improvising.

Some Ancient Melodic Formulae

Composers often use musical formulae as containers into which they pour their musical elements or to structure their ideas. One of the oldest ways of organizing melodies in some types of ancient music, especially chants, involved an *axial melody* in motion *around* a central pitch. Although not strictly governed by exact intervallic motion, ancient axial melodies demonstrated the idea of centrality—expressed at the melodic level—that is related to some modern approaches to composition. Steve Coleman's related idea of mirror symmetrical movement will be discussed later in this chapter. In both cases, melodic motion alternately rises above and sinks below a central pitch, always eventually returning to that pitch. Although this approach renders the axial schema a balanced formula, its melodies tend to have a static quality.

Another type of ancient melodic formulae is the *melodic arch*. Unlike the axial melody, the *melodic arch* is a form of melodic schema that generally does not use pitches below its central tone. Instead, tones rise to a climactic height before descending back down to the point of origin. Melodic arches usually develop a fairly linear pattern of tension that distinguishes them from axial melodies. The melodic arch has various positions at which its climax is located, but it rarely occurs at the end. Because a melody can only move upward for a limited length of time before reaching a point of reversal, eventually leading back to the pitch from which it departed, an ascending phrase always needs sufficient time to descend before ending.

A third type of ancient melodic structure used throughout world cultures is the *gap-fill* schema. The *gap-fill* schema is based upon the metaphorical idea that an ascending melodic leap leaves a void or gap that then has to be filled by a descending conjunct motion that both fills the gap and balances release of tension. The assorted qualities of gap-fill melodies are determined by the ways its downward pattern is elaborated.

All such formulae provide systematic ways to organize compositional content. In contemporary musical environments, most such prefabricated approaches and structures need contracting methods to maintain interest and keep the music from becoming too predictable. Music that is too formulaic generally sounds as though prescription is involved.

The Essential Value of Contemporaries, *Griots*, and Personal Mentors

In most traditional societies, the sources of musical origin or inspiration should be acknowledged. In traditional African villages socio-cultural information was most often passed along from mentor to neophyte through oral tradition. Many Ethiopian composers wrote ancient music and poetry then humbly attributed the work created to their most revered master, Saint Yared (born in 525 A.D. in the city of Axum), simply because he taught or inspired them. Crediting their esteemed Master Yared with the work that these younger composers produced demonstrated their sincere respect.

In contemporary society identifying the foundation of musical learning and development becomes more complex because artists do not study with a single mentor but, rather, draw from a number of individual, institutional, and virtual sources. In the West, partially as a result of slave era politics, people unfortunately tend to claim the ideas of others as their own without acknowledging the source. In the twenty-first century, music piracy is an example of stealing and misappropriating the intellectual property of others and is becoming an increasingly greater problem. The information in this book comes as a result of decades of absorbing and contemplating the ideas of those colleagues, thinkers, masters, recordings, and mentors with whom I have associated, performed, spoken, read, or studied.

This book is largely informed by information garnered from my personal mentors and influences. Throughout my career, I have benefited from the formal and informal knowledge and guidance gained from many wonderful teachers and mentors. Of course, many people influence your development throughout life, but a few are particularly special. Among my numerous musical influences there are those I never had the privilege of meeting, such as Bach, Mozart, Beethoven, Debussy, Ellington, Mary Lou Williams, Bird, Miles, Coltrane, Billie Holiday, Dolphy, and Mingus. Perhaps those who had the most memorable direct impact on my development as a spontaneous composer were jazz masters Louis Jordan, Buddy Collette, Joe Henderson, Cecil Taylor, Dr. Nelson Harrison, and Dr. Donald Byrd. My direct contact with Cecil was mostly focused within the time I met him after an outdoor duo performance he gave with dancer Min Tanaka on Mercer Street (in New York) and the amazing week he spent at Cornell as guest artist with my Experimental Lab Ensemble in the mid-1990s. Cecil deepened my understanding of musical applications of abstract symmetry and the symbiotic relationship between music, life, and poetry, and placed me in close proximity to hyper-intense musical individuality.

Both Nelson Harrison and Donald Byrd have contributed many ideas to my overarching creative and philosophical perspective, thus nurturing my general understanding of relationships between the outer and inner sectors of the musical and general universe. Nelson is an African-American *griot* who has also continually fed my spiritual and metaphysical intellect. His integrated perspectives on music, metaphysics, psychology, education, politics, and sociology harmonize with my own. Nelson was the first musician I met who clearly articulated the distinctions and interrelationship between the two hemispheres of the brain.

Dr. Byrd is another African-American *griot,* scholar, art collector, educator, pilot, and Renaissance man. Dr. Donald T. Byrd has a wealth of experiences and stories that chronicle the history of jazz from the "inside track" and contemporary music. Donald worked with the creative artists and innovative geniuses he often discusses. He began performing jazz at an early age and made scores of recordings with many of the most renowned innovators of the twentieth century. Dr. Byrd more recently evolved a system of musical composition based on mathematical symmetry and has a deep respect for the power of ancient and modern symbols. As a master composer, performing artist, and thinker, Donald Byrd codifies the multi-dimensional relationships between music, math, visual arts, business, history, education, and politics in erudite fashion.

Some musicians strive primarily to please their audiences at all costs. The primary motivation that propels many other artists is continuing musical evolution, interest in experimentation, and a need for self-expression. Joe Henderson, who first gained recognition in the 1960s, was perhaps my most influential teacher. After studying for a year at Kentucky State he transferred to Wayne State in Detroit to finish his degree in music. While there he often worked with Donald Byrd, Yusef Lateef, Barry Harris, and Hugh Lawson. After he was drafted in 1960, Henderson played bass in a military show that traveled worldwide. In 1961 he performed with Bud Powell and Kenny Clarke in Paris while serving that tour of duty. He was discharged in 1962, settled in New York, and began his historic musical association with Kenny Dorham. Henderson strictly taught by example, and his lessons are best expressed by direct contact with the music that emerged from that study. Henderson did not analyze that music, but instead let the musical etudes speak for themselves.[11]

Steve Coleman's Approach to Balance and Symmetry

In discussing balance and symmetry, composer and saxophonist Steve Coleman observes how our beautiful world offers a multitude of forms (with countless variations on simple themes), and suggests ways that related forms of natural balance can be achieved musically. He aims to achieve architectural balance musically, on both the micro to macro levels, by combining intuitive and logical methodologies. Because symmetry occurs throughout nature, artists can easily find an endless array of archetypes

---

[1]   See Appendix, Figure 3. "Round Midnight" (head melody) and solo Figure 4. "Round Midnight" (solo, transcribed from a lesson with Joe Henderson).

Figure 2. A Solo to "Donna Lee" Written in the Hand of Joe Henderson

Figure 3. Blues Changes (just a few assorted possibilities)

1	2	3	4	5	6	7	8	9	10	11	12
F7	F7	F7	F7	Bb7	Bb7	F7	F7	C7	Bb7	F7	F7
F7	Bb7	F7	C-F7	Bb7	B°7	F7 / C-7 F7	D7 / A-7 D7	G7 / D-7 G7	C7 / G-7 C7	F7 Bb7	F7
F7	Eb7	Db7	Cb7	CbM7	Bb-7 Eb7	A-7 D7	Ab-7 Db7	G-7	C7	F7 D7	G7 C7
F7	G7	A7	B7	BbM7	B-7 E7	AM7	Bb-7 Eb7	AbM7	G-7 C7	F7 D7	Db7 Gb7
F7	Bb7	A-7 G-7	F#7 B7	Bb7	Bb7	F7 E7	Eb D7	G-7	F7	F7 D7	Db7 C7
FM7	E-7 A7	D-7 G-7	C-7 F7	Bb7 Ab7	Db7 E7	A C7	F7	G-7 C7	Db-7 Gb7	F Ab	Db Gb7
F F#°7	G-7 Ab-7	A-7 D-7	C-7 F7	Bb7	Ab7	Gb7	F7	G-7 C7	Eb-7 Eb7	F7 Ab7	G7 Gb7
FM7	EbM7	DbM7	CbM7	F-7	Bb7	E-7 A7	Eb-7 Ab7	D-7 G7	Db-7 Gb7	F7 Eb7	Db7 C7
FM7	GM7	AM7	BM7	Bb7	E7	F-G-7	A-7 Ab-7	G-7	Gb7	F Ab	B D

in nature to accommodate concepts that align with melody, rhythm, tonality, form, harmony, timbre, texture, dynamics, and other elements of music. With regards to balance, Coleman wrote:

> We live in a world of immense beauty. There are a multitude of forms with countless variations on simple themes. I want to speak here about balance and make some comments about how balance can be achieved musically. There are countless ways that architectural balance can be musically achieved from the micro to macro level. Since attention to detail has always been an important factor for me, and these things are not usually discussed, I would like to initiate some dialogue on this subject. The most obvious kinds of balance that come to mind are the various forms of symmetry (i.e., bilateral, etc.) that can be applied musically, using intuitive and logical methods. Symmetry is a fact of nature and one of the oldest fascinations of humanity. Some of the more obvious ways in which symmetrical musical balance could be realized are through melody, rhythm, tonality, form, harmony, and instrumentation. As well as the structural considerations of symmetrical musical forms I will also discuss these structures from a dynamic point of view, i.e., as they progress through time.[22]

In Coleman's article, "Melodic Material Generated by Symmetrically Derived Laws of Motion," he explains how symmetrical expansion and contraction of melodic tones around a central "axis tone or axis tones" behave in accordance to gravity of motion within a "melodic system that obeys its own laws of motion." His system of symmetry can be applied to tonal harmony. Coleman describes his method of balance and symmetry, which began with a focus strictly on melody:

> When I first started dealing with symmetry I only dealt with the laws of motion produced by the system without any regard for other types of tonality. This is how I would suggest others learn the system to get a feel for thinking in these terms. Also a complete knowledge of intervals and their relationships (always thinking in terms of semi-tones) would be extremely helpful.
>
> I began by writing symmetrical exercises for myself. Then I practiced these exercises to get my fingers and ears used to moving and hearing these ideas. It was only after doing this that I practiced improvising within these structures playing at first in an open manner (not based on any outside structure such as a song). Later I adapted these improvisations to structures and forms. I did this by slowly integrating the ideas with the more traditional improvisational style I was already playing. My goal was not to play in a totally symmetrical

---

2   http://www.m-base.com/cnmat_ucb/Symmetry_Movement.html

style (as this would be as boring as playing all major scales) but to integrate the style and give myself more options when I improvise. The basic system involves what I call two spirals. They are tones that move out equally in half steps from an axis (which is always at least two tones).

If the axis of the first spiral is the two tone C-C unison (one octave above middle C, it could be in any octave) then from that unison C, you move out (spiral out) each tone in a different direction in half steps, i.e., C-C, then B on the bottom and C-sharp on the top; B-flat on bottom and D on top; A on bottom and D-sharp on top; A-flat on bottom and E on top; G on bottom and F on top; G-flat on bottom and F-sharp on top (at this point you are at the beginning of the spiral again, or the symmetrical mirror image of the spiral); F on bottom and G on top; E on bottom and G-sharp on top; E-flat on bottom, A on top; D on bottom and A-sharp on top; D-flat on bottom and B on top; C on bottom and C on top (this is your starting point one octave above and one octave below your original tones). You're thinking two tones at a time and they're spiraling out together. This I call spiral number one.

As you spiral out from C-C (the axis) and you think of the interval between the tones, then C to C is a unison. The next tones in the spiral are B and C-sharp, the interval between B and C-sharp is a major second. Next in the spiral is B-flat on bottom and D on top, that's a major third. Then A on bottom and D-sharp on top, that's an augmented fourth or a tritone. Continuing, A-flat on bottom and E on top, that's an augmented fifth (could also be thought of as a minor sixth). Then G on bottom and F on top is a minor seventh. The next tones are G-flat on bottom and F-sharp on top, these tones are an octave apart and are really the same as the beginning of the spiral. All symmetry has two axes and in this system they are always a tritone apart from each other, more on this later. As you keep spiraling out until you reach the two C's two octaves apart the important thing about the spiral is not the tones themselves, but the intervals between each of the tones as you spiral out each half step. It is these resulting intervals that are formed in spiral number one (Unison, Maj 2nd, Maj 3rd, Tritone, min 6th and min 7th) that I call Symmetrical Intervals (see Figure 4a). This is important to remember as it forms the foundation for the laws of melodic motion. Note that beginning with the tones G-flat on bottom and F-sharp on top, the intervals of the spiral repeat themselves if you perform octave reduction on the intervals.

Figure 4a. Spiral 1 (from Coleman)

(Note: Author substituted enharmonic spelling.)

Coleman first thoroughly digested his evolving concepts and vocabulary before improving in that new language. Coleman also demonstrates how his approach to symmetrical movement is applied to situations involving two as the axis starting point (for example, C and D-flat instead of C and C), then spiraling out from each note as before. He then continued to create a variety of related permutations in similar fashion. He began his compositional process by writing symmetrical exercises for himself. He practiced his exercises to familiarize his ears with his new musical approach. He then improvised openly within his new structures, gradually integrating the newly created patterns with the more traditional improvisational style he was already used to playing. He then adapted them to more conventional improvisational structures and forms. Coleman did not intend to play or compose in a totally symmetrical style, but aimed to integrate his new findings with his old musical methods and concepts, thus providing himself with more options as a spontaneous and premeditated composer.

Figure 4b. Spiral 2 (from Coleman)

In addition to intervallic spirals that radiate above and below an axis, chords can evolve symmetrically from a fixed nucleus. For example, the triad composed of a major third, then minor third above C yields a C-Major triad (C-E-G) above the central axis (C); and the triad composed of a major third, then minor third below C yields an F-minor triad (F-A♭-C) below the central axis (C). In his section on harmonic material generated in symmetrical space, Coleman sums up his ideas about gravitational forces as they relate to this brand of axial construction, symmetry, and related aspects of balance in music:

Over the years I have been exploring several ideas, which could be expansions of the symmetrical laws of motion mentioned above. Most of these ideas are based on the various concepts of "gravity" and what can be generally called "binding" and "unbinding" (i.e., different types of laws of attraction). The melodic concept discussed above and other related harmonic concepts all deal with tonal centers in terms of spatial geometry, as opposed to the standard tonality which deals in tonal key centers in terms of tonics. These different approaches can be looked at as different types of "gravity." Here we could borrow two terms coined by music theorist Ernst Levy, calling the concept of gravity that results in the traditional tonic-based tonality Telluric Gravity or Telluric Adaptation and the concept of gravity that is at the basis of centers of "geometric space" Absolute Conception. In Telluric Adaptation our perception of gravity is based on laws of attraction that are influenced by our sense of "up" and "down." Thus we tend to look at the harmonic series only from the "bottom-up" perspective, with the "fundamental" on the bottom. This is a "terrestrial" mode of thinking influenced by the fact that we live on Earth and tend to localize our concept of space according to our everyday situation. In Absolute Conception what is important is the position of the tones in space and their distance. Here the harmonic series is seen as "spiraling" out from a "generator" (as opposed to a tonic or fundamental), so as to produce both an "Overtone" and "Undertone" series! Absolute Conception is based on a "universal" mode of thinking that results when you look at the Earth, other planets, satellites, and stars from the point of view of how they relate to each other in space. So the difference is the way the gravity operates from a "terrestrial" or "telluric" perspective (on Earth we tend to think of the gravitation pull in one direction, "down") and how gravity operates from a "universal" or "absolute" perspective (in space we tend to think of objects orbiting around a gravity source or being pulled towards the source from a multidirectional perspective). In Absolute Conception partials are thought of as "orbiting" around a generator tone, producing both overtone and undertone energy.

Thus the symmetrical relationships explored in the Coltrane Matrix (discussed in Chapter 2), and Donald Byrd's Math+Music=Art concept are given new omnidirectional implications. Expanding the notion that tones of a harmonic series spiral out from a "generator" rather than from a simple fundamental, and the resulting symmetrical overtone and undertone mirroring series, involves a consideration of the thesis that such a generator might also radiate sound waves in the way other orbital structures organize their orbiting worlds systematically. Active tones from one radiating series could also take a *quantum* leap to join a nearby or related series. Thinking in this fashion, rather than from a terrestrial or linear matrix, enables symmetrical matrices to form new nuclei and satellites from any central tone, at any time, and extend themselves infinitely in spiral helix. A two-dimensional representation of the carboxypeptidase (or other protein), where its longest "a-helix" could fit within the sphere, could serve as a model for such colonies of chord possibilities extending from any selected pitch. From flowers and larger organisms to subatomic particles, nature forms systems where structures radiate in assorted orbital configurations around a central nucleus. The resulting balance is always abstract in design (like the radiating petals of a rose), flexible, and resilient. In these regards, fundamental particles, such as electrons, generate energy in little bits, or quanta, and the vibratory things we know behave like both particles and/or waves, depending on your perspective. When an atom is pumped up with energy, electrons whizzing around a nucleus can become excited to the point of making discrete *quantum* jumps into new orbitals that fit together like a vibrating ethereal flower (Tweed 79).

Figure 5. Circle of Fifths

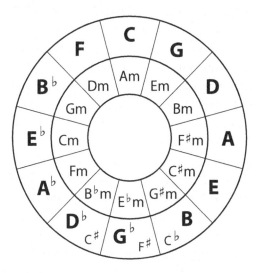

Music, Light, and Dark Matter

Our limited understanding of the Universe most certainly does not determine its capacity. Music involves a systematic study of the effects that sound vibrations have on humankind and the environment. It studies the mathematics of vibration from an intuitive perspective that includes empiricism. Music theory cannot organize music into an "exact" science because there are no exact sciences. Yesterday's science will be disproved, clarified, and extended tomorrow. We can experience phenomena that exist beyond the range of our senses and tools with our intuitive, subconscious, and higher senses if we refine those subtle abilities. Nevertheless, everything around us tells us something about universal order.

The behavior of light vibration may tell us something about the conduct of sound. If we think of the properties of light, gravity, and motion, and equate those characteristics with sound vibration, it may provide alternate ways of thinking about music's compositional resources and organization. Lunar influences on earth give a sense that radiating and gravitational planetary forces can have an effect on matter. Such forces may also affect chemical vibration, particle spin, sound vibrations, and various proportions and relationships within the solar system and beyond. Wavelengths of light (electromagnetic radiation) also produce measurable wave frequencies, and that radiation extends in all directions surrounding its source, just as sound waves radiate around their fundamental nucleus.

Like overtones and undertones of music, light waves are stratified. Wavelengths longer than infrared and very low energy are called *Radio waves*. *Infrared waves* form wavelengths longer than the red end of visible light and shorter than microwaves (roughly between 1 and 100 microns). Little infrared radiation reaches Earth's surface, but we can observe some degrees by telescopes on tall mountains or from a high-altitude aircraft. We refer to electromagnetic radiation at wavelengths visible to the human eye as *Optical* or *Visible waves* (we might think of them as related to the more accessible "perfect" intervals of the overtone series). People perceive this type of radiation as colors ranging from red (longer wavelengths about 700 nanometers) to violet (shorter wavelengths about 400 nanometers). *Ultraviolet* wavelengths are shorter than the violet end of visible light (we might pair those wavelengths with intervals of major and minor thirds and major seconds in partials immediately above the perfect intervals). Earth's atmosphere serves to block most ultraviolet light. As short wavelengths composed of very high-energy, *X-rays* have shorter wavelengths than ultraviolet light but longer wavelengths than gamma rays (they are like various chromatic semitones of the higher partials in the overtone series). *Gamma rays,* which are the highest energy and shortest wavelength of electromagnetic radiation currently known (like quarter-tone and smaller intervals that extend beyond the human range of hearing), are usually thought of as any photons having energies greater than about 100 keV (kiloelectron volts).

So much sonic information extends beyond our range of hearing that we may never understand. The affective influence that sound has on our emotions may be a result of vibration's higher orders of magnitude that is difficult to quantify or rationalize. Likewise, scientists are becoming increasingly aware that we have been observing only a minute portion of existence as we study the molecular universe. *Dark matter* is a fairly recent discovery that continues to confound astronomers and other scientists, as this mysterious essence is possibly everywhere but yet not easily detected or understood by anyone. Betsy Mason's August 24, 2006 article in the *McClatchy News Service* entitled, "Dark Matter Exists, New Research Confirms: Bent Light Key to Finding Particles," provides an introduction:

A purple haze shows evidence of dark matter—invisible particles—flanking a dense pack of galaxies known as the bullet cluster. . . . A team of scientists has found evidence of the mysterious stuff called dark matter that makes up about 20 percent of the universe by watching galaxies collide 3 billion light-years away. "This is the final, definitive proof that it has to be there," astronomer Douglas Clowe of the University of Arizona said earlier this week. Astronomers say dark matter consists of some sort of invisible particles. Most scientists have been convinced of the existence of dark matter for some time, but there are competing theories that gravity behaves differently on million- and billion-mile scales.

But what Clowe's team saw in these faraway galaxies cannot be explained by modifying gravity, said astrophysicist Marusa Bradac, a team member. . . . The team used NASA's Chandra X-ray observatory and telescopes to focus on a dense pack of galaxies called the bullet cluster. . . . By analyzing how the light from objects even farther away from Earth is bent around the colliding galaxies in the bullet cluster, the scientists could map out where all the mass is. . . . They found that most of the mass is located in invisible clouds on either side of the collision. "Those clouds must be made of dark matter," Clowe said.

"This shows pretty convincingly that there really is dark matter," said cosmologist Joel Primack of the University of California, Santa Cruz.

Sound and light consist of composite wavelengths that radiate waveforms in all directions from their source. Looking into space through a powerful telescope, scientists can observe the light energy emissions of electromagnetic radiation. Some of this radiation is the visible light we see with our eyes. Nevertheless, electromagnetic radiation exists in assorted wavelengths, as shown above (radio waves (the longest), infrared, optical, ultraviolet, X-rays, and short gamma rays). Since everything seems to vibrate, galaxies, nebulae, stars, trees, microscopic bugs, and anything else that can be measurably observed glows with pulsating energy at one of these wavelengths. In recent decades, however, scientists have become increasingly convinced that vast amounts of material in the universe do not glow. This mysterious "dark matter" is believed to be the most common substance in the universe, perhaps making up 90 percent or more of the total mass. Normal matter ("baryonic" matter) is made of atoms, which are composed of protons, neutrons, and electrons. Scientists suspect some dark matter is of the baryonic variety. This category may include brown dwarf stars and other objects that are simply too small or too dim to be seen from great distances.

Theorists often debate minute details in the measurement of overtone series intervals, and dismiss the existence of a corresponding undertone series in sound. An undertone series may exist as a mirror-image radiating system of sound waves whose influence extends far beyond the harmonic envelope of its own series, and possibly serving to balance a related overtone series above its own lower domain. Its presence could have a gravitational and interactive effect on its corresponding overtone series, with both lower and upper elements orbiting around a mutual fundamental nucleus (tone). Although dark matter does not emit enough energy to be directly detected with our current tools, researchers have noted its presence indirectly. Anything that has a mass exerts the force of gravity. Scientists at NASA's Goddard Space Flight Center conclude that dark matter, and perhaps other matter and forces that we have yet to discover, exert a gravitational pull on objects in and around distant galaxies. It even affects light emitted by those objects. Other researchers say the Coma Cluster of galaxies shows effects of gravity that can only be explained by the presence of some unseen dark matter. By measuring the effects of gravity, researchers determine how much "extra" gravity is present, and hence how much extra mass, or dark matter, must exist. In large clusters of galaxies, for example, scientists say that five to ten times more material exists than can be accounted for by the stars and gas they find. According to a NASA news release dated October 26, 2004:

> A growing body of evidence indicates that dark matter—which interacts with itself and "normal" matter only through gravity—is the dominant form of matter in the universe. According to the popular "cold dark matter" theory, dark matter consists of mysterious particles left over from the dense early universe that were moving slowly when galaxies and galaxy clusters began to form.

"The observed properties of NGC 4555 confirm that elliptical galaxies can posses dark matter halos of their own, regardless of their environment," said O'Sullivan. "This raises an important question: what determines whether elliptical galaxies have dark matter halos?" NASA's Chandra X-ray Observatory demonstrated this with the detection of an extensive envelope of dark matter around an isolated elliptical galaxy. This discovery conflicts with optical data that suggests a dearth of dark matter around similar galaxies, and raises questions about how galaxies acquire and keep such dark matter halos.

Most large elliptical galaxies are found in groups and clusters of galaxies, and are likely the product of the merger of two spiral galaxies. In such an environment, the dark matter halos can be stripped away by gravitational tidal force and added to other galaxies or the group as a whole. Therefore, it is difficult to determine how much dark matter the original galaxies had, and how much they have lost to the group as a whole through interactions with their environment.

If scientific discovery can reveal that the seemingly infinite portion of the Universe that we can verify by the measurement of light is but 10 percent of the matter that actually exists within the observable environments, what does that suggest with regards to our potential understanding of vibration of undertones or our understanding of spiritual aspects of our being? The fact that we cannot observe, detect, or monitor significant portions of existence with our senses and tools means little to the infinite Universe.

Hermann Ludwig Ferdinand von Helmholtz, Sensory Physiology, and Undertones

Some people do not dismiss the undertone series as groundless. Entertaining the notion that such a system of tones exists can at least alter the way we think about the radiation of tone. Hermann Ludwig Ferdinand von Helmholtz (1821–1894) was a German physician and physicist whose "life from first to last was one of devotion to science, and he must be accounted, on intellectual grounds, as one of the foremost men of the nineteenth century." Helmholtz, focused on the unity of mind and body, stressing the importance of materialism and sensory physiology. He looked for a connection between many aspects of science including empirical phenomena that exist beyond our usual range of perception. His investigation of the Universe included acoustics, physiology, ophthalmology, and aesthetics, and in 1863 he published his book entitled, *On the Sensations of Tone as a Physiological Basis for the Theory of Music,* exposing his interest in the physics of perception. Helmholtz invented the Helmholtz resonator to show the strength of the various tones through magnifying and cataloging the overtones and undertones he heard with the aid of his new tools.

Helmholtz also focused on the physiology of the senses. He published *Handbuch der Physiologischen Optik* (*Handbook of Physiological Optics*), a book that provided empirical theories on spatial vision, color vision, and motion perception that became an essential reference work in his field during the second half of the nineteenth century. Thus, in 1851, Helmholtz revolutionized the field of ophthalmology with the invention the ophthalmoscope, an instrument used to examine the inside of the human eye. His theory of accommodation went unchallenged until the final decade of the twentieth century. When Helmholtz moved from Heidelberg to Berlin to become a professor in physics in 1871, he became interested in electromagnetism. Helmholtz had predicted E-M radiation from Maxwell's equations, and the wave equation now carries his name, as does the Helmholtz Association, a large German association of research institutions.

In 1894, Helmholtz is considered the first person to put forward the idea of the heat death of the universe. Besides this and other later achievements, Helmholtz's first important scientific achievement was an 1847 physics treatise on the conservation of energy, written during his medical and philosophical studies. He discovered the principle of conservation of energy while studying muscle metabolism and attempted to demonstrate that no energy is lost in muscle movement. That theory was inspired by the implication that no *vital forces* were necessary for muscle movement, which was a rejection of the speculative tradition of *Naturphilosophie,* a dominant philosophical paradigm in nineteenth-century German physiology. He published his theories in his book *Über die Erhaltung der Kraft* (*On the Conservation of Force,* 1847).

Musicians are also interested in the relationships that exist between musical tones, our senses, and ancient philosophical and metaphysical ideas. Composer Dane Rudhyar felt that if the series of whole numbers reveals a universal principle, then selecting from the variety of possibilities revealed by the series solves the problem of choosing tones for our scale selection. Rudhyar said that, " The relationship between the Fundamentals have to be measured: they take on the objective character of intervals between entities spread in visual space. The Pythagorean monochord—which may have been used in Chaldean and Egyptian sanctuaries before Pythagoras—is the simplest and most characteristic instrument for identifying sounds and numbers and for experiencing descending and ascending series of tones. In China, decreasing or increasing length of tubes of bamboo served the same purpose" (80). Rudhyar concluded that two procedures were possible.

The first is to select a section of the harmonic series bounded by two sounds in octave relationship and to use only the overtone within this octave interval. This is the kind of natural intonation Kathleen Schlesinger believed was universally used before theorists formulated a more intellectual system. Natural intonation implies the primacy of instrumental music, for it is only through man-made instruments that overtone can be measured. Yet the earliest production of intentional series of tones (such as mantrams) was undoubtedly by human voice. True, a specially trained human voice can produce overtones (as in Tibetan sacred chanting), but such a deliberate production seems to belong to a later period. Above all, its overtones cannot be directly and concretely measured. Moreover, within a scale, no two intervals represented by two successive whole numbers constantly diminish.

In the second procedure, the relationships between primary numbers are used as interval units on which to build a scale—an archetype of relationship. The primary numbers one, two, three, and four constitute the Pythagorean tetraktys, a sacred symbol for the Greek philosopher. These numbers define the octave (the ratio 2:1), the fifth (3:2), and the fourth (4:3) (82).

Musicians tuning their lyre and other instruments and writers attempting to represent Pythagoras' ideas have often assumed that the proper procedure was to start from the fundamental bass tone C and move upward a fifth to G, then descend by a fourth from G to D. The interval of a whole tone between C and D produces a 9:8 ratio. By adding a whole tone above D the note E would be reached, leaving a semitone between E and F to complete the series, with the interval C to F (a perfect fourth) enveloping the lower tetrachord in the ascending scale). Rudhyar points out that, "Greek tetrachords were always presented as a descending sequence of four notes. Pythagoras perhaps sought to establish a structure indicating that humanity had reached a point at which man could reproduce the descent of the creative power of Sound by an upward kind of resonance symmetrically reflecting the first steps in the creative process, from the ineffable One, to the two, and from this mother tone to the three, the cosmic mind" (84).

Contemplation 6: African String Instruments

Musical instruments are vehicles through which the soul of humanity expresses itself. When the spoken African languages were forbidden in North America, Africans transmitted many of their thoughts through the musical voices and instruments they had, made, and found in their new environment. Each European musical instrument eventually adopted by African-American performers and composers had an ancient African musical equivalent. The winds, strings, and percussion instruments that Europeans developed in the West have ancient chordophone, aerophone, idiophone, and membranophone equivalents throughout the ancient world. Thus, Africans in America could readily relate to each European instrument they found in North America and through its basic form and stylistic characteristics from African tradition were thus relatively easy to transfer to European instruments whose functions were modified to suit African-American music.

We know African music evolved from linguistic influences—its languages and vocal chants that established sound patterns that were later imitated by ideas expressed on musical instruments. Africans who were abducted and relocated in the Americas carried on a similar pattern of musical development. Vocalists in particular retained and perpetuated features of African melodies, harmony, rhythm, and form within sea shanties, field hollers, children's game songs, spirituals and blues, during their "New World" transition. In America the African voice set the musical parameters for the various African-American instrumental styles that evolved around them.

Music-making worldwide probably most likely began with the production and organization of vocal sounds. Anthropological evidence suggests that humans performed music for ages in the form of chanting. Chanting (which came before speech) requires only lungs and vocal chords—physiological conditions that archaeologists have found to exist in skeletal remains from 580,000 years ago. Speaking demands considerable dexterity of the mouth and tongue, and such developments did not occur in humans until around 80,000 years ago. Since many early instruments were probably made of wood, gut, reed, horn, or other natural materials that readily decompose, the precise nature of the first instruments humans used for music-making remains speculative. Most likely, however, the invention of musical instruments was born out of a basic curiosity about sound and sound creation. Archaeologists found a group of mammoth bones that had been used as drums in Siberia that dates back 35,000 years before the last ice age (including the very large hip and shoulder joints). The most resonant spots that produced sounds when struck were clearly marked. A beater (drumstick) and two small flutes from that epoch were also found; all were carved out of bone (Hammel and Kahn 3).

Musicological Research on African Strings, the Structures of African Rhythms

Rhythm is the most important factor in African music. Even melodic patterns often serve rhythmic functions. An inclination towards ensemble playing lends itself to a wide assortment of vertical rhythmic relationships with African music. This results in a stylistic predisposition towards the use of hemiola and polyrhythms, and even in solo performances at least two independent rhythms are maintained. Additionally, each line may contain its own independent beat pattern that may not coincide cyclically with the pattern of the other complimentary lines. Polyrhythms have several sovereign rhythmic points of reference that anchor broader rhythmic phrases framed by distinct points of departure. Hand clapping or another central unifier may provide an underlying binding element.

African music has rich vocal, string, and drum traditions. Strings were very popular instruments in early African-American culture until the beginning of the twentieth century, due to their general accessibility. African retention in work songs, sea shanties, and spirituals was transferred to the blues vocals and instrumental music. Much of the harmonic language also came to the American South by way of the banjo and musical bow, both originally African instruments. In his book, *Africa and the Blues,* Gerhard Kubik discusses elements of his extensive research on African music and used his findings to explore the relationship between African string music and the development of blues strings in the United States. Early banjos were constructed from materials at hand.

> I well remember that in Virginia and Maryland the favorite and almost only instrument in use among the slaves then was a *bandore,* or, as they pronounced the word, *banjer.* Its body was a large hollow gourd, with a long handle attached to it, strung with catgut and played on with the finger (Kubik 8).

And one observer transcribed a "couplet" from one of the musician's songs:

> Negro Sambo play fine banjer, Make his finger go like handsaw. (Cited in Epstein 1973:76)

Africans from varied continental African cultures were used to spike-lutes and other string instruments, and they transferred some elements of their musical traditions, styles, and knowledge to the Western violin (fiddle), banjo, and guitar. As time passed, and gradually fewer numbers of Africans were abducted and brought to North America, continental African instruments became increasingly rare in the Americas. Most Africans were abducted from the West African region labeled the "Gold Coast." In his research, Kubik found spike-lutes across west-central Sudan. Spike-lutes are associated with Hausa minstrels and found in nearby Cameroon and northern Nigeria. Wolof musicians in Senegambia call their version *xalam* (Coolen 1982; Charry 1996). Spike-lutes were probably models for long-necked plucked lutes from the cultures of the western and central sections of the Sudan area. Related lute traditions have survived into present day and Hausa traders in northeastern Nigeria used to call a related lute-like instrument *garaya* (Kubik 9).

Africans immediately recognized the similarity between the European-made violins and a variety of related string instruments from their own traditional culture. Musicologists have traced the roots of fiddle playing in America to African one-stringed fiddles and other traditional prototypes:

> Epstein discovered a report from Virginia in the 1690s in the Accomac County Records, telling, "of a Negro fiddler playing for the dancing of the whites." We do not know what kind of fiddle this was. Probably it was a European fiddle, but in all likelihood it was also a conceptual extension of the west-central Sudanic *goje* or *goge* (one-stringed fiddle) as played by Hausa, Dagomba, and other minstrels. The expertise and specific style of this musician must have come from somewhere, after all to make him attractive to "whites" as an entertainer. Many of them would certainly have played the current Euro-American popular tunes, to which their audience was accustomed, and not any African music, but with novel accentuations, techniques, and improvisations that would have struck such audiences as "virtuoso." Indirectly, therefore, this source also suggests that techniques inherited from playing of one-stringed fiddles common in the west-central Sudanic belt would ultimately be transferred to status-enhancing European instruments, noticeably the violin. Expertise on such instruments could make a performer of African descent a prodigy in the eyes of his startled audience. Eventually this would result in a revival of African musical professionalism, though now for a different public and with a different repertoire (Kubik 8).

African-American music performed for European Americans was often diluted to accommodate Eurocentric sensibility; filtered through European aesthetics and theoretical conception. Such tendencies still remain in contemporary musical practices for similar reasons (labeled smooth jazz, acid jazz, nerd jazz, elevator jazz, etc.).

During the slave era, Eurocentric history attempted to erase Africans' traditions, culture, and memory. African drums were outlawed after they successfully transmitted messages that lead to a number of slave revolts in America. Of course, efforts to erase collective and individual memories were not entirely successful. Traditional music remained subtly disguised in many forms and a few traditional African instruments arrived continually from Africa as long as some continental Africans continued to arrive in the Americas. Africans in America left mouth-resonated bows and a number of other traditional instruments in communities through which they traveled over the years. Consequently some African instruments or their descendants were discovered within a number of European-American communities:

> The westward migration of English-speaking farmers and their slaves to Alabama, western Tennessee, Mississippi, Arkansas, northern Louisiana, and eventually to east Texas, for a life on the regimented cotton plantations can also be followed up by numerous "dropped leaves" on the path. Some of these were documented recently by Richard Graham (1994) in the Appalachian and Ozark mountains, in European-American communities. Graham studied mouth-resonated bows, and he expanded his field data by archival work uncovering a number of nineteenth- to twentieth-century written sources. The remote ancestry of these musical bows in specific African bow traditions is perceptible to the naked eye by an Africanist who is familiar with musical bows on that continent, in spite of the considerable mutation in organology and playing technique they have undergone in the course of time. An example was recorded by Alan Lomax in 1959 in Arkansas, and it has persisted to this day. The convex side of the bow's stave (instead of the string) is turned towards the player's mouth. We have come to the conclusion that the remote genealogy of these bows points in the direction of mouthbows in central and southern Mozambique, such as the *nyakatangali* and the *chipendani*. Two different playing techniques are found with the *chipenani*: striking the string with a stick, as for example among the Tsonga, or pulling it with thumb and index finger, as among the Shona-Karanga and -Zezuru.

Mozambicans were certainly also deported to the United States. Graham quoted one source from 1804, i.e., four years before the legal importation of African slaves to the United States came to an end, testifying to the arrival of 243 Mozambicans in Charleston, South Carolina. The startling extent of the Mozambique slave trade in the early nineteenth century was researched by Antonio Carreira (1979) (Ibid. 12–13).

The richness and diversity of African music transferred to all African-American music to some degree. The knowledge of traditional African music and culture, which was continually replenished from the time the first slaves abducted from Africa arrived around 1600 until well into the eighteenth century, shapes the musical traditions that define contemporary jazz. Although fewer Africans were brought in bondage from southeastern Africa to North America, their musical and cultural influence on the development of African-American string tradition can still be measured. Africans certainly moved throughout their continent distributing their influence for thousands of years. Kubik found plausible evidence of such cultural effect as he discovered African musical bows in America:

> Characteristically there seems to be no memory among the present-day cultural bearers of those bows now sold to tourists as authentic "hillbilly"

artifacts of a possible African background. Kinship tradition is usually cited, and occasionally even Amerindian origins are suggested, contrary to compelling evidence that Native Americans in the southeastern United States did not use mouth bows. Graham's findings not only testify to the relative ease with which traditions can migrate from one ethnic group to another, but also to how quickly historical memory fades; no one among his informants suggested any African background to these bows.

How did knowledge of those specific types of musical bows take root among the mountains? My guess is that slaves from Mozambique, and perhaps also from Angola, during the late eighteenth to early nineteenth century spread this knowledge to the newly established scattered European communities. It was towards the end of the eighteenth century that the Atlantic slave trade shifted increasingly to areas south of the equator—to Angola and (to a somewhat lesser extent) to Mozambique. Captives from those areas were beginning to be preferred to those from the Guinea Coast. Musical bow playing seen among Mozambicans and southwestern Angolans, where the technique of passing the back of the bow stave by the lips is prominent, was perhaps first imitated by children among the European settlers. Children in many cultures are known to be in the vanguard of artistic innovation. When people of European descent migrated increasingly to the Appalachian Mountains, and later the Ozark Mountains in Arkansas, such critical experiences could have gained general acceptance, once contacts with Africans had become minimal. Tony Russell and Richard Graham have both suggested that such traditions could have been more easily assimilated in the European-American communities once they were settled far away from African descendants, and could thereby perceive such cultural interaction as "less threatening." This idea could be corroborated by the fact that the five-stringed *banjo,* and American derivative of western and central Sudanic plucked lutes, is also especially concentrated in that relatively small area of European-American communities "no more than one hundred fifty miles in any direction from Knoxville in eastern Tennessee," as well as in the Ozark Mountains extension of this region (Kubik 15–16).

The history of the musical bows in the Americas demonstrates that the fluidity of African musical influence throughout the African continent makes it difficult to generalize specific regional influences on the development of African-American music. Knowledge of musical bows and other one-stringed instruments of African heritage survived especially among African-American children and most notably among communities in Mississippi where rural progenitors evolved the blues in the Deep South. Musical bow and quill player Eli Owens discusses the mouth-resonated musical bow he used earlier in the South during his youth, and its associations with the children's game of hide-and-seek (Evans 347). Memories of such musical associations are examples of

African retention that surface throughout New World Global African culture. In the case of Owens above, the association transferred from one type of one-stringed instrument (the monochord zither) to another (the mouthbow) (Kubik 17). His technique seemed closely related to the stylistic characteristics of the Khoisan Region Bushmen of the Kalahari Desert. No Bushmen were abducted and transplanted in the Americas. Slave traders in Angola despised these Africans in particular. But Gerhard Kubik concludes that:

> Southwestern Angola was a major slave-raiding area in the eighteenth century, and Bantu-language speakers such as the -Nkhumbi, -Handa, -Cipungu, and others, had been living in an economic symbiosis with the !Kung' for hundreds of years and—as is testified by the research of my Angolan colleague Marcelina Gomes—adopted essentials of bushmen musical-bow techniques. They then took their knowledge to New World destinations. To my surprise, when undertaking a systematic trait-by-trait analysis of an African-American musical-bow player, Eli Owens, recorded by David Evans in 1970 and 1973 in Bogalusa, Lousiana, we discovered that the closest African parallels that emerged were to be found in bushmen-related bow techniques of Angola and Namibia.

There are several partially derived tonal-harmonic systems in use across Africa. What they sound like depends on multiple variables: first, whether the system comes from vocal discoveries (formants of human speech or overtone singing) or from the use of an instrument; second, if its origins are in instrumental techniques, whether it is based on one, or more than one, fundamental; third, if there is more than one fundamental, what their interval relationships are; and finally, how high up the series of partials the tones are selectively reinforced.

The futility of restricting the source of African musical style or influence on African-American musical evolution to any one area of Africa applies to all aspects of musical development. Along with the retention of other musical elements, the blues matrix grows out of an African Matrix that absorbs harmonic concepts from a sinuous historical progression that reflects the trade roots, conquests, and coalitions that blended African language and cultures over thousands of years. Kubik points out that:

> In 1998, a flyer was circulated announcing the appearance of the Garland Encyclopedia of World Music. On that leaflet, the publishers subjected readers to a test with five questions under this heading: "How Well Do You Know World Music?" The first of these questions in statement form was "American jazz borrows its harmonic structure from European classical music." Readers were supposed to mark whether the statement was true or false. The answer given on the back of the flyer for those still in doubt was "True." Thereby was endorsed one of the most tenacious stereotypes about jazz, the

all-embracing notion that harmony in jazz and other African-American music was "European" in origin, while the rhythm was "African."

Unfortunately, the facts are much more complex. Before the topic called "jazz theory" became part of the curriculum in jazz schools across the United States, harmonic practices in jazz were not always so Western or "European." Chord symbols such as [Gm. sup.9], [G.sup.09], [E.sup.o7], [E.sup.(7[flat]5)], and so on, with their implicit reference to Western music theory, had served jazz musicians as a useful notational set, just as the Roman alphabet is useful for writing English, French, Latin, and Kiswahili. These symbols are coins with a hidden face. Jazz chords and progressions have functioned like the system of the orixa in Brazil. To a Catholic, the orixa can be explained as a set of Catholic saints, but a Yoruba from Nigeria will recognize all of them as transcendental beings in the Yoruba religion, and Afro-Brazilians in the Candomble religious meetings will think both ways.

Melville J. Herskovits (1941), to whom we owe much insight into the processes of culture contact, called such phenomena syncretism. Herskovits's terminology, embracing selection, retention, survival, reinterpretation, syncretism, and cultural focus, is still very useful, although occasionally with some necessary conceptual modification. Syncretism, for example, should not be understood as a blend or merger of different cognitive systems; rather, it is, at least originally, an attempt at a parallel, "bilingual" presentation of ideas that one can read in either of the two codes.

> From a standpoint in Western music theory claiming universal applicability, it is often difficult to comprehend that jazz musicians have always converted the tonal-harmonic resources provided by the Western instruments that they played to suit their own concepts, strongly rooted in blues tonality. From my viewpoint, as someone who has spent a lifetime in African cultures and recorded some twenty-six thousand items of African music since 1959 in eighteen countries, jazz harmony at its structural and aesthetic level is based predominantly on African matrices, although it must be added that individual jazz performers, ensembles, and composers vary in the degree to which their harmonic practices and understandings are more African- or more European-derived. It may vary even from one work to another or one performer to another (Kubik 83).

The characteristic style previously applied to performance of one traditional African instrument was transferred readily to any other musical instruments available in America, or incorporated into newly invented instruments that Africans made out of any materials at hand in their new daily environment. Apparently this brand of transference was also true with regards to adapting stylistic elements of traditional African harmonic, rhythmic, and melodic construction to jazz and other African-American music.

Composers can assign meaning to musical instruments that give added depth to their creations. Music is a very diverse means of communication that carries multiple symbolic meanings. In African musical tradition it is most often associated with consecrated deities and practice. Music symbolized sacred personalities in ancient societies and musical instruments were often assigned specific purposes in ancient times. Ancient iconography reveals a great deal about the significance of music in ancient Egyptian society and Lise Manniche has studied the relationship between the sacred and secular music of ancient Egypt. She first explains that the appearance of the Egyptian goddess in many different aspects reflects the Egyptian way of approaching issues from multiple angles. Hathor and many other deities were versatile and adapted to whichever situation the theologians assigned. Towards the end of the Pharaonic Period, Hathor frequently shared her attributes with Isis. Isis was a member of an important Egyptian trinity. Isis was the wife of Osiris, King of the Underworld, and she was the mother of Horus whom Osiris engendered posthumously. Although not identified by name, Isis most likely played a vital part in the depiction of the resurrection on a coffin of the Roman Period, as she is most probably playing the trumpet in that iconography, where a female sounds the trumpet to Osiris to the extent that the great god is crying (Manniche 62–64).

Although few gods are depicted playing instruments, Egyptian temple musicians are often represented in paintings and other artistic works. Frequently lone musicians are shown performing directly to a god on private monuments as an act of devotion. In such cases the name of the musician can often be established. Manniche reveals some names that she found:

> A certain Harnakht of Mendes plays a double oboe before the ram-headed god of his town; harpist Harwoz plays to Haroeris; Zekhensefankh plays the harp to Re-Harakhti; the chief singer Raia plays to Ptah. Other representations include a man playing the lyre to Sakhmet; a lutenist named Pedekhons who is represented with his instrument on a statue of the god; a trumpeter on a statue of the goddess Wazet. The single harpist playing for his god is so common an image that the subject deserves special consideration and a whole chapter is devoted to it (58).

Manniche also discovered an inscription on a statuette of Amenemhab (nicknamed Mahu) that refers to him as chief of singers of Amun and shows Mahu playing an arched harp to the sun. The deity (named Re) is shown as the sun-disc and Mahu is specifically called "singer of the noble harp of Amun." Mahu was probably in office near the end of the eighteenth dynasty, possibly just before the Amarna Period. The following text reveals that the sun is setting on the western horizon, while Mahu is singing praises to the sun god in order to obtain a favor:

Praise to you millions and millions of times!
I have come to you, adoring your beauty.
Your mother Nut [the sky] embraces you.
You are joyful as you traverse the sky and the earth.
May the gods of the Underworld worship you [and sing] your praise
When you hear my words which worship you every day,
So that you endow me with a burial in peace after enduring
old age and my *ba* being among my ancestors, following [the king]
(Manniche 60).

Numerous musical instruments are seen in both secular contexts and in scenes of Egyptian religious ceremonies and festivals. In some cases the nature of particular musical ensembles is difficult to distinguish. Manniche also discusses a little steatite bowl dedicated to the "Lord of Coptos" by Petearpocrates from around 500 B.C. It has a relief with a row of musicians proceeding towards a shrine containing a large portrait of Hathor. The musicians form a chain 'round the bowl and are shown playing a round tambourine, lyre, one-handed clappers, and the double oboe. One musician slaps her bare buttocks in lieu of playing an instrument. Their dress suggests that all are female, with the oboist perhaps being the exception. It is not clear if the performers were an official attachment to the cult of the goddess, or if they were part of a popular procession. Manniche says:

Another scene showing musicians performing in honour of Hathor comes from the Graeco-Roman temple at Medamud, eight kilometers north of Thebes. Three women play the angular harp, a minute barrel-shaped drum and a lute; a fourth woman plays no instrument but appears to be singing. Preceding the whole group are two ladies adorned with flowers; one, who raises her hands, is called "the one who sweetens evil," a phrase which must surely proclaim the role of music in this particular scene. The caption for the drummer and harpist is unusually eloquent: "The members of the choir take up their instruments and play them. The songstresses in full number adore the Golden Goddess and make music to the Golden Goddess: they never cease their chanting." The lutenist and gesticulating lady are accorded the following lines "We dance for you; we dance for you, O mistress, the words required by the adorers." This suggests a mime expressing words in praise of the goddess (62–63).

A hymn concluding with universal adoration of the Golden Goddess, written behind the performer of the lute and the singer, reveals a bit more about the performance:

Come, O Golden Goddess, the singers chant
(for it is nourishment for the heart to dance the *iba*,
to shine over the feast at the hour of retiring
and to enjoy—dance at night).

Come! The procession takes place at the site of drunkenness,
this area where one wanders in marshes.
Its routine is set, the rules firm:
nothing is left to be desired.

The royal children satisfy you with what you love
and the officials give offerings to you.
The lector priest exalts you singing a hymn,
and the wise men read the rituals.

The priest honours you with his basket,
and the drummers take their tambourines.
Ladies rejoice in your honour with garlands
and girls [do the same] with wreaths.

Drunkards play tambourines for you in the cool night,
and those they wake up bless you.
The bedouin dance for you in their garments,
and Asiatics [dance] with their sticks.
The griffins wrap their wings around you,
the hares stand on their hind legs for you.
The hippopatami adore with wide open mouths,
and their legs salute your face (64).

The flute and oboe seem to have been Egyptian instruments of choice for temple musicians. The end-blown flute, that seems appropriate in a religious setting, is found frequently in secular scenes of the Old Kingdom but rarely in later periods. Other Egyptian iconography often shows a single flautist in an intimate setting, performing before a god in the presence of a worshipper; or a pair of male flautists playing together at the festival, such as that of Sokaris, a funerary deity. The oboe is often found at ritual ceremonies, especially where a priest consecrates an offering to a deceased person. Manniche describes,

A musician of Hathor may follow the priest, blowing her double pipe. This is reminiscent of the use of the aulos in Greek temples, where offerings were accompanied by this instrument in lieu of the human voice. It is interesting to note in this context, too, that the double oboe was one of the instruments banned from the shrine of Osiris at Philae, but allowed to sound in the neighbouring temple of Hathor (64).

Of all of the instruments mentioned above that are found in secular as well as religious scenes, none have more specific sacred associations than the sistrum. The sistrum is a rattle that also served as a cult object in its own rite in ancient Egypt, frequently bearing the effigy of Hathor. The instrument evolved in two forms. The older "naos-shaped" sistrum dates back to the Old Kingdom, and was made from faience and consisted of a straight papyrus-shaped handle with a frame on top in the form of a miniature chapel, or naos. The volutes flanking the naos may mention Hathor's horns. Within the frame were bars of metal supporting metal discs. The sistrum's sound would have been delicate.

"Power is the ability to make change."

—Geneva Overholser

References

Beaugrande, Robert de. "The Processes of Invention: Association and Recombination." *College Composition and Communication* 30 (1979): 260–7. Blesh, Rudi. *Shining Trumpets*. New York: Knopf, 1958.

Bodin, Ron. *Voodoo: Past and Present*. University of Southwestern Louisiana, Lafayette, Louisiana, 1990.

Bruchez, Margaret Sabom. "Artifacts that Speak for Themselves: Sounds Underfoot in Mesoamerica." 4 April 2006. *ScienceDirect*. November 2007 <http://www.sciencedirect. com/ science?_ob=ArticleURL&_udi=B6WH6-4JMVHY0-&_user=10&_rdoc=1&_fmt=&_ orig=search&_sort=d&view=c&_acct=C000050221&_version=1&_urlVersion=0&_userid =10&md5=ba3318d1623be6106a087a734799f96c>.

Budd, Malcolm. *Music and The Emotions: The Philosophical Theories*. London: Routledge, 1992, 37–39.

Bundy, Murray Wright. "'Invention' and 'Imagination' in the Renaissance." *Journal of English and Germanic Philology* 29 (1930b): 535–45.

Caernarvon-Smith, Patricia. *Audience Analysis and Response*. Pembroke: Firman Technical Publications, 1983.

Cassimere, Raphael. *History of St. Louis Cemetery*. Compiled by Raphael Cassimere, Jr., Danny Barker, Florence Borders, D. Clive Hardy, Joseph Logsdon and Charles Rousseve. Sponsored by New Orleans NAACP, Carrollton, New Orleans, 1980.

Chun-yuan, Chang. *Creativity and Taoism: A Study of Chinese Philosophy, Art and Poetry*. London: Wildwood House, 1963.

Conway, David. *Ritual Magic: An Occult Primer*. New York: E. P. Dutton, 1972.

Cope, D. *Virtual Music—Computer Synthesis of Musical Style*. Cambridge, MA: MIT Press, 2001.

Cosentino, Donald J. ed. *Sacred Arts of Haitian Vodou*. Los Angeles, CA: UCLA Fowler Museum of Cultural History, 1995.

———. *Vodou Things*. The Art of Pierrot Barra and Marie Cassaise. University Press of Mississippi, Jackson, 1998.

Davidson, Basil. *Africa in History: Themes and Outlines*. New York: Collier Books, 1974.

Davis, Wade. *The Serpent and the Rainbow*. United States of America: Warner Books, 1985.

Deren, Maya. *Divine Horsemen: The Living Gods of Haiti.* United States of America: McPherson and Company, 1953.

Diccionario de la lengua española. Real Academia Española. Madrid: Editorial Espasa-Calpe, 1992.

Dictionary of American Regional English. Volume I. Introduction and A-C. Cambridge, MA, and London: The Belknap Press of Harvard University Press, 1985.

Dictionary of American Regional English. Volume II. D-H. Cambridge, MA and London: The Belknap Press of Harvard University Press, 1991.

Farr, Tyler. "Vincent Herring's Symmetrical Saxophone Solo on Straight Street." *Down Beat* (August 2008): 90–91.

Fiehrer, Thomas, ed. *Plantation Society in the Americas: An Interdisciplinary Journal of Tropical and Subtropical History and Culture. Carnival in Perspective.* New York: Athens Printing Company, 1990.

Gandolfo, Charles. *Marie Laveau of New Orleans: The Great Voodoo Queen.* New Orleans, LA: New Orleans Historic Voodoo Museum, 1992.

Grassi, Ernesto. *Rhetoric as Philosophy: The Humanist Tradition.* Trans. John Michael Krois and Azizeh Azodi. Carbondale: Southern Illinois UP, 2001.

Hall, Manly Palmer. *The Secret Teachings of All Ages: An Encyclopedic Outline of Masonic, Hermetic, Qabbalistic and Rosicrucian Symbolical Philosophy.* New York: Jeremy P. Tarcher/ Penguin, 2003.

Hurston, Zora Neale. *Mules and Men.* United States of America: J. B. Lippincott and Company, 1935.

———. *Tell My Horse.* United States of America: J. B. Lippincott and Company, 1938.

Jourdain, Robert. *Music, the Brain, and Ecstasy: How Music Captures Our Imagination.* New York: HarperCollins Publishers, 1998.

Khan, Hazrat Inayat. *The Mysticism of Sound and Music: The Sufi Teaching of Hazrat Inayat Khan.* Boston: Shambhala, 1996.

Kubik, G. *Africa and the Blues.* Jackson, MS: University Press of Mississippi, 1999. Langer, Susan. "Building and Weaving: Esthetic and Technical Metaphors as an Index to the Essential Unity of the Arts." *The Journal of Philosophy* 39.25 (December 3, 1942).

Lateef, Yusef. *Method on How to Perform Autophysiopsychic Music.* Amherst, MA: Fana Music, 1979.

Lee, Byong Won. *The Sinawi Performance in the Kut: Universality and Idiosyncrasy in the Korean Shaman Ritual Music.* The University of Hawaii. Unpublished manuscript, 2005.

Lee, Yong-Shik. *Shaman Ritual Music in Korea.* Seoul, Korea: Jimoondang, 2004.

Lewis, Ralph M., F. R. C. "The Function of Ritualism." *Rosicrucian Digest* (February 1986): 23–26.

Maniktala, Rakesh. "Beliefs." *Spiritualism, Modern Science and Ancient History.* March 2008 <http://geocities.com/ancientscience/beliefs>.

Martinez, Raymond J. *Mysterious Marie Laveau and Folk Tales Along the Mississippi.* New Orleans: Hope Publications, 1956.

Molin, Son, Exc. Mgr. *Dictionnaire Bambara-Français et Français-Bambara*. Seine: Les Presses Missionaires, 1955.

Murphy, Joseph M. *Santería: An African Religion in America*. Boston: Beacon Press, 1988.

Ortiz, Fernando. *Glosario de afronegrismos*. La Habana: Editorial de Ciencias Sociales, 1990.

———. *Nuevo cataura de cubanismos*. La Habana, Cuba: Editorial de Ciencias Sociales, 1985.

———. *Tomado de la primera edición*. La Habana: Imprenta "El siglo XX," 1924.

Overstreet, H. A. *The Mature Mind*. New York: W. W. Norton and Company, Inc., 1949.

Pachter, Henry M. *Paracelsus: Magic into Science*. New York: Collier Books, 1951.

Parker Rhodes, Jewell. *Voodoo Dreams*. New York: Picador USA, 1995.

Pelton, Robert W. *The Complete Book of Voodoo*. New York: Berkley Publishing Corporation, 1972.

Petit Larousse. Librairie Larousse. Paris, 1964.

Powell, Cory S. *God in the Equation: How Einstein Became the Prophet of the New Religious Era*. New York: The Free Press, 2002.

Prose, Francine. *Marie Laveau*. New York: Berkley Publishing Corporation, 1947.

Rigaud, Milo. *Secrets of Voodoo*. New York: Pocket Books, 1971.

Saxon, Lyle, Robert Tallant and Edward Dreyer. *Gumbo Ya-Ya: A Collection of Louisiana Folk Tales*. New York: Bonanza Books, 1945.

Stevenson, David B. "Freud's Division of the Mind." *The Victorian Web*. Brown University. 1996. <http://www.victorianweb.org/science/freud/division.html>.

Tallant, Robert. *Voodoo in New Orleans*. Gretna: Pelican Publishing Company, 1983.

———. *The Voodoo Queen*. New York: G. P. Putnam's Sons, 1956.

Valduran, Albert, Thomas A. Klingler, Margaret M. Marshall, Kevin J. Rotet. *Dictionary of Louisiana Creole*. Bloomington and Indianapolis: Indiana University Press, 1998.

Varela, Beatriz. "The Lexicon of Marie Laveau's Voodoo." *Organo Oficial de la Sociedad de Amigos del Pais*. (1998). February 2008 <http://www.amigospais guaracabuya.org/oagbv004.php>.

Wilmore, Gayraud S. *Black Religion and Black Radicalism*. Maryknoll, NY: Orbis, 1983.

Chapter Eight
Secular and Sacred: Ascension

The LAW of KARMA (Balance, Proportion, and Decision)

All human actions/deeds performed voluntarily or involuntarily are termed as **Karma.** Broadly, karma is divided in two categories.

1. **Nishkama Karma**—performed as a duty, without expecting any "karma-phal" (result/benefit) out of it. Karma of highly evolved yogis falls into this category.
2. **Sakama Karma**—where the performer wishes a particular result out of the karma. Karma of most humans falls into this category only. It can be good, bad, or mixed type of sakama karma.

Categorizing as per mode, human beings perform three types of karma:

1. "manasa"—by thought
2. "vacha"—by speech
3. "karmana"—by actions

Hindu scriptures consider nishkama karma to be the highest form of karma that leads the soul towards salvation.

"Meditations": Ritual and Magic with Music

Endless interconnected phenomena inspire creativity. Inspiration often comes during periods of meditation, and meditation can lead to transcendence. Meditation, transcendence, spirituality, magic, and ritual are often associated with music. Some people automatically associate magic with superstition. Superstition attributes an array of phenomena to supernatural forces, often to such an extent that demons, saints, or gods constantly interfere with the eternal course of nature. Paracelsus believed that all natural phenomena have a natural cause and "are determined by immutable laws, accessible to investigation by experiment and to understanding by the human reason" (64). Music may provide an opportunity to observe the intersection between reason, transcendence, ritual, and magic, and to witness the effect that this mixture has on listeners when balanced successfully.

"Musicism" involves an ecumenical, cross-cultural, and interdisciplinary approach to binding music conceptually with magic, science, mathematics, spirituality, philosophy, and psychology. Thus "Hesterian Musicism" entails a personal decision to approach music in an interdisciplinary, eclectic, and ecumenical way. Tones and words have a long history of magical, mystical, and spiritual applications. Magic was the forerunner of religion, rituals, and rites associated with magical practice. People at times find it difficult to differentiate between magic and religion, especially given that intangible dimensions are associated with both realms. Nonetheless, music is always intimately associated with both. In contemporary society, some feel that religion is a social phenomenon that has positive effects on society, while others consider magic a practice generally having detrimental effects on the community, much like superstition does. Residual elements of magical rites remain in some progressive religions. Magic often involves music and visual elements accompanied by verbal incantations intended to invoke esoteric spirits and objects. If nature's inherent forces are the causes of all manifestation in life, there is no magic. The magician ultimately seeks to do what the scientist accomplishes in the laboratory: to observe and duplicate natural phenomena. When magicians or spiritual practitioners incorporate music into their work they gain a sonic tool that provides intimate access to the esoteric realms of human consciousness. The magical process is intended to invoke natural forces directly, making them work to serve the magician's purpose. Author Ralph M. Lewis felt that the magician resorts to imagining primary causes that trigger natural forces into action. Lewis states:

> In religion, the individual courts the favor of a divine being by resorting to such rites as sacrifices, prayer, and praise. The religionist seeks not to gain his end directly, but through the intermediary of a super-natural being. Thus religion does have a beneficial effect on the individual, for he believes in the necessity of adjusting his conduct to the conceived requirements of the deity to whom he appeals. Thus he holds that only a good man can expect an answer to his divine supplications.

The magician, however, like the scientist, works entirely with impersonal factors. Like the scientist, the magician's procedure, basically, is to "influence the course of nature" by finding the connection between cause and effects (23).

Composers understand music's potential transcendent power and attempt to place musical elements where they work to obtain desired results, but the ultimate outcome can never be fully anticipated. From one perspective a ritual is an emotional and mysterious celebration that evades empirical analysis or plausible explanations. Ritual is also directed towards the compartments where the logical and intuitive realms of the mind struggle or compete. We all engage in daily or seasonal rituals, even when we do not label them as such. We use music to accompany routine daily rituals such as driving to work, exercising, making love, or eating dinner.

Rituals were observed in a broader range of contexts in early societies. References to rituals are often associated with religious doctrines and dogma. Modern rituals and ceremonies, that receive the greatest sense of reverence, conscientious observance, and emphasis in contemporary society, are those associated with religious and spiritual worship. Worship often evolved into routine activity, objectified in gesture and symbolism, to convey the notion of a deity or to invoke a supernatural power. Habitual formulas were transmitted from priests or tribal heads to their constituents as a means of spiritual intercourse that aspired towards communication with spiritual beings. Music was most often an important and inseparable part of such ritual drama and transcendence. Most of the time music enjoyed greater freedom and flexibility than the words and actions associated with formal religious ceremonies and situations.

Music evolves slowly because humankind adheres strongly to established patterns and tradition. Prehistoric and modern people share this strong attachment to routine, security in connection to the past, and alignment with the familiar. Rituals demonstrate respect for those acts practiced by forebears of particular traditions. Rituals permeate compositional and performance practice outside traditional ritual settings as well. The roles of instruments in a rhythm section, the practices of "trading fours" or "stop-time solos" are examples of musical performance procedures established in early jazz that are traditional routines still maintained in some circles. The choice of instrumentation, costumes, and the assorted implements worn by performers, body movement, rhythms, and other performance factors express sounds, feeling, or beliefs that often perpetuate familiar traditions. Certain circumstances are retained as ritual behavior perhaps due to a desire to preserve cherished memories. Innovators often ground their artistic thinking in the spirit of such traditional rituals while finding new ways to construct fresh artistic versions that reflect their contemporary world. Traditions were often perpetuated through myths and other forms transmitted orally during earlier periods of human history.

Myths are products of the imagination and are devised to explain phenomena for which no physical causes have been perceived. Myths are given objectivity and brought into the realm of experience and reality by means of the ritual drama. A ritual drama is often more than a portrayal of the myth. It is thought to be a means of invoking the efficacy attributed to the mythological characters. In other words, ritual dramas have a way of sympathetically relating the observer or participant to the mythological beings so that he shares in whatever powers or virtues these beings are thought to have. It is a vicarious act in that we put ourselves into the place of those beings thought to be of another realm (Ibid.).

Many myths were preserved in songs. Music fortifies and augments experiences in our memories. Ritual can help focus our subconscious mind while also exciting our emotional and psychic nature. Rituals performed on stage with music can stimulate a passive audience enough to transform a performance hall into an inspirational communal arena of human interaction. Rites and rituals introduce symbolic expressions of concepts that generate a universal language capable of being understood by a wide range of people. The sounds, gestures, and symbols of rituals transfer in ways that transmit enhanced clarity of function and idea when music is involved. Today, people around the world perform, listen to, and enjoy music from regions of the world they may never visit. Youth throughout the world emulate and memorize hip-hop culture and songs (and even the particular speech and body movement associated with certain popular artists), even despite an inability to translate the words into their own spoken language. The spirit and emotional message of such music is thoroughly understood. Ritual in music making, therefore, is potentially a powerful communicative tool whose effectiveness extends beyond words.

A great deal of human communication expresses emotions. In prehistoric times rituals may have served to pantomime intangible or inexplicable feelings and ideas. Music can use aural, visual, and kinetic ritual elements to heighten musical experience, sending performers and listeners on magical journeys. Although rituals attempt to free the spirit and create an environment where magical phenomena manifest, spontaneous composers often use concrete flexible structures and clear parameters that help performers for such events maintain logic, balance, and continuity. Responsibility increases exponentially as degrees of musical freedom increase and expand. There are a number of ways to practice creating conspicuous structures that provide guidance for listeners while allowing greater freedom of expression for adventurous artists.

Responsible Freedom

Premeditated composers have the luxury of time, but spontaneous composers do not. An improviser employs many of the same skills that a premeditated or spontaneous composer does, but both spontaneous composers and improvisers must make use of their acquired knowledge and developed skill more rapidly and with great accuracy. Spontaneous composition and improvisation involves varying degrees of responsible freedom that evolve through a process of individual and collective development. Learning jazz theory, improvisation, and mastering the practice of spontaneous composition/performance in a variety of styles can begin with emphasis on inventing new ideas, elemental structures, and procedures over the framework of the twelve-bar blues form, modal materials, and melodic derivatives of assorted harmonic progressions. Musicians can also explore methods that use chance operations and indeterminate procedure as motivation and structures for spontaneous performance. Spontaneous composers also explore methods designed to allow sounds (timbre), dynamics, and other fundamental elements to stand unencumbered or enhanced by dramatic framework, personal expression, and psychological underpinning. Electronics often serve a major role in defining the textures, dynamics, and structural parameters of spontaneous composition.

Various forms of structure are important, as they provide a musical framework with which to operate. With recognizable landmarks performers can refer back to previous musical elements or anticipate structure-providing compositions with an organic logic and continuity. Musicians should work towards building melodic, harmonic, and rhythmic vocabulary quickly through imitating masters of the traditions they are exploring. Like language, musical vocabulary is learned in part by imitating fluent "speakers" before developing personal styles. At its best, spontaneous composition can evolve as naturally as speech or conversation, as the Charles Mingus/Eric Dolphy duets on "So Long Eric" clearly demonstrate.[11] The composition was conceived as a temporary goodbye letter for Dolphy, who decided to stay in Europe indefinitely after the band's upcoming tour there. The same composition soon afterwards became a tribute to Dolphy when he lapsed into a sudden diabetic coma in Berlin and passed away at the age of thirty-six. Dolphy was an original voice in African-American music on all instruments he mastered, but he cut precious few sessions as a leader.

The preconditions for imaginative and flexible spontaneous composition are well-known among experienced performers. Musicians engaged in spontaneous composition or structured improvisation dig deeply into their minds and spirits to blend new ideas with sturdy old ideas. Their music is often infused with fervent enthusiasm (spontaneous adrenaline) that can keep both performers and audiences on the edge of their seats with magical and eternal features. Achieving such an elevated level of artistic effectiveness demands mature instincts and good will on the part of all ensemble members involved. Developing effective improvisation strategies requires much more than common sense, and musicians must acquire a broad set of expertise. A masterful improviser or spontaneous composer is thus a skilled craftsman and great actor who must continually make something beautiful out of little or nothing. Spontaneous composition is dependent upon a cultivated ability to draw upon a backlog of concepts, skills, and repertoire of music, training, and experience. All performers must share a vision, and all performers must be proficient at comprehending the multifarious cues that guide the direction of a performance. Lack of skill, cooperation, or imagination on the part of any performer within the group can stifle the success of a spontaneous performance. Perpetual culture of curiosity, persistent review of procedures, instantaneous decision-making, and an obligation to set aside premeditated routine exist. Successful performance necessitates focused attention and flexible action directed towards the goal of creating beauty, logic, and organic process. Learning takes place continually throughout the collective environment as members of the ensemble interpret signals

---

[1]   Listen to "So Long Eric" on *Charles Mingus Sextet With Eric Dolphy: Cornell 1964* [Blue Note; 2007] to hear an example of this composition.

and assess what is needed to bring about aesthetic success. We can begin by developing skills within conventional frameworks:

I. How do we combine components of a successful spontaneous music-making adventure? Creating interesting musical backgrounds with one and two distinct levels of stratification is an unusual but productive place to begin. After considering supporting structures, then move to the production of foreground features.

    A. Learning major, minor, and modal scales is essential to navigate through the basic chord constructions of tonal and modal harmony. The principles involved will also apply later as you evolve towards "symmetrical scales," such as the diminished and whole-tone constructs.

    B. Try incorporating various elements from all musical knowledge accumulated to create accompaniment figures.

    C. Learn to dialogue with all ensemble members rhythmically, melodically, and harmonically.

    D. Try inventing interesting free melody (with attention directed towards pitches, rhythms, duration, and space). Develop the ability to perform any interval that you conceive in your head. This ability enables musicians to perform any melody heard, which is an important tool when improvising and interacting confidently with ensemble members.

    E. Key fluency involves inventing melodies constructed with respect to underlying harmonic structure. Learning intervals in all keys is critical to navigating chord structures with assurance. The point is to develop the ability to create principal linear ideas involving elements of pitch, rhythm, and density with respect to underlying harmonic structures. Expand this skill by first taking familiar melodies and transposing them to different keys by ear.

    F. Next, develop a musical vocabulary by listening to recordings of selected jazz soloists and transcribing and memorizing their solos; relating the solo transcription to the composition's chord changes. Include all the nuances or tone, articulation, and rhythmic variation involved.

    G. Record all stages of your learning process. Listen back to your recordings and identify things that do not sound satisfying, and then analyze your music to figure out why it does or does not work. Decide if particular notes or rhythms may have provided more gratifying results.

II. Developing basic piano skills is *very helpful*. Nothing fancy, just work out common seventh chord types (minor 7, dominant 7, minor 7 w/flat fifth, dominant 7 w/flat ninth, major 7). Being able to recognize the "flavor" of a chord rapidly will increase your response speed in constructing a melody with respect to the harmony.

III. Understand the dominant/tonic (V7—I) relationship and cycle of fifths. This is an underpinning of Western tonal music. Learning to recognize and execute ii7-V7 chord progressions (and their substitutions) will enable you to perform the most common harmonic structure in early and modern jazz and popular music.

IV. Thinking of an ii7-V7 progression as a key area or "chunk" of information enables you to consider a construct, such as a B7 E7 progression, as the key area of A major, as opposed to considering each scale and chord choices individually. Ultimately this will allow you to understand that a melodic line should both reinforce the chord tones of B7 and E7 respectively, and move with a strong sense of good voice leading, linear logic, and melodic direction as well.

V. Following the Lead Soloist:
  A. Begin by identifying the fundamental tone of any given region (tonic, root, etc.); at first, keep musical contributions simple and secondary to the broader compositional goals.
  B. Be responsive, not self indulgent; self indulgence rarely produces meaningful composition.
  C. Changing conceptual, melodic, or harmonic directions requires a broad vocabulary.
  D. There ARE wrong notes! Logic must remain clear rhythmically, melodically, and harmonically. However, don't be reluctant to employ repetition and dissonance to provide variety, continuity, and color.

VI. Taking Breaths, Creating Balance, and Maintaining Interest:
  A. Live in the moment, vary your melodic contour and motion (similar, contrary, and oblique), and breathe by leaving sufficient space to listen to what's going on within the ensemble, enabling you to gain ideas about what to play next.
  B. Keep levels of ensemble stratification clear in function and always harmonious.
  C. Supporting and enhancing the soloist is the first priority.
  D. Sound and silence are mutually important considerations that both require careful attention.
  E. Think carefully about variety of timbre (avoid incessant or monotonous instrumental sounds).
  F. Structural concepts should be mutually understood (pitch sets, rhythmic modes, mood, message, location, etc.) if all musicians are painting a mutual canvas.
  G. Determine a conceptual outline carefully before performance.

VII. Create one-, two-, and three-minute spontaneous compositions for a trio maintaining all musical considerations mentioned above.
  A. Practice ii7-V7 patterns through the cycle of fifths accurately then develop associated etudes and melodies individually and as an ensemble.
  B. Practice ii7-V7 patterns, etudes, and melodies descending and ascending by whole steps; descending and ascending by half steps; descending and ascending by major and minor thirds, etc.

VIII. Orchestration—Instruments have their own personalities and natural roles. However, we should try to break out of restrictive molds and have instruments assume roles they rarely assume. This helps with balance, creativity, empathy, and variety in a composition.

IX. Whether a composition is completely written out or spontaneous, the end result should be the same sonically: the music must be beautiful, well-constructed, and interesting. Spontaneous playing should sound as if it were premeditatedly composed. Players should strive to improvise with interesting and well-constructed melodies, rhythms, and harmonies.

For many artists and philosophers the interaction between harmony and dissonance (tension and release) is the motivating creative force behind beauty, wisdom, and the evolution of knowledge. The definition of consonance and dissonance is arbitrary, relative, and culturally specific. Although there is some agreement around the world based upon fundamental aspects of the overtone series, sounds that are consonant to one set of ears may be dissonant to another. The nineteenth-century physicist Herman von Helmholtz proposed a theory of consonance and dissonance based on qualities he called beating and roughness within the harmonic series. Many cultures have noted that ratios involving relatively small integers (e.g., 1:1, 2:1, 3:2, 4:3, 5:3, 5:4, 6:5) produce what they mutually consider "harmonious" intervals (or consonances) within their respective music. In 1863, Helmholtz proposed that the degree of dissonance produced by an interval is related to the degree of roughness produced between the partials. In the even-tempered system, for instance, a separation of two frequencies by one semitone produces the most roughness in the middle register, with a separation of two semitones considered the next most dissonant interval.

For some, beauty occurs only when all physical components are in relative harmonious balance. Others equate qualities—dissonance and consonance—with more subjective perceptions of morality and human nature. Many people associate sacred music with compositions written primarily in tonal harmony. The tones and intervallic structures that evolved from European tonal harmony became an intricate array of harmonic interconnections that form a somewhat arbitrary foundation for governing tonal harmonic. The acceptance of a musical system is ultimately determined by mutual agreement based upon the short-term memory of listeners, the tolerance range of the human ear as it evolves within a musical culture, and the various manners in which tones and melodies are perceived. After all, concepts of good, bad, beauty, ugliness, consonance, and dissonance are in the ear of the beholder.

The world is called beautiful and its Creator is designated the *Good* because good perforce must act in conformity with its own nature, and good acting according to its own nature is harmony because the good which it accomplishes is harmonious with the good which it is. Beauty, therefore, is harmony manifesting its own intrinsic nature in the world of form.

The universe is made up of successive gradations of good, these gradations of good, these gradations ascending from matter (which is the least degree of good) to spirit (which is the greatest degree of good). In man, his superior nature is the *summum bonum*. It therefore follows that his highest nature most readily cognizes good, because the good external to him in the world is in harmonic ratio with the good present in his soul (Hall LXXXI–LXXXIV).

Music is a language that can speak articulately across cultural lines. Musicians spend years learning musical vocabulary before becoming fully capable of fusing scales, chords, rhythms, and other elements into the emotions, ideas, and expressions that later form poetic or complex musical expression. While all language can convey abstract thoughts and feelings, music transcends the limitations of spoken vocabulary and is capable of conveying ideas limited only by human imagination. Not all agree that musical expression constitutes valid language. Susan Langer suggests that, "Although we do receive it as a significant form, and comprehend the processes of life and sentience through its audible, dynamic pattern, it is not a language, because it has no vocabulary." She continues:

> Perhaps, in the same spirit of strict nomenclature, one really should not refer to its content as "meaning," either. Just as music is only loosely and inexactly called a language, so its symbolic function is only loosely called meaning, because the factor of conventional reference is missing from it (Langer 151–152).

On the contrary, music is a language that conveys meaning that is understood more universally than spoken language. Just as the language of love can be felt intimately, clearly, and strongly in ways that transcend the limitation of words, translating musical language and meaning into spoken language is impossible, nonetheless. Subconsciously, people have always appreciated the power of music. Some composers and other artists create inspired works that possess unworldly qualities that ancient people often associated with the supernatural. The intrinsic qualities of some artistic creations transcend time and cultural orientation. Knowledge and inspiration that generate some artistic manifestations are often based upon ancient esoteric traditions handed down over thousands of years. The healing and therapeutic capabilities of music involve and contain such ancient wisdom. Manly P. Hall suggests that Greek initiates gained their knowledge of the philosophic and therapeutic aspects of music from the Egyptians. In Egypt, Hermes was considered the founder of art and Isis and Osiris were patrons of music and poetry. According to Hall, Plato declared that songs and poetry existed in Egypt for at least ten thousand years, and that:

> These were of such an exalted and inspiring nature that only gods or god-like men could have composed them. In the mysteries the lyre was regarded as the secret symbol of the human constitution, the body of the instrument representing the physical form, the strings the nerves, and the musician the spirit. Playing upon the nerves, the spirit thus created the harmonies of normal functioning, which, however, became discords if the nature of man were defiled (Hall LXXXI–LXXXIV).

The ancient Greeks were not the first to develop the idea that music could be used to heal. Older world cultures used elements, vibration and music to govern aspects of daily life. Some investigators of Egyptian pyramid construction speculate that Egyptians used the power of vibrations to help glide the large limestone slabs to their resting places during the building process. Aristotle thought the sound of the flute could arouse strong emotions and thus serve as a catalyst for cathartic release. Ancient Greeks thought that the music of zithers aided digestion and used its music to accompany meals. Some musicians thought that the Greeks' Aeolian mode could aid in the treatment of mental disturbance and induce sleep. The Lydian mode was considered ideal for children and could soothe the soul. It was Pythagoras, however, who developed the concept of healing through melodic intervals and rhythms in Greece.

The behavior of melodic intervals is often a key determinant in leading our minds on musical journeys. The way tones are approached and left are principal factors for determining intervallic function. Thus a three- or four-note grouping can form a basic unit of a melodic grouping, especially when analyzing motivically derived melodies. Such melodic groupings are more distinguished when the size of the second interval is different from the first one. When the second interval is identical in size and direction to the first, the third interval then becomes the most important element of distinction.

Analysis of melodic groupings enables us to see how each tone proceeds to the next most inevitable one, and allows us to study the ways grouping boundaries are formed. When melodic grouping boundaries are vaguer they become less predictable, elastic, and poetic, and they enhance the integrity of melody. Because a musical phrase is frequently most interesting as a continuous gesture, the seams between its smaller components must not be too obvious.

A listener's expectation of melodic continuation, repetition, or reversal is often stimulated by a variety of minute internal melodic factors. Elements such as pitch, intervallic relationship, and the direction of melodic motion generally guide the listener's ear. Pitch motion is continued by moving in the same direction (ascending) or reversed by moving in the opposite direction (descending). Likewise, interval can continue in mixed directions with a similar interval (ascending major thirds with descending major thirds) or reverse itself with a contrasting interval (ascending major thirds with descending major seconds). Interval sequences may also imply forward motion and continuity, or suggest a reversal of direction and motion. When a melodic motion involves similar intervals in the same direction, greater continuation is implied. Whenever significant changes in interval size or direction of motion occur, segmentation is implied.

Developing Our Perception of Consonance, Dissonance, and Time

People have often wondered how the brain deals with musical information. Physical, emotional, cognitive, and subconscious factors are involved in all stages of music production and listening. Our perception of consonance and dissonance will most likely continue to evolve, as world societies grow accustomed to a greater range of musical intervals and sonorities. This will constantly test existing theories that the concept of relative dissonance has grounding in neurology and acoustics. Acoustical explanations revolve around the natural qualities of the overtone series. Almost all intervals of the overtone series, its lowest partials, were considered dissonant by certain cultures in remote times. Human ears have gradually evolved to accept increasingly higher frequency combinations from the overtone series as consonant: first the perfect intervals, then the major third, minor third, etc.

People are capable of discerning a vast and diverse array of simultaneous harmonics and sounds that form individual and collective sonic experiences within our aural capacity. Although we can recognize the distinct sounds of an owl while simultaneously hearing the sounds of several conversations, traffic noise, and musical instruments, the ability to remember and reproduce such a complex of sound is complicated. Spontaneous composers must respond immediately to horizontal and vertical movement of tones, rhythmic patterns, dynamics, timbre, and form as these elements unfold in time. Carefully shaping and tracking musical patterns and designs provides compositional orientation and control. Assorted parameters used to analyze, create, and develop melody can be readily applied to systematic thinking with regards to rhythm. In discussing *rhythmic groupings, rhythmic contour,* and *rhythmic tension,* Snyder outlines several helpful ways of thinking about rhythmic organization:

> *Rhythmic groupings* are the actual patterns of time intervals and accents that form music. An accent or larger time interval in the ongoing flow of events will usually form a rhythmic grouping boundary. Paralleling the terms *melodic grouping* and *melodic phrase* in chapter eleven, the terms *rhythmic grouping* and *rhythmic phrase* indicate, respectively, the lowest and the next higher level of grouping in the rhythmic dimension. Rhythmic phrases, then, consist of one or more rhythmic groupings; they are distinguished from these by stronger, more closural boundaries, often delineated by longer event durations or by pauses. Rhythmic (temporal) and melodic grouping factors interact with melodic grouping forces to a large degree, and a particular grouping is usually the result of the interaction of both of these forces. Rhythmic grouping boundaries are the primary factor in establishing the repeating accent patterns of meter.
>
> *Rhythmic contour* is the profile of changing timing patterns in a rhythmic grouping, metaphorically thought of as having a "rising and falling outline" formed by changes in time intervals between events. Faster rhythms with shorter time intervals form the high points of a rhythmic contour. The "height" of a rhythmic contour indicates the amount of purely rhythmic (nonmetrical) tension present at any given moment.
>
> *Rhythmic tension* is tension established within a rhythmic grouping by rhythmic contour. The larger the number of events occurring in a given amount of time, the higher the rhythmic tension. Rhythmic tension is completely

internal to a rhythm, and is *not* dependent on comparison with meter. Hence it is different from metrical tension. Rhythmic tension can be established without a meter or pulse, in a situation of *free rhythm,* where events are organized into patterns without meter, pulse, or both, that is, without the possibility of inferring any regularly repeating accent or pulse structure (237).

How does our brain process musical information? The ability to accurately perceive and remember distances between harmonic and melodic intervals increases as we learn to categorize them intuitively or by rote. Generally, in the West, we categorize individual frequencies as aligning with one of the twelve tones of the chromatic scale. We develop a sense of relative pitch when we can identify the position of a given pitch relative to any starting point in the spectrum of tones. Some musicologists and scientists theorize ways in which musical elements are processed in our brain. Although his analysis is restricted to mostly European classical music, Robert Jourdain attempts to take a somewhat broad and mechanical approach to the question: "What is music?" Jourdain concludes, for instance, that harmony is absorbed in the right brain while rhythm registers in the left hemisphere.

How does the brain go about perceiving chords and cadences? In earlier chapters we saw how harmonic analysis is focused in the auditory cortex of the right brain. Overtone-rich tones are processed predominantly in this hemisphere. By comparison, pure-frequency tones are processed equally on both sides of the brain. Intermediate cases, such as the overtone-poor notes of the flute, are lateralized less than those of other instruments. Behind our harmonic skills are tens of millions of years of evolution applied to identifying animal calls, and hundreds of thousands of years applied to decoding vowel sounds in spoken language. Such sounds change their harmonic content as they unfold, and this has meant that our brains have had to become expert in following harmonic transitions (111–114).

Jourdain intermingles examples from science, psychology, music theory, and philosophy to suggest why music speaks to people and captivates us in ways that supersede words, accounting for our robust connections to it. Jourdain seems to consider music as a mood-enhancing phenomenon people utilize in numerous ways. He suggests that music has evolved universal features that enable composers to use specific brands of music for film scores that can highlight love, fear, suspense, humor, or anger, while remaining personal enough to distinguish one person's invigorating song from another's monotony or annoyance. Although dissonance is arbitrary to a degree, certain qualities of sound have common effects on our ears. Neurological explanations of dissonance focus on the interaction of music and sound with the cochlea or inner ear. Jourdain suggests that:

> A loud pure-frequency sound stimulates a wide-range of receptor cells along the cochlea's basilar membrane. The membrane is most deformed, and the

receptors most activated, at the point along the membrane associated with the particular frequency. But receptors on either side also fire. This range of activation is called the *critical band* for the sound. It has been found that two frequencies form a dissonant interval when their critical bands overlap. By falling so close together along the cochlea, the two sounds upset each other's perception.

The phenomenon goes far in explaining why tones close in frequency are dissonant. The half step [sic] from middle C to D, somewhat less so. Dissonant flags only at three half steps, from C to D-sharp (a minor third), where the second tone falls entirely outside the critical band of the first. For lower frequencies, however, the cochlea crams a broader range of frequencies into a critical band, and tones need to be farther apart to avoid dissonance. At the bottom end of a piano keyboard, tones as much as a fifth apart (seven halfsteps) are dissonant. Harmonious music can hardly be written in this frequency range, and composers normally keep bass tones well separated (111–114).

Musical vibration affects our physical bodies. Intonation is the way frequencies are assigned to specific tones. Intonation can be expressed in an infinite number of ways. Intonation can add color or mood to music. Intonation can also provide different moods to music by introducing musical ideas in different keys. Different frequencies and sound combinations produce consequent and sympathetic (consonant and dissonant) vibrations on all aspects of our physical environment. The name "Jericho" conjures up images of Israelites marching, trumpets sounding, and walls falling down from a well-known biblical story of faith and victory. Of course, the concept of dissonance is not restricted to combinations of certain intervals and chords. Another kind of dissonance involves a simple physical phenomenon called *heating*, where two tones, at slightly different frequencies, conflict because they experience their moments of maximum out of synchronization. At regular periodic intervals (for example, at twice per second), however, the moments of each sound's maximum intensity coincide. The combined force of an arrangement of two such sounds push somewhat violently at your eardrum, causing momentary intensification of the overall sound. When similar sounds fuse at even higher frequencies they produce increased abrasive auditory friction. In melodic voice leading higher the intonation of a leading tone creates greater attraction towards the target tone above it; listeners feel such a dramatic pull. Conversely, low leading tones tend to give a more lackluster sound to music. Intonation also has a profound effect on the degree of dissonance within a dissonant harmony and on the consonance a consonant harmony yields. Consonances can promote a feeling of tranquility and resolution in music, while dissonance often serves to provide heightened contrasts, instability, or disturbance.

The process of spontaneous composition is a natural one for people because spontaneous creation occurring naturally is evident throughout all portions of the perceivable universe. Spontaneous composition, unlike improvisation, demands originality from the seed idea to finish, guided by creativity and individual expression. Improvisation involves mastering the ability to provide appropriate musical content to existing musical ideas usually derived from some form of aurally prescribed or written musical material. The source of improvised material need not be original. Many students may initially learn to improvise by mastering "licks" (or by generating well-rehearsed patterns) that they apply to contexts where minimal musical reference material is provided. The most effective and innovative African-American music is rarely contrived or conservative. It is more akin to conceptual aspects of what some call liberalism, because it encourages its own brand of character development and structure. Overstreet says liberalism's practitioners attempt to "understand the physical-spiritual workings of the universe and to work out, first, a relationship to that universe that comports with his creative human status and, second, a relationship to his fellow man that will express in practice his conviction of human dignity" (122–123). Demands on musicians increase exponentially when a dual-natured approach, involving physical and spiritual dimensions, is factored into the creative formula. The universe consists of much more than material and chemical forces, mechanical processes, cells, and the perspectives generated by human society. However, related themes and patterns seem to resound throughout existence. Solar systems are the microcosms of larger universal systems. Cellular systems and microorganisms give the impression of sharing (in microcosms) organizational and gravitational characteristics with certain aspects of solar systems. In both of the latter cases, material revolves around a nucleus that functions as the chief administrator of that system.

If we call experiences outside the context of our body "objective reality" and phenomena experienced inside the context of our body "subjective reality," then we at once realize one duality of dual existence. Happiness, love, anxiety, fear, and other moods and emotions are of the subjective realm. Music is a powerful force capable of reaching multiple levels of human consciousness. We can amplify and project our thoughts and emotions through music that penetrates our objective, subjective, and subconscious levels of body, mind, and spirit. Malcolm Budd states:

> If someone who listens to music is powerfully affected by the music that he comes to think of it as animate and perceives it as something which is in an emotional state then this falseness in his consciousness is an instance of the pathetic fallacy: the strength of the feelings has led him to project the emotion that he feels into the music. However, if the fact is that music arouses emotions in the listener, it is hard to see how he could be genuinely under

the impression that the subject of the emotions he feels is the music and not himself.

Pratt's solution to this problem is in outline as follows. There are movements both of and in the body: our body can move about and it is itself a locus of movements. Some of these movements we feel by kinesthesis and organic sensation. The fact that we can feel bodily movement kinesthetically and organically, is chiefly responsible for the many words which, when used to describe how we feel, signifies the dynamic character of movement (37–39).

Duality resounds throughout existence in an infinite array of forms. Spontaneous composers develop music that evokes kinesthetic, organic, and emotional responses, but it is difficult to measure or define the quality and range of effects produced. Nonetheless, developing an understanding of the physical, mental, and spiritual processes that music stimulates gives us a more intimate relationship with, and understanding of, its power and potential.

Musicians often say, "Music is the healing force of the universe." Many cultures produced rituals where music was a primary catalyst in the cleansing of the soul. Although little is known about the precise relationship between music and healing, it is clear that people throughout the ages have felt that music helps to quell physical, emotional, and psychological ailments. David Cope suggests that music itself does not contain soul but, rather, that it is a mirror reflecting our own souls.

> The bigger question for me, however, is not whether Experiments in Musical Intelligence compositions have soul but whether *human* compositions have soul (note that I deliberately avoid the question of whether humans themselves have soul). With such a vague definition of soul, I cannot see anyone arguing convincingly that the notes gathered on a page of music contain in them a "principle of life, feeling, thought, and action." No, the soul we perceive when we hear a deeply moving musical work, if "soul" is even the right word, is *our own soul* (91).

Indeed music would have no soul without the receptive ear of a listener whose soul is moved by an auditory experience. Thus, music helps to remind us that we are alive and potentially makes us aware of our soul or spiritual innerselves. It also reminds us of the greater, life generating force that surrounds us. The spiritual base of artistic creation does not involve a singular direct line of development, however. Some modern philosophers and musicians investigated modern esoteric views that challenged traditional ontological notions. "Liberalism invites humankind to feel, moreover, not the sinfulness and worthlessness of man, but the high powers of sociality and rationality that exist in man and bid for release. Liberalism asked humankind to grow up to the full stature of a self-governing and self-fulfilling human being" (Overstreet 122–123). If humankind is a microcosmic reflection of greater macrocosmic systems, then does this suggests that the universe needs to be self-governing, self-disciplined, and self-fulfilling, those qualities that seem to drive human existence?

Qualities of liberalism overlap with compositional concerns. Although love and spirituality are empirically immeasurable, their conspicuous effect on the subconscious, subjective, and object realm of human existence is undeniable. Some musicians and other artists are advocates of love and spirituality through their work as means through which concepts of proper fitness, personal balance, and general well-being are promoted. For certain artists, passion is a fundamental principle that motivates their work, and the concept of love is an element intimately intertwined with zeal and delight.

Physicians are well aware of chemical balance and study the physical requirements involved to maintain physical and psychological wellness. They know how to stay healthy themselves because the medical profession has systematically discovered shrewd ways to avoid and treat such common ailments as a cold by eating the right diet and taking appropriate dietary supplements. Physicians understand that proper amounts of sunshine, motion, and rest are required to maintain the overall flow of body fluids and energy that check such things as the accumulation of cholesterol in the bloodstream. They can help their patients tailor specific and aggressive anti-aging programs for themselves that give their bodies a relative sense of timelessness. They can prescribe dietary supplements that counteract anemia and have evolved measures and suggestions that help people become better balanced, less cluttered (physically and mentally), and more relaxed.

Musicians can also bring the healing forces of music to aid humanity. Composers and performers develop reliable musical styles and approaches that make people dance, nurture psychological wellness, and lift the spirits around them. To generate healthy music, many musicians also know how to stay healthy themselves and know that they must feel healthy to sound healthy. Drumming, wind playing, conducting, and other physical musical activity promote beneficial mechanical movement and proper breathing associated with the health and development of the body. The meditative state of mind that music generates for some performers and listeners alike helps to encourage the removal of mental clutter, focused consciousness, and helps people reach transcendence.

Despite a strong emphasis on spirituality and religion throughout the development of world society, modern Eurocentric societies generally have gradually grown increasingly more skeptical about spirituality than Afrocentric counterparts and other global societies. This is perhaps due to the role that Christianity played in supporting the brutality associated with colonization. Ironically, however, Eurocentric Christianity has dominated much of Global African culture throughout the past several centuries.

To a degree, Einstein's views reflect the ideas held by many atheists and agnostics. He felt that many of the ways in which societies conceive of God conflict with the needs of humanity. He also thought that, "If this being is omnipotent, then every human action, every human thought, every human feeling and aspiration is also His work; how is it possible to think of holding men responsible for their deeds and thoughts before such an almighty Being?" (251). Questions involving self-determination, fate, and the power of the human are also aimed at explaining the function of and reasons for the existence of our subconscious and intuition. Einstein concluded that, "The further the spiritual evolution of mankind advances, the more certain it seems to me that the path to genuine religiosity does not lie through the fear of life, and the fear of death, and blind faith, but through striving after rational knowledge" (251).

Some people reject the "religion of fear" as a primitive and destructive stage in the spiritual development of humankind. Einstein wrote in 1932 that he could not "imagine a God who rewards and punishes the objects of his creation, whose purposes are modeled after our own—a God, in short, who is but a reflection of human frailty" (252). He also felt that most religious conceptions of God also conflicted with the demands of science by potentially interfering with the predictable operation of natural law (253).

Of course, the omnipotent totality of existence does not have to be governed by a "Being" or anything else that we can conceive to still manifest as an actuality. The concept of a Creator, God, or Creative Source are indeed strictly symbols for a governing principal whose true essence will always extend far beyond our limited imagination or apprehension. Some African-American musicians and many others are less inclined to reduce their understanding or conception of spiritual concerns strictly to any form of intellectual analytical processes alone. Such people tend to apply a more holistic approach to their contemplation of a Creative Source where science, math, spirituality, morality, and aesthetics intertwine. Our expressed emotions, thoughts, and physical movement may be a direct reflection of our kinetic, visceral, cognitive, and spiritual nature. For example, Yusef Lateef tends to combine aspects of the soul, intuition, physical sensations, and our personal feelings into his phrase "emotional memory":

> Emotional memory is a vital tool in the science of self-expression. In this exercise, the musician reconstructs a highly emotional experience from the past or present life so as to recreate within the feelings associated with it.

The assumption behind autophysiopsychic music, as I see it, is that a value exists which can be transferred to performance.

The reproduction of intense emotionalism in such exercises proves that the musician is capable of experiencing certain feelings. It also testifies that the musician possesses a nervous system and a memory and that in isolated circumstances the two can combine to reproduce the physical sensations occasioned by a past experience. It is important for a musician to know just how much he/she can feel, if only to point out emotional limitations, but it is misleading for a musician to assume that the ability to undergo emotionalism automatically implies the ability to reproduce it. (If the manifestation of emotion were all that was required then the civil servant, the carpenter and the bus driver could compete with the mature musician.) The point is that the skilled musician is not just a mechanical, emotional dispenser, but an interpretive artist creating organically.

A valid audience does not go to hear a musician for the sake of just being on the scene. They go to hear music that is filled with life, and if the musician is geared to his/her role, body, mind and soul, his/her music will be charged with interest.

The emotional memory selected by the musician at any given time must be identical with the music being performed. If the resemblance between the music and the personal experience is striking, they will correspond and therefore the performance will be nourishing.

Emotionalism is never analogous to the degree that one feeling can serve the turn of another. The death of a goldfish does not stir the same sense of loss as that evoked by the death of a mother, and the death of a mother is not precisely the same as the loss of a wife. The sense of disgust prompted by an open maggot infested garbage can is not really akin to the revulsion produced by an unfaithful lover. The exultation, which marks the appearance of an old friend believed dead, is of a slightly different temper than that produced by the discovery of a lost wallet. For the emotional-memoirists these are analogous experiences, and as such, considered useful.

The emotional-memory exercise can be a sort of spiritual inventory of a musician's innermost feelings. The richest of these memories (from an artistic standpoint) may be rooted in the most painful incidents: The effects of a trauma, the result of an old hysteria, the sudden release of pent-up suppression, etc. The musician, in foraging about in these memories is expected to treat red-hot emotional coals as if they were functional artistic blocks. S/he is expected to skillfully filter his/her most profound sensations in order to extract their properties and recompose them in performance. This is a process that compels the musician not only to recall his/her feelings, but to analyze and understand. If we look at the emotion-memory squarely, we see not only an aesthetically expressive tool, but a great boon for the ego, a therapeutic toy.

The alternative to the conscious injection of emotional-memory is a full-bodied, deeply rooted, mentally aware sense that is a vital tool of human expression.

It is a man's experience of life (the coming together of sensibility and circumstance) which produces the sum total of his/her expression. When these contacts occur, these experiences yield drama. Every musician's expressions demand a series of emotional strata which demands a natural gravitation from one stratum to the other. This is their architecture, and they are designing for themselves (3–6).

Lateef's description has broad implications. Some musicologists attempt to define musical parameters much more simply and narrowly. Empirical thinkers reject things they cannot verify through experience. Some people feel that the musical expression of joy, sadness, or love requires not only particular musical spacing in time and pitch, but also particular levels of amplitudes arranged in what they consider "appropriate" or "essential" form. Of course narrow notions and descriptions about the forces of life may at best be narrowly perceived as "culture specific." No universal determinants reconcile our thoughts, actions, and movement with music that impinges upon the hearts and souls of humankind worldwide. It is especially difficult to quantify spirituality, emotions, and any specific brand of musical influence, therefore. Some generally effective therapeutic applications of music may exist, but these too are difficult to contain and must certainly have a somewhat unpredictable and diverse range of effectiveness; just as various drugs prescribed in medicine have a variety of reactions and effects on different people worldwide. Drug effects depend on their individual chemistry and other such factors and how they react with an individual's own physical and psychological chemistry. We cannot always reduce complex things to simple formulae. Although we are made to devise a symbolic set of standard emotions for actors during the Baroque era, some modern thinkers also attempt to reduce human feelings to seven emotions: anger, hate, grief, love, sex, joy, and reverence. Once emotions are blocked out in such a fashion, it does not mean that we can quantify all of our feelings into such fixed parameters. Thus, composers may recognize that certain chords, intervals, tempi, modes, and timbers may have developed a certain set of musical associations over the years, but attention to the finer details of music, not musical clichés, render works effective and convincing.

Attempts to reconcile science and religion lead to endless questions, paradoxes, and dilemma for those who try to filter all experiences through cognitive tools alone. Might not all manner of invisible vibrations of various forms of unknown energy extend in a multiplicity of directions that evade our inadequate senses and tools? If we cannot physically monitor the physical vibrations that ripple throughout the Universe, perhaps that is why we direct our non-cognitive human sensors towards understanding and evolving our meditation, prayer, and telepathy. Perhaps Einstein's skepticism about God serves only to keep us from defining the Creative Source too narrowly. In his book, *God in the Equation: How Einstein became the Prophet of the New Religious Era,* Cory Powell discusses ways in which science and religion also overlap. He says:

> Joel Primack, a cosmologist at the University of California Santa Cruz, who studies the formation and evolution of galaxies, offers an unusually trenchant description of the relationship between sci/religion and its wobbly predecessors. "Rather than assuming science and spirit are separate jurisdictions, I assume that reality is one, and that truth grows and evolves with the universe of which it speaks," he writes. "Every religion is a metaphor system, and like scientific theories, every religion myth is limited. Perhaps progression in religion can occur as it does in science: without invalidating a theory, a greater myth can encompass it respectfully, the way general relativity encompasses Newtonian mechanics. In the next few decades, powerful ideas of modern cosmology could inspire a spiritual renaissance, but they could also be totally ignored by almost everyone as irrelevant and elitist." If Einstein's cosmic religion fails to find an audience, that will be a terrible loss not just for the devout

researchers on a quest for ultimate knowledge, but for everyone seeking a more just and peaceful world.

More than three hundred years ago, the rationalist philosopher and theologian Baruch Spinoza described the dangers inherent in the biblical description of an interventionist God who responds to prayer. This description led people to believe that God acts to bring about certain goals, a notion Spinoza considered inherently corrosive. "Everyone thought out for himself, according to his abilities, a different way of worshipping God, so that God might love him more than his fellows, and direct the whole course of nature for the satisfaction of his blind cupidity and insatiable avarice. Thus the prejudice developed into superstition, and took a deep root in the human mind," he wrote. Because God did not reliably respond to these prayers, worshippers adjusted their superstition and came to believe that the Lord's judgments are beyond human understanding. "Such a doctrine might well have sufficed to conceal the truth from the human race for all eternity, if mathematics has not furnished another standard of verity in considering solely the essence and properties of figures without regard to their final causes," Spinoza concluded (252).

Nonetheless, we cannot forget that prayer and thoughts are indeed two forms of vibrations that we can control. In turn, all vibrations must have immeasurable affects on the extremely higher and lower frequencies extant throughout our action–consequence universe. In music, dealing with religious, spiritual, and metaphysical issues related to those with which science grapples incessantly are constantly relevant concerns. Ironically jazz was labeled "the devil's music" even as it evolved from the vocabulary of the ancient African religion and "Negro Spirituals," and while serving to uplift and inspire the souls of people around the world for over a century. A broader understanding and perspective may direct people to consider the multitude of social causes, conditions, and psychological reasons that African-American music evolved from its socially oppressive conditions in America into such a powerful transformative social and political force.

Ritual and Spiritual Movement

The word "ritual" is contained within the word spiritual; this is no accident. Rituals are often concerned with controlling all aspects of the physical, intellectual, and spiritual environment and use music, dance, lighting, incense, masks, visual arts, costumes, and other stimuli to create an altered environment. Both words (ritual and spiritual) suggest various methodologies for cultivating ancient and modern transcendental aspects of human existence that extend beyond the mundane world. Rituals have long been employed in ancient cultures for spiritual connection, invoking the higher spirits, seeking blessings, and advancing personal and collective renewal. From the Eurocentric ritual in England that involved placing coins beneath a foundation stone that insured a prosperous future life in that dwelling, to a Brazilian witch doctor's sacrifice of a chicken for related reasons, an array of rituals continue to shape many aspects of our lives.

The ancient Chinese felt the world was filled with spirits that surrounded us in our homes, work places, and other locations in our daily lives. They too felt that ritual insured our alignment with the Creative Source and brings protection to us from this spiritual realm. In *Feng Shui,* ritual is an integral part of the adjustment of physical space. Such beliefs allow humankind power to reconcile universal harmony with the spiritual realm. As spiritual power has become severely eroded in today's environment, modern human society seems increasingly more on the verge of an enormous moral, social, and cultural breakdown—as we lose touch with our ancient honoring of unknown forces that surround us.

Kinetic arts have an equally long history of bridging ritual and spiritual domains. From ancient shamans to the energetic contemporary African-American gospel choirs, rhythmic and poetic body movement has long been integrated into spiritual practices. The Middle East has several traditions of spiritual movement. Many contemporary dancers incorporate associated movement into their spiritual expression. Some choreographers and dancers may borrow from popular and traditional sources of traditional Middle Eastern and African ritual, while others prefer to focus strictly upon their own new spiritual creations. Music often labeled "trance dances," is perhaps better referred to as "movement meditations" or "rituals." In Morocco, the *Guedra* is performed as a ritual of blessing and, according to its oral tradition, its practice is many thousands of years old. The *Guedra* is part of the traditions associated with a sub-grouping of the nomadic Tuareg known as the Blue People because of the indigo powder they use to dye their clothing. Music is inseparable from dance and is a vital part of the *Guedra.*

When spontaneous composers and other musicians perform with dances they must use a fluid vocabulary to match the movement. All musicians and dancers feed off each other's creativity as the watch, listen, and leave room for individual and collective inspiration. Ritual and spiritual events, therefore, should result in ample room for our subconscious minds to absorb inspiration. We can better understand musical meaning through examining the foundation of certain rituals. Voodoo and Santeria involve African-based rituals that developed within Global African cultures in the Americas.

Voodoo and Santeria

Eileen Southern, Samuel Floyd, Hildred Roach, and many other scholars have traced the journey of African music into the Americas thoroughly and systematically. Gerhard Kubik discussed an integrated approach towards West African music and oral literature in his early fieldwork on Yoruba *chantefables* in Nigeria (Kubik 129–82). Difficulties in producing meaningful historical records arose when the racist tendencies of slave era politics dismissed or distorted the value of African and African-American music, history, and culture, while attempting to replace their true values with misinformation, negative associations, and stereotypes. In America such flawed historical documentation became the basis of destructive typecasts formed during minstrelsy of the late nineteenth century.

Despite such distortions of culture, early African-American music often contains modern parallels to ancient African social and historical traditions. Jazz music shares a common origin with voodoo music because they both come from Africa. Blues lyrics are a source for the perpetuation of African-American news and history, just as the information transmitted by African *griots* and *jalis* contained related sociocultural information. Blues also retains aspects of traditional African themes, melodic structure, and tendencies towards metaphors. These tendencies, in turn, have influenced other forms of twentieth-century music. The familiar situation concerning "a pact with the devil," often negotiated by a mythical blues musician at a midnight crossroads, is an example of folklore that displays a specific type of dynamic somewhat reflective of African myths. However, the closest traditional African cultural mythological parallels do not always tend towards extreme polar concepts such as the "Devil" versus "God" association. The black and white polemic of good versus evil is more reflective of European and European-American interpretation and suggestion (Kubik 24). In a recent study, Kubik discussed the relationship between African music and the blues:

> So far, the African background of the oral literature dimension of the blues has been studied mainly in one specific area, "magic" and "Voodoo," including the permeating presence of the "devil." A basic thesis of Finn and Spencer is that blues is "devil's music," as it was popularly called, demonstrates a process of reinterpretation of the Yoruba and Fõ, and in Nigeria among the Yoruba has taught me to exercise restraint when faced with the pleasures of freewheeling thought associations. Traditionally, *Èṣù* and *Legba* have no negativistic connotations such as "the devil." *Legba* mud sculptures found in the courtyards of many houses in Dahomey and Togo function to warn the inhabitants through dreams about any imminent danger of illness, even early death, caused by witchcraft. *Legba* is also intimately connected with the *fa* (in Fõ; *ifa* in Yoruba) oracle. A communal *Legba* called *Tolegba* is put up some two hundred meters from the village to protect against epidemic disease and arson, even harmful insects. *Legba* is a male being in love of truth. Nothing can be hidden before him, not even one's sexual organ. He himself is usually shown with a pronounced male sexual organ.

African-American studies seem often to pass through a stage in which the cognitive worlds of several distinctive African cultures are mixed up and grossly reinterpreted by the authors, with the Guinea Coast and particularly Nigeria providing the most easily accessible materials. What for a long time had been a dominant trend in the literature of Afro-Brazilian cultures is now being repeated in the United States: the Nigerianization of African-American studies, notably since Henry Louis Gates Jr.'s *The Signifying Monkey* (1988). It is true that the Yoruba òrìṣa (transcendental being) called *Èṣù* and the Fõ *vodu* equivalent called *Legba*, about whose connotations Danhin Amagbenyõ Kofi has informed us through firsthand observations, were variously targeted by Christians in Africa and in the New World and re-categorized as "devils." Somewhat later, anthropologists labeled them "trickster Gods." But they have shared that fate with some other religious ideas in Africa. For example, in southeastern Angola *Kavole*, one of the masked characters appearing during the season of the *mukanda* initiation rites for boys, was reinterpreted by Christians as the "devil." In Venezuela certain masks used in carnival manifestations with (possibly) remote African components are called "devils' masks." In Malawi and Zambia, Seventh Day Adventists and other Protestant American churches have been in the vanguard up to the 1990s in calling the traditional masks of the Achea and Amaŋanja people *zausatanta* (things of Satan).

Probably no one will suggest that all those African religious traditions, variously stigmatized by Christians as "devil's things," must have survived in the back of the mind of blues singers. But why then also pick *Èṣù* and *Legba*, who incorporate religious ideas from just one delineated culture area of West Africa? Surely Yoruba and Fõ religious ideas have had notable extensions in the Caribbean and in Brazil, but little nineteenth-century presence in the United States. Even in Louisiana the concept of *vodu* imported with Haitians was soon reinterpreted and made into something quite different, now popularly called "hoodoo" (21).

Christianity was clearly eager to reject any African spiritual belief as either incompetent as a religion or associated with devil worship. Such negative connotations extended themselves into blues and other forms of African-American music through African–Christian contact.

Voodoo

In Africa, drumming and singing played a significant role at ritual ceremonies in inducing states of transcendence, possession, and trance. Voodoo ceremonies in some areas of Haiti and the American South involved African-style drums until both the drums and ceremonies were finally banned. Before legislation barred Voodoo ceremonies from Congo Square in New Orleans, groups of African Americans gathered there frequently to celebrate their African heritage. As a result, the festive and spiritual qualities of Voodoo ritual survived and—along with other important elements of African tradition—found their way into African-American blues, jazz, and other African-American music. The degree to which Africans were free of Eurocentric influence was directly proportional to the Africanisms retained in African-American music, art, and culture. The free jazz styles of Ornette Coleman, Albert Ayler, John Coltrane, and others reflect Afrocentric free associations and tendencies towards sustained intensity akin to interrelated qualities of Voodoo ritual. Music's function in the rituals of other cultures serves correlated purposes, as Professor Byong Won Lee explains in his discussion of Korean ritual music.

Musical performance in shaman ritual serves several different functions. It provides extraordinary aural experience for the novice. It provides an interlude while the fatigued shaman is taking a break. Often the musical performance at the shaman ritual is merely a background functioning in much the same way as mood music in the barbershop or movie theater, during which the shaman prepares for the ensuing act. However, the most important function of the music is probably the facilitation and intensification in reaching a trance state. Most shamans have dual functions: healer and entertainer. Thus, music provides auditory stimulation in the brain, which in turn facilitates the trance state, the same music may enliven the entertaining act of the shaman (5).

In the West African Fon language Voodoo means spirit. Voodoo is a religion that emphasizes nature. The praying to *Vodu* generally means invoking a "spirit god," a state of "possession," or being "caught by a spirit." Voodoo ceremonies usually begin with drum sound inaugurating the movement towards the trance state that will allow a practitioner to be possessed by a spirit. Once possessed, they will visit the spirit to obtain advice. The Voodoo Spirits are invisible forces who serve as mediators between the highest gods and humans. These forces are responsible for a wide range of diverse conditions in the air, in the forest, in the water, and within humans themselves. Practitioners use appropriate articles in connection with certain rituals to acquire good fortune in love, health, and wealth.

Women make up over 50 percent of the Voodoo spiritual leaders in the West, which is contrary to the male-dominant leadership in the mother religion from which it was derived in West Africa. Although it is difficult to separate fact and fiction in Marie Laveau's life, she is certainly the one responsible for the popularization of Voodoo in the United States. Some people consider Laveau a witch who consorted with Satan, a thief, and a procuress. This viewpoint is not surprising considering the prevailing racist attitudes that surrounded any African-based worship in the Americas; European Americans considered the practice of Voodoo "Satan worshipping" and attached a host of negative connotations to the practice of Voodoo. Voodoo was the cult that most European Americans loved to hate. To many Voodoo practitioners and others, however, Laveau was a kind, benevolent woman who cared for a great many victims during the yellow fever epidemics and visited for decades the prisoners in the parish jail, bringing them food and clothing as well as voodoo trinkets. Marie Laveau could most likely read and write, but that was probably the extent of her education. Nevertheless, she brought Voodoo from the shadows into mainstream New Orleans culture; and her capacity as a hairdresser to the rich French and American ladies of her time enabled her to become a wealthy Voodoo queen and transformed her into a renowned celebrity of New Orleans history and folklore.

Voodoo remains a religion existing throughout the Southern United States, Brazil, and the West Indies. Enslaved western Africans brought the spiritual practice to the West, and it eventually acquired a host of different names according to the region in which it was practiced. Its spelling is also very irregular: hoodoo, houdou, vaudoo, vodou, vodu, voodoo, voudou, and voudoux. The forms adopted in the United States are voodoo and hoodoo. In French it is spelled "vaudou" and in Spanish "vodú" or "vudú." Voodoo priests and priestesses take years to learn the ways of Ifa priests, who often cast the sixteen sacred palm nuts (ikin Ifa) or shells to determine which subsection from the Odu Ifa they must consult, and the corresponding sign is traced in the iyerosun powder on the diviner's tray (opon Ifa).

Marie Laveau was called a free *mulatto,* which was the common way of referring to first generation offspring of biracial African and European. Doctor John, a voodoo priest with numerous aliases, detested mulattoes because "they were neither black nor white, they're mules" (Tallant 35). In Louisiana, the mulattoes with nice hair and of light skin color were referred to as "high yellow" Negroes. Marie Laveau was also called a *quadroon,* meaning one fourth black. The endings of this term and of *octoroon* were adopted from the Spanish *cuarterón* and *ochavón* through the French language (quarteron and octavon) (Varela 6).

In certain social contexts, Voodoo conveniently allowed Africans to maintain their worship and reverence for the lesser, personal gods (*Loas*) that surrounded the supreme African deity. Displaced African people outside the African continent at times were able to identify these lesser gods with the saints of the Roman Catholic Church in veiled form. That system of disguise enabled them to psychologically base their sacred world and spiritual beliefs upon something far more familiar to them than the idols of new European religions encountered in their new environment. In Voodoo rituals, the instruments "talk" as they invoke the gods (the *Loas*). The music inspires possession and "becomes effortless, but 'hot,' a West African linguistic survival referring to trance" (Blesh 21). An amazing similarity exists between the spirit and practice of Voodoo rituals and the rites of the black Pentecostal Church service (Wilmore 20–25).

Voodooists serve the Iwa and beseech their assistance. The hundreds of Iwa divide themselves into two families. *Rada* include benign ancestral spirits from ancient West Africa, and *Pethro* involve fiery spirits who represent Central African and Creole traditions. Spirits often express themselves as triads. The characteristics involved in such triads include ancestors, souls of twins, mysteries, and the divine personification of nature. A priest or priestess "feeds" the sacred Rada, Pethro, and Congo drums to strengthen them (Rigaud 105).

Many of the African spiritual traditions that survived the Middle Passage are embedded in Voodoo. The name "Voodoo" is inherited from the Fon kingdom of what is now Benin (once Dahomey). Their neighbors to the east, the Nago (a Yoruba speaking people) also influenced Haitian Voodoo. The Fon and Kongo kingdoms of West and Central Africa gave Voodoo its basic form and content. Fon names for "temple," "priest," "priestess," and "servitor" (*ounfo, oungan, mam'bo, ounsi*) are among the Rada elements retained in Voodoo.

The highly conspicuous presence of Voodoo in New Orleans may account for the birth of jazz in that region. Voodoo kept the rhythms of Africa alive at Congo Square in New Orleans and elsewhere. Consequently, African-American musicians in New Orleans maintained firm proportion of Afrocentric roots while also exploring the wide range of other influences that life in the cosmopolitan Crescent City provided.

Another new dual-natured tradition emerged in America serving, at once, as covert resistance to Catholic physical and spiritual oppression, a shield against Catholic values, and a means through which to sustain traditional Yoruba worship. Santeria refers to "the way of saints" because its devotions to the *orishas* were also disguised within the images of the Catholic saints. Eventually, a spiritual practice that began as subterfuge became a genuine universal religion. Thus, just as Yoruba spiritual practice became Lucumi in Cuba, it later emerged as Santeria, an attempt to worship and perpetuate the gods of Africa in a land dominated by Catholicism.

Several ethnically distinct Afro-Cuban religions emerged to preserve their African past. The Efik of the Niger delta established the Abakua society, or *nanigos*. Congo people created the *nganga, mayombe,* and *palo monte* traditions. The Fon founded assorted Arara cults. Esteban Montejo worked as a slave on several plantations in the nineteenth century. He voiced his impressions of the Afro-Cuban religions:

> I knew of two African religions in the barracoons: the Lucumi and the Congolese. The Congolese was the more important. It was well-known at the Flor de Sagua [an ingenio] because their magic men used to put spells on people and get possession of them, and their practice of soothsaying won them the confidence of all the slaves. . . .

The difference between the Congolese and Lucumi was that the former solved problems while the latter told the future. This they did with diloggunes which are round, white shells from Africa with mystery inside. . . .

The Congolese were more involved with witchcraft than the Lucumi, who had more to do with the saints and with God. The Lucumi liked rising early with the strength of the morning and looking up into the sky and saying prayers and sprinkling water on the ground. The Lucumi were at it when you least expected it (Murphy 32).

In western Africa, the major ethnic groups abducted and brought to Louisiana were Ashanti, Bambara, Dahomey, Ewe, and Ibo. Several of them, like Brer Dahomey, appear in state folktales. Others, like Ewe and Ibo, have become deities. *Hounfort* is the voodoo temple and its surroundings (Hurston 192–193). During the nineteenth century, Voodooists celebrated two important festivities, which are still observed in Louisiana today. The twenty-third of June, the Eve of St. John the Baptist, is the most important date on the Voodoo calendar. When the drums started playing, the Voodoo queen would start the Creole dances, with a boa constrictor across her shoulders. The different choreographed steps were performed by all attending the ritual, which went on 'til the early hours of the morning.

The Afrocentric spirit of freedom and ritual inherent in Voodoo and Santeria is reflected in performance rituals of some of the most striking African-American musical styles. Blues, the spirit of these spiritual celebrations, influenced New Orleans jazz, be-bop, and free jazz as marked pivotal musical periods on their evolutionary road towards greater degrees of musical freedom. Liberating individual expression was critical to the survival of an oppressed people.

Korean Shaman Ritual Music

Composers can expand the range of their artistic imagination and their palette of artistic resources by carefully examining traditional music styles, history, and contexts from around the world. Folk music from around the world sometimes shares related musical elements.

At first glance, the rich and colorful embellishments and ornamentation inherent in Korean traditional music may seem far removed from traditional African musical styles. With regards to musical timbre, however, both Korean and African music use a broad range of articulations, pitch modulation, rhythmic and metrical flexibility, and share a preference for sound that includes a rich collection of overtones. To a certain degree, the musical instruments used in traditional Korean music also resemble some of those found throughout the African continent. Korean flutes, such as the transverse *daegum,* *sogeum,* and vertical *dahnso,* are similar to the *fula* (played by the Fula and other West Africans) and *kwela* found in Malawi and other parts of southeast and southern Africa. The double-headed and hour-shaped Korean *junggu* finds related counterparts in the similarly constructed West African *gan gan* or *dondo* (talking drums). The strident sound of the conical double reed Korean *hojok* (or *taepyongso*) has a sound somewhat akin to that of the *orutu* (wooden Luo harp of Western Kenya) and a shape in common with the North African *mizmar* and West African *alghaita*. The *gayageum* of Korea has a shape that is not unlike the *enanga* (trough zither) played throughout the African Congo and Eastern Cattle Area. One-string African bowed fiddles, such as the long neck *njarka* of Mali and the Ethiopian *masenqo* (with its diamond-shaped sound box), share common features with the Korean *haegum* (two-string fiddle). In his paper, en-titled "The Sinawi Performance in the Kut: Universality and Idiosyncrasy in the Korean Shaman Ritual Music," Byong Won Lee tells us that:

> Music is an inseparable component in most of religious services. Even [though] musical activity is discouraged by the orthodox Islam, the stylized and heightened manner of chanting of the *Qoran* is definitely very musical to the ears of laymen and musicologists. The magical power of songs is all too well-known as a universal element in most of shaman rituals (4).

Various forms of pentatonic (often with fixed final tones) and other non-diatonic scales are common in traditional folk music throughout both Africa and Korea. Since much of the music from both regions evolved from work (used to coordinate and ease labor) and often used call and response patterning, it is reasonable to expect that the rhythms that evolved to support this brand of folk melodies might be interrelated in fundamental ways. Given that folk music is most often sang in communal settings, the reason that the general gamut of tones involved in folk melodies would be relatively small is clear. A small range can more readily accommodate an entire community of male and female voices. Simple structures and melodies also leave room for high levels of embellishment, another typical characteristic of the performance of folksongs. Timbre also becomes an interesting and distinctive focal point when other basic core melodic elements are simplified. The characteristically hoarse timbres of *Pan-Sori* singer voices or the shaman's nasal voice quality in Korea are distinguishable regional differences in timbre. Thus, the various styles and dialects that evolve from the old three Kingdoms in Korea all have unique musical characteristics just as geographical areas in America produced various regional blues sounds in the Delta (Mississippi-Alabama) and The Territories (Texas-Louisiana-Arkansas-Oklahoma-Missouri).

African *griots* and *jeli*, as well as the full range of African-American blues singers, also employ a wide variety of personal sounds rich in defining overtone mixtures. Neither the traditional vocal quality of African-American blues or Korean folk songs strived to obtain the characteristically more uniform "covered tone" of classic European singers as they aim towards a more "sine wave" purity in the voice. "Crying," tempered "screaming," and other raw emotional and expressive sounds prevail in Korean folk singing. Primarily through religious indoctrination, European Americans attempted to suppress Afrocentric cultural qualities during the slave era, just as the Japanese tried to force its traditions upon Korean culture. Nevertheless, both Koreans and African Americans retained the most salient expressive features of their respective musical legacies while also reluctantly absorbing certain qualities of the music of their oppressors. Nonetheless, just as water and oil do not mix, fortunately many of the original cultural features remained clear and distinct in both cases.

In *Gogok* "Pyellak" text places emphasis on emotions with subtle intensity, much like that expressed in African-American blues. For instance, there is much care placed on describing the emotion of a bird with a broken wing as a fox chases it. The metaphor contained within the bird's struggle is broadly applicable in human society. Aligned with traditional belief systems in most regions of Africa, Korean Buddhism considers no distinction between realms of the living and the dead. African texture also resembles Korean Buddhism music's multi-layered textures within the bright colors of its ritual costumes and ritual setting. Most traditional music notated in print leaves a wide degree of latitude for stylistic interpretation (much in keeping with the approach to reading big band charts). The songs of Korean *Pan-Sori* have close ties with nature just as with the Mbuti of the African Ituri forest. While untying unresolved sorrow and emotion through music, *Pan-Sori's* master musicians perform at higher levels when inspired by "master audiences," just as master jazz musicians do when they sense that their audience is astute and harmonized with their music.

The narratives in Korean shaman ritual are akin to the narratives of African *griots* and *jelis,* as well as the short stories that serve as free-narrative preludes to many early African-American blues songs. In addition to the use of related "blues-sounding" pitch sets and general tonality, the sliding between tones and other related means of embellishment applied to pitch and tones involved in shaman music also occur in blues and jazz. Visually, the magical power of Voodoo ritual musical qualities, in terms of effectively aiding participants in their journeys towards transcendence, has a number of other factors in common with Korean shaman rituals. Both styles of ritual seem to lead its participant towards similar trance states. The ritual ingredients such as the involvement of chickens, presence of fruit, candles, and the mixture of highly colorful costumes for some participants, blended with the white "uniforms" for others, are typical in both Voodoo and shaman ritual.

In Korea there are two general types of shaman: the hereditary shamans of the North (who pass their tradition on to their offspring) and spirit-descended shamans (who become shamans only when possessed by the appropriate spirit) who engage in *sinawi* rituals south of the Han River. In the *sinawi* style heterophonic melodies and asymmetrical phrasing blend musical elements involving unity, diversity, and sustained intensity that gradually lead the shaman towards ecstatic possession. For musicians involved, there is always a degree of freedom to introduce new melodic and rhythmic material into the mix and to produce thematic variation on the loosely fixed melodic material. Thus, in some ways, aspects of the *sinawi* performance practice are comparable to the heterophony of the early New Orleans jazz style of the early twentieth century.

Figure 1. Korean Shaman Ritual (Televised)

Authentic shaman rituals are long and require tremendous stamina on the part of the shaman. Trance is the basis of shamanism, and shamans traditionally use the power gained while in trance state to influence their either malevolent or benevolent purposes. Although shamans in northern Korea (north of the Han River) generally use percussion alone as accompaniment, shamans in the south often use pitched instruments for their trance dance ritual music. As with Voodoo ritual, idiophones or membranophones are common in the accompanying ensembles for shaman ritual. A variety of other melodic instruments are optional. The power, incessant presence, rhythmic complexity, and overtone structure of driving drum sound, in particular, become the most stimulating components of the psychological "cocktail" that captivates ritual participants. Shaman rhythms often employ 12/8 rhythmic feel akin to Afrocentric "swing" rhythmic patterns. Throughout the past, ancient shaman musical nuances have been passed on through oral tradition. Within the spirit possession, which is of paramount importance in both Voodoo and shaman rituals, the deities of both spiritual worlds are very powerful. In his book, *Shaman Ritual Music in Korea,* Lee Yong-Shik says:

> Deities in the Hwandghae shaman world are almighty in the control of human affairs and reveal their intentions by speaking through the shaman in such a way as to foretell the future. *Gongsu* is the divine message of the descended deity as spoken through the medium of the client. Unlike shaman songs, which are learned behavior from the spirit mother, *gongsu* is an action *acquired* from the shaman's tutelary spirit.

Gongsu is quintessentially a set of powerful words, known only to the shaman herself, and enunciated only when the deities possess her. After a shaman symbolically leaves the secular world and changes from human to divine, she is able to give *gongsu* to her clients. At this moment, the movements and expressions of the shaman are not those of a human, but those of the deity within her. The language used in *gongsu* changes to reflect the status of the descendent deity. The voice comes from the shaman's body, but the words come from somewhere outside it—from the deity (184).

Sinawi is an instrumental ensemble in which the voice becomes one of the instruments when it involves a style of singing related to the rhythmic syncopation and "blues" tonal inflections of African-American scat-singing. Instrumentation for a *sinawi* ensemble for shaman ritual usually includes a *changgu* (hourglass-shaped drum), *ching* (large gong), *taegum* (transverse flute), *p'iri* (double-reed pipe), *haegum* (fiddle), *ajaeng* (bowed zither), and voice. The *taegum* and *p'iri* typically play relatively short melodic patterns; *haegum, ajaeng* the voice perform more sustained melodic phrases; *changgu* provides prescribed rhythmic patterns embellished with free rhythmic variations; while the *ching* punctuates the metric groupings for the rhythmic patterns.

The *sinawi* performance and ritual develops through spontaneous creativity where traditional rhythmic formulas and abstract modal patterns evolve into extensive improvisation with no fixed rules. The tempo fluctuates continually and subtly through intricately interwoven ritual music until tension builds to the point of inducing supernatural power in the shaman. Voodoo participants dance more freely and actively at rituals than at Korean shaman rituals, however; where Korean spectators tend to observe the proceedings rather than partake more directly. Since most Korean shamans were female and the *sinawi* musicians were male, many *sinawi* musicians and shamans of the past were married couples.

Meditation and Breathing Theory

Whether or not a performer's instrument requires direct breathing to vibrate, the act of breathing is always an essential part of the dynamics involved in music making. Breath is the means through which life enters and leaves the human body, thus it animates our being. Proper breathing is the key element to proper health and must be factored into effective musical performance. In music, breath is not only important for tone production, articulation, and dynamic effects; it provides a psychological basis for shaping various parameters of musical construction and phrasing. Breathing is important in establishing the natural pace that renders music more assessable and convincing to listeners. Musicians all benefit from the stimulating and inspiring effects of deep breathing and meditation. The effect that breathing has on the performance of wind players in particular is very direct and conspicuous. Spontaneous composition requires an especially keen sense of concentration, clarity of mind, and physical coordination/control. Learning self-control and mental stillness through deep breathing, meditation, and contemplation are harmonious keys to musical enlightenment. Hazrat Inayat Khan taught:

> The secret of composition lies in sustaining the tone as solidly and as long as possible through all its different degrees. A break destroys its grace, power and magnetism, just as the breath holds life and has all grace, power and magnetism. There are some notes that need a longer life than others, according to their character and purpose (162).

Taoist concepts of *hsing* and *ming* provide additional means through which psychic circulation supports the composer's musical and personal development. The cleansing properties of age-old breathing exercises designed to use the full capacity of the lungs are important aspects of many metaphysical and spiritual disciplines practiced in the East. Taoists use the concepts of *hsing* and *ming* as the basis for their breathing theory. These two qualities represent a manner of psychic circulation where, through deep breathing, the practitioner lengthens their life span, or *ming*. Taoists combine concentration on "nothingness" to awaken their cosmic consciousness to spiritual revelation. Taoist meditation is based upon a view that humankind is a microcosmic universe, reflecting the macrocosmic universe about them.

The *Huai-nan-tzu,* dating from the second century B.C., is the earliest Taoist classic. This work describes humankind's place in the Universe as a background to a system of meditative breathing:

> What is spiritual is received from Heaven while the body and its material form are derived from the Earth. It is harmony of the spirits of yin and yang on which all harmony depends. . . .
>
> Heaven has four seasons, five elements, nine divisions, three hundred and sixty days. Similarly, man has four limbs, five internal organs, nine orifices, and three hundred and sixty joints. Heaven has wind, rain, cold, her; man similarly, has joy, anger, taking, giving. . . . Man forms a trinity with Heaven and Earth, and his mind is the master. . . . In the Sun there is a bird standing on three legs, and in the Moon a toad with three legs. . . .
>
> The five elements move in a circle in proper order, each of them performing its specific functions. Therefore, wood is located in the East and characterizes the ch'i or ether of Spring. Fire is located in the South and characterizes the ch'i of Summer. Metal is located in the West and characterizes the ch'i of Autumn. Water is located in the North and characterizes the ch'i of Winter. . . . Earth dwells in the center and is called Heavenly Nourisher (a natural source of nourishment for the four elements). . . .
>
> When the ch'i in the universe is condensed, it becomes One. When it is divided, we have yin and yang. When it is quartered we have the four seasons. When it is further divided we have the five elements. Each element has its own movement. On account of this difference in movement, we speak of the five movers (138).

The five movers are identified with a set of numbers that correspond to organs of the body. *Yin* and *yang* circulate throughout the five organs; therefore, the breathing movement is a cyclical one. Perhaps the fact that most cultures worldwide have music based upon various pentatonic scales is related to this ancient principle of structural organization around the number five.

Natural musical phrasing on wind instruments (including voice) is enhanced by taking breaths to develop the marking of musical phrase endings. Breathing, when combined with meditation and contemplation, brings music into an inner world (microcosm) in which the physical, mental, and spiritual realms of consciousness merge. The realm of sacred reality has aligned with music throughout time. Some societies believe that human beings did not originally belong to the physical world. Like the angels, they formerly dwelt in a realm where they could rejoice in the intuitive comprehension and glory of God's mystery. Unlike the passivity of angels, whose humility and adoration makes them appear more docile to humankind, people were endowed with an independent will, a privilege formerly reserved exclusively for God Himself (Conway 37). Reflecting upon the dual-natured combination of independent will and meditative humility can potentially lead the spontaneous composer towards greater clarity, inspiration, and creativity.

Vibratory Frequencies at the Human Level

Performing music spontaneously requires intense and uninterrupted concentration. For musicians seeking to apply a maximum degree of focused attention to their composing and performing, it may prove just as beneficial to meditate before a performance as it may be to warm up physically on one's instrument. Humans can alter their individual vibratory patterns and harmonize their body, mind, and spirit through practice of "mental alchemy." Mental alchemy is the process of transmuting thoughts to improve people's lives and expand their minds, and spiritual alchemy is the process of transforming a less evolved soul personality into a more refined one. During the Middle Ages people believed that alchemists sought to transform base metal into gold as they searched for an elusive substance referred to as the philosopher's stone, which would bring about the conversion known as alchemy. However, initiates of the ancient mystery schools realized that alchemy was primarily an allegory for the real work of spiritual and mental alchemy.

Vowel sounds or mantrams are potent vibrations that produce changes in the aura, body, and spirit of the person who uses them. The vibrations in the aura and those in the vowel sounds are at different frequencies, but harmonization occurs because the overtones of the mantrams align with those of the aura. Thus the mantram stimulates the aura by irradiating harmonic overtone vibrations of the basic mantric vibrations. During meditation, as one concentrates upon a nuclear thought (eliminating all extraneous thoughts), that nucleus intensifies until it eventually stimulates consciousness of related harmonic overtone vibrations.

Each successful meditation is like an initiation, because it is a simple ceremony that attunes the inner consciousness with the higher principles of the Universe, and reveals to the consciousness the Creator's laws. Sensing such vibratory results changes an individual's fundamental frequency much as irradiation of atoms and molecules causes vibratory modifications at the atomic or molecular levels. If the Creator represents the fundamental frequency of existence, the first cause—and if the Omnipotent Being contains all harmonic vibration in the cosmos—then, mathematically speaking, the vibration of the Creator would be the principal quantum number or the fundamental tone (or "fundamental vibe"). Composers use mathematics in subtle ways to create musical compositions to enhance compositional beauty, balance, logic, unity, and structure. The most basic connections between math and music are perhaps rhythm and the overtone series.

In the eastern areas of the Sudan in Africa, music often involves embellished pentatonic melodies that unfold over a single tonal center as voices and instruments of musicians depart from, then return to, a fundamental tone. This ornamented pentatonic scale orbiting about the nucleus of a single tonal center is an ancestor of rural blues tonality. Pentatonic scales can arise from the ascending projection of the interval of a fifth through harmonic space (F - C - G - D - A). If blues melodies are extracted from the chord resources that accompany it, the relationship between its own melodic tendency towards ornamenting the embellished pentatonic scales, orbiting above and below the nucleus of a single tonal center, becomes increasingly clear.

Maintaining Responsible Freedom

Order, motion, and freedom are apparently unlimited in the Universe. Considering the gravitational forces that bind and govern cells, solar systems, and galaxies, the tendencies expressed within such structures may serve as general models for guiding compositional construction, concepts, and infrastructure. Maintaining responsible freedom becomes especially important as spontaneous composers consider music performance as an organic ritual affair, an expression of spirituality, an intellectual mission, or as an effective psychological catharsis. Learning to dialogue effectively with fellow performers, as musicians spontaneously invent and discover music rhythmically, melodically, and harmonically, requires maintaining a creative process that includes a sense of clear orientation and sense of structure, even as certain musical elements become increasingly ethereal, dense, and abstracted on the musical surface. A clear sense of direction and purpose is achieved, in part, when musicians are attentive to the directions established by the lead soloist and also respond actively to all other fellow performers. All efforts must be made to avoid musical self-indulgence. In free composition, if working within tonal domains, the spontaneous composer can begin by clearly identifying the tonic and those tones orbiting around that nucleus, and initially restrict individual musical contributions to simple ideas until certain other fundamental musical parameters are firmly established and gradually digested. To move effectively, free spontaneous composition requires mastery over a broad and flexible range of musical vocabulary in order to possess a sufficient musical backlog of memory and resources that enables musicians to facilitate the constant changes in musical directions and elements involved. Wrong notes are those that fail to properly fit a certain rhythmic, harmonic, or melodic pitch-set, grouping, or harmonic matrix in any realm of a musical composition. Logic must always remain clear structurally, rhythmically, melodically, and harmonically because the human consciousness realizes immediately when logic breaks down. Balance occurs when the spontaneous composer keeps track of all proportions of musical ingredients applied. Greater degrees of interest are maintained when performing artists attend to minute details of a composition, such as paying attention to its voice-leading, producing a variety of directions in musical lines (similar, contrary and oblique), and the like.

Spontaneous Music-Making in Bolivia

To gather maximum benefit from music of a given culture people need to experience music in the context of that culture. Most music around the world in the twenty-first century freely mixes traditional music with contemporary and experimental approaches to composition and performance. I discovered an effective and conscientious approach to teaching young children to intimately absorb both traditional and experimental music from the beginning of their musical study while visiting La Paz, Bolivia. An invitation from *Taller Boliviano de Musica Popular Arawi* to attend the third *Festival Boliviano de Musica Contemporanea* proved to be an exciting and invigorating musical and cultural adventure. As a composer and performer interested in ecumenical approaches to music and other art forms, my experiences in La Paz in both 1994 and 1995 expanded not only my understanding of traditional Bolivian music and its compositional evolution into twentieth-century experimentation, but also exposed the elusive living elements that manifest as inspiration and variable expression among the participants of all ages involved in that festival.

The geophysical setting and socio-cultural environment of La Paz is unusual, so the music that I found there was appropriate in its exotic range, beauty, and diversity. Arriving at the La Paz airport and then descending from the Altiplano to the city, I was first struck by the contrast between the poverty, the unusual mountains and landscapes during the drive from the airport, and then finally the beauty of the city of La Paz that suddenly appears 400 meters below. I encountered similar levels of contrast as I explored this interesting and friendly city, culture, and music. Much was revealed through simply watching the typical urban business people intermingle with the colorful community of Aymara people in their traditional dress (with British bowler hats!), in what became a persistent scene. The music heard between November 22 and 25 at the Theatro Municipal during the festival demonstrated similar levels of contrasts.

Shortly after our electro-acoustic performance of my new works to open the festival on Tuesday, November 22, students and faculty at the Arawi workshop treated my ensemble (Hesterian Musicism, featuring vibraphonist Cecilia Smith and trumpeter Bill Johnson) to a private performance of a variety of traditional Bolivian music. The performance was followed by an engaging discussion with the performers who provided one of the high points of my visit to La Paz. Equally rewarding were conversations with my hosts, Jesus Duran and his family; Oscar Garcia Guzman (both of whom are organizers and composers from the workshop), Director General de Cultura in La Paz; and Alvaro Montenegro, a composer and woodwind specialist on the faculty at the interesting conservatory in La Paz. Garcia, a guitarist and composer interested in electronic composition, was director of the Contemporary Orchestra for Native Instruments, founding director of the "Arawi" Bolivian Workshop of Popular Music (Taller Boliviano de Música Popular "Arawi"), and contemporary music director of ensemble "Madera Viva." The musical performances made the visits magical for me and gave La Paz deeper meaning. The acoustics in Teatro Municipal were superb. Each of the performances contributed unique compositional and performance perspectives fueled by sincere commitment to both traditional and experimental musical directions. My impression was that each composer and performer inspired the other.

Bolivia has maintained a great cultural and intellectual life well since pre-Colombian times. Architecture, ceramics, temples, and other creative examples scattered throughout the country give testimony to a rich cultural heritage. The *kollas* were not only the first inhabitants of the Andes Mountains and part of the highly organized Aimara family, but they also live alongside their first conquerors, the Incas. The Incas imposed their language (Quechua), art, and culture upon the Kollas. The Incas brought a new system of roads and aqueducts, hanging bridges, and surgical and medical practices. Other Inca influences included new designs and geometric shapes on clay objects; and new rituals and songs were also introduced.

Dance and music are the most popular cultural expressions found in Bolivia. Bolivian celebrations bring together a whole gamut of folklore and national traditions. Bolivians are especially joyous during carnival and the regional celebrations of both the *kollas* and the *yungas*. The mixture of indigenous and Spanish cultures gave birth to dances in honor of Our Lady of Copacabana, called El *Gran Sicuri,* which uses drums and flutes, and the puli-puli dance, where women dressed in the traditional flowery crest and feathers garments of the highlands. In the Oruro carnival, the *diabladas,* or devil-dancers, wear masks and costumes. These features suggested a connection with an African past that practitioners of Yoruba rituals must have introduced to the area. Small pockets of Bolivian citizens of African descent are sprinkled throughout the lower elevations. The dancers are typically accompanied by guitar, harp, flute, or a small guitar called a *charango.* During the evening there are *peñas* and nightclub shows in Bolivian cities such as Santa Cruz, Cochabamba, and La Paz. Outdoor cafes have folkloric dances and folkloric music. Improvisation is the basis of most of this music.

The Taller Boliviano de Musica Popular Arawi and Festival Boliviano de Musica Contemporanea are to be commended for routinely teaching children traditional music with various approaches to musical experimentation. The instructors always performed with their students and, as a consequence, the younger performers were well prepared, focused, and highly disciplined. A reviewer in one of the local newspapers criticized parents who brought their children to the festival because a couple of them were noisy. This was a bit ridiculous to me. The benefit of exposing children to the arts as early as possible prepares them for understanding and participating in ensembles such as those presented by the slightly older workshop students. The value of this type of exposure to future society certainly exceeds the occasional discomfort experienced by adults in the audience whose parents may not have taken them to concerts so early in life.

Composing and arranging have no fixed rules. The novice composer and arranger will benefit from analyzing and transcribing recordings from as many varied sources as possible. A few simple guidelines are helpful when attempting to write arrangements for the first time, nonetheless. The main principle applied in all such approaches is balance. In Eurocentric counterpoint, balance is systematically contained within sets of fixed rules as the specific set of voice-leading possibilities for each note composed is carefully considered. Due to the greater degrees of freedom allowed in jazz in general, a symmetrical harmonic technique can often work in the wind sections of big band arrangements because the rhythm section and soloists are free to provide counterbalance in the form of similar, contrary, oblique, and other motion based upon artistic sensitivity, experience, personal aesthetics, and spontaneous craftsmanship.

Something as simple as making certain that musical lines are not rhythmically "flat-footed" often serves to enliven *melody lines*. Melody lines can sound dull if they always start and end on a beat. Beginning and ending melodies with syncopations (that is, on the "e" and/or "a" subdivision of a given beat) helps keep musical ideas buoyant and afloat. Of course, this syncopated approach to phrasing too needs to be balanced with opposing rhythms. A mixture of rhythmic positions from which phrases begin and end keeps melodic movement from becoming overly predictable or too regulated.

Harmonic progressions should follow the path outlined by the melody line and the dictates of the chords prescribed. At times, notes in a melody are non-chord tones; nevertheless, the accompanying chords supporting such tones should consist only of chord-tones. Student arrangers should begin by stacking all supporting chords in root position. *Bass lines* should initially be written in straight quarter notes and should place the root of each chord at the beginning of each measure. Initially, the bass roots that occur on the first beat of each measure should be approached either by a perfect fifth above or perfect fourth below. Alternately, bass roots can also be approached by upper or lower scale-tones or leading tones (from the fourth beat of the preceding measure). For the sake of variety and interest, neophyte arrangers can also use eighth notes sparingly in the bass line.

Figure 2a. Arranging Example 1 of 2 (Bass Line)

(Continued on next page →)

Figure 2a. Arranging Example 2 of 2 (continued)

Figure 2b: Notice (in the chord progressions that follows) chords that are only one accidental removed from each other often easily substitute for each other. Thus major chords often morph into dominants that share the same root, and minor seventh chords that share common roots often replace dominant chords.

Figure 2b. Arranging Example 1 of 2 (Bass and Chords)

(Continued on next page →)

Figure 2c: The *voicing of chords* can be explored to provide particular musical effects. Some common four-voice approaches to harmonizing a melody are four-voice close, four-voice spread, and drop-two harmonization. In four-voice close, chord tones are stacked as close as possible to each other, creating more opaque melodic hues. This

arrangement unifies the melody and its harmonizing chords so tightly that they sound as though one is the extension of the other. In four-voice spread, chord tones are spread over as wide of a range as possible. Each instrument is heard more distinctly as a result and the harmony is more transparent. Drop-two harmonization is often used when the melody and harmony want to remain clearly distinguished from one another. This is useful in situations where the melody is highlighted and wants to stand clearly above the accompaniment.

Figure 2c. Arranging Example

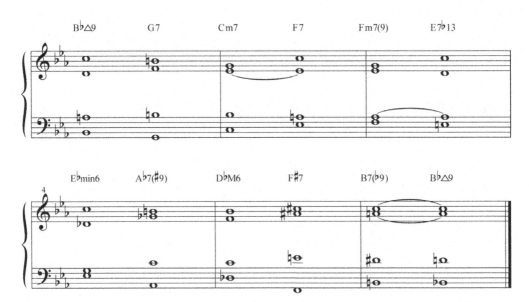

As mentioned earlier, melodies are rarely derived from chord tone exclusively. There are simple ways to harmonize passing tones, upper and lower neighbor notes, suspensions, and other non-chord tones. If we begin by filling in all chords supporting our melody with either a "chromatic approach" or "diminished approach" to harmonize non-chord tones, we add a rich set of chords to the harmonic mixture. In the chromatic approach we first find all non-chord tones that reside a half-step above or below subsequent basic chords. For non-chord tones that are located a half-step below, we build a chord comprised of notes that are all a half-step below or above each note of the subsequent chord. For all other non-chord tones we build a diminished chord from the given melody note to construct our chord (resulting in the construction of a symmetrical chord comprised of tones that are all a minor third away from each other).

Figure 2d. Arranging Example

Many contemporary jazz musicians, such as alto saxophonist Vincent Herring, use symmetry in the systematic construction of their solos (Farr 90–91). A number of other ways to approach harmonization in easy systematic ways exist. Some arrangers in high-pressure studio situations requiring short deadlines rely upon a series of formulas that enable them to produce quick, beautiful, and efficient results. The Schillinger method of composition is based upon a seemingly infinite array of mathematical formulas applied to musical composition. Such formulas are applied to rhythm, dynamics, melody, and harmony in ways reminiscent of total serialization that grew out of the music of composers from the Second Viennese School (Arnold Schoenberg, and his pupils Alban Berg, and Anton Webern) at the beginning of the twentieth century. The Schillinger process provides composers another systematic tool with which to harmonize a fixed melody in a tonal environment. The harmonic progression below first involves a basic harmonization (measures 1–6), then incorporates a Schllinger-styled pitch rotation over the same chord progression (measures 7–12). Interesting symmetrical patterns and voice-leading are produced in each voice of the pitch rotation. Voices follow their own fixed four-note rotation cycles as follows:

Soprano: 7–3-5–1
Alto: 3–5-1–7
Tenor: 5–1-7–3
Bass: 1–7-3–5

Figure 3. Schillinger Rotation

Composers need to know the range and transposition for each instrument. In addition to developing a familiarity with soprano, alto, tenor, and bass clefs, musicians should be acquainted with some of the most common intervals of transposition: transpose concert parts to B-flat by moving up a major second (or down a minor seventh); to E-flat by moving up a major sixth (or down a minor third); to F by moving up a perfect fifth (or down a perfect fourth); and to G by moving up a perfect fourth (or down a perfect fifth).

> B-flat—Soprano and bass clarinet, trumpet and flugelhorn, soprano, tenor and bass saxophone, etc.
> E-flat—Sopranino and alto clarinet, alto and baritone saxophone, etc.
> F—Bassett horn, English horn, French horn, etc.
> G—Alto flute, etc.

Other Harmonic Implications of the Blues

Blues melodic constructions have clear harmonic implications, certain linguistic qualities, and retentions from various African traditions that shape the tones of both vocal and instrumental blues styles. Such factors, along with a general relationship to the overtone series, transfer to all traditional and modern blues forms over time. A symbiotic relationship formed between melodic and harmonic interchange in blues demonstrates that the melody does not contain harmonic contradictions, but simply refuses to conform to the alien and inappropriate restrictions of European tonal harmony. Blues can be interpreted as having multiple fundamentals (C, F, and G are fundamentals of three successive seventy chords of a blues progression in C), just as in some regions of Africa, melodies revolve around two or multiple fundamentals. All chords in a blues progression can also be considered harmonic extensions of a single fundamental tone, just as African music has firm grounding in the natural harmonics series. In both cases the music resides outside the arbitrary rules evolved from even-tempered scales and chord progressions characteristic of the European tonal system.

Tonal systems promoting the awareness of a basic tonal reference note are always indicative of a remote origin in the selective use of harmonics over a *single* fundamental. By contrast, where they include the idea of harmonic shift, tonal systems are often derived from the use of at least *two* fundamentals, such as are obtained on a mouthbow whose string is braced or stopped with a finger or stick. This is the background to many of the harmonic structures found in the music of Gabon, Congo, Angola, and South Africa. There may also be retentions of this experience in some forms of the blues (Kubik 128).

The particular nature of various musical instruments characteristic of a culture may determine the number of fundamentals (or tonal centers) employed. Inspiration for the harmonics-based music of the stretched string on the hunting bow played by Bushmen of the Kalahari Desert in southern Africa (and the harmonics-based music of other African tonal systems) is derived from performance tendencies that may have emerged from its vocal music, or vice versa. The nuanced vowel formation of human speech may suggest the key to understanding speech-derived timbre, rhythm, pitch tendencies, and harmonics. Kubik discussed his theory of the emergence of harmonics from the voice.

A vowel is a *voiced* sound in which the air passes freely through the mouth or as nasalization through the nose. The difference between vowels is created by different shaping of the mouth as a resonance chamber, altered by movements of the tongue and shaping of the lips. Thus, each vowel has its own particular sound spectrum, and it is defined as a difference in the selective reinforcement of harmonics; i.e., the vowel [a] differs from [u] by its harmonics, if sung to the same pitch. In Africa, not only multipart singing styles, but also *unison singing* can be based on scalar patterns generated by representations of speech-derived partials (harmonics) over a single fundamental.

Kubik says:

> Proceeding from this knowledge, I have developed a simple theory of the blues and about how scalar patterns from the west central Sudanic belt were perpetuated in the blues. First, the remote origin of these scales must be sought in speech. They do not derive from experimentation with instruments. Next, if such tonal systems are inspired by partials over a single fundamental, these

partials must fall into the comfortable middle range of the natural harmonic series. Both postulates also have the advantage of explaining the presence of a single tonal center in many of the Sudanic styles *and* in the blues, since all partials-based tones sung by the performer reinforce the idea of their fundamental, and thereby the tonal center. The C in a blues written in the key of C, therefore, represents the fundamental of a harmonics-derived scale (129).

"Thought" itself is the seed of most human endeavors, and musical instruments merely amplify our thoughts, emotions, and perspectives. Our subconscious processes are governed by a series of complex glands that most people know little about. Levels of consciousness have been subjects of study through the ages. Contemporary discoveries have led to a convergence of the views of material science and spiritual wisdom. We are largely unaware of the various levels of subconscious "thought" that move within us continually, including those that guide the most vital aspects of our lives. The fundamental subconscious engages in functions that keep us alive, such as breathing, seeing, hearing, touching, and tasting. These actions occur without the active participation our objective or subjective consciousness. Most of our routine problems exist unconsciously and we only apply our consciousness purposefully to alter our actions or thoughts from the routine. Music often reflects the heartbeat, rhythm of various motions, visual impressions of beautiful scenery, and other phenomena that register upon the brain.

Composers also try to express the human will and consciousness. Emphasizing the unconscious mind, Freud initially attempted to subdivide the mind purely in terms of different levels of consciousness. He later abandoned that theory in favor of his tripartite

Figure 4a. Levels of Consciousness (Enlightenment)

(after a document given to the author by drummer, dancer, metaphysician and educator Maurice Haltom)

Chakra	Gland	Level of Consciousness
7th	Pineal	Transcendent Consciousness
6th	Pituitary	Community/Cultural Consciousness
5th	Thyroid	Individual Consciousness
4th	Thymus	Intermediary Consciousness
3rd	Pancreas	Individual Consciousness
2nd	Adrenals	Community / Cultural / Group Consciousness
1st	Testes/Ovum	Transcendent Consciousness

Goal: To become conscious of all levels, through 7th Level.

division of the id, ego, and superego, but consistently considered that the different functions of the mind operated at different levels. The id does not stand for a delay in gratification. As babies emerge from the womb into the reality of life, they want only to eat, drink, urinate, defecate, be warm, and gain sexual pleasure. These urges are the demands of the id, the most primitive motivational force. In pursuit of these ends, the id demands immediate gratification: it is ruled by the pleasure principle, demanding satisfaction now, regardless of circumstances and possible undesirable effects.

The ego emerges with the eventual understanding that immediate gratification is unwise and usually impossible, which is ruled by the reality principle. The ego serves as an intermediary in the id's relations with reality, suppressing the id's urges as required until an appropriate situation arises. This repression of inappropriate desires and urges represents the greatest strain on the mind. While the ego is still in the service of the id, it borrows some of its psychic energy in an effort to control the urge until it is reasonably satisfied.

The superego uses guilt and self-reproach as its primary means of enforcement for the id's rules. Conversely, if we do something that is acceptable to the superego, we experience pride and self-satisfaction. While the ego may temporarily repress certain human urges desired by the id in fear of punishment, eventually these external sources

Figure 4b. Levels of Discipline (Study)

(after a document given to the author by drummer, dancer, metaphysician and educator Maurice Haltom)

Chakra	Yin / Yang	Discipline
7th	 ○	Meditation
6th	 ☯	Natural Law / Religion / Mental Medicine / Tai Chi / Yoga
5th	 ☯	Music / Art / Aesthetics / Culture
4th	 ☯	Psychology / Philosophy / Social Science / Anthropology
3rd	 ☯	Math / Physics Natural Sciences / Physical Medicine
2nd	 ◐	History / Karma
1st	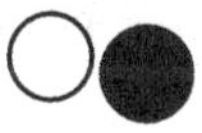 ○ ●	Geology / Earth Science / Planet Formation / Fossil Study

Goal: To grasp all levels of study; though any one can provide an individual jump off point through Level 7.

of punishment are internalized to such an extent that a child will not steal the candy, even when unwatched, because he has internalized punishment.

The superego is sub-dividable into two parts: conscience and ego ideal. Conscience tells what is right and wrong, and forces the ego to inhibit the id in pursuit of morally acceptable, not pleasurable or even realistic, goals. The ego ideal aims the individual's path of life towards the ideal, perfect goals instilled by society. In the pursuit, the mind attempts to make up for the loss of the perfect life experienced as a baby (Stevenson). The following chart lists glands and the levels of consciousness some metaphysicians suggest these organs effect.

So both musicians and listeners might consider whether or not the music they create or listen to is beneficial and making them healthier. People might begin to ask themselves, "Is the music that I am digesting helping to expand my awareness?" The functions of music in ritual demonstrate that it certainly helps to create a certain type of environment. The next question might be, "How is this sonic environment affecting the people within it?"

> "Music expresses that which cannot be said and on which it is impossible to be silent."
>
> —Victor Hugo

References

Beaugrande, Robert de. "The Processes of Invention: Association and Recombination." *College Composition and Communication* 30 (1979): 260–7. Blesh, Rudi. *Shining Trumpets.* New York: Knopf, 1958.

Bodin, Ron. *Voodoo: Past and Present.* University of Southwestern Louisiana, Lafayette, LA, 1990.

Bruchez, Margaret Sabom. "Artifacts that Speak for Themselves: Sounds Underfoot in Mesoamerica." 4 April 2006. *ScienceDirect.* November 2007 <http://www. sciencedirect.com/ science?_ob=ArticleURL&_udi=B6WH6-4JMVHY0-1&_user=10&_rdoc=1&_fmt=&_ orig=search&_sort=d&view=c&_acct=C000050221&_version=1&_urlVersion=0&_userid =10&md5=ba3318d1623be6106a087a73479 9f96c>.

Budd, Malcolm. *Music and The Emotions: The Philosophical Theories.* London: Routledge, 1992, 37–39.

Bundy, Murray Wright. "'Invention' and 'Imagination' in the Renaissance." *Journal of English and Germanic Philology* 29 (1930b): 535–45.

Caernarvon-Smith, Patricia. *Audience Analysis and Response.* Pembroke: Firman Technical Publications, 1983.

Cassimere, Raphael. *History of St. Louis Cemetery.* Compiled by Raphael Cassimere, Jr., Danny Barker, Florence Borders, D. Clive Hardy, Joseph Logsdon and Charles Rousseve. Sponsored by New Orleans NAACP, Carrollton, New Orleans, 1980.

Chun-yuan, Chang. *Creativity and Taoism: A Study of Chinese Philosophy, Art, and Poetry.* London: Wildwood House, 1963.

Conway, David. *Ritual Magic: An Occult Primer.* New York: E. P. Dutton, 1972.

Cope, D. *Virtual Music—Computer Synthesis of Musical Style.* Cambridge, MA: MIT Press, 2001.

Cosentino, Donald J. ed. *Sacred Arts of Haitian Vodou.* Los Angeles, CA: UCLA Fowler Museum of Cultural History, 1995.

———. *Vodou Things: The Art of Pierrot Barra and Marie Cassaise.* University Press of Mississippi, Jackson, 1998. Davidson, Basil. *Africa in History: Themes and Outlines.* New York: Collier Books, 1974.

Davis, Wade. *The Serpent and the Rainbow.* United States of America: Warner Books, 1985.

Deren, Maya. *Divine Horsemen: The Living Gods of Haiti.* United States of America: McPherson and Company, 1953.

Diccionario de la lengua española. Real Academia Española. Madrid: Editorial Espasa-Calpe, 1992.

Dictionary of American Regional English. Volume I. Introduction and A-C. Cambridge, MA, and London: The Belknap Press of Harvard University Press, 1985.

Dictionary of American Regional English. Volume II. D-H. Cambridge, MA and London: The Belknap Press of Harvard University Press, 1991.

Farr, Tyler. "Vincent Herring's Symmetrical Saxophone Solo on Straight Street." *Down Beat* (August 2008): 90–91.

Gandolfo, Charles. *Marie Laveau of New Orleans: The Great Voodoo Queen.* New Orleans, LA: New Orleans Historic Voodoo Museum, 1992.

Grassi, Ernesto. *Rhetoric as Philosophy: The Humanist Tradition.* Trans. John Michael Krois and Azizeh Azodi. Carbondale: Southern Illinois University Press, 2001.

Hall, Manly Palmer. *The Secret Teachings of All Ages: An Encyclopedic Outline of Masonic, Hermetic, Qabbalistic, and Rosicrucian Symbolical Philosophy.* New York: Jeremy P. Tarcher/Penguin, 2003.

Hurston, Zora Neale. *Mules and Men.* United States of America: J. B. Lippincott and Company, 1935.

———. *Tell My Horse.* United States of America: J. B. Lippincott and Company, 1938.

Jourdain, Robert. *Music, the Brain and Ecstasy: How Music Captures Our Imagination.* New York: HarperCollins Publishers, 1998.

Khan, Hazrat Inayat. *The Mysticism of Sound and Music: The Sufi Teaching of Hazrat Inayat Khan.* Boston: Shambhala, 1996.

Kubik, G. *Africa and the Blues.* Jackson, MS: University Press of Mississippi, 1999.

Langer, Susan. "Building and Weaving: Esthetic and Technical Metaphors as an Index to the Essential Unity of the Arts." *The Journal of Philosophy* 39.25 (December 3, 1942).

Lateef, Yusef. *Method on How to Perform Autophysiopsychic Music.* Amherst, MA: Fana Music, 1979.

Lee, Byong Won. *The Sinawi Performance in the Kut: Universality and Idiosyncrasy in the Korean Shaman Ritual Music.* The University of Hawaii. Unpublished manuscript. 2005.

Lee, Yong-Shik. *Shaman Ritual Music in Korea*. Seoul, Korea: Jimoondang, 2004. Lewis, Ralph M., F.R.C. "The Function of Ritualism." *Rosicrucian Digest* (February 1986): 23–26.

Maniktala, Rakesh. *Spiritualism, Modern Science and Ancient History*. March 2008 <http://geocities.com/ancientscience/beliefs>.

Martinez, Raymond J. *Mysterious Marie Laveau and Folk Tales Along the Mississippi*. New Orleans: Hope Publications, 1956.

Molin, Son, Exc. Mgr. *Dictionnaire Bambara-Français et Français-Bambara*. Seine: Les Presses Missionaires, 1955.

Murphy, Joseph M. *Santería: An African Religion in America*. Boston: Beacon Press, 1988.

Ortiz, Fernando. *Glosario de afronegrismos*. La Habana: Editorial de Ciencias Sociales, 1990.

———. *Nuevo catauro de cubanismos*. La Habana, Cuba: Editorial de Ciencias Sociales, 1985.

———. *Tomado de la primera edición*. La Habana: Imprenta "El siglo XX," 1924.

Overstreet, H. A. *The Mature Mind*. New York: W. W. Norton and Company, Inc., 1949.

Pachter, Henry M. *Paracelsus: Magic into Science*. New York: Collier Books, 1951.

Parker Rhodes, Jewell. *Voodoo Dreams*. New York: Picador USA, 1995.

Pelton, Robert W. *The Complete Book of Voodoo*. New York: Berkley Publishing Corporation, 1972.

Petit Larousse. Librairie Larousse. Paris, 1964.

Plantation Society in the Americas: An Interdisciplinary Journal of Tropical and Subtropical History and Culture. Carnival in Perspective. New York: Athens Printing Company, 1990.

Powell, Cory S. *God in the Equation: How Einstein Became the Prophet of the New Religious Era*. New York: The Free Press, 2002.

Prose, Francine. *Marie Laveau*. New York: Berkley Publishing Corporation, 1947.

Rigaud, Milo. *Secrets of Voodoo*. New York: Pocket Books, 1971.

Saxon, Lyle, Robert Tallant, and Edward Dreyer. *Gumbo Ya-Ya: A Collection of Louisiana Folk Tales*. New York: Bonanza Books, 1945.

Stevenson, David B. "Freud's Division of the Mind." *The Victorian Web*. Brown University. 1996. <http://www.victorianweb.org/science/freud/division.html>.

Tallant, Robert. *Voodoo in New Orleans*. Gretna: Pelican Publishing Company, 1983.

———. *The Voodoo Queen*. New York: G. P. Putnam's Sons, 1956.

Valduran, Albert, Thomas A. Klingler, Margaret M. Marshall, and Kevin J. Rotet. *Dictionary of Louisiana Creole*. Bloomington and Indianapolis: Indiana University Press, 1998.

Varela, Beatriz. "The Lexicon of Marie Laveau's Voodoo." *Organo Oficial de la Sociedad de Amigos del Pais*. (1998). February 2008 <http://www.amigospaisguaracabuya.org/oagbv004.php>.

Wilmore, Gayraud S. *Black Religion and Black Radicalism*. Maryknoll, NY: Orbis, 1983.

Chapter Nine
Blues: One Down, One Up

Unity of Macrocosm and Microcosm (The Individual Soloist and the Orchestra)

The knowledge of God is eternal, and is present everywhere around us in energy form. So are the past and prospective futures. These can be "tapped in" by sufficiently spiritually advanced individuals. Without the spiritual development, knowledge and science always decay.

Jazz, Math, and Musical Order

Numbers bind our understanding of the material Universe into systematic patterns. They represent a form of analysis that we apply to certain symbols that communicate certain notions and principles that ostensibly have universal meaning. Just as the colors we view are simply different frequencies of light, numbers may be just as distant from understanding the true essence of the phenomena they attempt to describe or represent. We can reduce the human body to a number of "precise" calculations and still have no clue as to the formula that animates our being. Nonetheless, they have served our daily purposes very well.

Although music symbols are specialized tools designed to suit a select set of stylist approaches, they each represent an intangible mathematical quantity that denotes aspects of musical time, frequency, amplitude, and the like. The characteristic patterns associated with various systems of numbers can support ethereal notions of musical imagery, qualities, and situations that inform and inspire many aspects of composition. Technical organization can provide supporting structure for the elusive psychological or emotional content of musical expression.

Humankind cannot invent effective new languages that are completely devoid of tradition out of thin air. Spoken language and the language of music reflect a long line of human evolution. Basic truths are not altered rapidly or haphazardly from era to era, although our understanding or interpretation of certain concepts is perpetually modified as our individual and collective knowledge evolves. Despite existing languages having been time-tested by billions of people worldwide over many thousands of years, we are each still inimitable beings with unique ideas and creative perspectives to share.

Music expresses a broad spectrum of emotions and ideas. Perhaps the language of music is universal because it represents natural laws recognized and confirmed by listeners throughout human history. The overtone series anchors and unifies musical language and laws. If styles of music reflect the socio-cultural freedom and limitations existing within an environment, innovative artists may merely extend existing musical languages to develop their personal ideas, individualized aesthetic perspectives, and evolving stylistic approaches. Africans in America were among the few modern people poised and compelled by social circumstances to combine disparate spiritual, cultural, intellectual, and free expression into an international language capable of eliciting a response worldwide, with and without words, throughout the twentieth century. Jazz is a mirror that reflects African-American experimentalism, resilience, creativity, and loving nature that, in turn, represents positive human nature and spirit. Its history of struggle represents a way we view both the best and worst aspects that impact upon our individual and collective thoughts, emotions, and experiences. It reflects the experimentalism, resilience, creativity, and loving nature of many people throughout the world. Musicians worldwide have continually expanded this musical language through creating musical portraits that reflect the contemporary world around them. The characteristics and laws governing music worldwide can be reduced to numerous common factors, and mathematics is one means through which principles of music can be measured physically or intuitively.

Appreciation for jazz will increase in the twenty-first century as it gains greater exposure and as its matrices of fractal geometry are better understood. With the computational ability of today's computer programs, the sounds produced in jazz performance will soon reveal to our eyes (in music notation or other analytical forms) some of the subtle and precise factors involved in spontaneous composition that have already attracted many believers through their ears. The highly evolved ritual, structural, technical, and communicative powers of jazz have caught the attention of many educators, scholars, business executives, and others who recognize the significance that the music holds as a prototype for political and business modeling. Kabir Sehgal recently wrote a book entitled, *Jazzocracy: Jazz Democracy, and The Creation of a New American Mythology.* Sehgal is a jazz bassist who toured with Wynton Marsalis during the summer of 2004. Marsalis has been talking about the democratic nature of jazz for many years and Sehgal seems to have expanded upon some of the trumpeter's views. President Jimmy Carter said, "Kabir Sehgal brilliantly shows us how both jazz and democracy require an environment of free exchange and collective ingenuity (front cover)." Sehgal not only extrapolates the many lessons that society can potentially take from jazz, but does not shy away from discussing the socio-cultural milieu in which

African-American music evolved to clarify the role that it has played in reflecting the nuances of a racist American culture. Of the "Myths of Unjust Treatment" of African Americans he says:

> These myths portray a people oppressed by the dominant group in society. They focus on the tragic collective experience of a particular nation—like the Holocaust in Nazi Germany and slavery in the U.S. (Schöpflin 31). While the Jim Crow days have vanished, modern music still places African Americans in the stranglehold of stereotype. In the late nineteenth century, whites smeared their faces with burnt cork to mimic black entertainment—at times reinforcing a wretched stereotype. The modern minstrel show of Eminem must be recognized for what it is.

Sehgal says that Elvis Presley was not wholly innovative. He performed derivative black music. Elvis's first producer said, "[Elvis] tried not to show it, but he felt so *inferior*" (Bayles 122). He was a white blues singer who made hip contortions and dancing lips appetizing to white America.

Sehgal also feels that, while Elvis certainly possessed a modicum of talent as a musician, he was still mimicking black musicians. Like Elvis, Eminem mimics blacks and is arguably the modern day minstrel entertainer. Eminem translates the bad of the black image, the human experience, into the worst. He raps of women, "So b*** me b****." Maybe it is generous to say that Eminem raps of the human plight, as blues music once did, but he offers hardly any words of sympathy and commiseration. And rap rhythm is largely repetitive, monotonous, and predictable. The repeated drum-and-bass of vulgar rap grinds the message home and provides little sonic or melodic release.

The blues are special because the low lyrics are canceled out by the harmonic progression of tension and release. A slow song sounded pensive, not gurgling with rage. The imprecision of the lyrics of the blues ballad are offset by the focused tonality of the song. Bessie Smith used incorrect words, saying "rural" instead of "ruler" in *Yellow Dog Blues* (Murray 82). The effect of the blues ballad sings from the music, not the words (Sehgal 150–151).

While Sehgal misses some of the nuances of early rural southern United States blues vernacular speech in pointing out its "imprecision," he does touch upon the peculiar aspect of society that results in the majority culture's preference for diluted versions of African-American music over the original version, largely due to the color of a musician's skin. Sehgal also discusses several perspectives on the role of art.

Yeats questioned whether art could make its audience unhappy. John Coltrane explored and shared a range of emotions with audience members, often confusing and angering them. Pianist Bill Evans suggested to him: it is the artist's responsibility to select those emotions "most beneficial for his audience." Coltrane once believed that jazz should bring joy to the listener, even if it talked about "the blues." Artists are the emotional sieves for the audience (151).

The title to Martha Bayles' book, *Hole in Our Soul: The Loss of Beauty and Meaning in American Popular Music,* introduces a perspective that is echoed frequently when analyzing music since the mid-1970s (Bayles 89). Music has lost some of the rich nuances of earlier music, but this tendency is reflective of our times and changing socio-cultural environment. Rap (and other music) does not necessarily lack tension and release, but the proportion between those polar opposite qualities has just been minimized to obtain a certain effect. Coltrane's composition *Mars* has sustained intensity throughout. Many Global African spiritual rituals depend upon sustained intensity. It is impossible for anyone to get a full understanding of rap or any other music without having thorough comprehension of hip hop culture. Listening to an intense waterfall or a field of crickets chirping can sound like sustained intensity, without tension and release. Closer examination of any such phenomena inevitably reveals that systematic oscillation exists between tension and release operating within dense sounds of all variety. Following several decades where so much of what artists produced resulted in "deconstructing" certain things without ever "constructing" something to replace the disassembled concept, makes Sehgal's skepticism readily understandable.

Just as some listeners have blocked out particular music because of the color of a performing artist's skin, and other listeners have derived the opposite meaning from Coltrane's music than he intended, the meaning of music resides far beyond the mathematics suggested by the notes involved. Because of a wide range of potential musical interpretations, careful examination of African and African-American music can lead composers to think more deeply about the many dimensions that exist beyond the limitations of notation on a printed page. For instance, *duration* refers to the time between the onset of an event and its end. In performance of music, rhythmic interpretation may be either precisely aligned with grid points in a metrical scheme or more loosely interpreted in a variety of individual ways. Musical rhythmic sequences can have the same attack points, but the actual durations of the sounds can vary according to the particular nature, character, and stylistic interpretation of the voices or instruments performing. Thus, in measuring musical events through computer analysis, duration refers to the actual length of time that is filled with sound and not strictly limited to a particular established set of note values.

Mathematics is a formal investigation of number, pattern, form, and other elements inherent in the organization of analysis, composition, and performance of music. Mathematics was born out of ancient peoples' practical necessity to use numbers and counting to keep track of their daily schedules, herds, crops, and to conduct business at the marketplace. Most presumably, ancient people developed intuitive rhythm and metrical grouping before any language of music theory existed. In time, nonetheless, the routine counting and grouping involved in various forms of early mathematics inevitably affected musical organization.

The ancient Egyptians possessed one of the earliest forms of mathematics, inspiring all mathematical traditions that would follow in history. As one of the first civilizations in the world to take advantage of the benefits of numbers and mathematics, the work of the Ancient Egyptians truly stands out, especially because many results of this early math are still visible today in the form of the vast architectural achievements. At the beginning of the Egyptian "Old Kingdom" (around 3000 B.C.), when the previously separate nations in the lower Nile valley formed into a single nation under one pharaoh (the first was *Djoser*), the Egyptians already possessed a counting system using hieroglyphics. At the beginning of European mathematics, Pythagorean mathematics was first and foremost music-driven, and by the end of ancient music Pythagoras' school was established in 518 B.C. in Croton. In that school the science of numbers and many advances in geometry were devised and discussed. Plato's Academy (an institution which lasted over 900 years until it was closed down by Emperor Justinian in 529 A.D. as a pagan establishment) was set up to educate the future politicians and statesmen of Athens. Plato's laws and concepts for mathematical applications to life and education were far less radical than those expounded by Pythagoras.

Compositions evolve from seed material just as life forms do. The origins of life on earth evolved from the most humble essence. Single cells evolved into complex organisms, nonetheless, as flexible life forms found that the key to survival was adaptation. Heightened self-awareness was the key to success that separated humankind from other creatures on Earth. Creativity involves musical self-exploration that leads to musical answers. This movement towards heightened self-awareness involves a process of knowledge, flexibility, adaptation, and musical evolution. An Afrocentric approach to music usually allows content to define the overall structural dimensions (form), leaving ample room for intuitive impulses to determine and navigate musical decision-making. To compose spontaneously, theoretical factors that complicate music intellectually are replaced by simpler formulas that are thoroughly digested, and then systematically skillfully applied, ultimately giving rise to complex and varied music that reflects heightened musical self-awareness. Thus the slave era was a social cataclysm that ultimately led to many African-American musical innovations. The degree of freedom that emerged as a result did not divorce these musical forms from the systematic mathematics that govern other forms of music. Instead the Africans in America devised a system of musical experimentation that produced music resembling the mathematic organization of products arising from Fractal Geometry. Wolfram suggests that in the past the only kinds of shapes widely discussed in science and mathematics were those that are regular or smooth. However, beginning in the late 1970s, the geometry field began to emphasize the importance of nested shapes that contain seemingly arbitrarily intricate pieces, and argued that such shapes are common throughout nature. Although many systems produce shapes that are extremely complex and have no nested structure,[1] in Fractal Geometry we find a fair number of systems that produce such nested shapes (Wolfram 15).

We can also find extremely complex nuclei within cores of modern and contemporary jazz. Such approaches contain not only rich conceptual nuclei and poly-tonal and

---

[1]   Structures can contain other structures as members; in other words, structures can nest.

hypermetric musical episodes, but also a diverse and stratified spectrum of music fueled by overlapping dynamic and emotionally expressive sections such as those found in Ornette Coleman's "Free Jazz," Coltrane's "Om," Cecil Taylor's "Unit Structures," or any of a number of Sun Ra's compositions for his Arkestra. The potential for central structures to evolve based upon a number of nuclei becomes increasingly more pronounced as spontaneous composers use computers in their music. Since all of the central motivational ideas do not have to be memorized, performers can interact with a greater number of musical subjects. The complexity involved when working with a number of simple nuclei, where relatively simple ideas become profound and complex due to synergy and reciprocal exchange, multiplies the depth and dimensionality of musical organization exponentially. This melodic developmental idea is akin to ways that polyrhythms multiply rhythmic potential when stacking very simple but potent little independent rhythms together systematically. The computer itself has a similar composite seed that governs the simple binary combinations of zeros and ones from the center of its operational process. Wolfram describes related aspects of Nanotechnology.

Growing rapidly since the early 1900s, the goal of nanotechnology is to implement technological systems on atomic scales. But so far nanotechnology has mostly been concerned with shrinking quite familiar mechanical and other devices. Yet what the discoveries in this book now show is that there are all sorts of systems that have much simpler structures, but that can nevertheless perform very sophisticated tasks. And some of these systems seem in many ways much more suitable for direct implementation on an atomic scale (15).

Each social journey taken by African Americans in their new homeland—from plantations (field hollers and spirituals), to urban ghettos (blues, boogie woogie), slightly into integrated social life in America (swing, bebop, cool, hard bop, etc.), then back into contemporary economic segregation (hip hop and rap)—resulted in continued stylistic change, innovations, revolution, and musical evolution. The overtone series automatically introduces the mathematical arrangement of composite tone as a complete system of notes orbiting around fundamental tones arranged in a prescribed order. Africans generally approach the implications of this arrangement by absorbing musical theory through their ears, and with a practical genius, rather than in an overtly analytical or theoretical fashion, with created complex systems. Spiritual awareness is an integral part of this Afro-centric artistic practicality. Initiated wisdom simplifies while the novice makes everything overly complex. For instance, Egyptians felt that numbers had no place that extends into infinity because only the Creator is infinite (because reducing the Creator to any form of exact quantity or abstract calculation is impossible).

Among both peoples [Egyptians and Babylonians] was a similar geometric origin of their mathematics, but two different mentalities quickly arose. The Babylonians opened the door to a "scholastic" way of thinking in which the "supposition" slowly replaced the fact, the geometric technique.

The "problem" implies an awareness of the existence of an unknown. The method of finding it can only be by the substitution of an unknown value with a supposed value. The algebraic method does not give any quantity to x, but the Ancients affirm that the unknown has a value of One, therefore the elements of the problem can only be fractions. Fractions are "positive enumerations," not negative values. Adding is composing with elements, but multiplying creates growth which is geometric. In subtraction, the quantities to be subtracted are not negative but "inversely positive."

This is the whole mathematic philosophy of the Ancients, and it is this that allows them easily and simply to solve problems that our methods only complicate. Now simplicity demands clarity and clarity comes from mastery over the question, whereas the novice always tends to make things complicated (Lubicz 226).

The most prevailing numbers are akin to those symbolic recurring digits that seem to have served as organizational quantities throughout much of human society's history. As a consequence, the numbers of corners of the earth, days in a week, months of the year, sacred trinities, points of a star, and other familiar groupings correspond to and are most consistently used in formulating musical scales and intervals. These recurring values also appear in metaphysics and religion that enable us to trace the history of numerical archetypal patterns. Most religions, whether they be monotheistic or not, recognize some form of a Supreme Being. As the source quantity, the number *One* represents the Creator.

Just as the ancients affirm that the unknown has a value of one, African rhythm likewise extends from a single beat. From a single nuclear source, musical elements can combine to form poly-dimensional melodies, harmonies, rhythms, and textures reflective of the poly-dimensional aspects of the forests and environments from which the music emerged. Each layer of polyrhythmic stratification enjoys a degree of independence, yet each line derives its individual metrical orientation from a composite grouping of time. Rather than thinking in terms of complex or compound metrical arrangements such as: |7/8 - 5/8|15/8 - 7/8|3/8 - 4/8 - 5/8| etc., Global African music typically replaces abundant "metrical signatures" with cross-rhythms and syncopated accents that serve the same sonic purpose of disrupting rhythmic regularity even more emphatically than bar lines. In written notation, bar lines merely indicate stress points that organize rhythm into logical regular or irregular groupings. Likewise, a complex tone produced on a musical instrument is often made up of a complex of overtones that overlaps harmonic frequencies that are integer multiples of the fundamental frequency. In a related fashion, stratified individual and independent African rhythms combine as one composite polyrhythmic unit.

Music usually has an underlying framework and fabric against which varied rhythmic phrases, note durations, and melodic patterns are heard. *Beats* or *pulses* are mental temporal reference points. These musical markers do not have to be represented by a specific musical event. The regularly recurring beat in music typically involves a series of identical and isochronous pulses that are most often equally spaced in time. *Meter* is the organization of the beats of a pulse into a cyclically repeating pattern of accentuation.

In some styles, certain beats in a pulse may be emphasized more than others. Accents give a particular note or beat the more stress or emphasis. In placing greater importance or centrality on certain beats than immediately surrounding ones we divide pulse into a series of equally spaced strong and weak metrical markers. For example, beats 2 and 4 receive greater emphasis than beats 1 and 3 in jazz. Syncopation[22] upsets such cycles by placing unexpected and unorthodox accentuation within otherwise predictable metrical schemes. When time is perceived as equidistant because the prevailing pulse is regular, an infinite variety of rhythmic permutations may occur around the beat. A pulse always has a tempo. Tempo, often measured in beats per minute, is the measurement of the repetition rate of a pulse.

The basic beat is thus felt by a listener as the central organizing pulse in a piece of music. When grouping boundaries do not reinforce the established accent pattern of meter, we get syncopation and heightened metrical tension. Syncopation operates against the regularly recurring metrical pulse by introducing accents in unusual or unexpected intervals in time. Since accents frame metrical organization, syncopation essentially introduces new unexpected metrical groupings within the overriding or prevailing meter.

Metrical structure is a primary way of establishing important points of temporal reference in music. This is accomplished by accenting particular beats more than others, which makes them central temporal reference points. This forms a framework for rhythmic expectation, where the central beat is "listened forward to." In this sense, meter is a type of schema. The most strongly accented beat in a metrical cycle is usually found at the beginning of the cycle and is called the *downbeat*. One cycle of meter is referred to in Western music as a *measure*. Just as a pulse forms a basic structure of beats repeating at a regular interval at the lowest rhythmic level, meter can form a repetitive structure of accented beats at the next higher level. In a sense, meter is like a higher-level pulse.

Metrical tension is tension between the rhythmic groupings of actual musical events and the accent pattern implied by meter. It is established by producing an accent pattern within a rhythmic phrase that does *not* conform to the accent pattern implied by the meter—placing strongly accented events, such as beginning or ending events in a rhythmic phrase or grouping, on *weak* (unaccented) beats in the meter (Snyder 59).

Metrical patterns are thus established by accented events in the music that create forms of reference that can both stabilize the composition and propel it forward. In many musical styles, once meter is established, its metrical cycle tends to persist. An even more pervasive feature of meter is its reciprocal relationship with rhythmic grouping. The parameters in time that meter creates through its regularity and accents, interact with grouping and phrase boundaries that either conform to the accent pattern

---

[2]   Syncopation involves a shift of accent in a passage or composition that occurs when a normally weak beat is stressed.

of meter or form new syncopated, irregular, or overlapping groupings that produce tension and surprise.

In African-American music varied tone *articulation* is an important musical element. When such articulation is properly applied, instrumental music often begins to emulate nuances of spoken language. Articulation involves the relatively small and subtle differences in pitch, accentuation, timbre, dynamics, and duration of time that is given to each tone. Increased emphasis can be given to any of the grouping factors by introducing changes in melodic factors, such as introducing a disjunct interval (leap in tone sequence) into a series of conjunct (connected scale-wise motion) tones.

Music, Chaos Theory, and Fractal Geometry

Music applies mathematical measurement to sound vibration and its various modes of organization. Musicians experiment with vibrations that involve complex underlying mathematical equations that they resolve using their ears as the primary computational tool. Often, what may seem chaotic to the uninitiated indeed has underlying logic and form. The serial music created by the Second Viennese School certainly seemed random to many listeners despite the highly formulaic nature of the music. A popular tendency today promotes the "immediately attractive," the "simple" and straightforward, the "easily accessible," while quickly marginalizing music that is too "innovative," "different," "progressive," or that which is often the most creative. Chaos might be defined as turmoil, turbulence, primordial abyss, and undesired randomness, but today scientists understand that chaos is something extremely sensitive to prevailing environment conditions. Chaos invites the question whether or not making accurate long-term predictions about the way systems will behave is possible. A chaotic system can actually develop in a way that appears very smooth and ordered from an appropriate distance and perspective. Thus, with the proper distance, perspective, and understanding, listeners begin to understand that Alban Berg's *Lulu and Wozzeck,* John Coltrane's *Ascension* and *Interstellar Space,* or contemporary computer compositions are all immune to the label "chaotic."

Chaos can often be a gross error in human judgment. African polyrhythms were considered chaotic by Europeans when they were first heard. Contemporary jazz often seems chaotic to certain listeners today when the stylistic approach to rhythm, melody, harmony, timbre, etc., is foreign and complex. As a reflection of nature, the poly-dimensional disposition of many African polyrhythms, melodies, and harmonies provides an extrapolative glance into the structure of the blues matrix. The African poly-dimensional way of viewing life, spirituality, and music transferred into jazz in America reflects nature's fluidity, simplicity, and complexity.

Quasi-modal jazz and free jazz often involve recursive production; a type of musical recycling that leads to an abstract and organic entity that mixes anticipation, surprise, and grounding repetition. Simple motivic cells, intervals, and melodic fragments are combined freely to build larger musical forms. Close examination of nature reveals related construction, where simple elements combine to form assorted building blocks and organisms. If we look at the irregular shape of clouds or mountain ranges, then look closer at a small segment, we discover the basic structural components of the entire mountain (macrocosm) are repeated on a smaller scale in the rocks and grains of sand that form it (microcosm). Upon careful examination of most things, what at first may strike us as random construction or lack of order most often reveals dynamic, flexible, resilient, and logical forms in nature.

Many natural phenomena are described with a dimensional equation or symbol representing a position somewhere between two whole numbers. Chaos theory is much like jazz theory, where the true essence of the blues resides within the immeasurable swing rhythms and the infinite number of "cracks" between those fixed notes of the well-tempered clavier. The primary issue in chaos is whether or not making accurate long-term predictions of the behavior of any system is possible if the initial conditions are known to an accurate degree. In jazz, if the primary ingredients are known (for example, the melodic, rhythmic, and harmonic infrastructure), the material's treatment need not be predictable to maintain complete organic structural validity. Chaos theory describes complex motion in nature and the dynamics of sensitive systems. Although chaotic systems are mathematically deterministic by Nature, they are nearly impossible to predict. This factor affects neither the stability nor the viability of that system. Chaos is more evident in long-term systems than in short-term systems. Behavior in chaotic systems is a-periodic, meaning no variable describing the state of the system undergoes a regular repetition of values. Bearing in mind that a-periodic material does not necessarily suggest that a chaotic situation exists, listeners may discover alternative logical bases for musical construction. Simply watching certain screensavers on computers demonstrates ways that chaotic systems evolve material that appears systematic, smooth, beautiful, and poetically cyclical (Sunstein and Thaler).

Free jazz (also called "Energy Music" or "The New Thing") is a movement of jazz music that developed in the 1950s and 1960s at the hands of artists such as Ornette Coleman, Eric Dolphy, Cecil Taylor, Albert Ayler, Archie Shepp, Eric Dolphy, and other innovators. Some of the best-known examples of free jazz are the late works of John Coltrane. Musicians approached free jazz with musical freedom in mind, not chaos. They were simply tired of the old jazz harmonic and structural treadmills, well-worn and dated musical habits, and wanted to avoid conventional clichés in their new musical world. Ornette Coleman's album entitled *Free Jazz: A Collective Improvisation*, recorded in 1960, provided this new genre with an appropriate name. Coleman used two separate quartets (with one assigned to each stereo channel on the recording) where the rhythm sections play simultaneously, providing a multifaceted rhythmic nucleus. The succession of solos differs from the more usual procedure in jazz as all performers have opportunities to accompany soloists with freely invented musical commentaries. This process often leads into full-scale collective improvisation. The premeditated material is a series of brief fanfares for the winds at the beginning that also serves as derivative interludes between subsequent solos. Notably, *Free Jazz* was the first LP-length improvisation, lasting nearly forty minutes in span, which was unheard of during the late 1950s. Coleman's new approach to improvisation brought back the free heterophonic and polyphonic nature of continental African harmony and was also reminiscent of New Orleans-style early jazz. It later served as the blueprint for longer large-ensemble free jazz recordings, such as John Coltrane's *Ascension* and *Om*.

Approaches to free jazz varied widely, but the common feature was mutual dissatisfaction with the expressive and somewhat jaded possibilities of bebop, hard bop, and modal jazz. Ironically, most musicians today still rely on the older forms that these free jazz pioneers evolved during the 1950s and 1960s. Each free jazz progenitor adopted a unique methodology for breaking down or extending traditional jazz conventions. Thus free jazz players were described as playing "out" or "outside" of "jazz" conventions. Many musicians and record labels adopted these descriptive terms and many applied it to album titles, such as Eric Dolphy's *Outward Bound, Out There, Out to Lunch*; Jaki Byard's *Out Front*; and Jackie McLean's *Destination Out*.

Chaos theory also had a series of early pioneers. Ilya Prigogine showed that complex structures could come from simpler ones, ultimately suggesting that order could evolve from chaos. Henry Adams described this suggestion saying, "Chaos often breeds life, when order breeds habit." Many call Henri Poincaré the "Father of Chaos Theory" and consider Edward Lorenz an important early "chaos" pioneer.

The planet Neptune was discovered in 1846 and was predicted from the observation of deviations in Uranus' orbit. King Oscar II of Norway was willing to give a prize to anyone who could prove or disprove that the solar system was stable. Poincaré offered his solution, but when a friend found an error in his calculations, the prize was taken away until he could come up with a new solution that worked. He found that no solution existed. Not even Sir Isaac Newton's laws provided a solution to this huge problem. Poincaré had been trying to find order in a system where none was to be found.

During the 1960s Edward Lorenz was a meteorologist at MIT working on a project to simulate weather patterns on a computer. He accidentally stumbled upon the butterfly effect after deviations in calculations off by thousandths greatly changed the simulations. The Butterfly Effect reflects how changes on the small scale affect things on the large scale. It is the classic example of chaos, as small changes lead to large changes. An example of this is how a butterfly flapping its wings in Hong Kong could change tornado patterns in Texas. Lorenz also discovered the Lorenz Attractor, an area that pulls points towards itself. He did so during a 3-D weather simulation. This brand of action consequence drives free jazz. Rather than having any fixed parameters within its musical system, each element (musician) evolves the composition through reacting to the spontaneous gestures that constantly arise throughout the ensemble.

The geometry of the fourth dimension, or fractal geometry, was ultimately the brainchild of Benoit B. Mandelbrot. We live in three-dimensional physical space where three directions of free movement exist: 1) Left/Right, 2) Back/Forth, and 3) Up/Down; thus it takes three values to describe the position of any point (x,y,z). In two dimensions, we only need two points: (x,y). Each of these three directions is perpendicular to each other so that any of the directions is exclusive and not formed from aspects of any of the other directions. An object can move forward or backward freely without ever going either left or right, or up or down. If we were to consider a fourth dimension (x,y,z,t), it would involve a new perpendicular direction in addition to the three dimensional directions. The dimension of music grows out of its physical elements (aspects of melody, harmony, rhythm, form, dynamics, timbre, and other musical elements) that can be measured mathematically, but gains its fourth dimension from the intangible musical heritage that has always given music its mysterious power of communication.

Mandelbrot and the Geometry of Chaos reveal a connection between mathematical organization and the abstract complexity of music. Mandelbrot, who is now both an IBM scientist and a professor of Mathematics at Yale University, defied the academic mathematics establishment to propose his new theory. Mandelbrot's fourth dimension of fractal forms includes an infinite set of fractional dimensions that fill the gap between the zero and first dimensions, the first and second dimensions, and the second and third dimensions. This infinite set is akin to the infinite set of fractional tone dimensions that exists between any two given frequencies of sound. Mandelbrot proved that the fourth dimension includes the fractional dimensions between the first three. Mandelbrot coined the word "fractal" based on the Latin adjective "fractus" and calls the in-between or interval dimensions the *fractal dimensions*. The corresponding Latin verb "frangere" means "to break," "to create irregular fragments." He has shown mathematically and graphically how nature uses the fractal dimensions and what he calls *self constrained chance* to create the complex and irregular forms of the real world (Ibid.). That theory is now considered the true geometry of nature. Mandelbrot points out that the idea of *recursive self similarity* was originally developed by the philosopher Leibniz, and popularized by the writer Jonathan Swift in 1733 with the following verse:

> So, Nat'ralists observe, a Flea
> Hath smaller Fleas that on him prey,
> And these have smaller fleas to bit 'em,
> And so proceed ad infinitum.

Thus all "particles" can be subdivided regardless of their size. The fluid bending of sound on a blues guitar represents this continuum of sound subdivision. The fourth dimension, space–time continuum, is now considered reality in science. Within the fourth dimension the infinite number of solids in the Universe exists in relationship with each other through time and energy. Blues mirrors the traditional African tendency towards fluidity and multiplicity of sound related to this notion of a space–time continuum with infinite variation due to its elasticity. These fractal numbers continue the movement of the third dimension (past) to form a wave, constituting fractally the space–time continuum of the fourth dimension.

Figure 1. Sine Wave

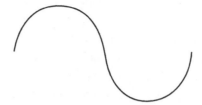

This symbol represents both fractals and the flexibility of each musical tone as a potential blue note. Music's oscillation between assorted factors of tension and release as it unfolds creates a brand of motion and energy that propels its molecular aspects into a virtual warp drive that aspires to inspire the listener through hyper-attentive manipulation of vibrations. The spirit of the imaginative composer resides in that electric field warp, between matter and antimatter (tension and release), and creates ideas that serve as the lightning-fast catalyst for ionizing animate sound. The Hypercube is the symbol used in mathematics to represent the fourth dimension in a two-dimensional drawing on a flat piece of paper (a plane) (Ibid.).

Figure 2. The Hypercube

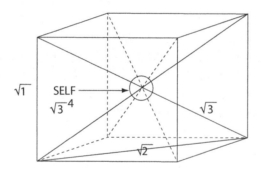

Basic chords from the blues matrices discussed earlier could find positions on the cube that suggest possible roots from any central chord to its related chords and harmonic variations. The evolution of chaos theory, which includes complex numbers and fractal geometry, begins in the mathematics and geometry of the fourth dimension. Consequently, Mandelbrot is the key Chaotician of our times who enabled us to understand what the fractal face of chaos (the fourth dimension) looks like. Earlier science and math was concerned with closed systems involving the first, second, and third dimensions, mathematical areas composed of line, plane, and solid elements. Free jazz tends to break away from the closed systems of prevailing Eurocentric structural, harmonic, melodic, metrical, and rhythmic notions that evolved from European tonal and modal harmony, twelve-tone, and serial approaches to music—just as the advent of Chaos theory broke shackles.

Mandelbrot's fractal geometry replaced the Euclidian geometry that dominated mathematical thinking for thousands of years. Euclidian geometry pertained only to the imaginary realities of the first, second, and third dimensions. Before Mandelbrot, mathematicians felt that most patterns of nature were too complex, irregular, fragmented, and amorphous to be described mathematically. The fourth dimension more closely aligns with the space/time continuum of human society and nature, where constant change based on perennial feedback is inevitable. As with music production, the fourth dimension in math is an open system where everything is interrelated. Premeditated composition requires left-brain theoretical principals supported by right-brain practical performance concerns. Earlier math emphasized left-brain algebra, but ignored right-brain geometry. After Einstein's theories emerged, mathematicians knew that even the third dimension solid bodies were just a model for reality and did not really exist. The world exists in the more fluid fourth dimension of the space–time continuum.

Mandelbrot went beyond Einstein's theories to discover that the fourth dimension encapsulated the first three dimensions and filled the fractal dimensions (the gaps or intervals between them). The fluid approach to tone in Global African music filled in the fragments between the inflexible constraints of even-tempered music of the European keyboards that evolved from the well-tempered clavier.

In earlier mathematics, geometry was relegated to an inferior position and academic math was dominated by arithmetic. Math existed comfortably within its own self-contained universe of numbers in detached and abstract isolation from nature. Some music put an equal distance between social sound and the fluid sounds of nature. Then Benoit Mandelbrot emerged to change math forever.

The ideas of self similarity and scaling embodied in these verses are critical to understanding the Laws of Chaos. Wherever we look in nature we find fractals with self similarity over scales. It is in every snowflake, every bolt of lightning, every tree, every branch; it is even in our very blood with its veins, and in our Galaxies with their clusters.

Thanks to Mandelbrot and other recent insights of Chaoticians, we now have a mathematical understanding of some of the heretofore secret workings of nature. We understand for the first time why two trees growing next to each other in the forest at the same time from the same stock with the same genes will still end up unique. They will be similar to be sure, but not identical. Just so every snowflake falling from the same cloud at the same time under identical conditions is still unique, different from all of the rest.

Countless good examples of instability: disease, political unrest, and family and community dysfunction. Disease is unstable because at any moment there could be an outbreak of some deadly disease for which there is no cure. This would cause terror and chaos. Political unrest is very unstable because people can revolt, throw over the government, and create a vast war. A war is another type of a chaotic system. Family and community dysfunction is also unstable because if you have a very tiny problem with a few people or a huge problem with many people, the outcome will be huge with many people involved and many people's lives in ruin. Chaos is also found in systems as complex as electric circuits, measles outbreaks, lasers, clashing gears, heart rhythms, electrical brain activity, circadian rhythms, fluids, animal populations, and chemical reactions, and in systems as simple as the pendulum. It also has been thought possibly to occur in the stock market.

Free jazz musicians seemed to take a very practical approach to acting out such universal tendencies towards individual uniqueness and the instability of all systems in a sonic environment. Very simple premeditated scores formed the basis of free jazz's spontaneous compositions. Mathematical concepts, like complex musical sound, can be reduced to simple formulae and symbols on a page. Mandelbrot's eclectic research is summarized by a simple mathematical formula: $z \rightarrow z^2 + c$, now called the Mandelbrot set. Euclidian geometry was concerned with abstract perfection that is non-existent in nature. It could not describe the shape of a cloud, a mountain, a coastline, or a tree. As Mandelbrot said in his book, *The Fractal Geometry of Nature* (1983): "Clouds are not spheres, mountains are not cones, coastlines are not circles, and bark is not smooth, nor does lightning travel in a straight line." Mandelbrot's formula, and the wisdom it represents, is the result of the computational power of modern computers.

The Mandelbrot set is a dynamic calculation based on the iteration (calculation based on constant feedback) of complex numbers with zero as the starting point. The order behind the chaotic production of numbers created by the formula $z \rightarrow z^2 + c$ can only be seen by the computer calculation and graphic portrayal of these numbers. Otherwise the formula appears to generate a totally random and meaningless set of numbers. It is only when millions of calculations are mechanically performed and plotted on a two-dimensional plane (the computer screen) that the hidden geometric order of the Mandelbrot set is revealed. The order is of a strange and beautiful kind, containing self-similar recursiveness over an infinite scale.

The sound of thunder, raindrops, the ocean, or a baby crying cannot be adequately described by any known form of music notation. Nonetheless, Ellington's trombonist Trick Sam Nanton and other musicians could imitate some human sounds convincingly on their musical muted instruments. Jazz musicians have never confined themselves to the written notation of any musical system because they understood that music cannot ever be fully expressed in descriptive symbols or words. The complexity of melodic, harmonic, and rhythmic sound generated by jazz musicians, that supersede notation, can now be captured in digestible two-dimensional form by computers. If the results of such tracking remain un-quantized, they become highly complicated when translated into standard notation or in graphic form. In the final analysis, it still does not fully represent the sounds generated.

Universal Connections

Universal connections and systems provide useful models that can be creatively applied to music, the arts, science, and religion. Mystics learn through carefully scrutinizing a broad range of natural forces, refusing to limit their investigations to strictly scholastic methodology. Many individuals throughout world culture attempt to live in harmony with the laws of nature. The Universe is a vast, delicate, interconnected web. It forms a multi-dimensional system filled with patterns, rhythms, and cycles that manifest as the seasons, weather, tides, our heartbeats, dreams, and lunar cycles. The source of the patterns always transfers its rhythmic and harmonic vibrations to air, water, ground, or another substance or medium in its vicinity. A phenomenon called resonance occurs when two sources of vibration performing similar cycles are placed in close enough proximity to merge their individual pulses into a unified composite rate. The harmonious relationships and patterns found, from the most microcosmic to the most expansive macrocosmic level, suggest that profound and intrinsic connections exist throughout all sectors and levels of the Universe (Hammel and Kahn 2).

Mathematical balance and proportion are found throughout art, despite the fact that artists most often are not thinking in concrete terms of numerical symbols and formulae when they create. Exploring the ways that math and music intersect is useful to spontaneous composers. In the book *Music and Math: Harmonic Connections* by Trudi Hammel Garland and Charity Vaughan Khan, the authors suggest that compositions are akin to geometric transformations. These mathematical forms include translation (which includes repetition of a sequence or theme), transposition (including the movement of an exact sequence of tones to another pitch level and location in time), reflection (where the mirror image of tones appear), inversion, retrogression (a musical sequence in reverse), retrograde inversion, and glide reflection (which is a rotation involving a translation followed by a reflection). Closely considering these ingredients again reveals the importance of repetition in music. Music, therefore, is highly reliant upon all the variants and permutations that can be applied to a theme or series of tones. This line of thought is useful in remembering composition techniques that provide direction, coherence, balance, and interest.

The composition of an enduring piece of music can be likened to the design of a classic painting or well-coordinated garden. It is not unlike the engineering of a sturdy bridge or a well-proportioned building. There is an underlying structure in all these cases that influences mathematics, sometimes more obviously than others, and sometimes more deliberately than others on the part of the artist, designer, engineer, or composer.

A basic procedure for achieving cohesion in a piece of music is the restating of a sequence of tones again—in variations, of course, to avoid monotony and to give the composition character. Care must be taken to assure that the transformed restatements are pleasing to the ear and interesting to the mind. If done well, these variations will help to make the musical piece more easily remembered. This will give it broader, more lasting appeal since the recognition of repetitive phrases is important to musical pleasure. Some of the techniques used to give a composition unity without making it boring are grounded in plane geometry.

Musical transformations are closely related to the four basic geometric transformations. A geometric transformation relocates a rigid geometric figure in the plane while carefully preserving its size and shape. The original configuration is not distorted by the manipulation (Garland and Khan 68–69).

The geometry of certain musical compositions is thus related to the architecture of the buildings where their intended performances are held. An example is Guillaume Dufay's medieval motet entitled *Nuper Rosarum Flores,* composed for the dedication of the Santa Maria del Fiore cathedral in Florence, Italy, on March 25, 1436. The architect of the cathedral was Filippo Brunelleschi (Hammel and Kahn 84).

Incorporating basic elemental musical designs provides a framework that allows musicians a means through which to control stratified musical dimensions and roles. After the subject material is introduced, the lead soloist sets the tone for the ensemble. Other performers follow and support each lead soloist while advancing the composition. All musicians involved respond simultaneously to various musical gestures supplied by fellow performers. Ideally the composite image of their musical interaction begins to resemble the natural action/consequence that occurs when the wind blows a string. To accomplish this level of synergy, balance, responsiveness, and proportion, each performer must bring the appropriate level of musical focus, flexibility, empathy, anticipation, and preparation required to paint their mutual canvas effectively. The ensemble members must leave appropriate melodic, harmonic, and rhythmic space for soloists while maintaining simplicity (economy of means), continuity, clarity, beauty, excitement, atmosphere, and logic. Learning to interact with fellow musicians communally is an important and demanding task for all spontaneous composers. The task extends beyond a strictly technical understanding of musical ingredients and vocabulary. To gain a rich assortment of conceptual models for general interactive dynamics, musicians and other artists can benefit from the exploration and understanding of human dynamics, mathematical balance, gravitational force, chemistry, and many other areas of their environment.

Responsiveness and Chemical Vibrations

In music we deal with personal "chemistry" as we work (and play) interactively and cooperatively with other musicians. In spontaneous composition interaction between members of an ensemble is extremely critical to obtaining convincing musical results. While establishing mutual music vocabulary and proper musical preparation help musicians complement each other intellectually, other more intangible qualities also contribute to the heightened telepathic interaction that takes place during effective spontaneous performances.

Both transmitters (performers) and receivers (audiences) of music readily perceive the chemistry of a group.

Can qualities of music be used to understand the vibratory processes of chemical phenomena? The contemporary chemist routinely studies an array of vibrations in molecules. In the program for his presentation of *The Chemical Ballet* at the 1939 meeting of the American Chemical Society in Baltimore, Donald Hatch Andrews, a professor of chemistry at Johns Hopkins University, stated, "Who would ever fail to understand the vibrations of hydrogen, if he had felt them while dancing with a beautiful living atom in his arms?" Later, in his book *The Symphony of Life* (published in 1966) Andrews said, "We are finding that the universe is composed not of matter but of music." The study of molecular vibrations enables chemists to identify the specific nature of molecules. Molecules have unique sets of fingerprints, based upon the frequency of vibration by which they are identified. Because music involves the physical, psychological, and spiritual applications of vibration, it holds several keys through which we can consider certain features of a chemical subject. Conversely, we might even gain insight into the interaction or "chemistry" between musicians in an ensemble through observing certain tendencies of microorganisms at the subatomic level.

Watching the chain of reactions set off by a cue ball in a billiard game suggests ways in which musical communication occurs within a successful jazz combo, especially during the relatively "free" sections of a spontaneous composition. A cue ball's rolling action has an even greater effect on other balls it contacts if nuanced with the spin of applied "English." Understanding the delivery of cue ball English is crucial to higher levels of play in billiard sports, just as understanding blues nuances elevates the performance caliber of musicians. A composition may begin with a short fixed melody, supported by a set of chord changes, that initiates the flow of action. Once this musical "cue ball" is launched, the majority of the compositional reaction occurs spontaneously as each musician responds to the initial musical forces and events that evolve around them. Each subsequent reaction then either generates or thwarts additional musical energy that, in return, effects, motivates, or retards additional action and reaction. When the opening burst of energy reaches its climax, all musical action gradually succumbs to the prevailing force of gravity (inertia). Musical interplay might also be compared with the particle spins and movement at the molecular, atomic, or subatomic levels.

One high frequency vibration that chemists find useful occurs at a frequency of 60 million vibrations per second. The vibration is used in a Nuclear Magnetic Resonance spectrometer, or NMR, an instrument that measures the exact point in a magnetic field at which the nuclei of particular atoms reverse their spins. The NMR is a useful device that allows chemists to monitor situations in which the same kinds of atoms reverse spins at different points depending on the quality, disposition, and behavior of atoms surrounding them. Apparently, the spin reversal depends not only upon the atom's own inherent tendencies, but also on its interaction with those of all the atoms in its immediate vicinity. This NMR experimentation demonstrates ways that vibrations can interact.

A related example of a social phenomenon occurs when a new person enters a room of people. A subtle, but distinct and noticeable change in the "vibrations" within the atmosphere takes place, as a result of the new presence or aura joining the others. The vibratory frequency of the new person's entrance into the social equation interacts with the harmonized vibration patterns of the others present in the room, creating a momentary disturbance with the introduction of the new composite pattern of vibrations. Musical tones are likewise affected by other tones entering their musical vicinity. Whether a musical tone has a consonant or dissonant function within a harmonic colony of tones depends upon the new tone's particular placement among other resident tones in a musical environment. The harmonic placement of tones is governed by the mathematical radiating sequences of the overtone series.

Jean-Philippe Rameau's Theoretical Concepts of the Overtone Series

Musicians sometimes cultivate and harbor musical theories and personal realizations based simply upon their relentless musing on music. For some, like John Coltrane, this direct, intuitive, philosophical, and technical exploration of musical knowledge evolves as they continually contemplate, practice, and perform musical ideas in real time. When composers choose not to reduce many of their musical ideas and artistic revelations to words, all that we may have to provide insight into their music through the limited potential of spoken words is often their short, cogent, and poetically descriptive titles, or perhaps their curt comments made during their conversations or interviews.

Music stands firmly on its own merit. The abstract nature of art is akin to nature's own abstract dynamic expression, in that analysis of music is not as important as direct musical absorption. Likewise, analyzing a sunset is not as important as the direct absorption of sun rays. Emphasis on written musical tradition means that musical ideas travel through the eyes before entering the ears. Often, in academic circles, writing about music tends to be on par with actually hearing the particular music under consideration. Nonetheless, because music cannot completely withstand the test of empirical scrutiny, due to its abstract essence, most musical theories are inevitably susceptible to criticism and failure. Analysis does possess tremendous pedagogical value when students are from cultures where reading about subjects becomes more important than acquiring knowledge directly by experience. Learning music through analysis is like learning anything through virtual reality; such processes reveal that all learning ultimately requires supplementation by direct experience at work on a subject. In the introduction to David Gray's article, "Work-Based Learning, Action Learning and the Virtual Paradigm," he examines the various definitions of what is known as work-based learning (WBL), and distinguishes WBL from traditional forms of classroom teaching. Gray concludes that, "As we have seen, one component in the process of action learning is the action learning set. McGill and Beatty (1996), suggest that such sets":

Focus on real problems: learning is based on grappling with *real* tasks (i.e., those which exist independently of their learning significance).

Provide for group reflection: learning with and from a group of others who are engaged in managing real problems.

Establish personal responsibility: the set is different from a project team or a task force, as members retain responsibility for solving their own problems.

Are action-based: members are concerned with implementing the actions explored in the Set, rather than simply seeking theoretical solutions.

Spontaneous composition demands that each participant take on a work-based, action learning responsibility throughout the duration of each creative performance, often in a context containing ample room for both traditional structure and responsible freedom. When dialogues about abstract musical ideas conflict sharply with reigning conventions, they can become targets for social criticism, and musicological warfare ensues. When composers discover significant and personal new musical territory, they often find that they have to defend his or her ideas before long-standing conservative institutions and within the narrow scope of conventional musical parameters. Thus, as a consequence of adventurous artistic exploration, avant-garde composers may find that they have invited upon themselves the daunting task of fighting an onslaught of mass criticism. Thus became Jean-Philippe Rameau's plight in defending his musical theories and ideas, some of which remain as difficult for some people to digest today as they were during his lifetime. Nonetheless, other aspects of his thinking about music remain closely aligned with theories of some contemporary composers, performers, and theorists who consider the overtone series as the primary basis of musical organization.

The allegorical representation of Rameau's theory of the *corps sonore* is found in the frontispiece to the *Code de Musique.* It is an engraving of three muses with the muse Euterpe plucking a lyre string in the center while listening to its overtones (the *corps sonore*). The muse to her right transcribes these musical ideas on paper, symbolizing the musician applying the proportions of these overtones to composition. To Euterpe's left, symbolizing all the sciences' reliance upon proportions and hence upon the *corps sonore,* a third muse measures the proportions of these overtones on her monochord. Rameau shared his theory on the resonant body and the one principle in 1760.

One principle governs everything. Any thinking person will have sensed the truth of this, though no one has yet explained it. In the conviction that there must be a universal principle, the earliest philosophers turned to music in their search for it. Pythagoras followed the Egyptians in applying the laws of harmony to the motions of the planets. Plato believed that the disposition of the soul was governed by these laws. Aristotle, his disciple, described music as a divine and heavenly thing, and added that it provided the explanation of the system on which the world was built. So impressed were these philosophers by the marvelous way in which the constituent parts of the universe harmonize, that they continued to look for the explanation in music, as the one thing in which proportion dwelt. For those objects that are perceived by the other senses are only the image of proportion, properly speaking. Movement, action, temporal relationships, and analogies can only be expressed in acoustic symbols. Unfortunately, the system that these great men adopted—far from bringing them nearer to the desired goal—only served to distance them further from it. There can be absolutely no doubt that they were unaware of the phenomenon of the resonant body (*corps sonore*) (189).

Thus Rameau identified the unalterable physical laws of the *corps sonore,* that is, the fundamental tone sounding in simultaneity with its prescribed order of harmonic overtones, a universal building block. During the European "Age of Enlightenment" Rameau involved himself with theoretical speculation that is, to some degree, related to fundamental principles aligned with those of the blues matrix. Both approaches mutually recognize that their foundational basis resides in harmonic structure of the overtone series.

Rameau was virtually unknown in Paris before the appearance of his monumental 450-page treatise, *Traité de l'harmonie* (1722) that launched his reputation in France and abroad. His *Nouveau système de musique théorique* (1726) followed up on his early theoretical ideas. As one of France's most eminent master composers, Rameau was considered highly knowledgeable and well-suited for analyzing and theorizing about structural aspects of musical practice. He felt that music, as an empirical body of acoustical evidence, could be rationalized theoretically through analysis equivalent to the scientific synthesis exposed by seventeenth-century scientists. In distilling chord movement to its basic progression, Rameau recognized the importance of the fundamental bass line in defining harmonic behavior. In the *Grove Dictionary of Music,* Christensen said:

> Inspired by the celebrated examples of scientific synthesis bequeathed by seventeenth-century scientists such as Descartes, Kepler, and Newton, Rameau believed music to represent an empirical body of acoustical evidence for which rational principles could be found. The "evidence" with which he was initially concerned was the burgeoning variety of chord "signatures" confronting any musician attempting to realize or compose a figured bass. As a young organist and music instructor in Clermont, Rameau wished to simplify the mastery of figured bass and composition for himself and for his students by reducing the plethora of signatures to a few fundamental types. At the same time, he hoped to be able to account for the behavior of most dissonant intervals and harmonic successions encoded in these signatures using a few basic prototypes. Towards this end, Rameau conceived of the *basse fondamentale,* which is perhaps less properly to be seen as an original invention than as a unification of received practical and speculative traditions in music theory.

Beginning with an informal heuristic of chord inversion (*renversement*) that can be found in many seventeenth-century thorough-bass manuals, Rameau invoked a more systematic notion of "octave identity" by which he could reduce most chord signatures to one of two fundamental types: the triad and the seventh chord. Taking disparate arguments of intervallic generation made by Descartes and Mersenne, Rameau further claimed that the lowest pitch class of each triad and seventh chord constitutes its fundamental sound (*son fondamental*). By displaying the succession of these chord fundamentals on a fictive bass line, Rameau could reveal the "fundamental bass" of any harmonic succession and show how it followed a limited number of paradigmatic cadence-like models.

It was in his pioneering *Traité de l'harmonie* (1722) that Rameau attempted to offer a more rigorous formalization of his empirical theory by casting it within a Cartesian-inspired deductive model based on a single "evident and clear principle." In the first book of the *Traité,* Rameau posited this principle to be the first six aliquot (harmonic) string divisions of a monochord. While successful in generating the major triad in this manner (as had Zarlino), Rameau's arguments quickly ran aground when he was unable to discover a satisfactorily consistent means of generating the minor triad. Generating the repertory of seventh chords he needed proved even more vexing, requiring Rameau to resort to eclectic arguments of third-stacking, "borrowed" fundamentals (for the diminished seventh chord), and "supposition" (wherein ninth and eleventh chords were explained as seventh chords with feigned roots "supposed" a third or fifth below their true fundamentals).

Had Rameau known today's theory of fractals he might have preferred to save his time trying to validate things he heard to the establishment. The natural overtone series extended its influence intuitively into Rameau's compositional practice, with a Euclidian-styled music theory as a tool. Thomas Street Christensen examines Rameau's ideas on the origins of music in his *Rameau and Musical Thought in the Enlightenment.* Throughout the 1750s, Rameau collected historical evidence to support and ground his theory. He was convinced that Chinese musical practice, Greek music theory, Egyptian science, medieval modal theory, and ancient biblical instruments all contributed some evidence that the *corps sonore* was the universal principle of music that extended throughout time. What his critics considered even more audacious was his assertion that the *corps sonore* was the principal progenitor of all the sciences (Christensen 294–295).

When Rameau came across Jean-Etienne Montucla's history of mathematics, in which Montucla argued that the geometrical and mathematical sciences originated in ancient Egypt,[33] he presented some of this new historical "evidence" in a short essay he published in the *Mercure* in 1762 entitled the "Origine des sciences." Rameau concluded that a cabal of Egyptian priests must have possessed knowledge of the *corps sonore,* and were consequently inspired to develop the sciences of geometry and algebra. Rameau's theory was closely related to Schwaller De Lubicz's later exhaustively

---

[3] The work is Jean-Etienne Montucla, *Histoire des Mathématiques dans laquelle on rend compte de leurs progrés depuis leur origine jusqu'à nos jours* (Paris, 1758).

researched hypothesis regarding the Egyptian's knowledge of musical proportion and its applications to mathematics and science. Rameau felt that listening to the *corps sonore* perhaps led the Egyptian priests to the discovery of the Pythagorean Theorem (long before Pythagoras' time), and thus, the square of the hypotenuse of a right-angled triangle is equal to the sum of the squares of its two sides.[44] Thomas Street Christensen concludes that:

> Rameau thought that in perceiving the arithmetic series 3 : 4 : 5 in the *corps sonore*, as well as their squares in the geometric progression, the Egyptians were led to investigate these relations, and thereby to the discovery that the sum of the squares of the third and fourth partials (9 + 16) was equal to the square of the fifth partial (25). But unfortunately these priests failed to share their knowledge of the *corps sonore* with others. Thus the true origins of geometry and algebra were soon forgotten except by a small and secretive sect of Pythagoreans (294–295).

Rameau originally felt that the Greek tetrachord was generated by the triple geometric progression and wondered how the triple geometric progression manifested itself in China and Egypt. In considering a widely circulated manuscript by the Jesuit missionary Joseph Marie Amiot concerning Chinese music (that arrived in Paris in 1754), Rameau became interested in Amiot's description of the theory and practice of Chinese music. Rameau extrapolated from this report that the Chinese pentatonic scale was generated by the triple geometric progression (e.g., the scale G A C D E could be generated by the geometric terms 3, 1, 3, 9, 3), and concluded that Chinese and Greek music must have evolved from the same source. Eventually Rameau speculated that Noah carried the triple geometric progression with him on the ark, and that perhaps, after the deluge, his sons were dispersed to the various corners of the world, and carried this knowledge with them (Ibid.).

Although Rameau may not have fully achieved substantiating the systematic theory of harmony towards which he originally aspired, his fundamental bass guided many musicians by the end of the eighteenth century, and eventually ranked as the dominant pedagogical music paradigm throughout Europe. Rameau felt that the fundamental bass generated major and minor scales. This position was necessary to underscore the pedagogical value of his fundamental bass, and to prove that harmony's influence surpasses that of melody. Thus, despite this emerging reputation, Rameau's theories were controversial. His ideas about the *basse fondamentale* led to a public debate in Paris on May 8, 1729 and caused other polemic exchanges, perhaps with Jacques de Bournonville, Michel Pignolet de Montéclair, and others. The Jesuit priest Louis-Bertrand Castel[55]

---

4   *CTW* IV, 289.

5   He was also a mathematician, physicist and scientific journalist.

took harmony lessons with Rameau. Castel probably introduced the composer to J. Sauveur's mathematical and acoustical theories.

After considering Sauveur's acoustical research (beginning with Nouveau système, 1726), Rameau became convinced that the harmonic overtone series detectable in many vibrating systems (*corps sonores*) contained a better principle to support his theory of chord generation. Rameau wanted to demonstrate that a single sound was a composite of harmonic overtones, through a more natural means of chord generation than monochord divisions, in a fashion equivalent to Newton's use of the prism to prove that white light was composed of a rich spectrum of colors. When Rameau was unsuccessful in justifying the production of the minor triad and seventh chords through his new theory, he conceived a variety of theses to solve this problem. Before eventually conceding "that only the major triad (*accord parfait*) was directly generated, and that all other harmonies had to be conceptually deduced by analogy using the natural harmonic ratios found in the *corps sonore* (*Nouvelles réflexions,* 1760)," one such theory involved an "undertone" series of arithmetic partials, double fundamentals, and functional borrowings (*Génération harmonique,* 1737; *Démonstration du principe de l'harmonie,* 1750). Thus, despite its original controversial nature, in the final analysis Rameau's *basse fondamentale* proved much more enduring than his efforts to ground musical harmony in the overtone series.

Utilizing the two fundamental chord types of the seventh chord and triad, Rameau conceived of the primary dynamic of music as a quasi-Cartesian mechanistic model of dissonance (displacement) and consonance (repose). As shown in the second book of his, *Traité,* this dynamic was best exemplified in the paradigmatic progression of the perfect cadence (*cadence parfaite*) in which a dominant seventh chord on the fifth scale degree (called the *dominante tonique*) resolves to a consonant tonic triad by a falling perfect fifth in the fundamental bass. Regardless of inversion, the "major" dissonance of the leading note (*notte sensible*) should resolve upwards to the tonic in this progression, while the "minor" dissonance of the seventh resolves downwards to the third. Seventh chords on other scale degrees (called simple "dominants") normally imitated the motion of the perfect cadence. Secondary cadence types related to the perfect cadence were also deduced by Rameau. The "irregular" cadence (*cadence irrégulière*) inverts the motion of the perfect cadence by ascending a perfect fifth in the fundamental bass from the fourth degree to the tonic, while a "broken" cadence (*cadence rompue*) thwarts the expected resolution of the dominant seventh chord with a deceptive cadence on the sixth degree. Of particular note was Rameau's observation that the intervals by which the fundamental bass progressed (primarily perfect fifths, secondarily major and minor thirds, with ascending seconds introduced by license) are those of which chords were constructed. This fact offered powerful support to Rameau's claim that his principle of harmony was indeed a comprehensive one, accounting for both the vocabulary and the grammar of music.

While the fundamental bass was conceived to explain localized chord connections, Rameau was also interested in more global questions of harmonic function and modal identity. The evolution of his thoughts on the subdominant (*sous dominante*) is an illustrative case. The importance of the fourth scale degree in the mode was initially singled out by Rameau in his *Nouveau système* (1726). Modeled by a "geometric" triple progression of connected fifths (1:3:9), the lower (*sous*) dominant was posited as a symmetrical counterpart to the upper dominant. In the *Génération harmonique* (1737), though, Rameau began to assign the subdominant a privileged harmonic function in his hierarchy of scale degrees, not only because of its important role in the irregular cadence (now dubbed the *cadence imparfaite*), but because of its importance in framing and defining a modal centre. Inspired by elements of Newtonian physics that were circulating widely in France during the 1730s, Rameau reconceptualized the tonic chord as a kind of gravitational body that was surrounded by upper and lower dominants. Each of these dominants was attracted to the tonic and at the same time helped constitute the mode. The subdominant could further play two different functional roles called by Rameau *double emploi*. Unlike the dissonant seventh added to the dominant chord, the "characteristic dissonance" added to the subdominant chord to distinguish it from a common tonic triad was the major 6th (*sixte ajouté*). While the bass note would be understood as the chord's fundamental sound when it resolved to the tonic as an imperfect cadence, the added sixth could also be inferred as a fundamental (on the second degree) if the chord moved to the dominant.

Although the blues is often constructed using only a series of dominant chords (and the ii/V harmonic embellishment, extensions, alterations, and substitutes that may embellish them), jazz musicians will announce "Blues in C" to suggest harmonic parameters revolving around the root (nucleus) of multifaceted harmonic progressions encircling the fundamental tone "C." Rameau also recognized that only one principal tonic (ton *régnant*) and its arpeggiation existed in any composition, while the movement of all non-tonic consonant triads represented secondary levels of modulation, depending on stratified degrees of cadential confirmation (called *censée tonique, tonique passagère,* etc.). Of course, any new music theory faces potential opposition from those with opposing views, orientation, aesthetic values, or any of a number of political inclinations. Nonetheless, in his searching for a conclusive solution, Rameau's theories involving interpolated basses, double employment, rearranging the order of the scale, and changing keys may not have provided him with a self-convincing solution, but he did explore a range of ideas about harmonic motion through and between keys that was referred to at the time as "modulation." His placing the fundamental tone and the harmony that revolved around it in the upper musical strata was a polemic assertion among those inclined to be melodically oriented in focus. In the final analysis, however,

Rameau seemed to always rely upon his ear to ground his musical thinking. Thus, his intuitive understanding regarding the principal tone remained unshaken until later in his career, when his ear guided him to a more flexible understanding of music's fluidity.

In Rameau's later writings, beginning with his manuscript *L'art de la basse fondamentale* from the early 1740s and particularly in the *Code de musique pratique,* his last and most comprehensive composition treatise (1760), Rameau loosened the rigorously deductive structuring of his theory. He allowed greater flexibility in the rules governing the fundamental bass (to produce, for example, various kinds of chromatic and enharmonic progressions). Of special note was his increasing willingness to explain chords of supposition as products of melodic suspension and his acceptance of equal temperament as a necessity demanded by reason and taste.

Rameau was never so obstinate a theorist that he would disregard his own intuitive musicality. Throughout his writings he continually invoked "the judgment of the ear" to resolve discrepancies within his theory, even if this meant reworking or abandoning various of his arguments. When Rameau became acquainted with the sensationalist epistemology of John Locke in the 1750s, his empirical views became even more pronounced, although his conviction as to the sensory potency of the *corps sonore* led him to make some extravagant claims on its behalf, to wit, that it might be the principle of all arts and sciences.

Rameau became ever more insistent in his claims as to the metaphysical priority and scientific validation of the principle of the *corps sonore*. Rousseau's arguments with Rameau took a more aesthetic, and ultimately political turn, and concerned the priority Rameau accorded to harmony. For Rousseau, the fierce partisan of Italian opera, Rameau's elevation of the "rational" component of harmony over the "passionate" component of melody perniciously inverted music's origins in natural language.

Although he later backed away slightly from his original intuition-based theory, Rameau made astute observations that could not be confirmed with conservative theory and material tools of investigation alone. Thus Rameau's bold earlier deductive reasoning may be roughly summarized this way:

> All universal phenomena are vibrating systems. (Major premise) Music is a model vibrating system reflective of universal principles. (Minor premise)
> Mathematic and scientific tools of investigation should be based on proportions derived from the overtone series. (Conclusion)

To raise such a hypothesis within music institutions that measure theoretical aspects of composition primarily with only objective and subjective tools of investigation was futile. Music and the Universe obviously cannot be contained within such narrow confines, given that music greatly impacts upon our objective, subjective, and subconscious realms of being. From 1752 until 1762 Rameau was in almost uninterrupted verbal combat with his critics and frequently bemoaned the loss of musical creativity. At that time he felt he should carefully conserve and direct his remaining energy towards his theoretical projects (Sawkins 66–91). Chabanon described the composer's solitary meandering through the Tuileries on his daily walk, lost in meditation upon his *corps sonore.*

Rameau's *corps sonore* had by now become a fixation. In his final treatise, the *Nouvelles réflexions sur le principe sonore of 1760*,[66] as well as his remaining essays—the "Origine des sciences" (1762), "Lettre aux philosophes" (1762), and the unpublished "Vérités interressantes" (1763–4)—Rameau sounds almost like a Rosicrucian when speaking of the *corps sonore*. It is the "key" that opens up the doors of all the sciences; it is sacred knowledge that can be traced back thousands of years to a small cult of Egyptian priests, but has since been hidden to mankind until Rameau himself revealed its glorious truth. One is tempted when reading Rameau's last writings to concur with Diderot's scornful assessment that they comprise "so much visionary gibberish and apocalyptic truth"—the products of a mad composer who has lost whatever sense he might have once possessed. But having followed Rameau this far, I think we can afford to be a bit more charitable in our assessment. (We will also shortly see that Diderot, too, retained a good deal of charity in regard to Rameau's theory.) Audacious speculations and profound mysticism need not be incompatible with scientific discovery. For Arthur Koestler, elements of the mystical, irrational, and subliminal have led scientists to brilliant insight and revelation, as his case study of Kepler richly shows. We could make much the same observation, I think, concerning Rameau's writings. It was because of his almost evangelical convictions as to the veracity of his *corps sonore*, that by relentless contemplation, imagination, and sheer force of will Rameau was able to draw from this phenomenon a myriad of insightful theoretical ideas and sensitive tonal relationships.

Still, the *corps sonore* was more than a phantasm. There was empirical evidence for it—evidence that he constantly wished to remind his readers was furnished or confirmed by those who now criticized him. D'Alembert's attacks agitated Rameau so much more profoundly than anyone else's not because his criticisms were either more malevolent or comprehensive—there were numerous other critics of Rameau whose criticisms were far more scathing or encyclopedic, including Bemetzrieder, Serre, Ducharger, Mercardier, and, of course, Rousseau—but because these criticisms came from a scientist who Rameau believed should (and at one time did) recognize his theory's obvious scientific validity. Rameau was so keen that the *corps sonore* be accepted as a *scientific* truth that when he realized d'Alembert was deserting his camp, he undertook strenuous efforts to secure approval from other scientific quarters.

Although everyone acknowledged the pedagogical significance, musical sensibility, and profound intellectual value of Rameau's theoretical output, facing the relentless opposition to his theories consumed much of Rameau's time and energy during the final decade of his life. Drawing upon an astonishing variety of arguments, Rameau circumvented music from a variety of musical and philosophical angles, ultimately

---

[6] Although the *Nouvelles réflexions* was eventually published as a kind of appendix to the *Code de musique pratique*, it must really be seen as an independent treatise—the last Rameau would publish in his lifetime.

producing some of the fundamental thinking that would serve as intellectual inspiration for centuries of tonal harmony.

Overtone/Undertone Harmonic Series and Ratios

Every organized system seems to have some kind of nucleus—a central gravitational force that binds all of its various components together in a way that distinguishes its communal relationship as a unified whole series. Musical vibration of the overtone series provides models of such a system that can potentially serve as reference points for the comparison and analysis of various other organized systems throughout the Universe. The overtone series begins with a fundamental tone (the nucleus) around which an omni-directional, systematic pattern of tones radiates in orbits at varying distances from the root. Overtone series not only provide harmonic determinants that guide the evolution of chord progressions, but they also become an array of sonic factors that, when subtly combined in different intervallic combinations, determine the distinguishing features of instrumental or vocal timbre.

String and wind instruments, with string lengths and finger holes spacing based on mathematical proportions, have been discovered in Egypt, Babylon, and Sumer as long ago as 3000 B.C. Ancient people understood that a ratio between two numbers is an entity, a concept essential in music theory. Ratios can represent the relationship between two tones. Many instrumental techniques worldwide are inclined towards just temperament, multi-phonics, harmonics, polytonality (as imbedded in blues harmonic tendencies), etc., and are shaped by a fundamental vibration-based actuality that appears to govern the Universe. The general African tendency is to incorporate as many overtones into a given composite sound as possible (as opposed to refining sound to come closer to a sine wave timbre). The whisper singers of Burundi, as well as the Fulani and South African "naka ya lethlake" flute players (both latter traditions use instruments that include two- or three-hole overtone flutes) are examples of African music traditions that regularly employ unusual collections of harmonics and multi-phonics into their timbre. Such tendencies towards musical grounding in the overtone series were retained in the timbre of African-American blues singing and instrumental performance that began well before the turn of the twentieth century. Instrumentalists generally imitated vocal techniques and phrasing (listen to the influence Bessie Smith had on Louis Armstrong's trumpet playing when they recorded together during the early years of the twentieth century).

The overtone scale series built from nature and even temperament, arrived with the well-tempered clavier only four hundred years or so ago. Most Western music uses tempered tuning today, which means that intervals of the overtone series were adjusted and restricted to reproduce the twelve major scales that fit the well-tempered clavier. Although born within the context of even tempered tuning systems, most African-American music has retained a natural tendency to incorporate harmonics and flexible approaches to tuning and pitch bending throughout its evolution. Performers on the so-called Jew's harp in rural blues incorporated an abundance of multi-phonics in its technique, as was the case when Africans originally performed on instruments of a similar type on the African continent. The "growling" technique Bessie Smith's voice used on occasion produces subtle multi-phonics in its timbre. The use of growls and mutes in instrumental jazz (trombonist Tricky Sam Nanton, Cootie Williams, et al.), were efforts established by early musicians to "dirt up" instrumental sound and increase the quantity of harmonics in their timbre. Bassists Slam Stewart and Major Holly sang an octave above their improvised based lines to produce a similar effect during the first half of the twentieth century. Rahsaan Roland Kirk used multi-phonics and harmonic fingerings on his flute (and sang while playing). Saxophonist Illinois Jacquet incorporated multi-phonics into his music in the 1940s. John Coltrane popularized the use of multi-phonics and harmonics during the mid- to late-1950s, after performing with Thelonious Monk. (Ironically, pianist Monk introduced the concept to Coltrane's experiments with harmonics and multi-phonics on the saxophone during the mid-1950s.) Related techniques and approaches were relatively common within traditional tendencies of the harmonics laden legacy of African-American music.

Tension and release create motion that propels life, cyclical patterns, and music forward. The classic yin/yang, positive/negative, sun/moon, and male/female pairings are but a few descriptive archetypal patterns representing duality and polarity. The duality formed by any polar opposite forces produces energy and motion. Such force, and its resulting motion, was symbolized in music by the sistrum and other instruments in ancient Egypt. The sistrum is an instrument designed to frighten off malevolent spirits. It consists of an oval or round frame, upon which little freewheeling metal rattle disks are suspended with a straight handle affixed at the end. In discussing the ancient mystery schools of Egypt, former Rosicrucian Imperator, Ralph M. Lewis, notes "At the height of the greatest culture and secret *learning* of the mystery schools, the sistrum became a symbol of universal or cosmic *motion*." It was conceived to remind us that all things must be kept in motion by nature, if they are to remain animate. When their motion ceases, so does their life force. Lewis concludes, "Here, then, in Egypt, a thousand years before the earliest Greek atomic theories were advanced, *a doctrine of motion* as the generation or cause of all matter was expounded" (5–6).

Our perception of tension and release is most often a conditioned response. At a fundamental level, music involves the constant manipulation of tension and release—action and reaction dynamic. Tension and release is present on all musical levels (rhythmic, melodic, structural, etc.), but one of the most conspicuous planes is harmonic. Harmonic tension relates to our perception of relative dissonance (in relation to movement against the lower partials of the overtone series), which is released by more relaxed consonance (in relation to conformity with the lower partials of the overtone series). The way we perceive music, in terms of consonance and dissonance; in terms of complementary aspects of a unified whole; and as alternating between positive and negative polarity, male and female qualities, light and darkness, and microcosmic and macrocosmic coupling (among other things), reflects processes in nature. Tension and release also involves the quality of distance between pitches in the overtone series, especially in melodic construction. The overtone series arises from the tendency of all physical objects to vibrate at integer multiples of a fundamental frequency. When a string vibrates at a fundamental frequency of 100 cycles/sec. (denoted 100 Hz), and you cut that string in half, for example, the fundamental frequency would be twice that of the original (or 200 Hz). This continues infinitely in a naturally prescribed mathematical order. The overtone series is formed from colonies of continuous composite pitches unified by a particular series of frequencies, and the entire series is subtly present during the production of every fundamental tone bowed, blown, or struck on a musical instrument. The first sixteen notes in the series above C are roughly:

C - C - G - C - E - G - B♭ - C - D - E - F♯ - G - G♯ - B♭ - B - C
1   2   3   4   5   6   7   8   9   10 11   12 13   14 15 16

Throughout history people have consistently examined relationships between music and mathematics because such connections are inevitable, clear, and concrete. Musical intervals and rhythms are measured in precise frequencies that organize, shape, and motivate musical languages and symbols. Due to the precision of such sonic calculations, these measurements are easily transferred to mathematical formulas. Henry Cowell employed simple overtone ratios to approximate customary systems of temperament in music notation. Jocelyn Godwin, like physicist Heinrich Helmholtz, expands the overtone series to include its reverse reflection in an inverse sub-harmonic series. Helmholtz proposed that our view of the harmonic series must expand to include its inverse reflection in a sub-harmonic series. Such a series of undertones is theoretically

Figure 3. Overtone/Undertone Series

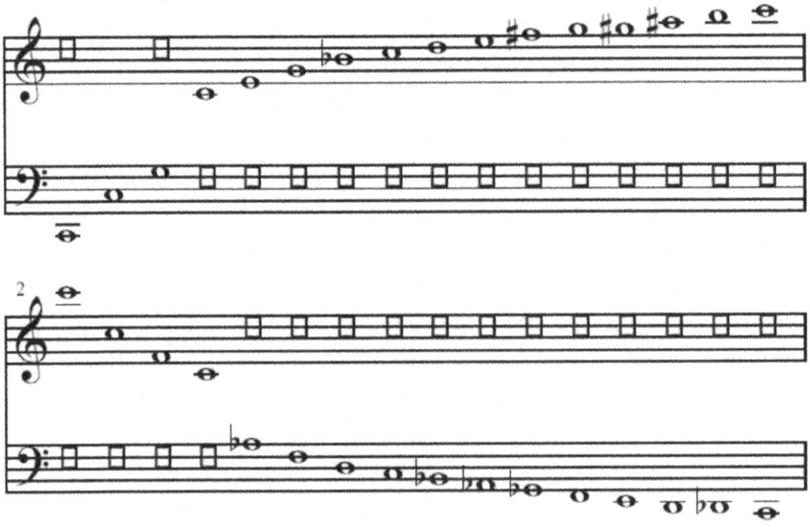

the exact inversion of the overtones, generated by a mirror-image arithmetical progression. Godwin's series also produces undertones that are the exact inversion of the overtones. It is generated systematically by an arithmetical progression regarded as a series of string lengths (Godwin 188–189).

Musicians, on occasion, draw upon the numerical systems inherent in nature in an attempt to achieve perfect proportion in their compositions. Henry Cowell used ratios of customary systems of temperament as basis for his rhythmic scales. Cowell's scales employed the simplest overtone ratios found to approximate each rhythmic interval (Cowell 98). Thus, the series of ratios upon which Cowell's rhythmic scales are formed reflect the harmonic proportions as follows:

Figure 4. Pitch Ratios of the Overtone Series

C:C	=	1:1	C:G	=	2:3
C:C♯	=	14:15 (C:D♭–15:16)	C:A♭	=	5:8
C:D	=	8:9	C:A	=	3:5
C:E♭	=	5:6	C:B♭	=	4:7
C:E	=	4:5	C:B	=	8:15
C:F	=	3:4	C:C	=	1:2
C:G♭	=	5:7			

Interestingly, the most common melodic building block intervals, those that hold strong positions in the development of melody over time, are the simplest ratios consisting of sequential numbers.

C:C = 1:1 (Perfect unison)
C:C = 1:2 (Perfect octave)
C:G = 2:3 (Perfect fifth)
C:F = 3:4 (Perfect fourth)
C:E = 4:5 (Major third)
C:E♭ = 5:6 (Minor third)
C:D = 8:9 (Major second)
C:C♯ = 14:15 (C:D♭-15:16) (Minor second)

Musical cultures generally progress from our most ancient basic tendencies towards singing the lower intervals of the overtone series (in unison and octaves, to the measured incorporation of ever-higher partials such as fifths, fourths, thirds), gradually towards forming pitch sets based upon small intervals of the higher portions of the overtone series. The use of chromatic, whole-tone, and octatonic scales (the latter combines both chromatic and whole-tone intervals) reflects human tendencies to formulate symmetrical systems based on the interval of major and minor seconds that occur at the upper end of a basic series. The history of music tends to progress very gradually from an acceptance of the lower partials of the series (first the and "perfect" intervals of the unison, octave, fifth, fourth, then the major third, minor third, and major second) to the increasingly smaller higher intervals, as the listener eventually grows accustomed to new combinations of tones derived from higher partials. Intervals considered dissonant during one era are gradually transformed into consonant intervals as the ear of the beholder matures through greater exposure to higher frequencies over time. Thus, harmony in cultures worldwide seems to have developed progressively from singing (or performing on wind, string, or percussion instruments) in octaves, to quartal and tertian harmony, etc., eventually to systems based upon symmetrical scales (whole tone, octatonic, chromatic, quarter-tone, micro-tonal, etc.). The following scale in an example of a scale that has symmetrical construction:

$$C\text{-----}E^\flat\text{-----}E\text{-----}G\text{-----}A^\flat\text{-----}B\text{-----}C\text{-----}E^\flat\text{-----}E\text{-----}G\text{-----}A^\flat\text{-----}B\text{-----}C$$
$$\text{m3}\quad\text{m2}\quad\text{m3}\quad\text{m2}\quad\text{m3}\quad\text{m2}\quad\text{m3}\quad\text{m2}\quad\text{m3}\quad\text{m2}\quad\text{m3}\quad\text{m2}$$

Music and the Pyramids

Egyptian tomb builders and their families enjoyed a relatively high standard of living for commoners in the ancient world. Workers and their families lived in mud-brick houses whose dimensions measured 15 feet by 45 feet. These homes had ceilings made of trunks and branches from palm trees, with whitewashed walls that were often decorated with plant or animal designs. Furnishings included baskets woven from reeds and pottery. Workers dressed in loose linen garments and wore papyrus sandals in hot weather, and they changed into their more sturdy leather slippers and wool cloaks when it got cool and windy in the desert. When the arduous work schedules were finished, many found time to play harps and flutes, take care of their pet cats and monkeys, and attend parties and festivals where they enjoyed home-brewed barley beer. Because a shortage of water always exists in the desert, a continuous procession of donkey caravans moved into the villages bringing tall earthenware jars filled with water.

The pyramids and the Great Sphinx rise mysteriously from the desert at Giza and other sites, relics of an advanced African culture. The largest pyramid was built for the Pharaoh Khufu around 2530 B.C. Pyramids of that status were intended to last an eternity, and Khufu's pyramid remained the biggest building on earth until early in the twentieth century. Over six and a half million tons of stone, including some in blocks as large as nine tons, were moved into precise positions, apparently with laborers equipped with only wood and rope. Each pyramid stands as a remarkable feat of ancient engineering genius and a testament to decades-long periods of human labor involving tens of thousands of Egyptian laborers.

Written at the end of the fifth dynasty (beginning around 2625 B.C.), almost 5,000 years ago, and continuing possibly to 2475 B.C., the Pyramid Text provides the oldest written chapter in human cognition preserved for humanity. The hieroglyphics that occupy the chambers, passages, and galleries in five of the pyramids at Sakkara furnish the most remote intellectual history that exists today. The information contained in these texts reflects an ancient knowledge that perhaps originally flowed up the Nile River from southern regions of the African continent. Egypt's isolation in the lower Nile valley permitted its civilization to develop for many millennia without the brand of outside interruptions that ordinarily marked the developmental growth of other early civilizations. This extraordinary evolution reflects a general tendency towards the development of all categories of Egyptian life (in aspects of its society's body, mind, and spirit). As we continually destroy some of the oldest places and artifacts on earth, including the rainforests and its ancient human inhabitants, we must remember that ancestral wisdom and knowledge contain the information that we must not forget if we are to survive as a species.

A number of theories exist on how sound vibrations may have been used to help move the enormous limestone slabs over long distances, from the Egyptian quarries to the specified sites of the ancient pyramids. Schwaller De Lubicz's intriguing and incredibly detailed research reveals an intimate relationship between music and math in ancient Egypt. A few interesting details divulge the importance that the ancient Egyptians dedicated to the power of music. Plato's perspective suggests that the union of the point 1:1 gives the initial tonic note, then 1:2 produces the octave, the ratio 2:3 creates the (perfect) fifth, and 3:4 the (perfect) fourth. When we combine these latter notes we have the first two harmonious intervals occurring between 1 and 2. By joining 4 to 9—or the square of 2 joined to the square of 3—we get an interval that spans two fifths. Finally, the ratio of 9 to 8 produces the value of a whole step (Timaeus 132). When applied to geometric segments of the Pyramids of Cheops and of Chephren, "This series, 1, 2, 3, 4, 9, 8, 27, which has often been taken as an anomaly or an error, is justified and demonstrated by this mathematical arrangement, 2 and 3 being the lines, 4 and 9 the squares, and 8 and 27 the cubes" (Lubicz 240). Lubicz examined the principle of volume in comparing the precise dimensions and capacity of certain ancient Egyptian cylinders (held in the Cairo museum) to the proportions of music's harmonic series. He found that:

> The musical scale, on the other hand, does not allow one to find the cube root of 3, but nevertheless the *khar* representing 2/3 of the cubic cubit, plays an important role in Pharaonic measures of capacity. Thanks to the use of the numbers of harmony, the problem can be resolved without having to extract the cube root of 3; knowing that for calculation of volume the Ancients divide the volume by a surface, the only unknown is the depth, or height. Thus, it is only a question of establishing two surfaces that are between them in a proportion that allows the definition of this height in whole numbers (Lubicz 254).

Thus the principles that apply the proportions of the harmonic series to formal structure are not restricted to music composition. Ancient Egyptian mathematical thought involved a level of unprecedented precision evidenced in the resilient pyramid construction that has survived for thousands of years. Of all Pharaonic calculation (Pharaonic geometry, trigonometry, proportion, the rule of three, etc.), the Egyptian Cosmic principle of musical harmony and volume demonstrates the potential broad-range implications of the harmonic series. Lubicz created an in-depth examination of the systematic calculation and measurement underlying the mathematical principles involved in the Egyptian master pyramid builders' grid.[7] Within his two-volume work, Lubicz explores the mathematical relationships between the measurements of pyramids (in cubits, for example) and measurements of musical tones (through the harmonic series). Regarding music's essential relationship to the laws governing nature, Lubicz says:

> Now, the intelligence of musical harmony is humanity's most sensitive tool of verification. The ear, as a sensory instrument, and hearing, as a means of judging, form the only sense that allows us to verify directly the harmony of two aspects of a phenomenon, what we might call the Verb, the essence of things. For all other verification we require objective experience.
>
> Hearing detects the subtle difference between sounds, the concord or the discord of tones, therefore of vibrations and wavelengths, and allows us to modify these sources of sound until a perfect harmony is reached. This gives a positive, experimentally reliable character to the sense of hearing that enables us to understand the importance that the Ancients attribute to musical harmony; it is this natural and innate criterion because any other means of verification, being objective, is fallible (Lubicz 250).

The Golden Ratio/Phi

Mathematical aspects of musical organization align with the theories of Leonardo of Pisa, who wrote under the pen name Fibonacci and lived around 1200 A.D. A sequence of numbers named after him centuries after his death consists of a series beginning with the number 1, where each subsequent number is the sum of the previous two (Numbers 1, 1, 2, 3, 5, 8, 13, 21, 34, etc.). People from a wide range of disciplines study the Fibonacci series and their related proportions in nature. The Fibonacci ratio involves any Fibonacci number divided by one adjacent to it (for example, 1/1, 1/2, 2/3, 3/5, 5/8, 8/13, etc.). The proportions that Fibonacci ratios represent are considered by many people to have a certain sense of balance and aesthetic appeal. They also represent the frequency relationships of some of the lower principal intervals from the overtone series. The universality of this order is referred to as the golden proportion, a ratio used

---

[7] Interested students can read *The Temple of Man* by R. A. Schwaller de Lubicz (Rochester, Vermont: Inner Traditions International, 1998).

frequently in art and architecture. Fibonacci ratios have also been observed in many structures of nature (Garland and Kahn 113).

Figure 5. An Example of the Beginning of the Fibonacci Sequence of Numbers Follows

1,	1,	2,	3,	5,	8,	13,	21,	34,	etc.
	0+1	1+1	1+2	2+3	3+5	5+8	8+13	13+21	etc.

The ratios produced also steadily grow closer to the three-digit decimal fraction 0.618, and the reciprocal fractions (which are all greater than one) gradually converge to the decimal 1.618.

$$1/1 = 1.000000 \ldots (+)$$
$$1/2 = 0.500000 \ldots (-)$$
$$2/3 = 0.666666 \ldots (+)$$
$$3/5 = 0.600000 \ldots (-)$$
$$5/8 = 0.625000 \ldots (+)$$
$$8/13 = 0.615384 \ldots (-)$$
$$13/21 = 0.619047 \ldots (+)$$
$$21/34 = 0.619047 \ldots (-)$$
$$34/55 = 0.618181 \ldots (+)$$
$$55/89 = 0.617977 \ldots (-)$$
$$89/144 = 0.618055 \ldots (+)$$
$$144/233 = 0.618025 \ldots (-)$$
$$233/377 = 0.618037 \ldots (+)$$

The Golden Ratio in the Fibonacci series, or *phi*, is found throughout organic life (but only rarely in mineral kingdoms) and was widely used in ancient art and architecture. Anything that is divided along the golden ratio proportion maintains a sense of fluidity and abstract symmetry. Phi occurs often in human patterns and in designs that we consider elegant. The dynamic symmetry of the golden proportion in nature (the asymmetric design of a Norway spruce tree and other phenomena involving natural cycles, for example) is also found in rectangles, pentagons, and other geometric figures. Artists suggest that visibly beautiful phenomena are also audibly pleasing. In the pentagram inside the pentagon in Figure 7 are two different types of broken lines. Phi divides the line in such a way that the ratio of the smaller section (a) to the larger section (b) is the same as the greater section (b) to the whole (ab).

The Golden Ratio is elusive to human calculation and is intriguing from musical, mathematical, and metaphysical perspectives. It is essentially 0.618, but because 1 divided by it is 1.618 (which is the same as adding 1 to 0.618), and 1.618 times 1.618 equals 2.618 (the same as adding 1 more), it can appear as any of these values (Martineau 22).

Phi is at the origin; it defines itself only by the harmony it engenders. The tone, that is, our experience of hearing the exactitude of the tone, is for us the absolute moment of 0, that which reason, that is, calculation, is unable to express. It is also for this reason that we can consider the intelligence of harmony as a supernatural state (Lubicz 241).

Figure 6. Pentagrams

```
              (a)         (b)
1.618    ------------|------------------------    a:b = b: (a+b)
           0.618...    1.000
```

Only *two numbers remain the same when they are squared,* namely **0** and **1**. Other numbers get bigger and some get smaller when we square them:

Squares that are bigger	Squares that are smaller
2^2 is 4	$1/2=0\cdot5$ and $0\cdot5^2$ is $0\cdot25=1/4$
3^2 is 9	$1/5=0\cdot2$ and $0\cdot2^2$ is $0\cdot04=1/25$
10^2 is 100	$1/10=0\cdot1$ and $0\cdot1^2$ is $0\cdot01=1/100$

A simple definition of Phi (the golden section number) is that to square it you just add 1 or, in mathematics:

$$\text{Phi}^2 = \text{Phi} + 1$$

In fact, there are *two* numbers with this property: one is Phi and another is closely related to it when we write out some of its decimal places. Phi can also be found in many geometrical shapes, but instead of representing it as an irrational number we can express it in the following way. Given a line segment, we can divide it into two segments A and B, in such a way that the length of the entire segment is equal to the length of the segment A as the length of segment A is equal to the length of segment B. If we calculate these ratios, we see that we get an approximation of the Golden Ratio.

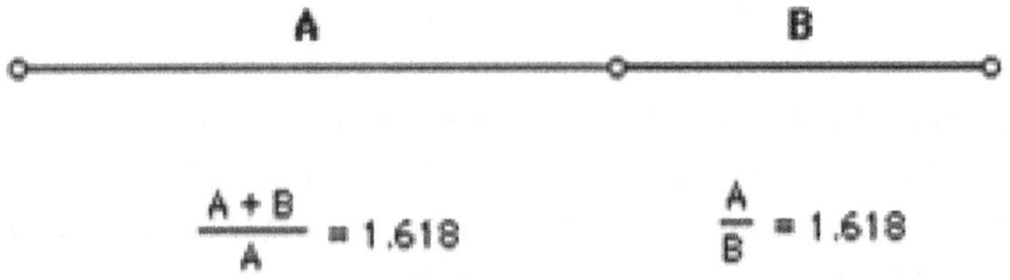

$$\frac{A+B}{A} = 1.618 \qquad \frac{A}{B} = 1.618$$

The golden proportion and Fibonacci numbers have operated as organizational and structural devices in spontaneous and premeditated musical compositions, as some modern and contemporary composers intentionally calculate related structural

Figure 7. Pentagrams

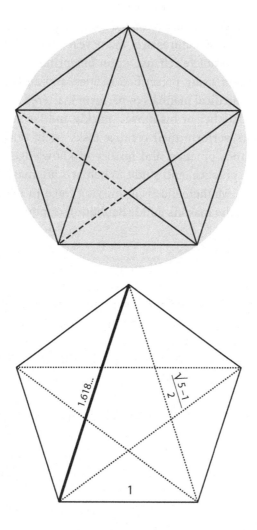

proportions to their work to assure "perfect" musical balance. The critical musical events of an entire composition can be subdivided into sections, determined by specific periods of time or number of measures at which the principal climaxes occur. Such sections may equal a particular proportion or a Fibonacci number of measures (Hammel and Kahn 114). Although Fibonacci structure has also been found in older compositions, no one has determined with absolute certainty that such occurrences were intentionally calculated mathematically in advance by composers, or if results that imply such balance are due strictly to an astute sense of aesthetic sensibility and intuitive considerations. For example, the careful positioning of the motto theme in Beethoven's *Fifth Symphony* may have merely been purely coincidental musically, and simply a result of the composer's highly trained ear and wonderful intuitive sense of balance and proportion, rather than a result of premeditated mathematical calculation (115).

Whether in music, horticulture, sports, chess, or culinary arts, a systematic, balanced, logical, and creative approach can enhance the success of any vocation or avocation. Each discipline is mastered through prolonged study, concentration, and practice. After building many complicated structures over many years, the master architect eventually learns to build without complete reliance upon blueprints. The master chef can fix a scrumptious meal without using prescribed recipes, and an experienced surgeon no longer needs to refer to medical manuals to perform mastered surgical procedures. The chess master can calculate her or his moves quickly and far in advance. Accordingly, spontaneous composers perform their creative tasks easily, once elements of musical composition, performance practice, and history of knowledge are mastered through years of concentration, practice, and study. When arts are mastered they become potentially transcendental. Mathematics is a unifying force in nature and, therefore, in music. In ancient times, the mason's guild (Bauhütte), responsible for Egyptian temple construction, felt that:

> There is a natural geometry and a mental geometry. The latter allows absolute circles and numbers, but natural geometry cannot allow these except by applying itself to what is fixed and dead. The impulse to all movement and to all form is given by Ø, since it is the proportion that summarizes in itself the additive and the geometric, or logarithmic, series. *Phi* is the impulse for the whole number 5, but starting from 5, Ø cannot be defined in rational numbers. It can only be defined *through the harmony it engenders*. Through musical harmony, and therefore only through our sensation of music, and not by reasoning, can we know absolute Ø. This fact indicates the way of the pharaonic mentality and the true Pythagoreanism developed from it. We have five senses with which to judge living reality. The mental concept would have cadavers, numbers, and arrested forms. It "supposes" invariables for points of reference. But nothing in the universe is invariable. Our science obviously knows this, but it still believes that we must approach the knowledge of matter with mental mathematics, when Ancients, more wisely than we, attained this knowledge through the metaphysical principles of their theology (Lubicz 229).

Throughout time, both spontaneity and the precision and mystery of numbers have inspired premeditated and spontaneous composers. Because systematic numbers calibrate frequencies of vibration, and music is intrinsically married to the structure of the overtone series, it is clear why the Egyptians studied carefully the relationship between music and mathematics. Calculating the measurements of the Pyramids of Cheops and of Chephren, for instance, make comprehensible the double series 1, 2, 4, 8, and 1, 3, 9, 27, (or combined 1, 2, 3, 4, 9, 8, 27) cited by Plato as the architectural essence referred to as the "Soul of the World." That essential numerical structure develops surfaces, volumes, harmonic numbers, and the ratios of musical harmony. The geometric series

1, 2, 4, 8 provides the values of one, two, and three octaves while 1, 3, 9, 27 results in an octave plus a fifth, then two octaves plus two fifths, then three octaves and three fifths (logarithmic function). Iconography depicting string lengths of the Egyptian Harp of Numbers precisely represents these calculations (as represented in the Bes of Philae). Thus:

Strings: 1   2   3   4   5   6

Interval: $\{5/8 - 3/5\} = \emptyset \{-1/-1\}$ = sound $\{3/2\}$ = perfect 5th $\{4/5\}$ = major 3rd $\{3/4\}$ = perfect 4th

Throughout history, various attempts have been made to compose music using the rules and logical structure of mathematics. Composers have utilized specific techniques, such as transformations and the calculus of probability, as well as more general ideas, such as assorted pattern, form, and repetition. One compositional technique uses an algorithm, which is simply a list of operations or set of rules for solving a problem. The etymology of the term *algorithm* is the Latin *algorism*, the archaic word for the rules used to calculate with Arabic numerals. One of the first composers to use a compositional algorithm was Guido D'Arezzo, a musical theoretician living in the early eleventh century. D'Arezzo devised a method for attaching Latin text to music through matching the vowels in the text with the notes in the double octave. A scaling fractal involves geometric objects that you can magnify repeatedly and perpetually, producing the same pattern and detail, although in varying scales. The self-similarity inherent in a fractal is apparent in the creation of the infinitely complex border of what is known as the Koch snowflake. The Swedish mathematician Helge von Koch, after whom the phenomenon was named, made his discovery in 1904 (Hammel and Kahn 126).

A very computationally intensive algorithm known as a *fast-fourier transform* (FFT) was used for such analysis of an acoustic sound. In 1822, the French mathematician Jean Baptist Fourier (1768–1830) came forth with a mathematical proof demonstrating that any waveform, regardless of its complexity, could be reduced to an infinite set of sine wave components. The FFT algorithms that run on personal computers today are based on Fourier's work and bear his name. Grey, Moorer, Risset, and other researchers first used computers to analyze the tones produced by acoustic instruments in the 1970s. Researchers are able to use computers to isolate the individual partials of a musical instrument's tone to demonstrate how each individual partial's amplitude progresses independently through time. Nature's unifying fluidity and infinite variety are readily apparent in music and mathematics because they are both products of the natural world.

Pythagoras

Pythagoras considered the natural division of the overtone series the determining factor for the fundamental pitch sets that form the bases for each Western musical system.

Thales encouraged Pythagoras to travel to Egypt, Mesopotamia, and India to broaden his understanding. When he returned home, he founded an academy devoted to the study of philosophy, mathematics, and natural science. Pythagoras' academy became an esoteric order with secret initiation rites that involved spiritual and mathematical observances. Composer Dane Rudyar suggested that the Chaldeans and Egyptians used an ancient instrument in sanctuaries that eventually evolved into the Pythagorean monochord. The monochord is a simple instrument used to identify sounds, numbers, and to distinguish between descending and ascending series of tones (Rudhyar 80–84). The transition from Pythagorean tuning to equal temperament (which took centuries to eliminate the Pythagorean comma) reveals the changing relationship between mathematics and music. Currently mathematics remains a basis for music theory throughout the West, although few modern musicians consider music a strictly mathematical discipline (Hammel and Kahn 36–37):

> Temperament is an attempt to reconcile two conflicting musical norms. One is the octave, which sets a definite, frame-like limit. The other is the bypassing of the octave by the accumulation of any other primary, scale-building interval. Temperament is the musical way of fitting an otherwise endless series into a definite space (Levarie and Levi 212).

Music was strictly a mathematical discipline when Pythagoreans developed his *quadrivium*. The Pythagoreans believed that music and math provided keys to the secrets of the world. Pythagoras believed "All is Number" and felt that all periodic and regular natural phenomena were musical. The Pythagoreans' considered the study of the relationship between natural phenomena and musical order the path towards divine understanding. Pythagoras and his followers promoted the doctrine of the "Music of the Spheres," which proposed that the human soul must be attuned to the laws of the universe. "Music of the Spheres" also held that heavenly bodies moving in space produce a spectrum of sounds that the Universe itself orchestrates. Plato (c. 427–347 B.C.) clarified this concept more fully in his subsequent writings, *The Republic* and *Timaeus*. The elusive Pythagoreans worshipped numbers, believed in reincarnation, participated in mysterious rituals, and remained individually anonymous by signing the symbol of the Pythagorean brotherhood (a pentagram) to everything they wrote or discovered (Hammel and Kahn 98). Pythagoreans agreed that:

> God has ordered the universe by means of numbers. God is unity, the world is plurality, and it consists of contrasting elements. It is harmony which restores unity to the contrasting parts and which moulds them into a cosmos. Harmony is divine; it consists of numerical ratios. Whosoever acquires full understanding of this number harmony, he becomes himself divine and immortal (Hammel and Kahn 45–46).

The ancients assigned seven musical notes in various symbolic arrangements to the seven heavenly bodies ("Harmoniae Mundi") most closely related to Earth. Kepler precisely calculated the orbits of these heavenly bodies and noticed that the ratios between planets' extreme angular velocities were all harmonic intervals. In 1968 A. M. Molchanov concluded that the entire solar system was a "tuned" quantum resonant structure, with Jupiter serving as the presiding force (Martineau 14).

Intervals created by the different pitches are arbitrarily determined to be those that are in agreement or that sound "good" (consonant intervals) and those that do not (dissonant intervals). Pythagoras found three pitch combinations he considered consonant intervals—the *diaspon* (octave), the *diapente* (fifth), and the *diatesaron* (fourth). In Western music these are referred to as perfect intervals. The primary numbers one, two, three, and four constitute the Pythagorean tetraktys, a sacred symbol for Greek philosophers. The frequency ratio between the numbers of the *diaspon* forms the intervals essential to musical systems throughout the world: the fundamental octave (the ratio 2:1), the fifth (3:2), and the fourth (4:3). Equal temperament or the twelve-tone tuning forming the even-tempered system frequently used throughout most Western societies is just one of many ways to assign intervals to a scale. While some forms of African music also divide the octave into twelve parts, other traditions in Africa and around the world maintain other independent forms of tuning systems that are distantly related to Western tuning.

Natural, Mathematical, and Symmetrical

Logistics involved in dealing with numbered events and sequences in music and math result in related systems of calculation. Likewise, in mysticism, numbers often express relationships between unity, multiplicity, and periodic cycles. Ralph M. Lewis discusses "the Unity," which represents "the Absolute" as a model that can be extended to represent the duality of man and the universe. The Unity and Absolute correspond to the nucleus or generative aspect of a system. Lewis concludes:

> Basic archetypal or Cosmic patterns are expressed in many forms in mythology, religion, literature, and art. The archetypal plan or pattern is manifested in created or mundane types that are realized by man in his awareness of the universe, himself, and the symbols he creates. These symbols, however, are influenced by the society and culture in which the individual lives, as well as by his own nature and personality (14–16).

Thus as we discover corresponding patterns and cycles in music and the universe, we often outline such discoveries in mathematical terms. Jazz often uses symmetrical patterns, scales, and chords. We have mentioned the octatonic (diminished), heptatonic (whole tone), and chromatic scales and their corresponding symmetrical chords. They are among the most conspicuous forms. The superimposition of two dominant seventh chords whose roots are a semitone apart creates a familiar blues scale. The full set of expanded major chord tones in jazz harmony [Cmaj13($^\sharp$ 11)] is constructed on a symmetrical set of alternating intervals of major and minor thirds:

```
C------ E ------ G ------ B ------ D ------ F♯ ------ A
1 ------ 3 ------ 5 ------ 7 ------ 9 ------ ♯11 ------ 13
     M3    m3     M3     m3     M3     m3
```

Symmetry and repetition are approaches that supply familiarity to a composition, while the alternation of musical features, events, and careful orchestration provide shifting focal points that create variety and interest. Music composition should never be a randomly evolved event if it truly reflects the workings of the mind that operated by association. Audiences know intuitively when logic, passion, and purpose exist in art.

In jazz we study the overtone series because it provides the harmonic basis that naturally aligns with certain other universal patterns. As spontaneous composers we are not machines set to do only predictable and prescribed work within fixed parameters. Potentially, we are designed to grow and evolve according to more flexible abstract balancing, from firm roots, in multiple organic directions as a tree does, in accordance with those inner forces and qualities that define and distinguish phenomena as particular living things. All matter is clearly subject to the vibration and gravitational solar, lunar, and planetary forces that surround us. As humans, our distinct quality of mind enables us to study, analyze, and understand these forces to a greater degree than other inhabitants of our Earth environment. Human minds and acquired knowledge potentially enable us to cooperate with planetary forces and to free ourselves from the dominant forces of nature to a greater extent than our fellow creatures. Using our minds and intuition, we learn to cooperate with the forces of nature. We gain musical freedom through a similar evolutionary process.

Accumulating musical knowledge, through focused study and practice, gradually enables the spontaneous composer to understand and eventually conquer certain musical circumstances that result in an increased range of musical communication and freedom of expression. Growth results in conditions that can render past situations obsolete. We often outgrow them. Considering life's progressive tendencies, to live constantly in the past is unnatural. We must have the courage to move forward. The human birthright of independence and creative freedom cannot be realized if we do not use our potential to continually grow and evolve.

If creation expresses itself through universal laws, patterns, and harmonic alignment that manifest in reflective ways that extend throughout creation at both microcosmic and macrocosmic levels, then those tendencies found within a tone's overtone series (microcosm) might reflect systematic planetary organization. Scientists suggest that a precise quantity of substance in the universe is organized in appropriate proportions and relationships to make it function automatically. The inherent abstract symmetry that we constantly discover and explore, and the relationship between microcosmic and macrocosmic fundamental forces in the universe, suggests that perhaps we were supposed to gradually realize that a creative force (Creator) carefully tuned existence to become increasingly more self-aware as it evolves in complexity, beauty, and harmony. Each universal action or alteration has a chain reaction of vibratory consequences. An organic approach to the musical quest for systematic order, pattern, and meaning provides a metaphysical, personal, and scientific mode of thinking with which to examine the nature and power of the universe at large. Music and geometry are closely related. Mathematicians, scientists, and composers throughout the ages have worked to identify examples of harmony and geometry in the solar system. Basic laws seem to govern the structure and content of music, math, science, and nature.

Just as the microscope reveals glimpses of universal law and order at the subatomic or molecular level, students since antiquity have explored the "Music of the Spheres" through examining cosmic law and order through the telescope, computer, and numerous other tools of extension. In his book, *A Little Book of Coincidence*, John Martineau reveals a series of planetary patterns that align with familiar elements of mathematical and musical organization. A few of his findings are summarized as follows:

1. The Sun and Moon are a unified couple of heavenly bodies. Along with our closest planetary neighbors, these heavenly bodies exert measurable influence on life on Earth. The mathematical precision contained within areas of these relationships is astonishing. The proportion between the closest and farthest distances between Earth and the Moon create a proportion that is invoked precisely by the planetary neighbors between which we orbit, Venus and Mars. The closest to farthest distance ratio that each of these heavenly bodies experiences of the other is, remarkably, 3:11, and 3:11 is 27.3 percent. The moon orbits the Earth every 27.3 days, which is also the average rotation period of a sunspot.

2. The musical *octave* (a halving or doubling of frequency or wavelength) can be represented by an equilateral triangle, as its inscribed circle has a diameter half that of the containing circle. Jupiter and Saturn's obits are in the proportion 6:11, the octave, or double, of the 3:11 Moon to Earth ratio.

3. The diameter of Uranus's bright outermost ring is twice that of Uranus itself, an octave. Neptune's innermost ring is two-thirds the size of its outermost, a musical fifth. As a reflection of those harmonic proportions, Neptune's orbital period is twice that of Uranus's, and Uranus's is two-thirds that of Pluto.

4. After the fundamental laws of the Egyptians enabled ancient Africans to produce pyramids, art, and a great civilization that lasted for many centuries, later the ideas of Kepler, Newton, and Einstein defined laws that formed the basis for modern science. Keplar sought a geometric or musical solution to the orbits of planets and observed that six heliocentric planets meant five intervals. The well-known geometric solution he attempted resulted in the five Platonic solids between their spheres.

5. Carl Von Weizsacker's 1948 particle-cloud formation theory of condensing the planets suggested hidden patterns between the elusive orbits of several planets. Scientists have calculated that two nested pentagons define Mercury's orbital shell, the empty space between Mercury and Venus, Earth's and Mars's relative mean orbits, and the space between Mars and Ceres. Three nested pentagons define the space between Venus and Mars, and Ceres' and Jupiter's mean orbits (14).

Of course, neither the music of the spheres nor the universe is so easily reduced to any formulae that humankind can ever understand or duplicate entirely. Nonetheless, we do learn from observing its laws, and creative people will undoubtedly always continue to unlock their mysteries. If we could monitor the Earth's beautiful sky over billions of years, we would undoubtedly discover an infinite variety of sunrises, cloud formations, colors, and sunsets. The cloud patterns and infinite variety of colors thrill us each day with their beauty, yet the ordering of the systems we detect never fall within empirical mathematical formulae that we can then apply to the architecture humankind creates. The infinite array of elements forming the sky patterns that occur continually throughout each day are based upon an infinite number of causes and effects, many of which we may never comprehend completely. Nonetheless, artists are inspired by the overpowering grandeur of such phenomena and channel their thoughts and feelings of these natural influences into the art they create. Few thinkers would consider the events that unfold in the sky chaotic, despite their inability to effectively control or accurately predict mathematically the natural beauty that unfolds each day.

The nature of sound vibration may hold the key to the nature of order within the universe, but we may never fully understand its true nature. However, a universe heavily governed by the occurrence of unpredictable actions and consequences should inspire more humility than delusions of certainty.

Musical intercourse is more engaging than many other activities in life because it fully challenges our capacity to align and reconcile our music perception with an understanding of surrounding environmental forces. Musical messages can also bypass our five senses and touch our souls. The most effective music evolves from the alignment of inspiration (which emerges in the subconscious or intuitive realm) with theories of music that have grown gradually and organically as humankind's ears advance in musical understanding through active and passive listening. Music cannot be effectively limited or reduced to scientific formulae or mathematical calculation. In music, theoretical laws and arbitrary rules would have to be universally verifiable and transferable to music worldwide, and throughout time, to actually be empirically sound laws. The tools used for empirical analysis of music cannot surpass intimate musical knowledge, wisdom, and understanding gained through the actual production of music.

As computers advance some theorists and scientists feel that machines are evolving to a point where they can imitate or duplicate biological systems and creative processes. They feel that the artistic process can also be measured and analyzed cognitively to a degree that enables a computer's artificial intelligence to effectively mimic the process of human composition. The implications established by such assertions not only usher in possibilities of a radically new brand of contemporary composition, but also generate waves of other changes in the nature of creative process, thought, and performance practice that extend to other aspects of contemporary world society. Stephen Wolfram discusses "A New Kind of Science" that is rapidly evolving (in his book of the same name):

> Ever since machines have existed, people have wondered to what extent they might be able to imitate living systems. Most active from the mid-1980s to the mid-1990s, the field of artificial life concerned itself mainly with showing that computer programs could be made to emulate various features of biological systems. But normally it was assumed that the necessary programs would have to be quite complex. What the discoveries in this book show, however, is that in fact very simple programs can be sufficient. And such programs make the fundamental mechanisms for behavior clearer—and probably come much closer to what is actually happening in real biological systems (12).

What may seem complex can usually be traced to relatively simple seed material in music and throughout the universe. Science too understands the limits of empirical tools that restrict their analytical method. Through close examination of chaos theory, certain contemporary scientists are beginning to contemplate such questions and related issues. In a chapter that discusses how "History Matters," in his book *Ubiquity*, Mark Buchanan observes:

> For centuries, physicists have sought to capture the fundamental laws of the universe in timeless and unchanging equations, such as those of quantum theory of relativity. While this project has been enormously successful, the ultimate simplicity of such equations points to a paradox: If the laws of physics are so simple, why is the world so complex? Why don't ecosystems, organisms, and economics reveal the same simplicity as Newton's laws and the other laws of physics?
>
> In the late 1970s and 1980s, scientists discovered at least part of the answer—chaos. When a pinball scatters through a pinball machine, the path is extraordinarily sensitive to tiny influences along the way. This is chaos. Inside any ordinary balloon, the molecules also move according to the law of chaos: give a tiny nudge to just a single molecule and in much less than a minute every last one will be affected. In the context of the Earth's atmosphere, chaos brings us the "butterfly effect," the incredible collision that the flapping of a butterfly's wings in Portugal now might just lead to the formation of an intense thunderstorm over Moscow in a few weeks' time.
>
> So here we have one mechanism by which complexity can grow out of simplicity. Predicting the long-term future of any chaotic system is practically impossible, and a chaotic process looks wildly erratic even if the underlying

rules are actually quite simple. Researchers have discovered chaos at work in the fluctuations of things ranging from lasers to rabbit populations, and in the late 1980s and early 1990s some scientists even hoped that chaos might finally make sense of the wild ups and downs of financial markets. But it didn't, for there is an aspect of the world's complexity that chaos leaves completely untouched. Not its unpredictability, but its upheavability. Chaos is limited in its ability to explain tumultuous events, as researchers had hoped it might, because chaos itself does not generate upheavals. Something more is needed if chaos is to give rise to tumultuous events, such as stock market crashes or earthquakes, and that something more is history.

To see why, think again about the famous butterfly example, but with one important difference: imagine the butterfly is inside a balloon. A butterfly could flap its wings for eternity inside a balloon and never cause the equivalent of a thunderstorm inside that closed space. This is because the air in the balloon lives in peace under unchanging conditions, in what scientists refer to as equilibrium. In equilibrium, it is certainly true that the individual molecules toss around in utter chaos, but that's pretty much the end of the story. No larger patterns ever emerge, nothing important ever happens, and so the idea of history has little meaning. For the air in the balloon, the past and future are essentially the same. In contrast, the air in the Earth's atmosphere is very much out of equilibrium. Far from being left in peace, it is continually stirred and agitated and energized by the influx of light from the Sun. The result is the rich and ever unfolding history of the weather and climate. Out of equilibrium, there is such a thing as history.

This gives us a clue about the cause of upheavability: it clearly has something to do with the way things work when out of equilibrium. For the most part, out-of-equilibrium physics remains a forest of the unknown. And yet, over the past two decades, scientists have forged a few remarkable insights, one of which cast upheavals we met earlier in this chapter into a fascinating light. The key idea is the notion of the critical state, a special kind of organization characterized by a tendency towards sudden and tumultuous changes, an organization that seems to arise naturally under diverse conditions when a system gets pushed away from equilibrium. This is the first landmark discovery in the emerging science of nonequilibrium physics—what we might equally call the field of historic physics (15–17).

Non-equilibrium physics apply when our notions of balance (tension and release) operate within the dynamics of the chaos that ultimately arises when any degree of freedom occurs; and some degree of freedom may always exist throughout the motion of existence. Although we experience a much greater degree of freedom in performing spontaneous composition than in premeditated composition, the artistic decisions made among experienced improvisers are rarely randomly derived. Despite our various systematic elements of musical control, the high interactivity among improvisers ushers in consequential poetic chaos that inevitably creates the "butterfly effect and affect" in performance. Such musical interaction provides the "out-of-equilibrium physics" that places the musical experience within "a forest of the unknown," where every moment marks a new beginning and introduces an additional element of surprise—despite the simple systems that may be in place. The effect is less radical and conspicuous in the performance of premeditated composition, due to its relatively fixed form (with its written score and conductors to guide most of the performers decisions), but chaos still takes place on a subtler scale and the affective unpredictability can run equally high in any music.

When practicing alone in a secluded room, musicians create a situation of extremely limited interaction, and this may seemingly result in a situation akin to "equilibrium." A performer (transmitter) never knows who is listening (receiver) or fully realizes the influence that the vibrations produce in relatively solitary confines have on the surrounding environment, however. Conversely, what may appear to be chaotic music to inexperienced listeners may actually shift, alter, or rotate a highly structured nucleus governing the chain of events. In the most interactive forms of spontaneous composition, orientation can remain fluid as the center of gravity shifts incessantly from each musical action or reaction generated by a melodic lead, then taken up by a rhythmic motive, then producing a sudden harmonic shift, and so forth. Constantly introducing musical ideas, and the consequential reactions they inspire, requires active listening, musical readiness, rapid decision making, and high levels of concentration. Generally speaking, few (if any) musical "accidents" happen within the high-caliber ensembles of artists such as those led by Davis, John Coltrane, Cannonball Adderley, and other music masters. Dr. Donald Byrd thinks that, "Musicians that are trained can hear the musical sounds when looking at the contours. They can identify melody, rhythm, and harmonic lines from a geometric standpoint" (Byrd 17). This process of spontaneous composition undoubtedly involves a general reflection of other related yet-to-be-discovered universal patterns of interaction. In Buchanan's chapter on "Accidents of History," we may wonder as to the degree to which a process is actually ever accidental:

> Toss a copper button into a pan of hot molten copper, and after a time there will be no button; it will have melted and its atoms will have dispersed into the liquid sea. After things settle down, the result is equilibrium: an unchanging steady state in which the copper atoms swim about in an unending, monotonous chaos. The liquid stays liquid, nothing interesting or different ever happens, and there is little to distinguish one moment from the next. In equilibrium, the notion of history has very little meaning.
>
> But suppose you disturb the peace by taking the pan of hot copper and placing into a bath of ice water. In an instant some of the molten copper will cool and a chuck of solid copper will begin forming again in the pool. The copper is now far from equilibrium, since the liquid "wants" to freeze into

the solid form, but hasn't managed it yet. Because of this imbalance, now there is such a thing as history, and the amount of solid copper will gradually increase with time. There is also something else—complexity. For as the atoms in the liquid fall over one another in trying to join the growing chunk of solid, they link up to form a weird and complex structure something like a snowflake, with all kinds of side-branches and whiskers. In a nutshell, this is what happens when something freezes very quickly: rushing from the liquid into the solid, the atoms pile up in an atomic scale traffic jam, and a mess of complexity is the result (48–49).

Cities such as New York, San Francisco, Los Angeles, Paris, Cairo, and other cosmopolitan places in the world are interesting because of their diversity. More homogeneous populations fail to generate similar degrees of creativity, interest, and knowledge. This was also true in the ancient world. Music works the same way. Jazz evolved so quickly and with such richness because Africans were like the molten copper thrown into the icy water. Eric Dolphy was like the catalyst for complexity described above when he joined John Coltrane's ensemble. Although the ambiance was already extremely innovative and challenging, Dolphy's presence introduced a type of "imbalance" that forced everyone in that group to take their music to another level of abstraction, concentration, beauty, and flexibility. What may be clear to many composers, scientists, and theorists is that the simplicity that seemingly binds many systems that we observe in nature either, 1) may have subtle depths involving imperceptible complex infrastructures at the quantum level, or 2) can serve as the simple nuclei that proliferates orbiting complexity. Coltrane's classic quintet was bound by both of those features. Its initial condition possessed a highly unusual sense of depth and readiness for the addition of Dolphy into the ensemble. Interestingly, Wolfram summarizes his notions of Chaos Theory this way:

The field of Chaos Theory is based on the observation that certain mathematical systems behave in a way that depends arbitrarily and sensitively on the details of their initial conditions. First noticed at the end of the 1800s, this came into prominence after computer simulations in the 1960s and 1970s. Its main significance is that it implies that if any detail of the initial condition is uncertain, then it will eventually become impossible to predict the behavior of the system. But despite some claims to the contrary in popular accounts, this fact alone does not imply that the behavior will be necessarily complex. Indeed, all that it shows is that if there is complexity in the details of the initial conditions, then this complexity will eventually appear in the large-scale behavior of the system. But if the initial conditions are simple, then there is no reason for the behavior not to be correspondingly simple. What I show in this book, however, is that even when their initial conditions are very simple there are many systems that still produce highly complex behavior. And I argue that it is this phenomenon that is, for example, responsible for most of the obvious complexity we see in nature (13).

Can Chaos Theory analyze the patterns of actions and consequences that unfold in the sky above our planet? Do the structures, patterns, and musical details of some creative approaches to spontaneous composition resemble or share things in common with the mathematical unfolding of such natural phenomena? In the least, the patterns in nature provide much over which composers can compare, explore, and contemplate.

Math + Music = Art

Dr. Donald Byrd has explored intersections between math and music for many years. He shared his thinking and experiments with me on numerous occasions beginning in 1993. "Tone's Tune" (on the album *Sacred Musicism*) and the composition "Byrd Math" on *Harmonious Soul Scenes 2000* were both influenced by Donald Byrd's particular systematic approach to music and math. Symmetry and mathematical logic replace common scales and chords and provide musical references easily absorbed and utilized by other musicians.

In his self-published book, *Math + Music = Art,* Dr. Byrd aims to introduce children to the importance and necessity of exploring the connections between music and math. His study gives educators a catalog of ideas to motivate, guide, and inspire their students towards an appreciation of music through the examination of basic mathematical principles. He shows young people ways things they use every day, such as phone numbers, can be converted into mathematical expressions then performed as musical ideas. Byrd says, "Music is created by using symbols. Music is also verbal and sometimes spatial or pictorial. Music can be seen in a pictorial way when seen in a graphic sense" (20). He also suggests that educators and students:

1. Make a statement on the necessity of learning how to read. This system will help to change your quality of life. The M+M=A will assist in taking you from a survival to success level.
2. The importance of numbers, and how numbers can be used to make music. Relate this concept to melody, rhythm, and harmony.
3. (215) 323–4211 = (215) (323) (4211)
   > SET A   SET B   SET C = algebraic symbols
   a. Use the algebraic operations, rules, and laws in performing the composition of a piece of music.
   b. Use permutations and other ways to arrive at a solution.
4. Changing the form but not the meaning. Go from numbers to notes. (Byrd demonstrates ways numbers are easily converted to scale tones or representative intervals by counting in groups of semitones.)

5. The three ways of learning arithmetic and mathematics are verbally, symbolically, and spatially.
6. Learning requires understanding, knowing, and remembering the words, symbols, and their usages.
7. In learning M+M=A, certain rules and operations are suggested. M+M=A is a way of translating words, algebraic, arithmetic, and other forms of mathematics symbols into music and musical forms.
8. M+M=A expressions are similar to algebraic expressions because they often involve more than one number or group of notes. M+M=A uses terms and factors just like algebra. Constants and variables are often employed (23).

Byrd often asks of anything that demands his time: "Is it going to make me play better?" I trust that the material under your investigation is always worthy of your time and indeed improves your cognition, performance, and compositional skill as you work towards becoming a better musician.

"There is nothing stronger in the world than gentleness."

—Han Suyin

References

Andrews, Donald Hatch. *The Symphony of Life*. Sunlight Books, 1966. In a lecture based on his book entitled, "Molecular Adventure: Message to the Science Community." May 2007 <http://www.molecadv.com/ach/webpage.cfm>.

Bayles, Martha. *Hole in Our Soul: The Loss of Beauty and Meaning in American Popular Music*. Chicago: University of Chicago, 1994.

Buchanan, Mark. *Ubiquity*. New York: Crown Publishers, 2000.

Byrd, Donaldson T. L. *Math + Music = Art*. Teaneck, NJ: Blackbyrd Publishing Press, 1999.

Christensen, Thomas. *Grove Dictionary of Music*. New York: Oxford University Press. Reprint of *Life Magazine* (April 17, 1939): 22. June 2007.

Christensen, Thomas Street. *Rameau and Musical Thought in the Enlightenment*. New York: Cambridge University Press, 1993.

Cowell, Henry. *New Musical Resources*. New York: Something Else Press, 1969.

Diderot, Denis. *Rameau's Nephew and Other Works*. Trans. Jacques Barzun and Ralph H. Bowen. Indianapolis: Hackett Publishing: 2001.

Godwin, Jocelyn. *Harmonies of Heaven and Earth*. Rochester, VT: Inner Traditions International, 1995.

Hammel, T. and C. V. Kahn. *Math and Music—Harmonious Connections*. Palo Alto, CA: Dale Seymour Publications, 1995.

Ho, Andrew. "Fractal Geometry: The Story of Benoit B. Mandelbrot and the Geometry of Chaos." School of Wisdom. September 2007 <http://www.fractalwisdom.com/FractalWisdom/fractal.html>.

Hosking, Geoffrey and George Schöpflin, eds. "The Functions of Myth and a Taxonomy of Myths." *Myths and Nationhood*. New York: Routledge, 1997, p. 31.

Jacobi, E. ed. *The Complete Theoretical Writings of Jean-Philippe Rameau* (CTW VI, 387–407) American Institute of Musicology, 1967–72.

Jowett, B. trans. *Timaeus, The Dialogues of Plato*. Oxford: Clarendon Press, 1953.

Levarie, Siegmund and Ernst Levy. *Tone, a Study in Musical Acoustics*. New York: Greenwood Press, 1981.

Lewis, George E. *A Power Stronger Than Itself: The AACM and American Experimental Music*. The University of Chicago Press, 2008.

Lewis, Ralph M. (The Imperator). "The Ancient Mystery Schools." *Rosicrucian Digest* (June 1986): 5–6.

Lubicz, R. A. Schwaller de. *The Temple of Man*. Original French text translated to English by Debra and Robert Lawlor. Rochester, VT: Inner Traditions International, 1998, p. 5.

Maniktala, Rakesh. Ancient Science "Spiritualism, Modern Science and Ancient History." Mahabharata (Vana Parva) Ch. 187, Vayu Purana 50–88, Shatpath Brahman 1-8-16. August 2007 <http://geocities.com/ancientscience/beliefs>.

Martineau, John. *A Little Book of Coincidence*. New York: Walker and Company, 2001.

Montucla, Jean-Etienne. *Histoire des Mathématiques dans laquelle on rend compte de leurs progrés depuis leur origine jusqu'à nos jours*. Paris: 1758.

Murray, Albert. *Stomping the Blues*. New York: Da Capo Press, 1976.

Rameau. "Nouvelles réflexions sur le principe sonore." *Code de musique pratique*. Plate 10.1 Frontispiece. *Code de Musique*. (1760).

Rameau, Jean-Philippe. "Rameau on the Resonant Body and the One Principle (1760)." "Nouvelles réflexions sur le principe sonore." *Code de musique pratique*. Paris: 1760.

Rudhyar, Dane. *The Magic of Tone and the Art of Music*. Boston: Shambhala, 1982.

Sams, Gregory. "The Fractal Art Gallery" 2007. *Chaos Works*. December 2007 <http://www.chaos-works.com/gallery.html>.

Sawkins, Lionel. "Rameau's Last Years: Some Implications of Rediscovered Material at Bordeaux." *Proceedings of the Royal Musical Association* 111 (1984): 66–91.

Sehgal, Kabir. *Jazzocracy: Jazz Democracy, and The Creation of a New American Mythology*. Mishawaka, IN: Better World Books, 2008.

Shaw, Jonathan. "Who Built the Pyramids?" July–August 2003. *Harvard Magazine*. <http://www.harvardmagazine.com/on-line/070391.html>.

Snyder, Bob. *Music and Memory: An Introduction*. Cambridge, MA: The MIT Press, 2000.

Sunstein, Cass and Richard Thaler. "Chaos Theory and Complexity Theory: A Non-Technical Introduction." *As cited on Complexity Pages*. January 2008 <http://www.mathjmendl.org/chaos/#intro>.

Wolfram, Stephen. *A New Kind of Science*. Champaign, IL: Wolfram Media, Inc., 2002.

Chapter Ten
The Industry: Interstellar Space

KNOWLEDGE is ETERNAL (Tension and Release)

At the end of every chaturyugi, there is always a **pralaya**—mass destruction in the form of natural or man-made cataclysms—in which most of the knowledge in physical form is destroyed. But humanity survives in the form of a few human beings to carry forward the human race into next chaturyugi, like **"Manu"** (**Noah**) did at the end of last chaturyugi **3,893,100 years** ago. (The Vayu Purana is a Shaiva Purana, a Hindu religious text, dedicated to the god Vayu (the wind god), containing about 24,000 shlokas.)

Music in a Global Context

Melodies, rhythms, timbres, and harmonies in music reflect the knowledge, wisdom, attitudes, and behavior of the people who produce it. Rhythm unites us with the rhythmic universal patterns and cycles. Musical instruments amplify feelings the soul longs to express. Samite Mulondo, a world-renowned musician from Uganda, once said to me that he first tries to "find its song in each flute that he plays." In Global African culture, music is a living force that reflects humankind's psychological and emotional evolution towards the higher planes of realization. Such an approach to music blends passion with the technique required to communicate personal expression and cognition. Emphasis upon the free expression of one's own personal ideas is the trademark of Global African music and provides the music's universal appeal.

Knowledge is often preserved and perpetuated through the word. The word is also a viable part of the musical tradition, and through an oral tradition most Afrocentric music is transmitted. The word is not strictly that which we speak or write down, it is also the ideas that we generate and transmit as we conceptualize about music, art, ontology, the functions of the universe, love, and the like. The wise Sufi asks:

What is the word? Is the word just what we speak? Is that the word? No, that is the word of the surface. Our thought is a word, our feeling is a word, our voice, our atmosphere is a word. There is a saying: "What you are speaks louder than what you say." That shows that man does not always speak, but his soul speaks always. How do the fortune-tellers read the future? They hear it. They say that they see it from the action of man. But what is it all? It is all a word. For word means expression, expression in voice, in word, in form, in color, in line, in movement: all are united in one thing and that is the esoteric side of mysticism (267).

No absolute mathematical equations or musical formulae remain unshakable throughout time. Thus life, science, spirituality, and music hold something in common: they are all susceptible to change. Mastery of these disciplines is based upon making and testing assumptions that eventually lead to conclusions based upon experience and logical reasoning. They all deal with belief systems and none of these approaches to ontological understanding of existence ever prove anything absolutely conclusive. Time eventually requires that all such conclusions be continuously tested, modified, and expanded. All such disciplines can provide a certain degree of convincing evidence supporting the efficacy of certain principles that are developed through many years of observation and discovery.

Knowledge is indeed eternal and humankind has created an infinite variety of ways to express its collective progress, motion, ideas, and emotions. Musical knowledge, therefore, could obviously never be completely defined or dominated worldwide by the influence of a single culture. Like the distribution of astrological qualities throughout the zodiac, the meaning of music is scattered incrementally throughout time and place worldwide. Each culture's music reflects its own history, style, aesthetics, temperament, and reasoning. The music that each region from all corners of the world creates provides an important piece of the abstract puzzle that humanity gradually evolves to reflect its collective consciousness. African-American music, like other art forms, absorbs from all of the disparate music and circumstances with which it comes in contact. Therefore, spontaneous composers can increase their knowledge and musical resources by examining all music worldwide. Each new bit of information becomes yet another tool, resource, or color among those continually accumulating within the minds of creative artists. The richer the contents within the bag of creative ingredients, the wider the potential capacity and range of musical communication becomes.

European Musical Connections

Music reflects all the particular elements of a historical era, culture, and the environmental matrix in which it is born and cultivated. It is becoming increasingly more likely that contemporary composers' music may expose their roots in multiple cultures, interdisciplinary arts, and global influences. Of course, music (like religion, education, commerce, and most other aspects of world society) can often be highly politicized—frequently to the point of irrational absurdity. Most people consider classic music to be that which has a lasting recognized value and ultimately serves as a standard of refined craftsmanship and artistic excellence. Throughout much of the twentieth century some people consider European music the only real "classical" music, thus politicizing the term "classical" within a narrow provincial definition. Likewise, most music departments in America did not teach music (of the world) until the latter half of the twentieth century, most often recognizing only European music while allowing only token representation of music from the rest of the world.

The precise qualities of music that render it enduring are those most difficult to define quantitatively. The depth of music along technical, emotional, logical, and psychological lines contributes to its longevity and effectiveness. Most composers seek innovative musical ideas that render it a "living music"; personal artistic expression that extends beyond prevailing traditional conventions. Thus, rather than simply preserving old and existing styles and ideas, innovative artists continue a forward motion that reflects other natural growth processes.

European composers popularized the tempered scale (created to equalize the tones on the piano keyboard by dividing the octave into twelve equal parts) during the Baroque era. As tonal music evolved within the framework of even temperament in the West, composers increasingly demanded that their audiences perceive ever more subtle harmonic nuances and track greater numbers of hierarchical key modulations over lengthening periods of time. By the twentieth century most serious listeners knew earlier genres of European music through their music education in most public and private schools. (In a segregated society, however, many people in America were unable to access African-American music in school). Some African Americans (especially those employed as servants in European-American homes) heard and learned some European music. Consequently, the majority of European-American audiences were not exposed to accelerated musical evolution through which secular styles of African-American music progressed rapidly from nineteenth-century blues and ragtime to

Figure 1. Sample Matrix of European Tonal Harmony

European Tonal Music

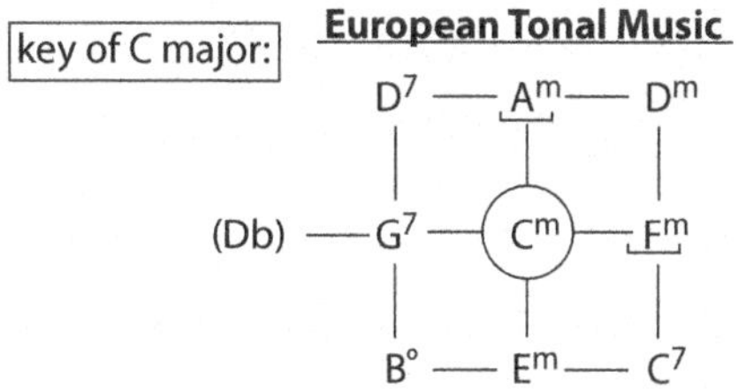

twentieth-century free jazz. A glance at the harmonic matrixes that governed European tonal harmony (**Figure 1. Matrix of European Tonal Harmony**) and African-American blues (**Figure 2. Matrix of African-American Blues**) demonstrates some of the basic harmonic nuclear patterns governing the musical orientation that ordinary people heard in segregated America by the mid-twentieth century.

After Debussy heard the Balinese gamelan at the Exposition Universelle, he began experimenting with composing music that deliberately avoided conventional tonal architecture and traditional gravitation towards conventional tonal centers. From this point in history the future of Eurocentric harmony was severely redirected and expanded. Debussy and other Impressionist composers employed the symmetrical whole-tone scale and augmented chords, while avoiding the traditional diatonic scale and the chords associated with that tonal environment. Richard Strauss and Maurice Ravel were among those other composers who also successfully pushed the boundaries and conventions of Eurocentric harmony.

Global African music had a significant influence on premeditated composition of the twentieth century in Europe and elsewhere in the world. A number of European composers recognized and utilized the creative resources of the rich "black" music idioms. Debussy was clearly inspired by ragtime technique in his "Golliwog's Cakewalk" and in his pianoforte suite *Children's Corner*. Stravinsky began to borrow from ragtime in 1918 after Ernest Ansermet's glowing reports of Sidney Bechet's clarinet playing in London in 1919 inspired him to compose his *Three Pieces for Clarinet*. Stravinsky also wrote his *Piano-Rag-Music* for solo piano and *Ragtime for Eleven Instruments* during that period (1919).

While in New York, as director of the Conservatory of Music, Dvorak was "captivated by black music in America" and all the main themes in his *New World Symphony* are the melodies of Negro Spirituals. Within the members of the Second Viennese school, Alban Berg's Lulu: Act I Scene 3: "Ragtime" displays the influence that early African-American style had on that composer's approach to serialism. Steve Reich has often discussed how heavily his approach to minimalism was influenced by "Black music" after he became aware of African music via a composers' conference that was held in 1962 in Ojai, California, while he was still a student of Luciano Berio's at Mills College. Reich embraced his new aesthetic "rhythm as melody" after studying West African drumming in Ghana. Electronic dance music soon followed suit and Reich and other minimalist composers gradually moved from simplicity to more complex combinations of cross-rhythms and polyrhythms as a result. Other composers influenced by jazz, blues, spirituals, and other music from the Global-African cultural experience include George Gershwin (*Rhapsody in Blue, An American in Paris,* etc.), William Grant Still, Eric Coats, Billy Mayerl, and many others.

The importance of a seed idea cannot be over-estimated. Einstein, in his penetrating study of Mozart, tells us that "Mozart needed only the beginning—his imagination and unerring taste provided the appropriate continuation" (136). Artists give the impression that novel ideas do not spring from the intellect or from conscious calculation, but

Figure 2. Matrix of African-American Blues (Excerpt)

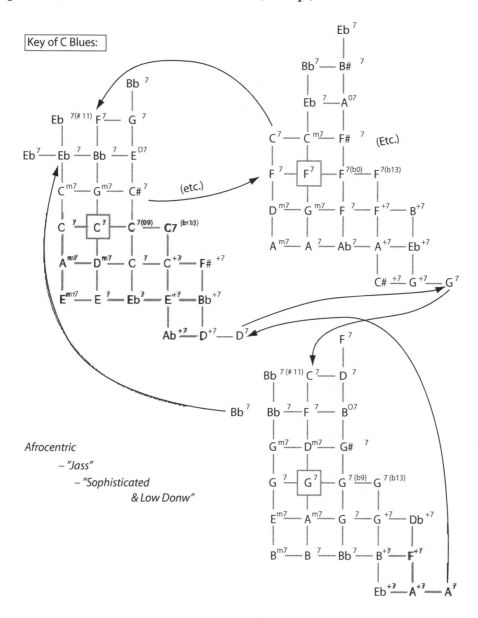

come from full-bloom, often unbidden, from "mysterious corners of the mind." Hard work and logical thought do not enter the creative process until after the idea is born. Then it must be written down, painted, composed, choreographed, improvised upon, or otherwise artistically transmitted.

The overtone series, as theoretical basis for harmonic evolution, seemed to reach its pinnacle in the evolution of European tonal harmony by the beginning of the twentieth century. Some European composers continued to experiment with interesting approaches to extending tonality to its limits. Nonetheless, a new generation of composers pressed forward, abandoning the familiar gravitational force of the harmonic series. Essentially there were two schools: some composers modified the earlier "classical" theoretical systems while others abandoned it entirely. The "neoclassical" approach of Stravinsky, Hindemith, and others extended harmonic freedom systematically, while retaining certain more staid aspects of traditional music structure and form. The second Viennese School, launched by the Austrian composer Arnold Schoenberg, took a much more radical departure from traditional Eurocentric tonal music. The direction of serialism, as some of these musical experiments were labeled, completely abandoned tonal centers. This is accomplished by giving all twelve tones of the chromatic scale equal weight, resulting in an "atonal" music (Schoenberg preferred the term "pantonal"). The blues matrix also allows equal weight to all twelve tones, but the paths available from each tone's position must be explored systematically in accordance with the prescribed order of tone alignment in the overtone series. Serial music worked with tone rows that could use twelve tones in a random order.

The lack of tonal centers, and a seemingly tacit agreement among European composers to proceed with an absence or lack of attention to emotional concerns in much of their serial music, destroyed all traditional hierarchies of intervals and left many audiences cold. Further disorientation was caused when serialists discouraged repetition of any kind. As a result, although some found the serial approach "interesting," few audiences throughout the twentieth century were moved emotionally or enjoyed serial music the way they had appreciated tonal music in previous generations.

Twentieth-century African-American music enjoyed a different brand of success, even while racism in the United States tempered the audience's expression of appreciation. While late nineteenth- and early twentieth-century European composers explored the upper partials of the overtone series (ninths, elevenths, thirteenths, whole-tones, octatonic scales, etc.) in relatively curt fashion, the blues began by incorporating what European tonal harmony standards deemed "unstable" as its harmony was founded upon various series of dominant seventh chord progressions. By the 1940s, every conceivable alteration was systematically attached to the basic blues harmonic matrix. By the 1950s and 1960s, however, even the structure of the extended blues matrix was challenged by innovators who formerly digested traditional ideas but later refused to be limited by them.

An Overview of Schenker's Theory

The analytical thinking in Europe that is closest to that of a jazz composer's frame of reference is *Schenkerian Analysis*. Schenkerian Analysis is a theory of musical construction developed by Heinrich Schenker (1868–1935). Schenker was a piano teacher, music theorist, and composer whose theory was grounded in music pedagogy. He was concerned with representing the musical structures that underlie tonal music composition, rather than directing our focus to the surface musical events, and Schenker devised modified musical notation specially adapted to accomplish the task. Schenker aimed to show musical structure in strictly musical terms. His theory suggests that musical structure unfolds in ways analogous to fractals, involving synergy where the whole is reflected in the hierarchical stratification of its parts, and also contained within the simpler levels and details of its structures.

Traditional Western musical notation uses a half-note to represent a duration of two beats, which is twice as long as a quarter-note, which represents one beat. In Schenkerian Analysis, the half-note is used to represent a structural pitch at a higher order of structural importance than one represented in quarter notes. Quarter notes, in turn, are more structurally significant than notes represented by note-heads without stems. This stratified system of notation is used to describe musical motion that occurs on several levels. Schenker concluded that what we hear when listening to a musical composition is a series of more or less complex elaborations of simpler underlying structures that supports various levels of surface musical events. Schenker's theory thus attempts to clarify these underlying levels of motions and demonstrate that they involve laws of musical motion similar to those governing the foreground, if often in more rigid ways. The experienced jazz performer hears a background of fundamental and secondary tones that serve as a structure for shaping the details of their improvising and spontaneous composing.

Traditional theory and teaching concentrates on two aspects of pitch: harmony and counterpoint. Schenker's study of harmony is mostly theoretical, while his study of counterpoint is largely based on a European teaching method called Species Counterpoint that has existed for several centuries. His aim was ultimately to bring harmony and counterpoint together in a study of what he called "free composition." Schenker explored the most controversial part of his theory—the fundamental structure—near the end of his career. The part of his theory that initially had the most impact in the English-speaking world was his theory on what he called parallelism. Motivic analysis had traditionally looked for how themes and motives were inter-related on the surface. Schenker examined ways in which musical ideas held more cryptic underlying and structurally significant similarities. It shifted musical perspective to the background structures, much as the blues matrix focused attention upon the fundamental tones that serve as nuclei for the overtone series that govern harmony.

Harmonic Series

To a degree, the basic principles underlying chord and scale tones that outline Schenker's approach differ from those that shape the blues matrix. Nevertheless, both approaches have related fundamental standards. Schenker began with the harmonic series. Theorists and composers understand the harmonic series' contribution to the formation of timbre and harmony, realize that there comes a point beyond which overtones cannot be heard by human ears, and are aware that not all notes of the series correspond to the limited range of tempered notes of the Western scale. Schenker argued that only the first five tones of the overtone series were readily audible, and that particular composite of notes made up the basic unit of tonal music: the triad (C, E, and G, and he attributed almost mystical properties to this "chord of nature"). In fact, Schenker considered the basic root position triad as a conceptual abbreviation of nature because it appears spread across three octaves in the harmonic series.

Schenker argued that the harmonic series demonstrates that the rising fifth is the basic motion of tonal music; and that, after the tonic, the dominant is the most important chord. In tonal harmony, this theory conforms to crucial functions of the dominant in cadential formulae progressions. Thus, the rising fifth key system aligns with what is called the circle of fifths. The rising fifth from the harmonic series suggests an ever-expanding movement upwards (i.e., C - G - D - A - etc.) around the circle of fifths. Schenker's explanation for the effect that (what he considers) natural phenomena have on the process of making music was a departure from traditional theory and, consequently, controversial. He felt that tonality would quickly become incompressible if it followed this continual upward expansion of fifths. Schenker concluded that for this reason the artist employs motion in the opposite direction (descending fifths). Thus this descending fifth brings music to a close in European music with a perfect cadence (V-I), defying the continuous expansion suggested by nature. The blues matrix, with its emphasis on that same array of rising fifths from the harmonic series, absorbs both

Figure 3. Harmonics 1–5

1st through 5th harmonics of a vibrating string

1st through 5th harmonics of a vibrating string

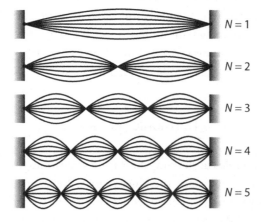

$N = 1$

$N = 2$

$N = 3$

$N = 4$

$N = 5$

ascending and descending fifth spirals in a system that allows freedom of movement between all dominant key areas through chord substitutions (such as tritone substitutions), chord extensions (such as flat-nine and flat-thirteen), and dominant chord equivalents (diminished chords, augmented chords, suspended-four, etc.).

> Ascending fifths: C-E-G-B, G-B-D-F, D-F-A-C, A-C-E-G, E-G-B-D, B-D-F-A, F-A-C-E, etc.

> Descending fifths: C-E-G-B, F-A-C-E, B-D-F-A, E-G-B-D, A-C-E-G, D-F-A-C, G-B-D-F, etc.

The motion of the scale step is also a critical part of Schenker's theory of harmony. Schenker criticized Roman numeral harmonic analysis because it portrays music as constantly modulating sequences. His emphasis on scale tones within a single key is also related to fundamental jazz procedure, where the introduction of closely related notes or chords is simply embellishments of a given musical event or environment, rather than modulations. (Note: For example, all arpeggiations above are from the same scale, so they may be thought of as closely related to each other harmonically.) Therefore, where some theorists may consider music to have changed key (modulated into the dominant region or relative major), Schenker and contemporary jazz musicians hear these relationships on a much broader scale and consider such movement to related harmony as extensions of the central or fundamental key. In other words, where traditional Western theory might consider moving the tonic key towards the relative minor and then the dominant, Schenker would determine the same progression beginning in the tonic going towards scale step III of the tonic, then to scale step V of the tonic; all while remaining in the tonic area.

Comparing Elements of Premeditated Compositions to Spontaneous Solos

In Chapter Four, we examined an analysis of W. A. Mozart's "Symphony in E-flat." Observing structural elements of Bach, Mozart, and other influential compositions enhances our ability to associate structural elements of premeditated compositional approaches with various approaches to spontaneous compositions, because the logic inherent within excellent musical craftsmanship is perceptible, enduring, and effective universally regardless of prevailing stylistic approach. Bach's "B minor Partita No. 1" (Corrente) is subjected to Schenkerian analysis below in an attempt to expose its basic underlying structure. Traditionally, Schenkerian analysis breaks down European composers' music to expose the background, middle-ground, and foreground compositional features. Other related analytical charting includes separate harmonic, melodic, and rhythmic reductions that add to the search for structural clarity. Through various approaches to analysis we begin to find relationships between the "structural hearing" of premeditated composers and the underlying stylistic approaches used by spontaneous composers. The specialized symbols of Schenkerian analysis present a systematic portrait of the three stratified levels of compositional structure and distill the most structurally significant features. Study the results while listening to recorded examples of Bach's Corrente. Spontaneous composers might then apply related "structural hearing" approaches to examining other musical organization. A clear sense of structure and direction enhances musical orientation, continuity, balance, and confidence while improvising, keeping all elements of spontaneous music fresh, logical, and organic. Compare the features of the two compositions beginning on page 391. Can you determine how one is derived from the other?

"Mellow Bossa" (Figure 8) represents the original short composition from which the longer and more elaborate composition "Muse" (see Appendix, Figure 7) was born. Knowing this, then approaching "Mellow Bossa" as a formal outline structure for "Muse" makes it easier to separate the melodic elements of "Mellow Bossa" from the foreground details that were later applied to embellish and extend the "Muse" framework. Comparing "Mellow Bossa" (as the formal framework for "Muse") with the Schenkerian analysis of the Corrente of Bach's "Partita No. 1 in B minor" above, we find similarities of structural design. Of the most conspicuous observations to make is that both compositions have strong melodic and harmonic cores elaborated by less stable middle-ground and foreground embellishment. In terms of formal structure, the thematic construction of "Mellow Bossa" involves an introduction, departure/expansion, and return that is closely related to the exposition, development, and recapitulation sectional divisions of Mozart's *E-flat Major Symphony*. In sorting out compositional construction, isolating the basic backbone structure of a composition is a good place to begin. Composers from around the world have more features in common with regards to applying structural form than with any other element of music. Theme and variation, binary, and ternary structures are common formal structures that occur in many compositional styles worldwide.

Analysis of Corrente in B Minor from J. S. Bach, Partita No. 1 for Solo Violin (BWV 1002)

In the earlier discussion involving recombinant music we saw ways to isolate various stylistic features of a composer's music. The use of figured bass symbols to guide portions of compositions during Bach's time; his own inclinations towards spontaneous composing; and the frequency at which he composed great music for weekly church services and other such occasions are related to the demands placed upon contemporary spontaneous composers to produce masterful music instantaneously.

Bach's "B minor Corrente from the Partita No. 1" for solo violin contains the incessant running figures in an alternating melody/accompaniment texture (in a quick 3/4 meter) that confirms the movement's Italian flavor. Notwithstanding, we might interpret certain rhythmic elements of the piece as a shifting of accent from the 3/4 (triple) feeling to the 6/8 (compound duple) feeling. This subtle instability of rhythm (which will be dealt with in particular later) resembles the *hemiola* often found in the French *courante*. Whether or not theorists argue in terms of this composition's particular "type," it is clearly a complex and colorful piece of music in which the composer employs an amazing economy of means in creating an exciting musical work.

Let's explore the bass movement to see its impact on the composition's structure. Spontaneous composers often listen intently to bass lines to determine the nuclei of their harmonic and melodic directions. I divided the composition into two parts, the second part beginning after the first repeat sign. Part I has a bass (lower voice) that moves from the tonic, through a third progression, to the dominant. Although Part II begins on this same dominant, it soon moves back to the tonic. From I, the bass moves to the subdominant region (prolonged by a motion to the mediant neighbor) before reaching the dominant (suggested in measure 74 and confirmed in measure 78) and, finally, the concluding tonic.

In composing spontaneously, each musical gesture should likewise have a specific goal. An important goal of the first half of Part I involves the top voice motion from the opening scale tone 1 to structural 3 in measure 18. From there, structural 2 is quickly obtained in the following measure and prolonged (by means of a descending octave line) to the end of Part I. The opening scale tone B moves scale-wise creating two series of parallel tenths with the lower voice, as indicated on the chart in Figure 5. These opening six measures consist of three two-measure sequences that lead to a series of 9–8 suspensions (in measures 7, 8, 9, and 10) after a brief and inconclusive cadence in the mediant area. The suggestion of D major (measures 17 and 18) does not impede the general momentum towards the dominant, which is reached in measure 19 and that supports structural 2 to the end of this section. Both scale tone 2 and 5 in the bass are carried over into Part II, which begins with a contrasting descending arpeggio.

We find symmetry, tension and release, balance, and deception on multiple levels of Bach's compositions. After the dividing dominant, which leads into Part II, a cadence on the tonic is reached in measure 35 with scale tone 3 in the top voice. From this point, a series of parallel tenths extends into measure 44, serving as a prolongation of the tonic (see Figure 5). This eventually leads to a cadence on the subdominant in measure 48 supporting a neighbor note motion in the top voice (from 3 of the tonic chord to E, its upper neighbor F), which returns to the principal tone in measure 51. Figures 4–7 that follow enable us to better understand the stratified structural, harmonic, symmetrical, and rhythmic levels of the Corrente.

Figure 4. Corrente (from BWV 1002)

Corrente in B minor

J.S. Bach

Figure 5. Schenkerian Analysis (by Karlton E. Hester)

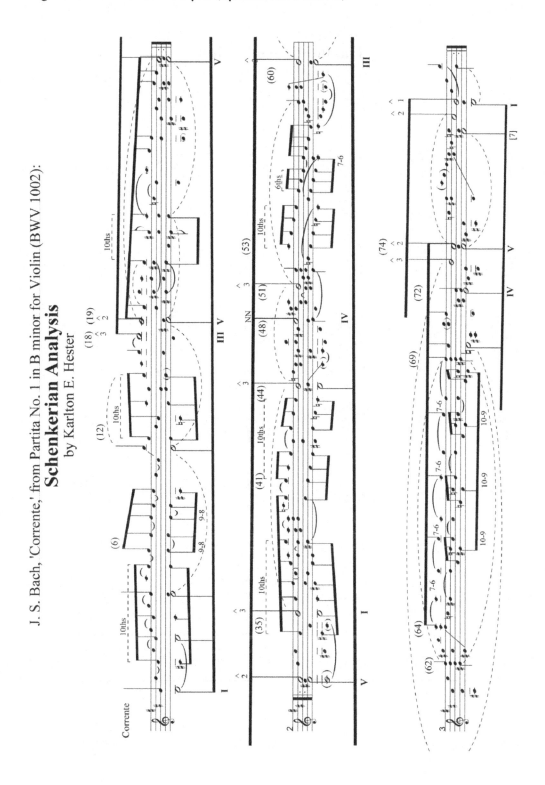

J. S. Bach, 'Corrente,' from Partita No. 1 in B minor for Violin (BWV 1002):
Schenkerian Analysis
by Karlton E. Hester

Figure 6. Harmonic Reduction (by Karlton E. Hester)

J. S. Bach, 'Corrente,' from Partita No. 1 in B minor for Violin (BWV 1002):
Harmonic Reduction
by Karlton E. Hester

Figure 7. Rhythmic Reduction (by Karlton E. Hester)

Rhythmic Reduction
by Karlton E. Hester

At measure 53, another series of parallel tenths is initiated and the interval is inverted (forming parallel sixths) in measure 55. Scale tone 3 is prolonged throughout this mediant chord in measure 60. This subdominant chord predominates between measures 48 and 72. Another chain of 7–6 suspensions arises in the top two voices (beginning in measure 64) that soon creates a double suspension when the third voice enters in the following measure (on the third beat of measure 65, with G-sharp) creating an additional 3–2 suspension between the outer voices. During this entire process, the top voice descends an octave line, once again from the C-sharp in measure 64 to the octave below in measure 74, where structural 2 is confirmed over a V (dominant tone) in the lower voice. Both the C in the bass and scale tone 2 in the upper voice are then prolonged throughout the events that lead to the concluding cadence in measure 79.

We now know that patterns and imitation are characteristic of most compositional styles. This helps familiarize the listener with the composer's most essential ideas. The two-measure sequences that occupy the opening six measures of this movement contain three important motivic elements that remain as primary building material throughout this composition: 1) the ascending two-octave arpeggio that usually begins in root position or first inversion; 2) a striking, downward motion involving three large leaps; and 3) a descending conjunct motive that involves four notes. The former feature (the ascending arpeggio) and the descending four-note motive both occur fairly frequently throughout Parts I and II. In both instances, the motive generally originates in the lower voice near the beginning of the piece. The three broad leaps begin on the downbeat of even-numbered measures (i.e., measures 2, 4, and 6) in Part I, but are inverted and situated on the third beat of the measure upon a few occasional appearances in Part II (i.e., measures 73 and 75).

Balanced mixtures of conjunct and disjunct motion can also become important tension and release-producing factors. Because much of the melodic and accompaniment material moves by leap in Bach's composition, the more rarefied occasions of step-wise motion stand out as the striking and unusual elements when they appear. The four-note motive in the second half of the composition, in measure 2, is the first case in point. This motive is an important one in both parts of the movement. With the exception of measure 76, each time the motive occurs it is both approached and left by leaps in the opposite direction of its own motion, thus isolating its conjunct feature from the more disjunct surroundings. Each of the dozen or more situations that involve this motive (in its various forms) begins on the second half of the second beat of the measure. The significance of this particular rhythmic characteristic will be discussed presently.

In contrast to the four-note descending motive just mentioned, the seven appearances of the full ascending arpeggiated chords (which occur on odd-numbered measures 3, 5, 11, 25, 61, and 79) all descend step-wise after they have completed themselves. A notable exception to this procedure is the final arpeggio, which continues to ascend by leap to the final scale tone B. The sequential figure introduced in measures 7 and 8, which is found in modified versions throughout Part II, is expanded to its greatest length in measures 65–69. In a fashion similar to the rhythmic disposition of the conjunct four-note motive examined earlier, this rhythmic pattern also draws attention to the hemiola grouping of the beats (i.e., towards a quasi 6/8 feeling) that somewhat resembles the subtle rhythmic quality of a French courant.

In a fashion akin to that often used by Thelonious Monk, Miles Davis, and other modern spontaneous composers, Bach is a master of exploring a single musical idea's permutations in infinite variety. As we observed, despite the extremely complex nature of the construction of this Corrente, the economy of means employed in the movement is remarkable. Most of the material is derived from three motivic elements. Nevertheless, the variety and contrasts that Bach achieves with this basic material are so rich that listeners might fail to perceive some gestures as exact repetitions that occur within varied contexts of the piece (compare measures 25 and 63 or measures 3 and 79, for example).

Other repetitions of melodic materials occur in different octaves (compare measures 18 and 60) or at other pitch levels (compare measures 25 and 62). The chart in Figure 6 is simply a harmonic reduction of the chord movement, while the chart in Figure 7 attempts to demonstrate the basic underlying rhythmic patterns and contrasting shifts that occur. The increased harmonic pacing during these remarkable rhythmic episodes adds to their importance and attraction. Within this movement, melodic elements often become responsible for the unusual and structurally significant rhythmic features that contribute to the overall aesthetic beauty and architectural design of the composition. Rhythm clearly serves as interesting bridges and links that contribute to the forward momentum of the music.

The rhythmic functions are designed to merge with the rich contrapuntal and harmonic construction of the work to form musical moments that are illusive, yet memorable, in nature. Within these dance moments we discover Bach's concern for prolonging the musical line (as briefly indicated in mentioning the two-octave lines in Part I and Part II, and the general pacing of the overall harmonic motion of the Corrente) and, once again, his complete mastery over all such compositional elements at his disposal.

Influences on Music as a Reflection of Culture

Technical mastery over music notes covers only a basic understanding of musical vocabulary, but deeper knowledge ultimately develops only when infused with the life-giving force of the imagination. Unity, precision, and discipline are qualities that all musicians must display before comprehending the deeper levels of musical knowledge. The Kingdoms of ancient Egypt displayed the power of unity, precision, and discipline for thousands of years. Traditionally, in African music, Nature herself provided the fertile source of inspiration and examples of universal principles of polarity and proportion. If music is a mirror of both our innermost spirit and the external environments through which we travel during a cultural lifetime, then the music of Asia, Europe, or any other music is similarly affected by the things and events surrounding it.

The influence of personality and culture is perceptible in music to a degree. Cultures that emphasize conformity, or hold extraordinary social control over its individual constituents, create music that reflects such tendencies. Highly literate cultures that experience the world more through the social constructs absorbed predominantly through the eyes, rather than initially through the ears or other senses, create music that is learned first through the eyes and not through the ears. Societies who live closer to nature, and thus organize their daily affairs more spontaneously, are more inclined to approach music more empirically, as an experiential encounter based upon aurally and visually generated experience, thus allowing greater degrees of musical spontaneity and freedom reflective of their social inclinations. People who spend the majority of their lives within square-shaped boxes (homes, offices, schoolrooms, restaurants, etc.) will

Figure 8. "Mellow Bossa" by Karlton E. Hester

Mellow Bossa

c Karlton E. Hester 1980

produce music that resembles the geometry of that experience. Those who spend most of their lives outdoors with nature create music, dance, and visual art corresponding to those social and environmental configurations as well.

Because everything in the universe apparently vibrates, it is plausible that most of the things that we sense in our environment, with or without tools that enhance, extend, and magnify our senses, generate various types of waveforms. Waveforms tend to radiate around a central core. The Milky Way, with its seemingly infinite array of stars and other heavenly bodies, conforms to a spiral organization. The shape of an egg is composed of an infinite number of spiral rings, distributed below and above its equator, that suggest the organization of frequencies of the overtone and undertone series above and below a fundamental frequency. Afrocentric music rarely involves square musical rhythms. Whether applying polyrhythmic layers, syncopation, 12/8 rhythmic feel, or the illusive quality of "swing," most Afrocentric rhythms are based on more circular or spiral rhythmic implications of triple division.

Virtually all African-American music allows performers varying degrees of freedom. In Eurocentric "serious" music, the premeditated composer attempts to control almost all performance parameters and details through detailed symbols of instruction of a score. During certain historical periods, European and European-American composers granted performers a considerate measure of freedom, such as the use of Baroque era figured bass or in twentieth-century compositions involving indeterminacy (such as the compositions of John Cage). As African-American music evolved from African roots through field hollers and blues, spirituals and gospel, barrelhouse music, ragtime, New Orleans jazz forms, boogie-woogie, rhythm and blues, bebop, hard bop, free jazz, various fusion styles, hip-hop, and other stylistic forms, twentieth-century music worldwide witnessed a rapid metamorphosis and general evolutionary progression towards increasingly greater degrees of freedom. Over the course of several hundred years European music moved gradually through an equal number of styles, from medieval mono-phonic music to a total abandonment of all tonal principles.

Many composers abandoned tonality for twelve-tone and serial approaches at the beginning of the twentieth century, particularly in certain of the most innovative periods in Schoenberg, Berg, and Webern's atonal music. Over time futurism, nationalism, the electronic revolution, and new pluralism (which gradually admitted jazz, rock, popular music, and "ethnic music" into previously more exclusive Eurocentric music histories on twentieth-century music) all moved towards the incorporation of increasingly greater degrees of freedom. Minimalism and other styles followed, creating paths towards other new approaches, vocabularies, and musical freedom. Improvisation was still not extremely important within Eurocentric composition, however, except among a small group of composers (such as John Cage). From the 1970s onward, music vocabularies began to merge across cultural boundaries to greater extents. Spontaneous and premeditated composers worldwide began to explore mutual artistic concerns in a contemporary shrinking world. Composers continually explored new concepts, musical tools, and fresh and ever-broadening aesthetic palettes. The electronic revolution also encountered mutual international interest in compositions that used tape recorders, synthesizers, and computers to expand the range of possibilities. Although some composers reverted to nationalism, neoclassical forms, or others retrospective styles, a strong tendency among others by the end of the twentieth century was to regain traditional ancient connections between music, interdisciplinary arts, ritual, and magic. Periods of extremely esoteric music, composed for a small sector of listeners and inaccessible to the masses, usually enjoy short lives. Therefore, developing an ability to create innovative music that communicates more broadly is a skill worth acquiring.

Exploring new musical concepts and vocabularies requires spending time together as ensembles. In jazz, fewer musical ensembles emerged during the last quarter of the twentieth century than in any other period in the development of African-American music. There were no equivalent ensembles to the early New Orleans-style combos such as King Oliver's; no style-setting swing bands like the Count Basie or Duke Ellington organizations; and no Charlie Parker/Dizzy Gillespie bebop "collectives" learning revolutionary new styles at places like Minton's. For the most part, the period between 1970 and 2009 has remained the age of the freelance musicians forcing musicians to rely upon old traditional frameworks in the absence of conditions conducive to creating innovative styles. Perhaps this paucity of distinct and groundbreaking musical styles may be due to a severe breakdown in the typical jazz mentor/student relationship. It may also reflect social politics and changing economic trends in America. Prior to the age of the computer the level of musical innovation produced by blues, swing, bebop, and other "jazz" masters was overwhelming for most younger musicians and audiences to digest. Computer technology has equipped future generations with powerful computational tools that can move music into exciting new territory when coupled with the knowledge gained through learning through mentoring during the development of imagination. Some critics may consider this new technology responsible for creating isolation among those who sit alone with their computerized machinery at the cost of diminished human interaction. Nonetheless, creative thinking can usher in ways to use technology to bring people together in various new ways enabling them to develop new capabilities.

Technology, in its many forms, is a particularly useful teaching and social-interaction tool among younger people. Children with autism have trouble listening and responding, but scientists are working on using technology to help them. Contrary to some popular opinions that suggest that gaming is turning teenagers into anti-social loners, some argue that new experimental technology could also help previously isolated kids make connections in the real world through video games that help them engage with friends and community. The Pew Internet study of U.S. teenagers found that few play alone and most join up with friends when gaming. It found that many used educational games to learn about world issues and to begin engaging in politics. The report also found that gaming had become an almost universal pastime among young Americans.

Christian Gold submitted an article entitled, "Effects of Music Therapy for Children and Adolescents with Psychopathology: A Meta-Analysis," for the *Journal of Child*

Psychology and Psychiatry. The objectives of this assessment were "to examine the overall efficacy of music therapy for children and adolescents with psychopathology, and to examine how the size of the effect of music therapy is influenced by the type of pathology, client's age, music therapy approach, and type of outcome." Eleven studies were analyzed, covering a total of 188 subjects for the meta-analysis. The study found that:

> After exclusion of an extreme positive outlying value, the analysis revealed that music therapy has a medium to large positive effect (ES = .61) on clinically relevant outcomes that was statistically highly significant ($p < .001$) and statistically homogeneous. No evidence of a publication bias was identified. Effects tended to be greater for behavioral and developmental disorders than for emotional disorders; greater for eclectic, psychodynamic, and humanistic approaches than for behavioral models; and greater for behavioral and developmental outcomes than for social skills and self-concept (11).

Spirituality and Healing Force

Musicians often say, "Music is the healing force of the universe." Certainly music has often served as a primary defense against oppression and heartache, and has supplied a critical psychological tool that fortified enslaved Africans in America and others during periods of suffering. Although little is known concretely about the relationship between music and healing, people throughout time have acknowledged that music helps to quell physical, emotional, and psychological ailments.

Our heartbeat is one of our personal rhythms. As the rhythms of life impact us, our bodies crave to move and dance in harmony with our surroundings. Music can serve as a vehicle that enables us to harmonize the mind, body, and spirit to the vibration of its own intuitive rhythm and flow. Flow provides health and regeneration and, conversely, we flow in sync with life when healthy. Conditions of imbalance can often impede our flowing with the natural course of life, and eventually lead to some form of disease. Everything vibrates, and the higher the flow, the greater the life force contained within us. Music provides a way of harmonizing with the universal vibrations of existence, and through sound and breathing, and using musical instruments to enhance our musical expression, we can channel our flow in a way that enhances our health and wellness. Thus, through sound we can find healing vibrations.

It seems that often periods of suffering result in heightened degrees of spirituality and creativity. The disappointment and continued suffering experienced by African-American communities after the Emancipation Proclamation managed to produce yet a stronger brand of music: the blues. Early African-American religious thought, like Gnosticism and theories expressed in various occult literatures, was diametrically opposed to the theory of evolution. Forced to go deep within the wellspring of their subconscious mind to survive intensely adverse physical conditions, oppressed people have often preferred to align themselves with the position of empowerment that faith in a transcendent mind, force, or power provides. David Conway discusses ways many people considered themselves especially close to the C re at or.

Part of this tradition maintains that human beings did not originally belong to the physical world. Instead, like the angels whose incorporeal nature they once shared, they formerly dwelt in the astral light where they could rejoice in the intuitive comprehension of God's mystery. However, unlike the angels, whose passive adoration makes them seem like docile sheep, mankind was endowed with a will of its own, a privilege God had otherwise reserved only for Himself. And it was this will, the divine spark within them, which persuaded men to revel against the benevolent authority of God. Here we have the old story of spiritual pride, as a result of which, according to the occultists, human beings were demoted to the world of matter and, supreme indignity, clothed in flesh. Since then each one of us has inherited the blot of original sin which can be expurgated only after repeated incarnations in this valley of tears (14–15).

A spiritual foundation for artistic creation does not involve a singular or direct line of development, however. People within an assortment of world cultures adapted to a wide range of spiritual and philosophical directions and influences. Many investigated modern views that challenged traditional ontological notions. Liberalism and authoritarianism suggest a structure that challenges humankind to understand the physical–spiritual nature of the universe. Liberalism attempts to establish a relationship to the universe that "comports with his creative human status and, second, a relationship to his fellow man that will express in practice his conviction of human dignity. It invites him to feel, moreover, not the sinfulness and worthlessness of man, but the high powers of sociality and rationality that exist in man and bid for release. Liberalism asked man to grow up to the full stature of a self-governing and self-fulfilling human being" (Overstreet 122–123).

Although love and spirituality are immeasurable empirically, their conspicuous effect on the subconscious, subjective, and objective realms of human existence are undeniable. Some musicians and artists advocate for love creating health and well-being. Love, as an element intimately related with health and spirituality, is a fundamental principle that motivates their work. John Coltrane's *A Love Supreme* is a celebrated example of modern music based upon this universal principle. In his book, *Healing Words,* Larry Dossey, M.D., reminds us that "tender, loving care," throughout history has uniformly been recognized as an important element in healing.

David McClelland, Ph.D., of Harvard Medical School, has demonstrated the power of love to make the body healthier through what he calls the "Mother Teresa effect." He showed a group of Harvard students a documentary of Mother Teresa ministering lovingly to the sick, and measured the levels of immunoglobulin A (IgA) in their saliva before and after seeing the film. (IgA is an antibody active against viral infections such as colds.) IgA levels rose significantly in the students, even in many of those who considered Mother Teresa "too religious" or a fake. In order to achieve this effect in another way, McClelland later discarded the film and asked his graduate students simply to think about two things: past moments when they felt deeply loved and cared for by someone else, and a time when they loved another person. In his own experience, McClelland had been able to abort colds with this technique. As a result of his personal experiences and research, he became an advocate for the role of love in modern healing (Dossey 109–110).

Music is now a cornerstone of Global-African communities. African Americans experienced intensely emotional circumstances during bondage in the Americas that severely limited normal modes of personal interaction and human expression. This psychological adjustment forced African Americans to channel much of their thoughts and feelings into musical expression to exercise their minds, bodies, and spirits. The African *jali* (also *jeli* or *griot*) was centered at the nucleus of musical life in many parts of traditional Africa. Music making in traditional African culture was a communal affair in which all community members were mutually involved. This brand of democratic interaction made its way into the functioning of the African-American jazz ensemble. The stratified dynamics of communal African villages were reflected in Global-African music. The roles of each instrument within a New Orleans style combo are clearly distinct, independent, and well defined, but they are all involved in a truly synergistic relationship. All members of the ensemble provide integral components. A healthy community reflects the harmony, wisdom, effectiveness, stratification (of responsibilities), mutual respect, and the rich diversity of such synergism. A healthy jazz ensemble usually consists of members who have each been initiated into similar musical experience, principles, and training without losing their individual musical ideas and identities. The elders of a particular school of musical evolution and thought are often innovators who form the nucleus of future stylistic directions. New musical initiatives bring a healthy and inevitable sense of rebellion, fresh energy, and new perspectives.

Aesthetics

For many artists and philosophers, the interaction between harmony and dissonance is the motivating force that creates beauty. For other beauty occurs only when all components are harmonious. Author Manly Hall feels:

> The world is called beautiful and its Creator is designated the *Good* because good perforce must act in conformity with its own nature; and good acting according to its own nature is harmony, because the good which it accomplishes is harmonious with the good which it is. Beauty, therefore, is harmony manifesting its own intrinsic nature in the world of form.
>
> The universe is made up of successive gradations of good, these gradations ascending from matter (which is the least degree of good) to spirit (which is the greatest degree of good). In man, his superior nature is the *summum*

bonum. It therefore follows that his highest nature most readily cognizes good, because the good external to him in the world is in harmonic ratio with the good present in his soul. What man terms *evil* is therefore, in common with matter, merely the least degree of its own opposite. The least degree of harmony and beauty. Thus deformity (evil) is really the least harmonious combination of elements naturally harmonic as individual units. Deformity is unnatural, for, the sum of all things being the *Good,* it is natural that all things should partake of the *Good* and be arranged in combinations that are harmonious. Harmony is the manifesting expression of the *Will* of the eternal *Good* (Hall, LXXXI–LXXXIV).

Unlike painting and other visual arts, which exist largely in actual and virtual space, music depends heavily upon our witnessing music unfold over the passage of time. Its languages and musical elements form temporal sequences expressed in written and aural symbolism that construct artificial temporal relationships between tones. Poetry comes to life through a different means, using arbitrary symbols of a different type to affect the souls of humanity. Each art form wields a force that combines with space and time to energize metaphysical and mathematical laws that people are conditioned to comprehend and appreciate over time. Combining various artistic languages in inter-disciplinary presentation is powerful because multiple levels of "meaning" are intensified. The difficulty involved in defining the relationship between music and language is evident in the struggle some composers have when reconciling music with words. De Schloezer discussed Scriabin's dilemma:

> Scriabin could not set a ready-made text to music, because he could not and would not subordinate the process of musical thought to an unrelated entity. Any adjustment to words was to him a violation of the essence of music; every time he heard an art song, he listened to it with mixed irony and disdain. Sometimes he was asked by people who did not know him well why he never wrote for voice. He usually evaded the question; it was unthinkable to him that his music could be united with words in a relationship in which the former would be subordinated to the latter. But if it was impossible for him to set words by someone else to music, why did he not himself, like Wagner, write both the poetry and the music? The reason for this self-denial (which he reconsidered only in the last years of his life, in the *Acte prealable*), I believe, was the inadequacy of his verbal expression. He became aware of this inadequacy by the failure of his only attempt to set words to music which was in the finale of his First Symphony (89).

An even greater dilemma than reconciling music and words is our understanding the relationship between aesthetic artistic phenomena and our emotions. Our emotional realm is quite a complex mystery, but music penetrates it with ease. We saw earlier that each person is regarded as both a physical and spiritual being in Yoruba religion. The physical body of the person is known as *ara.* The spiritual aspect is described first as emi, or "breath," and second as *ori,* or "head." Emi is that power that gives life to the body. The human body would be incapable of thought and unable to communicate with the world of religious power without *ori.* The aspect that connects *ori* to the course of life of the individual is one of its most important features. According to the Yoruba, human identity, fate, and one's general life plan are determined before birth. This individual identity (that is also identified with that of an ancestor), has a heavenly origin and serves as an individual's personal guardian. Thus, people are considered the reincarnation of an ancestor (Lawson 67–68). Malcolm Budd explores the affect music has on moods and the emotions in *Music and The Emotions: The Philosophical Theories:*

> In *The Meaning of Music,* Carroll C. Pratt posed in the following way the problem of the apparent ascription of emotional qualities to music. Let us say that what a person experiences as outside his body is for that person objective and that what is experienced as belonging to or inside his body is subjective. By this criterion, moods and emotions are subjective for the person who feels them: what someone feels when he feels worry, anxiety, uneasiness, fear, and joy belongs to or lies within his body. An emotion is subjective in the sense that what is felt is located within, rather than outside, the subject's body. When a person experiences an emotion he feels the contraction of his brow, the tension of his muscles, the pounding of his blood, or some other happenings in or to his body. But moods and emotions are sometimes spoken of as though for each person objective—in particular, as though they could be properties of music. Yet it cannot be literally true that music embodies emotion, for it is not a living body which feels its own bodily processes. How, then, are we to understand the characterization of music as agitated, calm, wistful, seductive, restless, pompous, passionate, somber, triumphant, or yearning? (37–39).

Manly P. Hall suggests that Greek initiates gained their knowledge of the philosophic and therapeutic aspects of music from the Egyptians. In Egypt, Hermes was considered the founder of art and Isis and Osiris were patrons of music and poetry. According to Hall, Plato declared that songs and poetry existed in Egypt for at least ten thousand years, and that:

> "These were of such an exalted and inspiring nature that only gods or god-like men could have composed them. In the mysteries, the lyre was regarded as the secret symbol of the human constitution, the body of the instrument representing the physical form, the strings the nerves, and the musician the spirit. Playing upon the nerves, the spirit thus created the harmonies of normal functioning, which, however, became discords if the nature of man were defiled" (LXXXI–LXXXIV).

The Greeks defined music and poetry as artistic domains over which the Muses presided. Perhaps ancient people throughout the world realized the futility of arguments over whether or not phenomena are "science" or "art." Similarly, no established criteria for determining whether music is valid, pleasing, purposeful, expressive, or intelligible exist. Aesthetic impressions differ not only between various cultures around the world, but a myriad of perspectives on a single work of art often exists within any single culture. Therefore, each individual is capable of setting personal parameters for deciding what constitutes pleasing music. In the book *Music of the Whole Earth* author David Reck suggests a definition worth noting:

> Music is *mostly* (but not entirely) sound, that it is organized in some way, that it may be intimately and inseparably though loosely connected with what we in the West consider separate phenomena (namely, dance, body movement, visual arts, religion, mysticism, power, medicine, astronomy, mathematics, architecture, group interaction, social structure, language, cooking, sex, walking, magic, psychology, being, thinking, or any other of a perhaps infinite number of possibilities), and, finally, that although all the peoples of the world have music in one form or another, many of them do not have even a roughly equivalent word for it! (13–14).

People can set aesthetic limits for themselves. The greater the exposure people have to a wide range of art, the more experience a listener brings to their personal artistic evaluations. Serious artists rebuke restrictive rules that attempt to determine what is beautiful or artistically valid. Many such rules are applied by theorists to European "art music" in the tonal tradition. Arnold Schoenberg has rejected arbitrary notions of aesthetics, and in the introductory chapter of his *Theory of Harmony*, Carl Dalhaus discusses some of Schoenberg's reactions:

> The esthetics that Schoenberg dismissed with a scornful gesture as superfluous chatter was a metaphysics of "the beautiful music," misused in journalism to defend an established situation. In the name of this esthetics, guardians of decayed traditions protested against the new music that they did not understand, music that they wanted to shut out of their range of hearing. On the other hand, the craft that Schoenberg contrasted with outworn esthetics meant to him precisely a central core of practices remaining within the bounds of tonality, the very language that Schoenberg had left behind as dead and finished, while traditional esthetics saw in tonality a precondition, given by nature or sanctioned by nature, of all intelligible musical expression. No matter how unceremoniously Schoenberg rejected the norms of a confining esthetics, he was still far from any tendency to subject composing to the rules of a theory of craftsmanship, for composing meant to him inner necessity and obeyed only the composer's conscience (1–2).

A total dismissal of tonality is also an unreasonable and biased rejection of aesthetics that simply fails to align with a particular stylistic perspective. Beauty cannot be defined from any singular point of view.

Music and Language

Music and language communicate ideas, emotions, and aurally descriptive information chronicling the history of human development. Thus, their inherent power, multidimensionality, and overwhelming influence cannot be restricted to the mastery of any set of rules and fixed techniques. Artistic expression often operates in poly-dimensional forms in an attempt to emulate nature. Drums speak in polyrhythms, winds perform over the polytonal and pantonal harmonic regions, and poetic language and song often apply the application of the double entendre.

In traditional African society, the tendency towards replicating nature's poly-dimensional temperament in its communal social organization and traditions is mirrored in the interconnection of the interdisciplinary art forms, religion, and expressive functions of daily social interaction between people. The resulting traditional patterns of life are related to the sights, sounds, and smells of the environment (such as the Ituri Forest or Kalahari Desert).

Music serves as a vehicle through which socio-cultural, aesthetic, spiritual, and mathematical experience unfolds. If music reflects humankind's most involved study, practice, and worship of vibration, perhaps sound deals directly with our comprehension of the Creator's omnipotent expression. ("And the Spirit of God moved upon the face of the water," from the King James Version.) Perhaps each nucleus of vibration extends in helical patterns radiating from a fundamental vibration. In any case, it matters not whether a musical composition conforms to European sonata form or to perfectly symmetrical serial construction if it misses its mark in moving listeners emotionally, physically, and intellectually.

Writing is capable of related power. A personal account infused with strong creative stimulus produces literature that elicits strong emotional or cognitive responses within the minds of readers. Constructing impressive sequences of sentences and paragraphs based on themes void of rich content, or that are not infused with passion are generally rendered less effective, regardless of levels of eloquent vocabulary or grammatical sophistication. Most often meaningful content trumps flawless form and structure. When words align with music, their power is mutually enhanced. For the listener, composer, and performer, music affects our senses along lines that no other stimulus can reach. Boris De Schloezer discusses the elements and forces applied by musicians to "communicate the incommunicable" in his book, *Scriabin: Aristist and Music*.

Scriabin's three modes of self-expression included the thinker, the artist, and the mystic, all of which sprang from his inner experience. Scribabin's theoretical speculations gave his vision a philosophical foundation. Nicolas Slonimsky (Schloezer's book's

English translator) felt that Scribabin's visions of *Mysterium* were intended to transfigure humanity but were not connected with this music in subject matter or development, thematic content or comment, theory or realization. They were parallel actions that enabled Scriabin to communicate the incommunicable. Schloezer wrote: "It is entirely possible that there exists a different relationship between the cognitive process and creative activity. Each may be autonomous and independent and yet linked to the other by a vital intuition, which is their common source" (8).

When a specific emotion, purpose, or directive motivates a given composition or creative project, it often achieves its objective with the listening audience. Ellington's composition, *Take the 'A' Train,* transports the listener onto that perpetual vehicle. Nevertheless, the listener supplies images and detail that complete the picture. The relationship between music, words, pictures, and color adds an additional layer to the instrumental exploration and investigation of expressive phenomena. H. Spencer Lewis (an imperator of the Rosicrucian Order) and others have systematically explored the relationship between music and the color spectrum. Fux considered the study of counterpoint a musical process related to the study of perspective. Studies in words, counterpoint, and perspective were important developments in Renaissance art, and interest in these areas reflects the rise of three-dimensional thought.

The medieval composer dealt with different voices of a motet in much the way in which the medieval painter portrayed different levels of landscape. The composition, in both cases, was an aggregate of parts rather than an entity conceived in depth. It is characteristic of medieval music that theorists speak of *discantus*—two-fold melody— even when they refer to a setting of more than two parts. Theirs was a two-dimensional approach to polyphony. The term discantus was the predecessor of the term counter-point. Early in its use, discantus had acquired the connotation of part-writing that left no room for improvisational freedom but whose rhythm was strictly measured note against note: *punctus contra punctum* (Fux vii–x).

Joscelyn Godwin likewise explores the relationship between words, tones, and color in her book, *The Mystery of the Seven Vowels.* Godwin asserts that the non-linear nature of vowels makes them more comparable to the color spectrum than to musical tones. She feels that color and vowels share certain extreme fixed points. The colors black and white or three primary colors represent fixed points while an infinite array of colors form a divisible range of shades between such points. She explains some of the notions upon which her somewhat controversial theories are based:

> The most famous attempt at a vowel-color parallel is the one proposed by the poet Arthur Rimbaud, who in early sonnet (circa 1870) on the vowels ("*A noir, E blanc, I rouge, U vert, O bleu*") assigns black to A, white to E, red to I, green to U, and blue to O. Much ink has been spilt in trying to explain why Rimbaud chose the colors he did. Perhaps he felt that the openness of the A gives on to the dark cavern of the mouth; it is the first of sounds, the un-formed place from which the voice emerges. The French E, verging towards

the A of sofa when it is not simply mute, is the most indifferent and colorless of the vowels. The intensity of the I (meet) is like the sharp sting of scarlet, though later in the poem Rimbaud makes it the "purple" of spat-out blood and of penitence. The French U or German ü, so foreign to English mouths, has the greatest range of audible harmonics, mysterious like the inexhaustible greens of nature. Robert Greer Cohn points out its innate tension, combining a bright, acute, male I with a relaxed, open, female receptacle, which is acoustically if not anatomically correct (one pronounces it by holding the mouth in the shape of hoot, then trying to say me).

And the deep and resonant O is like the azure bowl of the sky, the limit of our vision as the omega is the end of the Greek alphabet, and, apocalyptically, of all things (35–38).

Music is the universal language and the "flower of feelings." In ancient traditional African cultures, music was inseparable from spirituality, the arts, mathematics, healing, and entertainment. If the relationships between such disciplines were again reunited, that base of knowledge might produce models for teaching humanity creative techniques helpful in achieving world harmony, equality, happiness, and unity. Mathematical logic and natural laws that form the foundation for a technical analysis of music help foster a systematic understanding of certain universal principals involving balance and vibratory patterns.

We have seen how people have consistently examined relationships between music and mathematics throughout history because such connections are clear and concrete. Musical intervals and rhythms are measured in languages and symbols that are easily transferred to mathematical formulas. In mysticism, numbers often express the relationship between unity, multiplicity, and the systematic order of the universe. For example, the nature of the unity or the dyad facilitates an understanding of the nature of what Ralph M. Lewis calls "the Unity," which represents "the Absolute." This model can extend to represent the duality of man (microcosm) and the universe (macrocosm). Lewis concludes:

> Basic archetypal or Cosmic patterns are expressed in many forms in mythology, religion, literature, and art. The archetypal plan or pattern is manifested in created or mundane types which are realized by man in his awareness of the universe, himself, and the symbols he creates. These symbols, however, are influenced by the society and culture in which the individual lives, as well as by his own nature and personality (14–16).

Once we realize the infinite connections that exist between music, language, dance, and nature, then creative artists from various disciplines can benefit mutually from a wide range of shared experiences and information. A holistic perspective can enhance an artist's appreciation and understanding of the creative process.

Music reflects society. Psychological, economic, and physical influences affect socio-cultural development and, consequently, artistic production. Therefore, we must consider both the artist and the environment in which their work emerged to gain an understanding of the purpose and evolution of artistic expression. Dr. Donald Byrd has said to me, "Jazz has never been about playing forty- or fifty-year-old music." The exploration of new ideas requires experimentation that always reveals new frontiers. We learn and grow from conquering new equations.

Summary

This book contains just a single cell of information from a single perspective. It is a collection of ideas within an infinite and omnipotent universe of factors, events, and forces that contribute to the evolution of "organized sound." The creation of music involves dynamic processes in which its elements combine in infinite variety, because the natural world is composed of an infinite variety of dynamic systems. The weather, the delicate ecology of a rain forest, the migration of monarch butterflies, and phenomena throughout existence are examples of infinite dynamic systems that interact with the rest of the universe. The "butterfly effect" is but one example of how a single action projects waves of consequences that resound throughout the universe. Music reflects that synergy, order, abstraction, and diversity. Dynamic systems display a wide range of tendencies, from seemingly stable illusions to the unpredictable phenomena we sense as chaotic.

A dynamic system in nature also leaves fingerprints, which are an abstract puzzle that we try to understand through fractals that encompass an intangible balance between order and disorder. The blues matrixes and other musical systems provide related patterns of abstract symmetry that guide our understanding of information obtained through our senses and tools in search of order and beauty. Musical systems are based upon tendencies to discover polarity and balance between tension and resolution, stasis and motion, cycles and deviations.

Many musicians are great performers and improvisers but may not be strong composers (spontaneous or premeditated). Symphony orchestras worldwide are full of master performers who are extraordinary musicians. To compose and perform simultaneously is an approach to music that requires both strong performance skill and great craftsmanship and knowledge as a composer. The late twentieth century created an age of specialists where, in the medical profession, for instance, doctors who formerly looked at the entire patient in general practice have been replaced by a host of specialists who treat only individual parts of the body (and never the whole person). In jazz, conservatory-trained musicians are beginning to specialize stylistically as well. Young lions of the late twentieth century found opportunities to practice incessantly in universities and conservatories, enabling them to develop great "chops" (speed, agility, range, etc.). Nonetheless, the break with the system of mentoring that produced earlier innovative jazz progenitors created a conspicuous void in jazz of the last quarter of the twentieth century. Retrospection has often replaced innovation as a consequence. Thus there has been no name for a definitive jazz style for forty years (since jazz fusion of the early 1970s).

Jazz has influenced twentieth- and twenty-first-century world socio-culture in a multiplicity of ways beyond its more conspicuous effects upon music, language, dance, film, fashion, and visual arts. Jazz is about freedom and innovation, but it is deeply concerned with discipline, tradition, and preservation as well. In 1972, my mentor Louis Jordan told me that he liked to remember the earlier solos he played on certain tunes because he had no reason to totally discard his earlier beautiful ideas. Despite this preservation of his own musical moments through committing them to memory, he was the progenitor of rhythm 'n blues and always continued to evolve throughout his career. Jazz has never been a deposable music, and its innovators have always fortified themselves in past traditions while gradually forging new voices through reflecting the contemporary world in which their musical style evolves. Retrospective jazz focuses primarily upon recreating swing, bebop, cool, and hard-bop styles with slightly new embellishments and twists, however. Likewise, retrospective free jazz, produced by a handful of musicians in places such as New York's Knitting Factory, and other "avant-garde" music venues generally grasp a façade of the authentic 1960s and 1970s styles, but have yet to supersede those stylistic parameters. The point of innovation has never simply been to create music that was odd; rather, it places creative self-expression as a high priority.

Donald Byrd once asked me, "How many musicians play Wynton Marsalis compositions on their gigs the way earlier musicians frequently performed and promoted the music of their contemporary colleagues in earlier times? Everyone played Parker, Dizzy, Monk, Miles, Coltrane, et al., as soon as their new compositions were written and performed." In response to an article written by Marvin Stamm, jazz writer Willard Jenkins wrote to me in an e-mail:

> One thing that should be corrected from this piece is the perception that Wynton Marsalis has been a record hit maker. Nothing could be further from the truth. Despite his obvious success in so many endeavors, making records has not been nearly as large a part of that equation as some might imagine. Curiously, Wynton's recordings through the years have enjoyed at the very best modest sales records. In fact, with that huge spate of new recordings he/they released at the end of 1999 through 2000, his contract with Columbia reportedly ended. And there has been no news that it has yet to be renewed!

Neither of these comments is aimed at minimizing Marsalis' talent or contribution to music. They are intended to place the media's attempt to define that contribution within the context of the evolution of jazz. By bringing jazz to a wider audience, with an undeniable degree of integrity, technical virtuosity, and broad-ranged musicianship, Marsalis has certainly made a valuable contribution to jazz and "serious" European music. All musicians contribute to the evolution of jazz in their own way, but the jazz evolution has slowed its pace dramatically over the past thirty years. To understand this, jazz, in general, has to be considered within its historical context. Steve Coleman says:

> I've dwelled on history because, of all today's fusions, only jazz-and-classical has as much to draw from. I'd argue that third stream reached its peak not in its own era but in the early 1980s, by which point the emphasis in what was still being called free jazz paradoxically shifted to composition, ultimately producing Anthony Davis's *X*—not a jazz opera, whatever that might be, but a legitimate one in which jazz from ragtime to Coltrane and beyond played an integral part. Given the decelerated pace of jazz evolution, that period feels like just yesterday. Its strides forward and missteps are still being sorted out in clubs and concert halls (and on panels), even though Davis himself and others from his 1980s circle (their efforts color-coded as "jazz," rather than Philip Glass or Meredith Monk's "new music," by everyone except the jazz police) have taken refuge in academia, alongside the post-serialists and dodecaphonists who don't care if anybody listens—a luxury jazz has never been able to afford, and one it had better not covet. "If it sounds good, it is good," Ellington preached, and even if it appalls aesthetic conservatives among the jazz faithful, who can be as scornful of relativism as the Christian right, his subjective criterion is the only one worth applying to future jazz-and-classical hybrids. There figure to be lots of them. When haven't there been? (9).

Jazz and all other expressive art forms have no fear of extinction as long as they continue to flow naturally through the course of human evolution. The rich and fertile past that evolved jazz mirrors nature in many respects—in its freely juggling physical, cognitive, and spiritual elements of the universe and its managing successfully to manifest beautiful and useful phenomena. Its future is assured as long as it continues to honor self-expression and venerate nature and all its splendor as the ultimate model of the creative process.

"To live is so startling it leaves little time for anything else."
—Emily Dickinson

References

Budd, Malcolm. *Music and The Emotions: The Philosophical Theories.* London: Routledge, 1992.

Conway, David. *Ritual Magic: An Occult Primer.* New York: E. P. Dutton, 1972. ms. page 15.

Dahlhaus, Carl. *Studies on the Origin of Harmonic Tonality.* Trans. Robert O. Gjerdingen. Princeton, NJ: Princeton University Press, 1990.

Davis, Francis and Milchedik Fleishedik. "Jazzing the Classics and Classing the Jazzers from Jelly Roll Morton to Uri Caine." *Village Voice.* May 25, 2004 <http://www.villagevoice.com/content/printVersion/183770>.

de Schloezer, Boris. *Scriabin: Artist and Mystic.* Trans. Nicolas Slonimsky. Oxford: Oxford University Press, 1987.

Dossey, Larry M.D. *Healing Words: The Power of Prayer and the Practice of Medicine.* New York: HarperCollins, 1993.

Einstein, Alfred, Arthur Mendel, Nathan Broder. *Mozart: His Character, His Work.* New York: Oxford University Press, 1965.

Fux, John J. *Study of Counterpoint.* Revised edition. New York: W. W. Norton and Company, 1965.

Godwin, Joscelyn. *Harmonies of Heaven and Earth: Mysticism in Music from Antiquity to the Avant-Garde.* Rochester, VT: Inner Traditions; Bear and Company, 1987.

Hall, Manly Palmer. *The Secret Teachings of All Ages: An Encyclopedic Outline of Masonic, Hermetic, Qabbalistic, and Rosicrucian Symbolical Philosophy.* New York: Jeremy P. Tarcher/Penguin, 2003.

Journal of Child Psychology and Psychiatry 45.6 (July 19, 2004): 1054–1063. <http://www3.interscience.wiley.com/journal/118755409/abstract?CRETRY=1&SRETY=0>

Khan, Hazrat Inayat. *The Mysticism of Sound and Music: The Sufi Teaching of Hazrat Inayat Khan.* Boston: Shambhala, 1996.

Langer, Susan. "Building and Weaving: Esthetic and Technical Metaphors as an Index to the Essential Unity of the Arts." *The Journal of Philosophy,* 39.25 (December 3, 1942).

Lawson, E. Thomas and Robert N. McCauley. *Rethinking Religion.* New York: Cambridge University Press, 1993.

Lenhart, Amanda. "Computer Games Drive Social Ties." 16 September 2008. *BBC News.* March 2008 <http://news.bbc.co.uk/2/hi/technology/7619372.stm>.

Lewis, Ralph M. The Imperator. "The Ancient Mystery Schools." *Rosicrucian Digest* (June 1986): 5–6.

Mahabharata (Vana Parva) Ch. 187 Vayu Purana 50–88 Shatpath Brahman 1–8–16. Overstreet, H. A. *The Mature Mind.* New York: W. W. Norton and Company, Inc., 1949. Reck, David. *Music of the Whole Earth.* New York: Scribner, 1976.

APPENDIX: MUSICAL EXAMPLES

Figure 1. Scale and Chord Exercises for Spontaneous Etude Development

These drills should be practiced daily to increase aural and technical skills needed to perform all the sounds that one imagines. After gaining control over the notes, each pattern should gradually become a musical etude, avoiding routine interpretation and with the shaping of musical phrases and melodies as the primary aspiration.

I. Half Steps, Perfect Fifths, Tritones

II. Half Steps, Perfect Fifths

III

IV. Whole Steps

V. Major Sixths, Minor Thirds

VI. Chromaticism

VII. Chromaticism, Major Triads

VIII. Lydian Augmented Scale

IX. Diminished Seventh Chords

X. Dominant Sevenths, Diminished Sevenths

XI. Dominant Seventh Chords

XII. Major Triads

XIII. Blue Notes

XIV. Chord Study

XV. Major and Minor Sevenths (Relative Tonalities)

XV. Major and Minor Sevenths (Relative Tonalities) *continued*

XVI. Whole Tone Study

XVII. Augmented Chords

XVIII. Whole Tone Study

XIX. Whole Tone Study

XX. Fourths

XXI. Scaletone Fourths

XXI. Scaletone Fourths *continued*

XXII. Scale Tone Thirds (Major)

XXII. Scale Tone Thirds (Major) *continued*

Etude XXIII

Etude XXIV

Etude XXV

Etude XXVI

Etudes   c   Karlton E. Hester 2000

Figure 2. Scale and Chord Exercises for Spontaneous Composition Development

The seed material in this section should serve as nuclei for extended spontaneous composition. Each subject establishes a different mood, point in time, place, etc., that sets an environment to inspire and serve as a container for the musical material that it spawns.

Scale and Chord Exercises (Karlton E. Hester)

Figure 3. "'Round Midnight" (Head Melody)—for Melodic/Harmonic Analysis 1

Study the construction of the melody with repetition, balance, contrast, and polarity in mind.

'Round Midnight

Study the construction of the improvisation with repetition, balance, contrast, and polarity in mind as the music builds upon and extends ideas from the head melody.

Solo to 'Round Midnight

'Round Midnight by Thelonius Monk
Solo as passed on by Joe Henderson

Figure 5. "For the Affect of It"—Rhythmic and Counterpoint Analysis 1

Examine the ways in which contrasting meter serves as a means through which rhythmic liberation is promoted while also establishing a clear and firm rhythmic foundation.

For the Affect of It
(Flute Duet with Bass)

Figure 6. "Ancient and Future Incarnations"—Polyrhythmic and Counterpoint Analysis 2

Explore the musical elements of each part of "Ancient and Future Incarnations" separately to discover features of its individual musical construction and identity. Then understand that each part serves as a polyrhythmic component of the communal whole much in the way that West African polyrhythms are constructed.

Ancient and Future Incarnations

Karlton E. Hester
March 14, 2001

Ancient and Future Incarnations

Karlton E. Hester
March 14, 2001

Ancient and Future Incarnations:

African Polyrhythms

Karlton E. Hester
March 14, 2001

Ancient and Future Incarnations:

African Polyrhythms

{3} (Bamengoum Music; Lali)

Karlton E. Hester
March 14, 2001

Ancient and Future Incarnations:
African Polyrhythms

{IV} (Ibibio; Standard Rhythms)

Karlton E. Hester
March 14, 2001

Ancient and Future Incarnations:

African Polyrhythms

Figure 7. "Muse"—Comparative Analysis with "Mellow Bossa"

Align features of "Mellow Bossa" (from chapter 10) with those of "Muse" to see how the process of Schenkerian Analysis can be reverse engineered to produce a new offspring composition ("Muse") from a parent composition ("Mellow Bossa").

MUSE

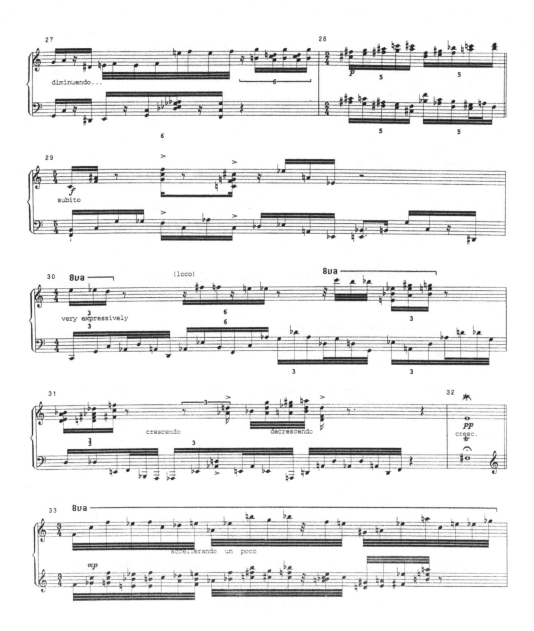

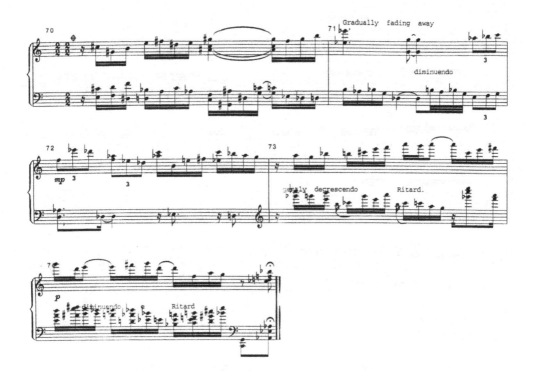

CPSIA information can be obtained
at www.ICGtesting.com
Printed in the USA
FSOW03n1819300915
11719FS